W9-DDD-827

BRITISH POETRY SINCE 1960

A Critical Survey

*edited by Michael Schmidt
and Grevel Lindop*

A CARCANET PRESS PUBLICATION

DALE H. GRAMLEY LIBRARY
SALEM COLLEGE
WINSTON-SALEM, N. C.

PR
611
S3

SBN 902145 73 8

On all Introductory Material and Conversations
Copyright © Carcanet Press Ltd. 1972

On all Essays Copyright © resides with the Authors

All Rights Reserved

First published 1972
by Carcanet Press Ltd.
Pin Farm, South Hinksey
Oxford

Printed in Great Britain
by W & J Mackay Limited, Chatham

Contents

Preface

A BOOK of this nature attempts to be comprehensive but necessarily fails. A few major names appear only cursorily. We felt in some cases that the neglected poet had not developed significantly during the sixties or contributed much to the decade; in others, we preferred to dedicate individual attention to poets as interesting as those more commonly discussed, but neglected because they are less popular or publicist in character. We have traced the most important movements. Others of a slighter nature, that have followed the patterns of the ones we describe, we note in passing. We have paid close attention to "the Group" because they manifest, as a sort of *multum in parvo*, many of the trends prevalent in the early sixties; and they have moved far enough away from "the Group" identity for us to assess the value of that movement in terms of a few individual talents associated with it.

We decided to compile this book in the belief that serious, extended criticism of contemporary poetry would help both writer and reader in a way which reviewers' comment cannot. We hoped to place the poet in a wider context of poets, and poetry in a critical context aware of more than literary criteria. We felt too that British poetry, its present and its potential, could be coherently assessed, and that a study of different areas by various writers might reveal the continued vitality of the British tradition despite the various cases raised against it. We hoped to discover if there was any significant "underground" in Britain, an alternative tradition, or whether, as in the past, the distinction amounts to that between "good" and "bad" poetry.

In all but a few cases, the essays have been commissioned for this book.

We are grateful to the editors of the *New Statesman* for permitting us to reprint Ian Hamilton's essay, "The Making of the Movement"; to Carol Buckroyd of Oxford University Press, and Merle Brown of *The Iowa Review* for permitting us to use Calvin Bedient's essay, "On Charles Tomlinson"; to Merle Brown of *The Iowa Review* for permitting us to print Jon Silkin's "The Poetry of Geoffrey Hill", originally commissioned for this volume; and to POETRY for permission to reprint part of Michael Schmidt's article, "A Defence", in the first section of the Introduction.

Alan Brownjohn's essay, "A View of English Poetry in the Early Seventies", is an expanded version of an "Opinion" article in *The Review*. Terry Eagleton's essay, "Myth and History in Recent Poetry", draws on material from two *Times Literary Supplement* reviews.

This book is the first in Carcanet's critical series. It will be followed by *New Irish Writing, a survey*, to cover the complex developments in recent Irish prose and poetry; and *American Poetry since 1960*.

Introduction

BRITISH poetry has ever more regularly come under fire in the last few years from several quarters, primarily American. The British malady has been variously diagnosed, though the nature of the illness, expressed in sweeping generalities, is seldom illustrated with specific textual symptoms. The medic, carrying the capacious black bag of American poetry, assumes an easy critical stance, denounces our failure of scope, of ambition, of originality.

One of the more recent and generously condescending visits has been paid us by Louis Simpson who—in the "Opinion" pages of *The Review*—offers us tea and comfortable advice. His essay reveals not only the inconsistent tenets of the main case against contemporary British poetry. It also provokes in the reader, by reaction, a clearer sense of what many British poets are in fact attempting and achieving—how they differ in ambition, temperament, and "technique" (a word brandished frequently by the detractors) from the Americans whose criteria are wished upon them.

Simpson laments the lack of any substantial *movement* in British poetry:

> . . . a movement means some discussion of technique. Without an involvement in technique, the practice of any art must degenerate into a desperate exertion of mere personality.

Americans, he informs us, are concerned with technique. English poets are not. English poets express opinions, make remarks (conditioned, we're told, by public-school-induced glibness); and remarks—on the authority of Gertrude Stein—are not literature.

Simpson reveals what he and his co-religionists mean by "technique". We may expect they mean some "mechanical process". Nothing so dull as that! They mean "the exact opposite" which is "writing with the living breath"—

> The life within the poet is his subject, and his individual breathing determines the line and shape of the poem—not a concern with love, or God, or asparagus.

If this is the case, *technique* can hardly be discussed at all—it is beyond the range of criticism. Each poet determines and is justified in his own technique or "breathing". It remains to the critic to differentiate between good and bad breath, perhaps, but he cannot approach the process, the self-determined breathing, the empirical technique which is impregnably situated in the poet's lung or whim, and which has proved, painfully in many cases, "a desperate exertion of mere personality". Simpson slips from his unresolved discussion of technique into a discussion of subject matter. He declares,

> From [William Carlos] Williams a poet, especially an English poet, could
> learn how to write of his perceptions rather than his opinions.

No specific examples substantiate this verdict. We would suggest that, in
this context, "perceptions" are no more or less than imagistic or surreal
remarks—perceptual "opinions" individually as valueless as single, unrelated
intellectual opinions; that the virtue of many British poets—certainly of those
given prominence in this anthology—is not in any pithy, offhand opinions
they express but rather in their attempt to make structures of imagery and
language in which words and images impart significance to one another and in
so doing relate to a wider context. Critics of Mr. Simpson's persuasion would
have poetry of description, surreal evocation, dream or fable; of poetic aloof-
ness from social and even physical reality; a finding of voice or "breath"
without establishing a context in which to exercise it. This they call "percep-
tion" and "poetry of juxtapositions". What they eschew or fail to comprehend
is the poetry of synthesis, in which images are expressed in a language more
highly charged than translators' English; where words hinge by implication
various areas of experience or significance, and many meanings choose one
word; where the poem attempts to transmit an experience of thought or per-
ception accurately *as* experience, not as having-been-experienced; where,
finally, the poem enacts a process and is not enacted by a poet insistently
present in the pulmonary system of his poem.

The argument for clear form—not necessarily prescriptive or traditional,
but unobtrusively functional—in such a synthetic verbal process is strong.
The varied achievements of Geoffrey Hill, Charles Tomlinson, and Philip
Larkin—to name three radically different formalists—fully justify this asser-
tion. But Simpson and his comrades urge on the British poets "free forms"—
an oxymoronic phrase at best. The assailants' voices sound uncomfortably
and indefinitely prescriptive, revealing preference rather than critical insight,
devoid of significant example.

The British poet—it seems—is urged to write either impregnably private
or, conversely, vatic poetry, where the poet is the point on which we focus,
not himself focal onto a significant, common world. For the poet, writing the
poem is an assertion of identity, "I am a poet", rather than an act of com-
munication, in the first instance. Such critics prefer the Ted Hughes of the
Crow myth, or W. S. Merwin's recent work, where he chooses to pull up
anchor and swim in the circumambient gas, to Jon Silkin's poems of relation-
ship, or Douglas Dunn's and Brian Jones's social poems, or Peter Porter's
complex satires—all poets for whom the social, historical, legendary, local,
and physical serve as *materia prima*, who subdue themselves to these realities
and serve them as integrities rather than using them without regard for their
actual nature.

This difference seems one aspect of a radical difference between the school of American poets most critical of British poetry and the British poets themselves. One might typify the distinction as that between the geographic or descriptive eye and the historical eye. The former, which is characteristic of the hostile camp, can be illustrated by poets as different as Robert Bly, Ed Dorn, and W. S. Merwin, and certainly by many followers of Pound. They make history spatial and travel through it as though it were flat presence, as though it were an alternative geography on a plane with the physical or present world. Historical incidents, like places and natural objects, are images wrenched from context, falsified in the service of allusion. Or time, history, social reference, are annihilated and private symbolism or myth prevails. This sort of poetry, which requires "spontaneity" or "truth to living breath" as well, in some cases, as the rigorous suppression of transitional material, often fails to generate a structure significant to anyone but the individual poet—if to him. It is not interpretative but more accurately descriptive of a private world. It lacks, as well as a sense of time or history as distinct from presence, a sense of *context*. When it steps into the area of "meanings" it swaggers with the surreal rhetoric of Bly's political utterances or Dorn's epic attempts. If it interprets, the interpretations are projected, not detected structures of significance. Description, a quality these poets prefer to "meanings", implies imagistic or surreal decoration, linguistic surrealism that upsets syntactical and structural expectation but fails in the process to supply a significant alternative. The poetry is essentially private, even in public readings; in its authoritarian voice it is conservative, emphasising the individuality of the poet—whereas, say, Robert Lowell's more traditional approach to form and syntax is capable of socially radical statement.

British poets, at least those who seem significant to these editors, are historical in imagination. By this, we mean that they are aware of and active in or against—but aware of—the continued presence and vitality of literary tradition. Their plane of constant reference includes the social, the historical, the legendary (but usually not the mythical). If, as Geoffrey Hill does in *Mercian Hymns* or Jon Silkin does in *Amana Grass*, they attempt to synthesise areas of history with present experience, they do not drag it piecemeal into the present. They describe a continuity, a presence of history or, one might say, a permanence of historical fact which is indeed *fact* and is historical. The structure is discovered in time and place as time and place are differently and inexorably constituted, not imposed on them. In a sense, their best poems apply the community of experience to the community.

Partisans of Mr. Simpson give the image the full weight of their critical emphasis. And the major weakness of their argument is that they take little account of the potential of language as itself capable of being employed as a complex image: the verbal structure as a metaphor for an emotion, perception, process. Simpson, and the poets he chooses to quote from in his essay, have come to write a sort of poetic esperanto which, if sometimes rhythmically convincing, is often nearly devoid of connotation in itself. This is often the language of literal or superficial translation, without compression or accuracy. The images do the talking—can be called up in any language. A language is necessary but, in the final assessment, nearly irrelevant except as it conjures images or takes the poet's breath, like a balloon. When we drop "meaning" or what these critics prefer to call "opinion", we dump with it other things— like structure, which by relating images syntactically and rhythmically—by relating *ideas*—to one another, interprets as well as perceives, and needn't become trite or sententious in the process.

It might not be invidious to suggest that an insularity parallel to that enjoyed by England as recently as 1964 is developing in America, where certain prescriptive orthodoxies which generalise and dismiss work not immediately in their range will increasingly prevail. Certainly only a few American journals seem seriously involved with modern British poetry or more than a narrow range of translated poetry. If "two traditions" seem to develop, the impetus for the apparent development will be largely American.

ii

For the new and established poet the last decade provided a number of unexpected opportunities and temptations. The retrenchments of the Movement were almost forgotten. Poetry readings, poetry and jazz, little magazines and presses, poetry in translation, proliferated. Poetry seems to claim wide popular attention. Certainly more people from a variety of backgrounds now confess to writing poetry than before.

Poetry readings have had a varied effect on poets and audiences. Grevel Lindop, in his essay "Poetry, Rhetoric, and the Mass Audience", explores their effect on the Liverpool poets. One of the first large-scale organisers of poetry and jazz occasions, Jeremy Robson, is fortunately a person with a strong preference for written poetry, and he tended to treat the jazz at his first successful happenings as sugar on a serious pill. He had good readers, judging from his little anthology, *Jazz and Poetry*. His success led others less sophisticated to emulation. Michael Horovitz started a similar movement at the same time, on a more ambitious scale, but with far less intelligent presentation. As the phenomenon spread, various poets began writing for performance—poets as different as Adrian Mitchell and Christopher Logue, Alan Bold and Adrian Henri.

The reading circuit has had its effect on the primarily literary poets too. John Wain's recent, linguistically lax "Feng" poems seem to be far more for live presentation than for the page, their ultimate destination. George Macbeth and Ted Hughes among others have at times debased their poetic currency by writing poems primarily for the spoken voice. In much of their recent work verbal tension is at low ebb, rhetorical or flashy devices carry points in such a way as to falsify the poem, failing to contain the complex balance which makes a poem *true*—that bringing into tension, and retaining in tension, of contrasts or opposites, the showing of both sides of the coin at one time. One would not be far wrong in suggesting that Hughes' *Crow*, like Macbeth's "The Auschwitz Rag", are sentimental in the sense that they state with one-sided rhetoric or with hilarity (perhaps this is the language of the extremist school) a very limited area of an experience, and yet they pretend that they are making a total statement in the one case or a wittily true one in the other. Their respective responses reveal a failure of sensibility to the human and moral implications of the subject matter which is vast, primary, almost unbearably painful. They do not help us to assimilate or understand the experience. They reduce it. They simplify for an audience instead of clarifying for a reader *and* an audience.

Various little magazines have lived and died during the decade. Besides those discussed by Harry Chambers in his essay (p. 85) and Jon Silkin in conversation (p. 193), two demand special mention. *Akros*, still living, is an energetic forum for Northern and Scots writing, edited by Duncan Glen. Its achievement, particularly in helping to restore Hugh MacDiarmid to prominence and in critically encouraging young poets, is one of the substantial periodical achievements of recent years. Peter Jay's *New Measure* was another notable magazine for new poets. Peter Jay ran the magazine for ten issues, afterwards founding Anvil Press Poetry to publish the poets he discovered during his years as editor.

His is one of the various little presses that have been active during the last few years. Regrettably, many little presses concentrate on established talents rather than on discovering new ones. In some cases, poets—especially from "the Group"—appear with monotonous regularity in lovely little broadsheets and pamphlets. The more important presses, like Fulcrum, London Magazine Editions, Trigram, and Anvil, are not altogether blameless here. Fulcrum's list bristles with mythical Americans. Its discoveries among new British poets have been negligible, though it has published some important work by Michael Hamburger, Christopher Middleton, David Jones, Basil Bunting, and Stuart Montgomery (its proprietor). There are at present over one hundred small presses active in Britain, and poets have seldom had a better chance to be published—and seldom a worse opportunity for being read seriously.

As if to destroy the image of a culturally insular Britain, translations of poetry and criticism have been proliferating. In 1963, *Modern Poetry in Translation* was established by Ted Hughes and Daniel Weissbort, introducing many of the now popular Eastern European poets. In the same year, Penguin Books initiated their series of modern poets in translation, a series which has yet to receive its critical due. Nathaniel Tarn initiated the Cape Editions, too—texts primarily in translation, with interesting results. Tarn was made unjustly the whipping boy of many xenophobic critics for taking Breton, Neruda, Lévi-Strauss and Olson seriously, and for writing unexpected poetry himself which—whatever its quality—deserved more intelligent reading than it received. The validity and effect of translation on recent British poetry is discussed in conversation with Jon Silkin (p. 193) and Peter Porter (p. 202).

With these new opportunities, the poet's situation has not changed radically during the decade. It has altered only, perhaps, in this respect: that the poet can, if he chooses, be a more public figure than before. There are larger spin-offs financially from writing poetry or being identified as a poet, in the form of bursaries, reading fees, and fellowships; but there are so many thirsty poets lolling at the waterhole (to use Peter Porter's image) that only a handful profit from the benefits. Though it is easier than ever to be published, it is still likely that the new poet will be little read. The surface conditions have altered: larger audiences are interested, more money is available, more presses are rolling. But there are so many poets that the new opportunities hardly constitute in themselves a more credible context than before for individual self-assessment or development.

iii

Despite the numerous coteries which have congregated and dissipated during the sixties, only one significant "movement"—one with critical biasses more or less consistently adhered to—has emerged. It is a group not for social reasons but because it gravitates around an exacting critic whose effect on the poets prominent in his magazine, *The Review*, is marked. The critic, Ian Hamilton, is his own best poet, with Hugo Williams a close and not altogether docile second. Mr. Hamilton is his own best critic too, and the effect of his movement has been, in its achievements, primarily critical, maintaining through influential public organs exacting critical standards. The astringency of the standards has told upon the poetry of the group generally, an achievement close to negligible except in the case of the two poets mentioned above. Even Hamilton's poems, in the assessment of Martin Seymour-Smith, are almost "casualties of their own cautiousness"; or as Anthony Thwaite said of Hamilton's individual poems, "in their brevity they seemed almost refined beyond reticence, stripped down to something so taciturn as to be practically silent". This is one form of what Santayana called "penitential art"—though lacking both the awe and the innocence.

Hamilton encourages a fresh form of imagism, where the fusion is not between sea and fir tree or petals and faces but usually between the poet and another party in, or at the dissolution of, a relationship. The poems are, to this degree, social poems—moments of human recognition or perception within a relationship. In diction there is a close analogy with the practice of the early Imagists, a terseness and complete concision, though the scope is slightly wider than that of the "pure" Imagist, allowing for tone of voice, attitude, even abstraction. Nonetheless it is a narrowly conceived poetic incapable of significantly prolonged utterance. Unlike early Imagism, a point of intersection at which various different talents—Pound's, HD's, Lawrence's, Marianne Moore's among others—reached a certain stage of their development at one time, coincided, then passed on in their individual courses, adapting a basically similar technique to different ends, *The Review*'s brand of imagism has become uncomfortably prescriptive, and poets who join the ranks find themselves in a restricting *cul-de-sac*. This is a critical extreme rather than a point of intersection. It will elevate minor poets like Geoffrey Grigson for praise because they write trenchant criticism. Unfortunately, as a critical persuasion, it has not developed a strong style of its own. The witty and *humane* trenchancy of Randall Jarrell's critical writing, though admired, is not emulated, perhaps because Jarrell's standards, equally high, were capable of wider application: he had in his prose and verse access to a more developed verbal imagination. Nonetheless, the movement is powerful, if not strong, provocative and consistent. It approaches experience in its poems with a linguistic shyness and a conscious restriction of the scope of significance the experience can have. So in its criticism—the knife is sharp, deft, though it sometimes inflicts only surface wounds on its victims.

During the 'sixties other groupings of poets developed, though no other one with the coherence of a "movement". The varied achievement of "the Group", for example, was not stylistic but social—providing the poets involved with a sort of poetic group therapy, from which some emerged with a chronic sense of Audience (Adrian Mitchell and George MacBeth) and others with a more constructive preoccupation with form and the discovery of more ample forms (Alan Brownjohn, Peter Porter, Peter Redgrove). Roger Garfitt treats the individual achievements of six of these poets in his essay (p. 13). The Group itself proved a sort of *multum in parvo* of the various tendencies and preoccupations present in the early 'sixties throughout British poetry.

Groupings exist outside London as well. In Newcastle, in the Mordern Tower precincts where poets like Tom Pickard and Barry MacSweeney sow their aesthetic seed in sparse enclosure soil, there exists a more exclusive élite than any establishment could be. Bill Parkinson, in his essay "Poetry in the North-East" (p. 107), considers the failure of these much-publicised poets to assimilate regional experience, their lip service to, and scanty understanding of, their poetic deities and their chosen techniques. In Liverpool a looser, more friendly aggregate whose achievement is as thin, thrives. Grevel Lindop considers them in his essay. (p. 92).

Beside the slender achievement of these regional literatures, the real success of Scots poetry in the last decade, traced by Edwin Morgan in his essay, "Scottish poetry in the 1960s" (p. 132), where he fails to include reference to his own substantial contribution, is noteworthy. Perhaps the breadth of the achievement—from dialect poems to concrete poems, with substantial results in every mode along the way—is due to a native Scots individualism which does not require grouping for confidence. Aestheticism is not bitter there, nor is the poet set over against his society or his tradition, as he feels he is in the North-East. And Scotland has a number of thriving periodicals. A similar development can be witnessed in Welsh and Anglo-Welsh writing, the subject of Glyn Jones's essay, "Second Flowering" (p. 122).

iv

Terry Eagleton, in his book *Exiles and Emigrés*, makes a point about artistic perspective relevant in this context.

> At the high point of their development, both realism and Romanticism were able to discover a point of operative distance from the partial interests and allegiances of their own cultures: a point of balance at which inwardness could combine with an essential externality to produce major art.

Great literature, he continues, needn't have broad perspectives,

> but it does seem to demand enough interaction between those convictions [i.e., of a limited class outlook], and the typifying problems and developments of the whole culture in which they are set, for them to appear representative rather than narrowly partisan.

A few poets sense and probe this inter-relation between themselves and their complex environment. Burns Singer wrote, "I carry that which I am carried by". Jon Silkin says, "the world not as I would have world/ But as it lay before me". They try to establish a relevant natural relationship between individual vision and the actual world it sees and is carried by—something a critic like Raymond Williams wrestles with semantically, trying to make an intransigent language speak beyond itself, beyond conditioned verbal structures, into linguistic potential. The attempt is to a degree subversive to thought patterns and perhaps, ultimately, to patterns of action. Anne Cluysenaar, in her essay "Post-culture: Pre-culture?" (p. 215), explores the possibilities of this mode of linguistic exploration, suggesting that some poets are approaching a valid reconciliation of the dichotomy in a poetry of hypothesis. Terry Eagleton, in his essay "Myth and History in Recent Poetry" (p. 233), describes this potential in different terms. A new criticism, aware of linguistic principles on the one hand and of the importance of relating contemporary poet and poem to a social and historical as well as a literary context on the other, is developing.

The most noteworthy poets since 1960 have explored consciously and unconsciously these areas of language and relationship, considering and responding to place, object, history, tradition, people. They have not gestured passively at these realities, overwhelmed by them. They have not been socially ignorant, spinning polite verbal webs, generating private myths, pronouncing vatically, or serving up popular aphorism in rhyme. These latter activities have been common—the product of a bourgeois self-regard that compels the poet to draw attention to himself as poet rather than through himself as a lens onto a clarifiable reality. The British poet as seer rather than abstract visionary, as focal rather than focus, the poet modestly concerned with his subject matter and language, is the one whose achievement since 1960 has been most real and—in some cases—least recognised. The poets given individual prominence in this anthology—Geoffrey Hill, Jon Silkin, and Charles Tomlinson—are among those who seem to us to transcend language and particular experience, not by dislocating the one to their ends or projectively falsifying the other, but by trying to find inherent in situation and language structures at once significant to them as poets and latent in their subject matter. They have understood in their best work the distinction between a personal and an exclusive, private world, opting for the former. They are literalists to begin with, and from the literal variety of the world, without erecting alternative realities or withdrawing into their dim psyches, they perceive, express, and in expression particularise and transcend those realities.

GROUPINGS

DALE H. GRAMLEY LIBRARY
SALEM COLLEGE
WINSTON-SALEM, N. C.

The Group

by Roger Garfitt

IT can almost be said of the Group that divided they stand, united they fall. The label "a Group poet" became a term of abuse in some quarters, yet leading members of the Group have gone on to establish considerable reputations. Anyone who writes about the Group as a literary movement has to start by pointing out that it wasn't one. The truth is that it was somewhat less than a literary movement, and rather more.

To begin with, the title "the Group" can refer to at least three things: a critical procedure, a category of poets, and a group of friends.

It was initially a critical procedure: a group of poets was organised by Philip Hobsbaum, first in Cambridge and then in London, to give each other's recent work the same rigorous examination that was given to classical literature by Dr. Leavis and critics of that school. The examination was made more thorough by the distribution of the poems on cyclostyled sheets, prior to the meetings. The Cambridge group was started in 1952, the London group, which became known as "the Group", in the autumn of 1955. In 1959, Edward Lucie-Smith succeeded Philip Hobsbaum as chairman of the London Group, and Philip Hobsbaum later founded a similar group in Belfast. "The Group", as such, discontinued when Edward Lucie-Smith resigned, but was re-formed as Poets' Workshop, using the premises of the Poetry Society. It continues to run, as Workshop Two, and some of the earliest Group members, Alan Brownjohn and George Macbeth, for example, still attend. The method was briefly explained by Philip Hobsbaum, with a quotation from a typical discussion, in *A Group Anthology* (O.U.P. 1963). It was fully discussed by him, with illustrations from recorded meetings, in *A Theory of Communication* (Macmillan, 1970).

A critical procedure, but never a critical orthodoxy. Edward Lucie-Smith writes in his introduction to the Anthology,

> we have tried to make it a rule that anyone who asked if he could come was welcome to do so. . . . The only principle to which we would all subscribe is that poetry is discussable, or, to put it another way, that the process by which words work in poetry is something open to rational examination. The acceptance of this principle is, of course, impossible to certain poets, and these do not come to us. But within this boundary we have many shades of belief: religious, political, and social, as well as literary.

The poets who first formed the Group were markedly diverse, and have become, if anything, more diverse since. The Group never had the stylistic cohesion of the Movement, and never wanted it.

The critical procedure itself is one that few would quarrel with. The introduction to the *Anthology*, citing "the notorious paranoia which afflicts all writers, and particularly the writers of verse", does suggest that the very existence and duration of the Group were remarkable. Caricatures apart, I doubt if, historically, the exchange of criticism between serious poets has been quite so rare. As for the Group approach, it is rather the product of its age. To discuss literature in this way is natural to anyone educated since the advent of Practical Criticism—and in this respect Lucie-Smith's reference back to the Rhymers' Club and Pound's sessions at the Café Royal is misleading. Surely the Group only brought together into a public forum the criticism that many poets exchange in private anyway. The achievement was precisely this, the establishment of a public forum, with its particular value for those who would otherwise have been in isolation.

There is nothing magical in the method itself: it takes its quality from those involved. And it does remain a subjective process, taking its character from them too. The character of the Group was felt to depend partly on the chairman, even on the venue. Peter Porter reflected, in an interview:

> Even the venue made a difference. In the early days, to turn out on a cold night and catch a bus down to Stockwell was in itself almost an act of commitment, a pilgrimage. When the meeting changed to Edward Lucie-Smith's flat, that was in the centre of Chelsea, and the whole atmosphere of attending a meeting was quite different.

Again, if one is to see recent poetry from Belfast as being in any way influenced by the group run there until recently by Philip Hobsbaum, then the procedure in Belfast generated poetry of a quite different kind from the Group poetry in London.

From being the name of a critical workshop, the Group became, mistakenly I think, the nomenclature denoting certain poets. The influence of this has persisted, so that most of them are grouped together in *British Poetry since 1945*. The particular danger of the grouping is that it links the concept of the critical practice with the style of certain poets. Conversely, some of the bitterness voiced by non-Group poets when the Group poets came into prominence was probably based on a feeling that the Group were making capital, in terms of publicity, out of standard practice.

The Group poets were centred in London, they established their reputations at about the same time, the early 'sixties, and the publication of the *Group Anthology* in 1963 brought them together in one volume, with a certain amount of publicity: these facts were quite enough, given the prevalence of the Conspiracy Theory among poets, to label them as a power group. There probably was a brief period when it seemed to provincial poets that a junta had captured the radio station and imposed control on the literary journals. This was not, of course, a putsch, but simply another literary generation, in the first flush of success, establishing its careers. Their activity was seen paranoiacally, in terms of power, and the human aspects were forgotten. It did not seem to occur to the disgruntled that George Macbeth needed a job, and probably enjoyed slipping a verse across Auntie, or that Edward Lucie-Smith was writing so many articles because he needed the money to furnish a flat. In any case, history has put the matter in perspective. If one must talk in these terms, it is only fair to point out that since the late 'sixties the provincial poets have carried out a more than successful counter-revolution.

The aspect of the Group that is hardest to document, and is probably the most fruitful, is that it became a group of friends, who influenced each other, not only in their writing, but in their reading, in their conversation, in the contrast of personalities. For those who had been to university it was a more realistic extension of the university experience, or a fulfilment of what that experience should have been: for those who came from outside university, it was a university in itself. It was far more lively, fluid and unpretentious than the picture which emerges from *A Group Anthology* or *A Theory of Communication*: these can only present, in fossilised form, the official hour of discussion. It was far wider in its sympathies than some of its detractors have imagined. For instance, some three or four years before the publication of *Hawk in the Rain*, at a time when no London publisher would touch it, Peter Redgrove was championing Ted Hughes's poetry, and the Group were discussing it with enthusiasm. George Macbeth, for one, has testified to its influence on him. Certain roles are those one would expect, though even these contrast: Philip Hobsbaum was respected for his critical rigour, George Macbeth for his versatility and panache, Peter Redgrove for his verbal power. Other cross-currents are more surprising: that the liveliest appreciation of Brownjohn's work should have come from George Macbeth; that of his contemporaries the one Peter Porter should have admired most as a poet—and admires equally still—is Peter Redgrove. Edward Lucie-Smith has given a hint of this aspect of the Group in his mention of "a sort of undeclared rivalry. Particular themes—School was one which had a long run—are taken up by several poets in turn, each apparently convinced that he alone has the key to it." The strength of the Group was not in uniformity, nor even in rigour: it was in diversity, in the exchange of energies, enthusiasms, skills; even, simply, of information.

It was this background of friendship and equality that made effective discussion possible. Later in the Group's history, as earlier members established reputations and later recruits regarded them with deference, the balance and freedom were lost. At Poets' Workshop, for instance, the discussions were often inhibited, as much by those who were better known holding back, as by those who were unknown hesitating. The particular quality of the Group as a literary event, and the indeterminable nature of its value, can be seen in this: as a cultural encounter, its effects have not yet terminated; as a cultural institution, there was a time-limit to its full effectiveness.

Some of the variety of the Group does get through to *A Group Anthology*. There is Adrian Mitchell, for instance, in an unexpected setting. His poem, "Veteran with a Head Wound", should silence recent accusations that he has jumped onto the bandwagon of protest, for it shows him at this early date struggling with exactly the same concerns: and whilst one may not approve of the style which he has since developed, it is quite apparent that the style of "Veteran", highly competent though it is on the page, just would not make an impact on a large audience. Some of the liveliest contributions come from other poets—Rosemary Joseph, B. C. Leale, Margaret Owen—of whom one has heard too little since. In fact, the established contributors do not show up well in this selection. It is a dull anthology, taxing the perseverance of the reader.

Partly, I think, the selection itself is at fault. It presents the whole spectrum of Group poets, but it does not do justice to their variety, presenting too great a uniformity of subject and style. Beyond this, despite the lack of any "Group style", there are certain weaknesses of style which one can fairly say are recurrent.

Putting together the experience of London and Belfast, it would seem that this type of critical activity favours established forms in poetry. In Belfast this has resulted in a convincing revival of strict techniques. For the London Group the question was undoubtedly complicated by a reaction against the formalism of the Movement: the assumptions behind formal tidiness were felt to be dubious. This reaction was an insufficient emancipation. Strict forms should have been reckoned with or dispensed with, taken as a challenge or as a point of departure: as it was, form nagged, an anxiety in the background. There are cases of what one might call "residual form", often where the style itself would have most to offer, if it had found its own voice. There are rather more cases where form is adhered to, but seems to have had a dissipating influence: the sense is not of form growing out of the struggle with the material, but of the material being stretched to fit the form. One can find this tendency even in a poet of the calibre of Alan Brownjohn, and in his later work:

> What is there underneath this tight and
> scarlet creasing at their eye-corners,
> as the mouth-stretching laughter-spasm holds
> and stacks each man's entire, shuddering
> body on top of his stomach folds?
>
> ("Old Company")

It seems to me here that the rhyme on "holds/folds" is too heavy, and works against the impact of the image, against any sense of physical convulsion; the line arrangement is not convincing; above all, the expression of the image takes too long, the impact is blurred over too many words. It is almost as meticulous, pedantic and undramatic as a policeman giving evidence, and this is something one finds too often in Group writing. The characteristic mode is

analysis, not synthesis. The characteristic vice is wordiness, spelling every-
thing out. To take an example from the Anthology, there is Philip Hobsbaum's
"A Journey Round the Inside of my Mouth":

> The teeth are tomb-stones for the probing tongue,
> ridged, jag-edged and uneven.

The image is arresting, but devolves, almost automatically, into a routine of
factual evidence. "Ridged" and "jag-edged" are accurate, but out of place:
they deflect rather than support the image.

> I retched. To think of that full-blown decay
> eating while I was eating—mould I should
> clear away quick if found under the sink
> blotched, damp and green—

What does "blotched, damp and green" add to one's imagination of the
mould? If anything, it is less than the reader's own imagination of it. Editing
does not seem to have been one of the Group's critical activities.

The Movement were right to insist on the everyday detail, as an honesty to
experience: but any technique for reflecting experience, once it becomes
familiar, becomes a technique for producing platitudes. It is, for instance,
rather disturbing that a poem like Christopher Hampton's "The Grand-
mother" should be so obviously sincere, so competently worked out, and so
unmemorable. One has only to compare it with Ian Hamilton's "Birthday
Poem", which has hardly more words than it has lines, to see the value of a
more searching approach to established procedures. The dynamic brevity of
the Hamilton poem is an accentuation of detail, beyond a sympathetic
photography, into a painful apprehension of reality.

As a sustained encounter between a number of young poets, the Group is
historical fact. It would be a misnomer to call it a literary movement, in any
but the zoological sense. It did involve the regular movement of litterati to
Stockwell and Chelsea, but it was not a literary movement. No one actually
makes this mistake, only the appearance of it, but that in itself is confusing.
The only logical approach to the poets who were Group members is to discuss
them as individuals, or in relation to other, more verifiable movements, and
that is my procedure for the rest of this chapter.

The allotment of space to each poet should not be taken as any relative
assessment of merit. It is strictly a matter of personal chemistry—I have
written most where I have reacted most strongly. I am uneasily aware that I
should perhaps have allotted space to Martin Bell, but I can only say that
whilst I find his debunking attitudes and his brusque irony admirable, these
damage the work itself. He uses languages as an instrument of offence,
choosing coarse textures, lurid highlights. The energy is self-hating. The aim
is to express disillusion: the effect is to reduce the sensibility. With Philip
Hobsbaum, as poet rather than critic, I am in a different quandary: of his

earlier work I could find little to say, beyond what I have indicated in this introduction. I would write about his recent work with considerably more eagerness, but there seems little point until the direction is confirmed, and a representative collection published.

Alan Brownjohn

The characteristic of Alan Brownjohn's poetry that critic and reviewer have stressed is his scrupulousness, and certainly to be precisely honest to the limitations of experience is basic to his achievement: yet this dry attribute, perhaps because it is rarely so precise, has tended to overshadow other fundamental qualities in his work; and unsupported, it becomes a deathly compliment. "A poet whom one reads with respect, but to whom one does not quite submit" (*The Poetry Review*): this, if it is not a misunderstanding of what poetry should offer, is certainly purgatory by faint praise. I think that we will make better sense of Brownjohn's achievement if we consider the resources and impulses that have been schooled by his concern for accuracy in response to experience.

The language is always strictly curbed, yet its rectitude masks a certain roguishness: on occasion, it can scathe slyly. Part of Brownjohn's commitment to contemporary poetry is a striving for the informal, colloquial voice. Yet there is also apparent an attraction to the formal mode of address—thus his interest in a form of perfectly-manicured aggression. In "Retirement", for instance, the mandarin style is itself an irony:

> Shuffle the four equal armies of the contentious cards
> and manoeuvre those

and its decorous restraint can be vicious:

> The minor consolations
> of the manageable evening arrive the faster
> for either, or both, of these applications of power.

The compassion here is as incisive as the final sarcasm.

In "Snow on Bromley" a not-quite-neutral topography,

> . . . the snow
> settles the outer suburbs now,
> laying its claim unhurriedly
> on gnome and monkey-puzzle-tree

which Betjeman could have furnished, hardens into direct social satire:

> . . . I fall
> into forgiving nearly all
> the aspirations of the place,
> and what it does to save its face

the calm and dutiful obsession
with what is "best in our position"

which Larkin might have written; but the real attack, the final scathing, is
classical in form, an achievement, not of topical accuracy, but simply of
language. The fifth stanza begins with the accustomed moderation,

The snow fulfills its pure design
and softens every ugly line,

then suddenly clinches the kill in two lines,

and for a while will exorcize
these virulent proprieties.

This, not only in the technique, the cramming of "i" and "r" sounds, the
thrust of the pent rhythm, but in the linguistic relish evident behind the
technique, stands as close to the poetry of Marvell as it does to the poetry of
the 'fifties. The achievement continues, by contrast, in the delicate rhythms
of the last stanza,

Within one mile of here there is
no lovelier place to walk than this,
on days when these kind flakes decide
that what it boasts of, they shall hide.

Attention to this possibility of style is not confined to the earlier poetry:
it recurs, for instance, in "A 202", in which the road, which we have followed
past

blackened
and not-quite-Georgian terraces,
shagged-out Greens of geraniums and
floral coats-of-arms, . . .

and which will become the subject of a disenchanted meditation,

. . . turns any ironic
observer's tracer-isotope of ecology,
sociology or hopeful manic

verse into a kind of mere
nosing virus itself.

is sharply summarised at the mid-point of the poem in a line that Webster's
Bosola might have been proud of:

. . . It is altogether
like a vein travelled by hardy diseases.

The style is crucial at this point because it is the point where the poem
turns from description to interpretation, from the objective to the subjective.
To put it another way, the line has to bridge two passages of different kinds of
writing, both characteristic of Brownjohn. The first is the pointed but essenti-

ally neutral descriptive style inherited from Larkin, and concerned with the
outer environment,

>   . . . wired-off bombed lots glossy
>   with parked Consuls

The second is description of the mental wasteland associated with it, a gift for
defining the inner nullity, which is particularly Brownjohn's own, and lies
behind poems such as "If Time's to Work" and "The Space".

In this case, both styles are heightened. The tone of the description is
sharper than it would be in Larkin, and the mood of the meditation more
abrasive than in poems where Brownjohn is solely concerned with definition.
From each side, scorn forces an apotheosis—yet both styles claim to be dis-
passionate: Brownjohn's solution lies in this effect of style, echoing an age
when panache was an attribute of the dispassionate. The formality of the
phrasing creates a stance, a detachment; at the same time the energy of the
phrase is conclusive.

Elsewhere Brownjohn seeks exactly that neutrality of statement that made
a line like Larkin's "Canals with floatings of industrial froth" such a flawless
evocation of contemporary England. In the second of the "Two Songs in
Homage to Louis MacNeice", for instance, on a level with the formal pastoral
of lines like, "Three day-owls scatter towards the approaching wood", and
"Rides of pines come thinly down to entreat at the hedge", there are these
lines, "Finished sacks, thrown down, glitter and litter on the field", and "Hay-
blocks provide for the month under polythene sheets", which both give a
domestic feeling to the rural imagery, a sense of the land being husbanded;
and, by implying plastic sacks, not hessian, and admitting polythene in place
of tarpaulin, allow that the land is actually farmed by modern methods.

This evenness of description is important, because it is far more convinc-
ing than mere outcry. There is outcry in Brownjohn—the "Ode to Felix", for
example. Granted, this poem is a response not simply to environment but to
pressure, to commercial insistence and popular distortion. It is one of a
number of poems in which Brownjohn speaks up in the persona of the ordin-
ary man; but the others, "A Hair-dresser", "Farmer's Point of View", and
"Diana and the Transmitter", are more successful because they approach
their anger more hesitantly, considering other responses first. This poem loses
its temper. Even then, rage could have a quality, "the basic squawk" re-
asserting itself against "their cute squeak". But in its haste the poem builds
on pre-suppositions, becomes itself a pre-packaged attitude, so that its
evidence, however accurate, betrays the intention in its very presentation:

>   the easy prototype of all
>   those smirking descendants, capering
>   in slick, flourished lines, richer
>   for the primary colours . . .

The poem is a masterly performance, but, like Felix, it does run on. Consider, by contrast, the light touch of "William Empson at Aldermaston", which gives it a haunting quality, rare in its genre.

The urban environment does not repay strident attack, for the same reason that it does not repay contemplation: that it lacks resonance. The essential claustrophobia is that our habitat is an understatement, which it is impossible to criticise without overstating. Brownjohn is particularly good on this in the second part of "A 202":

> It takes no clear
> attitude anyone could easily define
>
> so as to resist or admire it. It seems to hate you
> possessively, want to envelop you in nothing
> distinguishable or distinguished, . . .

Brownjohn portrays a similar helplessness in the cultural environment: "Somehow" or "Daines at a Party" contain not so much satire of cultural pretension—though that is there too—as a sense of the shared limitation of our cultural horizon, the secondhandness of our experience. When he turns to our emotional mores, the fashions in love or pity, Brownjohn has developed a form of statement that leaves the ambivalence of the situation unbiased. In "At the Time" and "Of Consequence" the effect is both satiric and healing. In "Tin Doll", the irony is piercing precisely because the good intentions of the charitable are given their full due.

In the poems where Brownjohn does comment, as in "Snow on Bromley" and "A 202", there is an interesting difference between the style of his comment, and the style that Larkin might use. Larkin, if he wished to comment on the environment presented here, would speak from inside it, using its own lingo: though the puncture would be wry, the deflation would be final. Brownjohn, in a sense, speaks from outside, and not to puncture, but truly to comment, for in a curious way he is committed to the continuance of what he sees around him. The irony is that Larkin's mind flies all too easily outside his environment, so he forces himself to confine his utterance to its terms: Brownjohn accepts that there cannot be any other environment, and then protects himself by stepping back from it. The step back is in the style.

There is, of course, a rhetorical tradition behind "A 202"—this is not meant pejoratively, but simply as a definition of method, for it extends even to a rather fine platform joke:

> Camberwell, Peckham,
> New Cross Gate; places having no recorded past
> except in histories of the tram.

and there is something of rhetoric in the line on which I have focused attention,

> It is altogether
> like a vein travelled by hardy diseases

The placing of "altogether" has some point here, but it does draw on its rhetorical ancestry, the summary pretension giving it a false strength; and it is certainly characteristic of what is a minor vice elsewhere in Brownjohn, the use of words such as "always", "ever", "somehow", slipped into a line to achieve a vague extension of vista, an extra resonance. There is also an occasional tendency to prolixity, occurring most often when one senses that he is writing a part of the poem that interests him least: it is a sort of reverse courtesy—where he feels dislike or uneasiness, he pays attention in too many words. Both tendencies come together in a quotation from "A Girl Counting":

> the struggle
> long lost before anyone ever
> began on those cool, implacable
> constructs of order and tabulation.

A more interesting lapse is the occasional sanctimony, which often seems to be an echo from Graves:

> a trick, in assistance of love,
> and no truth
> ("Apology for Blasphemy")

or this aside,

> (though no one should dare to aperse her skill)
> ("Breaking Eggs")

There are poems which draw heavily on the style of Graves—"No Good" and "For My Son" are examples—but these do not jar: within their chosen medium, they are individual, and certainly successful. The shock comes when the distinctive tones of Majorca sound suddenly through those of Baron's Court. The problem seems to be that Brownjohn has attempted to do two things: to harness the colloquial voice for poetry, and to forge a formal style out of everyday language. The two impulses work well enough apart, but they work against each other in the same poem:

> a trick, in assistance of love,
> and no truth

sits uneasily next to

> shells of deception, all a lie.
> My words did that.

In Graves the style is based not only on hard work, but on a pre-1914 education, which means that his very conversation, and doubtless the language of his thoughts, is more etched than ours. There is a certain elevation of tone open to Graves which he achieves effortlessly, without loss of naturalness: in a more recent generation, the effort produces diction. For Brownjohn the source of dignity is energy, not decorum: in "Eight Investigations", for example, particularly in "cliff" and "epistemology", the language is entirely natural, and yet achieved.

Brownjohn frequently achieves emphasis by displacing the natural word order:

> but that is not now so.
> ("The Railings")
> . . . the ten next minutes,
> ("Hedonist")
> Walk a razed block round nine times
> ("Two Songs")

and the ending of "William Empson at Aldermaston"

> That deep blankness
> was the real thing strange.

This is effective where it is almost unnoticeable: but in "The Railings", for instance, an otherwise perfect poem, the misplacement in the penultimate line creates a jingling rhythm, and inserts an American idiom into very English writing: "The principle will drain from out a place".

Awkwardness sometimes besets the poems at their beginning, for instance, the first line of "The Situation", "For it was that the cousins never came," or the first lines of "Breaking Eggs":

> It is as if she chose to exist
> to scathe forgiveable sins.

Two characteristics seem to come together here. The first is the striving after a formal style. The second is part of the scrupulousness. Brownjohn's lyrical poems only take off into lyric just at the end; it seems almost a principle that there has to be a long run-up. Sometimes it is like an elimination process: the lyric statement is reached only after all the other possible statements have been investigated—hence, of course, the quality of his lyrics, his ability to see the grace in "rapid and curt fingers" ("Breaking Eggs") or to see the squalor of the moon, or the woman, and still find them, not transcendent, but, more to the point, "acceptable" ("Twenty Third Day"). Sometimes a lyric is built on a preamble. This happens several times in "Eight Investigations". In "a junction" for instance, the preamble is ingenious, even painstaking:

> Not to meet, then. But can't we maintain
> one concessionary contact: of
> some meeting in theory—for instance,
> making an agreement to retain
> a *kind* of connection by a glance
> each day at some same landmark? Or have
>
> an intersection of routes planned out
> on journeys we are often making?
> This could be a place where we again
> —at quite different times!—could no doubt
> "meet";

but it is wrought into a memorable effect:

> (I would cross it like a night train
> crossing points—rapid, darkened, trembling.)

This idea, handled differently, might easily have made a commonplace poem: handled inventively, it is startling.

If the first lines are sometimes awkward, it is a similar dourness that gives the last lines their peculiar quality. There is a deliberate resistance in the language, the lyric has to be wrung from it. The resistance is in the last line of "Apology for Blasphemy":

> . . . and as

> your mouth just opened, now,
> in a slight surprise, all the lions'
> mouths on the bronze financial doors
> dropped their gripped rings.

And in the close of "Sestina in Memoriam Vernon Watkins", where the poem almost seizes up before it achieves its end:

> He had this sort-of quality—no-one's first

> virtue, and not *his* first, but one power his good-ness had,
> then as always: to give all quirks and details a sort of odd
>   wonder,
> each last, least, great thing asking wry gratitudes.

Partly the resistance is an insistence on accuracy of detail—if Brownjohn overwrites at all, it is in being over-specific—but by this the movement of an image is not so much curtailed as completed: it is directed back into its own particularities. This certainly is the effect in the last phrase of "Breaking Eggs":

> if she could not also, with a mere knife only,
> take up (precise and chilling miracle!)
> each omelette into surging fabric-folds.

If lyric is, as it were, a last resort, it seems logical that Brownjohn writes some of his best love poems out of fear. The fears are everyday, they are daylight cowardice, nightmare panic. The poems are wry, tender and unsolemn. Nevertheless, the sensation of fear does spark off the expression of love; even, in a sense, is its expression. This is the *raison d'être* behind "cliff", "Diana and the Transmitter", and "Pictures". Love is more consciously summoned to the aid of fear in "Winter Appointment", where the ordeal, real enough, is the dentist. With impressive variety of manner, the poet follows his own flurries of nerves and reassurance: there is a surreal quality of suspense,

> that quick, sinister, flicking parade of the wan street
> of my mouth, that tilting of searching mirrors . . .

there are the odd details that impinge on unease,

> a train grates, roars down
> the cutting outside, the smooth cat flops off the sill.

there's humour,

> . . . Christ! Anything *must*
> be painful to be salutary

and description of a chilling perfection,

> Pain accurately descends his cold, angled crane
> of quivering wires:

before the final delicacy of rhythm:

> With ball-point
> I fray his dotted line, sense comfort in the gift
> of this restored street in hopeful mid-afternoon,
>
> down which Diana could be ready softly to
> walk, as down some now-
> cleansed and part-shuttered Piccadilly, quite alone.

Movement tends to be positive in Brownjohn. One of the affirmative qualities in his work is that he often traces a situation down, or back, to a point of movement. In looking at her "Second Drawing", he remembers the moment when it was drawn:

> past these pencilled lines
> to their sudden, living start: your neat
> intent smile, your tensed fingers moving).

The pleasure of the "Hedonist" is

> . . . the sunlight, as an amiable event
> to walk out into after the thick
> complexities of his room, leaving cigarettes, stick
> and tablets and trusting, for once,
> to his own feet and the friendliness of distance,
> and to mere walking alone on the bright pavement.

This isn't anything as simple as optimism—the last line of "KAO U888", "flattering his feet with challenging distances", is sufficient evidence for that —but it is, at least, a refusal to stall.

The strength of Brownjohn is that irony and invention come to the assistance of accuracy. In some respects, he is a satirist, writing about things that are unfunny. Compassion is the off-shoot of irony, affirmation is the resilience of decay. He explores the everyday reality in all its lack of promise, and then, out of that very knowledge, not despite it, he makes the everyday a springboard for lyric.

His achievement is not an easy one. He has the gifts, and the temptations, of a classical lyricist, but he has been schooled by his concern to write of the world around him. His reticence is not a shortcoming, but a commitment, and the most truly fecund of his qualities. The *Sunday Times* critic accurately assessed him when he wrote of *The Lions' Mouths*, "these poems are altogether his own, their hesitant scrupulousness a crisp achievement".

Edward Lucie-Smith

Edward Lucie-Smith's first collection established him as a master of the modest, perfectly-articulated statement—modest in dimension, quiet in tone, but not necessarily limited in feeling or perception. His vignettes of childhood are delicate, and unsettling. His courteous, fluent irony can be a surprising guide, discovering grounds for tenderness where one might have seen grounds for satire—"Imperialists in Retirement" is an example—and revealing a shrewd honesty when one was prepared for pathos, for instance "The Lesson", when he learned of his father's death:

> I still remember how the noise was stilled
> in school-assembly when my grief came in.
> Some goldfish in a bowl quietly sculled
> around their shining prison on its shelf.
> They were indifferent. All the other eyes
> were turned towards me. Somewhere in myself
> pride, like a goldfish, flashed a sudden fin.

This shrewdness can be a saving humour, puncturing bluff almost in the Lucky Jim manner, but with a lighter, more amused touch: the portrait of "The Drill Sergeant" is almost affectionate. By contrast, it can unmask the separateness beneath the social game: the ending of "The Portrait" is bleak, though the writing is somewhat muffled by the adoption of period dress.

Nevertheless, beyond a certain range of statement, the style lacks muscle. The expression can be lean and agile, as it is for "On looking at Stubbs's *Anatomy of the Horse*", but it can also be mannered, inconclusive, prim: "Sir, I'd obey you—but these angers come", is a tame ending to "A Prophet On The Underground". Doubt, detachment, distaste, these are the limits of its effective range. The strain becomes apparent when the style reaches for the actual dynamics of horror:

> It was the warren's mouths began to shriek—
> I saw their breathless immobility
> ajar to the still sky stripped bare of birds.

"Breathless immobility" is the expected cadence of the style: it does nothing to prepare us for the monosyllabic fervour of the last line. From an awkward start on "ajar", the rhythm runs away through the reversed second stress, and the chosen consonants concertina in a bumper-to-bumper crash. It's fine writing, but it ends up as an elocution test.

Logical, then, the change to a more relaxed form, which allows a more ebullient line: thus, the adoption of the Browningesque monologue. Again the form is thoroughly mastered, and the handling of rhythm in particular gives vigour. Irony still is the most dependable tone, issuing as a sardonic tenderness,

> If the long years
> instruct me now in fusing tone with tone
> until the painted you seems made of flowers,
> my skill is nothing to you, just the years

a wry celebration,

> But when I go?—I see you plan already.
> Good Flemish thoughts stir in those aqueous eyes . . .
> ("Rubens to Helene Fourment")

Lucie-Smith certainly equals the achievement of Browning's monologues, but he does not transcend it, or even extend the medium, for he brings no new understanding to bear, only the old gusto. Even more than Browning's, Lucie-Smith's monologues are guided tours of the picture gallery. Browning chose rather complex characters as his central figures, and the focus rests as much on their unfolding paradox as on the catalogue of pictures. Lucie-Smith's characters are striking rather than complex, and even the forceful Caravaggio ends on a slightly smug note as he finds his last state prophesied by his last picture. Only the art collector is a curiosity in his own right, and his monologue, "Soliloquy in the Dark", is the most successful of the group. Lucie-Smith fails, as Browning did, to find a convincing idiom for the characters' compressed sequences of thought. Caravaggio has his moments of subtlety:

> I've lost my anger.
> It left, and left me empty

but they tend to blur into the jargon of the form:

> I greet smiling
> my new-found death.

Even the idiom of "Soliloquy in the Dark" is anything but natural:

> No pity! Alteration,
> that I admit. But how to keep accounts
> of loss and gain?

The concealment of artifice is vital to a monologue, but the wit to conceal is a virtue rare in its exponents. It is a dramatic form, a situation contrived to generate conflict, most often by a paradox of thought or behaviour. But if the contrivance is stressed, it becomes more like a masque than a drama. So here, Rubens' shrewd assessment of his young wife begins in a markedly artificial vein:

> Now sinking towards age, I paint your rising.
> Your flesh glows with my sunset.

Doubt and self-doubt, distrust of the outer world and inner vacancy, in short, the existentialist syndrome: these seem to be Lucie-Smith's real subject, and one wishes he had tried to explore these through his monologues, rather than counterfeiting states of confidence. Nowhere does he really come to grips with this theme: he states it often, but he does not explore it in any depth. The problem is that the material is intuitive, not logical, and does not readily submit to the rational procedures of his first style. One can sense at times that the real core of a poem is touched on in a line—"rivers of silence roaring in my ear" ("Cardinal Bird"), or "Today thoughts swim, but feelings drown" ("At the Roman Baths, Bath")—but then is lost again in the orderly progression of the poem, which is admirable but predictable. What is needed is a style—enigmatic it might have to be, and elliptical, but it should at least be lithe, plangent—which could explore this inchoate region. Perhaps Lucie-Smith's clearest treatment to date is via personal allegory, in "A Sort of Sickness".

Given this subject matter, a state of feeling both palpable and evanescent, his recent style, informal and direct, is a right development: but it is still portraiture rather than exploratory expression. As the earlier style had its rational procedures, so the new style has its own philosophical pretensions:

> I cannot tell if time
> is being washed away,
> or if this is time, made
> tangible as water.

On the other hand, there is less moral abstraction—the implications of fever are now more basic—

> Flesh becomes
> like the wet sacks out there,
> abandoned in the dark
> of the garden, lapsing
> slowly into the earth.

and there is a strong vein of curt humour—

> Hear
> your own noisy machine, which
> is moving towards silence.

Less idiosyncrasy, more common humanity: is this the resolution of the inner doubt? If so, it has come, perhaps, a little too quietly. One discovers in the work sympathy, not revelation. Lucie-Smith's talent is acute enough to set his own problem. He isolates exactly the blind spots in human consciousness: but what one demands, paradoxically, is a conclusive statement of the inconclusive, and this requires a penetration which, to date, he has not shown. It involves, perhaps, a risk he has not yet taken.

George Macbeth

Early in his career, George Macbeth acquired a reputation as the *enfant terrible* of English poetry, which his subsequent lively publicity has done its best to play up:

> We announce with trepidation yet another macabre collection from the pen of that ever-fertile verse *couturier*, George Macbeth. Admirers and detractors will need no reminder of his predilection for the surreal, his obsession with the obscure and the extreme, and his poker-faced Notes.

Sadly, if we ignore the sinister packaging, we find that Macbeth is not quite the diabolical revolutionary he is made out to be. A look at the poems themselves, rather than the notes on them at the back of the book, brings the expectant eye to focus on a rather traditional product: accomplished, but not in any important sense original. The poems strike a violent posture, to utter a mild truth: publicity by Mr. Hyde, poems by Dr. Jekyll. "The Son", for instance, has the following note: "A mortuary attendant rapes the body of a dead woman. He associates her with his mother, who died of a liver disease". Yet the poem itself is robustly healthy at its core, and familiar in its impulse:

> There was only
> the sun above me. I *was* the
> sun. The world was my mother, I
> spread my wings to protect her growth. She broke
> into wheat and apples
> beneath my rain. I came with my fire to
> the sea, to the earth from the air,
>
> to the broken ground with my fresh
> seed.

If there is an extreme here, it is in the direction of neo-Romanticism. The note and the poem together may make the social point that deviant behaviour is often the regalia of innocence, an attempt to express common emotions by uncommon means. Macbeth's note ends, "He believes in a concrete form of resurrection by the power of love", and throughout his early poems he is generous, or credulous, to the possibility of innocence in strange places, viz. "The Disciple"—but the point is that without the note, the climax of the poem is not particularly striking. In fact, as a love poem, it would seem crisp, but rather trite. The images, the silver column, the sword of blood, the cross of fire, are stock sub-religious properties, and as close to the paintings of suburban spiritualists as they are to Dali. (This may be deliberate: this group of poems seems heavily imbued with the atmosphere of backstreet chapels.)

The technique of these poems is not to match complexity with a complex texture, but to provide a powerful simplification. They refer complicated contemporary situations back to primal myth. The note to "A Dirge" reads, "the imaginary murder of Hitler by someone with an Oedipus-complex", but the poem gains its strength from images such as:

> There a black dog rolled
> by a cold hearth whose fire had gone.
> And I remembered how it licked my hand
> when I was in your fold.

This is a powerful image of Death, particularly of the outrage and squalor of death—the cold hearth—but it relies very much on the ancient setting, with its echo of the old Odysseus returning to Ithaca, to find his dog lying on the dungheap. In other words, it draws heavily on the Oedipus Rex half of "Oedipus-complex". The complexity belongs to the note.

There are exceptions: "The Killing" relates the ritual execution of Eichmann to the manufacture of the atomic bomb, the scattering of his ashes to the radiation effects on Bikini Atoll. The detail of the poem remains contemporary, within a slightly heightened style, and it is effective. The connection is an ingenious one, but gains ground as a paradox, the ambivalence of sympathy carefully respected:

> Let no Jew or Gentile believe that
> the fly in the brain of the
> bald man adjusting his earphones annuls his
> own nature;

"The Crucifix" also takes contemporary detail, but only to intone it as rhetoric:

> Tomorrow
> is the celebration of the
> rape in the mine-field. I condone
>
> Starace, forgive the nine men
> in Sheffield.

On the other hand, it does make a distinct attempt at perverse imagery:

> My black milk swells
> in the fallen candle, breaking
> over charred wood in the dark.

Generally, though, the diabolism is very much on a *News of the World* level: again, perhaps deliberately so. This is valid as an expression of social sympathy, but it is hardly a startling new force in poetry.

It is perhaps significant that there are a number of Science Fiction poems, for much SF writing is precisely what I have tried to indicate in Macbeth, the use of a complicated theory to establish a very simple human situation. It works at its best in a writer like Ray Bradbury, where the paraphernalia is kept to a minimum, and is strictly an imaginative device, a framework by which he restates basic human predicaments. It may be that some writers have decided that they can nowadays only express simple statements via complicated devices, or it may be that the impulse itself is naïve, and that the SF mechanism provides a protective outlet. Even SF writers of the calibre of Bradbury, or in poetry, D. M. Thomas, come very close at times to sentimentality. So here, in "Early Warning", where an Eskimo has reverently collected the pilot's bones from a crashed American A-Bomber, the disturbing conclusion is partly undermined by sentimental touches—"my friendly pack of dogs"—and the antiquated religious diction:

> Forgive
> my theft. I give thee back thy skull,
> thy scalding thigh-bone, god. Thou shalt
> own all I have, my hut, my wife,
> my friendly pack of dogs, if thou
>
> wilt only tell me why these green scars
> ache in my cheeks; why this grey mould
> forms on my herring pail; why this
> right hand that touched thy head shrinks up;
> and why this living fish I touched
> writhes on that plank, spoiled food for gulls?

"Mother Superior" is a monologue spoken by the principal of an order of pregnant nuns, whose duty is to bear uncontaminated children in the event of a nuclear war. It draws on another stock SF device, the description of a bizarre future in the tones of complete normality:

> Sisters, it will be necessary
> to prepare a cool retreat. See to
> it that several basins are filled
> nightly with fresh water and placed there.
> Take care that food for a long stay be
>
> provided in sealed jars. I know of
> no way to protect an outer room
> from the light but some must be tried. Let
> the walls be made thick to keep out the
> heat. Before the Annunciation
>
> Our Lord exacts no other service.
> It may seem prudent to wear a wool
> robe at all times, and to bow down when
> the Word comes.

The illusion is maintained by an appearance of practical instructions, which are, in fact, hopelessly vague. The purpose of the cool tone is to soften the reader up, for the poem derives its shock from the sudden transfer of religious terms, a sort of sanctimonious blasphemy. One of the chief delights of SF seems to be writing the litany of outrage. We see immediately how coy it is if we compare it with the sharp satire of Peter Porter's "Your Attention Please":

> . . . administer
> the capsules marked "Valley Forge"
> (Red pocket in No. 1 Survival Kit)
> for painless death. (Catholics
> will have been instructed by their priests
> what to do in this eventuality.)

The hopeless realism of that last parenthesis makes it still possible to imagine us all in our underground shelters, the walls papered with Government instructions, muddling before death as we did in life.

"Report to the Director", on an establishment for extracting information by torture, uses a similar technique, evoking horror from vague references to unspecified equipment. The style is informal jargon, an old hand reporting to his boss: this makes possible one or two amusing touches

> Evacuation
> very decent. An infinity of freshness
> in a little diffusion of bitter carbolic.

and the odd sinister note,

> I doubt if anyone smelled
> a rat in the whole building, or heard as much
> as a squeak from a plimsoll

—but generally the style is deadening. It has the normal fault of a monologue, that the conversational asides muffle the impact: it is dull just because the ordinary turns of speech *are* dull, whereas a true raconteur has his idiosyncrasies of phrase, which give life even to the mere business of the story.

"Bedtime Story", in which a giant ant tells one of its children how the last man was accidentally wiped out, is far more effective, simply because it is good storytelling, not a report. The scene is re-created in detail; there is suspense, surprise, pathos.

> Long long ago when the world was a wild place
> planted with bushes and peopled by apes . . .

The style is in good nursery vein, humorous and vivid, pouncing on its effects:

> There were no more
> men. An impetuous soldier had killed off,
> purely by chance, the penultimate primate.

The final cadence is a triumph, with an exhilarating echo of nonsense verse that is, given the subject, piquant:

> Where had the bones gone? Over the earth, dear,
> ground by the teeth of the termites, blown by the
> wind, like the dodo's.

Christianity seems to be an irritant to Macbeth. He tries to debunk it, but it's a frame of reference that he can't resist. It is used for a cheap image in "Drop", (and to spice the storyline in "A Confession"):

> You were strung up like Jesus
> Christ in the strings
> of your own carriage.

("Drop")

In "A Christmas Ring" it is little more than a decorative device. It is the basis of "The Disciple", who sees Hitler as the Messiah; and in "The Crucifix", Sigrid von Lappus is seen as the Madonna. In these poems it is the invariable symbolism in which new beliefs must clothe themselves, as if it has become an obsessive force in the collective unconscious. The roots of this in Macbeth's own experience are perhaps explored in "St. Andrew's", a dispassionate poem which, by describing exactly the barrenness of the mystery, expresses the hopelessness of established religion more vividly than the irony wrung from religion elsewhere. That Macbeth does have a certain animus against Christianity is clear. What is left obscure is the reason for this, and the relevance of it, beyond a convenient source of emotive references, to his poetry. Curiously, the thought comes closest to the surface in "Circe Undersea", a Science Fiction scenario; humans serve a Being whom they take to be Love, but who is in fact Destruction. Their intentions are good, but events are a system programmed for evil. This theme has obvious contemporary relevance, and relates to Macbeth's belief in essential innocence; but its possibilities are lost in a cumbersome structure of religious references—it's not an attack or a restatement, but a welter of punch-phrases. "The God of Love" is explicit, but rather clumsy; a herd of oxen enact a parable against repressive Christianity. The poem is sustained by some fine descriptive writing, but undermined by a stream of almost comically suggestive imagery:

> that a softer womb
> would open between far hills in a plunge
> of bunched muscles . . .
> if that hill of fur could split and run . . .

Here is one of the dangers of symbolic narrative. "King Uspud" is amusing, but again it fails because it is shallow: in order to dispel belief, it merely makes play with the materials of belief. The animus remains inarticulate, barren in its own spite. Macbeth has not harnessed his anger as a creative force.

Blake heaved a whole mythology upside-down and turned it against the object of his wrath. In *Crow* one perceives another positive demolition: Hughes ignores the accretions of belief, resentment and guilt, and simply explodes the foundation myth. He changes the terms of the game. Crow comes out from under the shadow of Platonic Ideals, Unfallen Adam, and suppressed Lucifer: he asserts his own unlovely identity, Himself Absolute.

God is not destroyed, but He's out of a job. Compared to these antagonists, Macbeth's enmity is footling: he is not a revolutionary wit but a hack satirist, dependent on the continuance of the Establishment. The pity is, there are signs he could have been something more. He has an unusual sympathy, but not the passion to drive him far beyond the obvious. He has an acute mind, but not a clear head, for it is buzzing with effects.

The tendency to elaborate the surface, rather than strike to the substance, is one that recurs throughout Macbeth. It is mirrored in his style, which tends more to an accretion of detail and an accumulation of verbal effect, than to one incisive choice or a single stroke of language. Despite, or because of, all the surface clutter, there is a distance from the object. The technique works well enough in a poem like "On the Thunersee", where the surface has become the substance, but in the sequence that Macbeth calls his own kind of white goddess poem it means that the goddess has no real presence: she inhabits the poem rather as the family name inhabits a stately home, vapid behind her furniture. This distance in the writing is probably a habit now, which Macbeth shows recent signs of trying to break, but initially the distance was deliberately sought, and not, I think, as an aid to perspective, but as a protective measure. Macbeth has been widely praised for his powers of invention. It is equally possible to see his work as a series of attractive diversions, skirting immense areas of silence.

A recent interview with Macbeth, in Pooter's column in the *Sunday Times*, suggests where the diversions may have started:

> In the early sixties I got interested in late Victorian monologues, and Browning particularly, and it gave me a way obliquely of dealing with the autobiographic but publicly violent material. The sense of a newly discovered power was very exhilarating.

In other words, the discovery of a distancing device acted as a release, made it possible to write about difficult personal material. The pity is that this is not a release but an evasion. A divorce grows between the impetus and the expression. Interest shifts from the real to the apparent subject, from the clarification of a complex experience to the forging of a simplified one. And so there is this division of energy in Macbeth, between the lurid façade of the note and the wholesome commonplaces of the poem. Presumably the real subject, the material that was of difficulty and might have been of value, lies lost somewhere in the cabbala of the note: and what we have in the poem is *kitsch*.

We can measure, I think, what we have lost in potential poetry by looking at the difference between "The Return" and "The Son". "The Return" seems to me a far stronger poem, and its points of strength are where it is closest to reality. The background of coal-town and sickroom, and the accuracy of description, are an active part of the dramatic style:

Before
another stroke he will come back in bone

and thin my heart. That soot-black hill will break
and raise him in his clay suit from the stone
while my chalk-ridden fingers dryly ache
and burn.

Even here, the expression at climaxes tends to be markedly traditional—"on this rush floor/he will come striding hotly. . . . I am sand/threading a glass with slow and even pace"—but there is the sense of an imagined event, not an elaborated scenario.

I am not suggesting that Macbeth should have become a confessional poet: what I am objecting to is his presenting us with a literary version of the truth. Often, in fact, it is a succession of versions, each one more ornate than the last. He has often been praised for his versatility. I'm not sure it isn't his worst enemy, for it seems to extend the fundamental dissipation of energy. There are several subjects on which he has written a cluster of poems, treating the same material in a variety of styles, from a straightforward selection from the facts through several degrees of decoration to extreme artifice. The neatest example is the sequence on the death of his cat: in quite a brief space of time he seems to have run the whole gamut. Here the critical conclusion is not simple: the precise account is moving, but the formal lament is even finer—only, beyond the lament, lie two more variations, a surrealist dream-poem of only moderate quality, and an intricately woven sequence of twelve sonnets that is quite preposterous. There are other clusters where one can simply say that the quality is consistently mixed. In the White Goddess poems he seems all the time to be circling his material, feinting as often as he attacks: intricate footwork, but only rarely does he draw blood. The ironic reflections on Christianity are similarly inconclusive.

The largest cluster of poems are those about the War and his father's death, and here, I think, we can see most clearly the dissipation of energy through varieties of style. First there is "The Shell", an elegy for his father, which harks back quite distinctly to Dylan Thomas. It begins:

Since the shell came and took you in its arms
    whose body was fine bone
that walked in light beside a place of flowers,

Granted this, and the rather obvious use of Shakespearian references,

There is no bell
to tell what drowned king founders. Violets bloom

where someone died

the poem is well written, and the grim reconciliation with which it ends almost redeems the style:

And I sense the flow
of death like honey to make all things whole.

Then there are "The Landmine" and "The Ward": these make clear the desolating nature of Macbeth's childhood experience of War, but the style is gross with rhetoric:

> And air moved as in bowers
> of cedar with a scented breath of smoke
> and fire. . . .
>
> . . . That day of ire,
> if it shall come, will find me on my knees.

By contrast, there's "The Drawer", a bare summary of the facts, formally arranged, very much in the manner of the *Group Anthology*:

> So this dead, middle-aged, middle-class man
> killed by a misfired shell, and his wife
> dead of cirrhosis, have left one son
> aged nine, aged nineteen, aged twenty-six,
> who has buried them both in a cardboard box.

This might seem conclusive, but in "The Compasses" (his father's drawing instruments) Macbeth moves away from it, following two characteristic tendencies: the yearning for a conclusion which is not quite so flat, and the decorative impulse, the obsession with shining up all the details. The ending is fine:

> These compasses should be there,
>
> not locked away in a box
> by an uninstructed son
> but like an Egyptian king's
> ready shield and swords
> beside his crumbling hand.

But as usual the decorative impulse seems to lead to irrelevant effects:

> In an inch of hollowed bone
> two cylinders of lead
> slither against each other
> with a faint scurrying sound.

Finally, under the guise of reportage, there is the extreme of artifice, *A War Quartet*, which piles up verbal effects but is nowhere as vivid as the four prose quotations which precede each book.

The point is, then, that here is crucial personal material, but from it has come no distinctive poetic achievement. The elegy and rhetoric are accomplished, but they can be referred back to the source in other poets. Where there is a resistance to decorating the facts, the writing is strongest: yet even here the achievement is at the level of competence, no more. Had his creative impulse been intensive rather than extensive, Macbeth might have given us at least one moment of utter reality, wrought into imperishable form. As it is, he has given us a body of verse, most of which is already disposable.

I have said that *A War Quartet*, under the guise of reportage, is the extreme of artifice. The point is made clear by one simple contrast, between the actual history of what the Second World War did to Macbeth, and what he has made of that War in his *War Quartet*. The *Sunday Times* interview gives us the biographical fact: . . . "as his father had been killed by a dud anti-aircraft shell on a night when Sheffield was not even being raided, and later he was bombed out of his home, he felt he had as direct a connexion with the war as a serving man." The facts are humbling: his father's death was precisely the sort of inconsequential tragedy that war abounds in. Bitterly futile and arbitrary as it was, it was part of the true fabric of hostilities. It belongs to the same reality as the poems of Owen, Rosenberg and Keith Douglas. Contrast with this the edifice that Macbeth has constructed in the *War Quartet*. The whole style is device: he attempts to order the progress of war by a reference to omens and the state of the weather. In expression he mistakes verbal activity for verbal action, and reintroduces every trick of overwriting that the War Poets were so careful to eschew. The final fault is the most telling: there is a distinct element of glory-mongering, and his fighting-men retain a certain romantic aura—up-dated, of course, with a routine reference to sex.

In his introduction to the *Quartet*, Macbeth is careful to point out that he writes at secondhand, and that what he is after is a kind of "documentary surrealism". This intention is borne out by the quotations that precede each section: they present a world in which corpses from a ballroom look like broken dolls, in which a roar of noise becomes a wall of silence, in which tracer bullets look like paper streamers. Here is the material for the "dream-like trauma" that Macbeth wishes to create. His failure is measured by the fact that these brief quotations are not only superior but different in kind to his verse extensions. Where they are reticent, he is wordy. Where they are direct, he is obscure. Conversely, where they are subtle, he is naïve. His machinery is too obvious and his characters are too blank. He does create a mood for different phases of the War, but only at the level of *All Our Yesterdays*. His mistake, surely, is to counterfeit an average man's reaction. It goes against his own declared interest in the detached, peculiar vision: and indeed, if war has any purgative value, it is this, that it burns away the average reaction.

Apart from the testimony that the prose quotations bear against Macbeth's verse, there is the evidence of an earlier poem, "The Drop", in which a French paratrooper describes a raid on the F. L. N.. True, this is written from the point of view of a professional soldier, not a citizen soldier, and it does make rather a rhetoric of barrackroom language, and it can be clumsy—"to feel the sick/flap of the envelope in the wind:/like galloping under a stallion's/belly"—but it does come close to the way a certain sort of soldier talks—"Half of Africa flushed/out and cocked/up; you could piss in its eye."—and there is a sense of physical effort, of real bullets flying:

> When the ground
> slammed you at eighteen feet
> per second you were out skedaddling for the first
> tree with your harness
> cut: the sten jammed whore-
>
> hot yammering out of your
> groin. You were implementing the drill
> balls: it was flog
> on till you blacked out dead.

Crude as this poem is, it shares with the War Poets one fact of war, the futility of the individual's contribution. The structure of Macbeth's *Quartet* might almost be an attempt to compensate for this fact.

Perhaps the fundamental failing of *War Quartet* was its distance from most of the material and its bookishness. "A Light in Winter" is an imagined narrative and uses all the devices of the *Quartet*, but at least it is set in a background which is close at hand, and verifiable in detail. Here too the seasons are a commentary on the phases of the relationship:

> and then,
> with no perceptible crisis, while
> the chestnut walls burst open, and green mines
> exploded mahogany on gravel, he
> felt a control come.
> . . . he
> slipped into winter, losing her.
> Now she
> was all one with the shed seeds, fallen in
> some drift of snow.

And there is a similar use of omens, though these can be ludicrous:

> In their eating, tumbling prawns
> with a barbed fork, hot feeling found
> its symptoms.

More interesting is the sense of a mechanism underlying human relationships, an impersonal rhythm, conveyed through a series of images in which the humans are matched with objects. This is basic to the rationale of the affair, in which desire and need are almost material possessions: the husband,

> only saw hard lust
> forged in a pouch for spending

and the mistress "opened her purse of illness." Illness is a force which governs the lovers:

> So she
> planned a disaster, helpless.
> In the quick
> under the covers, even as they humped

like spoons, in close liaison, it all soured
to a head

just as the mechanism of marriage links the husband to his wife

In thin poise, to and fro,
their union clicked and held.

The illness works itself out, and the end of the affair, like its genesis, is automatic:

So the other, when he came
in burned late August, was
inevitable, a laboratory.

Set against this impersonal mechanism is the husband's subjective reading of times and moods, in which he interprets the inanimate furniture as constraining him: as his frustration and anger grew,

he saw the hands
grip in the clock, stir, threaten.

Then, as "love swivelled",

In his panelled house,
. . . all
the brooches pricked and held still.

Identically structured as it is, "A Light in Winter" is far more successful than *A War Quartet*. It has energy, which perhaps comes from using a background closer at hand: and the attempt to impose an order upon experience is successful, both because the experience itself is more compact, and because the attempt represents, not wishful thinking, but a determinedly realistic view of a set of emotional convulsions. There is a concern to make sense, not to manufacture sense. The clear-sightedness is not all one way: there is a recognition, perhaps in rather fulsome terms, of the friendship that is basic to the marriage's survival: the mechanism is, "saturate with the oils of mercy".

"The Wasp-Woman", again, is total device, but a complete success. Macbeth takes over from the French poet Ponge the theme of Woman as a Wasp. The poem is exciting to read because it keeps on moving into new variations, refusing to be pinned down to one statement or one style. It continually surpasses expectations. The approach can be direct:

Like a taut string whose touch
burned or cut as it yielded its resonance,
she hurt as she moved.

or wry:

She was one of those wheeled machines
that at certain seasons ride
from farm to farm in the country, providing
refreshment. A little pump grinding on wings.

or ingenious:

> The electric tram moves
>
> on its rails. There is something deaf in repose
>   and loud into gear about
> it too. It breaks at the waist as she did. Is
>
> shrivelled by electricity like something
>   fried. And if you touched her, she
> pricked. No shock, the venomous vibration from
>
> all her pores: but her body was softer, her
>   flight wilder, more unforeseen,
> more dangerous than the even run of a
>
> thing on rails.

Even erudition is a source of energy:

> Such thirst perhaps from
>
> the slenderness of her waist. For the Greeks the
>   brain was in the waist. And they
> used the same word for both. If it was *sponge*, they
>
> were right.

Macbeth imagines, and tries to pre-empt, the critic's reproach of this poem: "piquancy without depth" he suggests. I think there is a certain depth, not finally in the thought, for it is behind the thought and the thought is merely a reaction to it; it is a personal presence, which resonates throughout the poem. Whether it is the personality of a particular woman or the spirit simply of Woman, it possesses the poem, with a presence strong enough to rile the poet.

In this sense of being inhabited by a personality other than the poet's, "A Wasp-Woman" is unique in Macbeth. Generally his poems are structures devoid of personal contact. Even in the sequence which begins the second section of his *Collected Poems*, the "White Goddess" section, the poems imagine particular histories and sets of personal attributes—they present themselves as love poems—but there is little sense of person addressing person. One feels that the unusual settings and the tragic attributes have invaded too strongly, and become almost the *raison d'être* of the poems. One can see the decorative impulse at work even in incidentals

> One winter night
> the wheels we hired were stayed on wet stone. Light
> flared in the stucco.
>
> ("The Heir")

and it reaches its apotheosis in "The Death-Bell", where the girl's entrance into an airliner is described thus:

> I see you enter through the silver door

under the tail. To where your throne
rests in its grooves, you move on naked feet,
alive, and well. Strapped in, you sit alone.
I see your toes, white worms along the floor,
carved as in glass.

In fact, this poem uses exactly the same technique as "The Son": via imagery
it ascends from the facts into associative symbols. Nonetheless, it has its
moments of quality,

All I own
sinks into this: that we are still at war
and burn like soldiers in the heat

just as in the ending of "The Heir" an astringent tone comes suddenly out
of a rather bizarre device:

Here it lies,
hard, wrinkled as a dried fruit's. And what shades
it with his body, is the wind that dies.

Reading this sequence is rather like listening to a distant radio station: an
odd phrase comes clearly through the buzz of literary static. When a phrase
does communicate, it is strong enough to make one wish the static away.

Perhaps the fault is in Macbeth's philosophy of writing. Pooter tells us
that he writes in concentrated bursts, night after night, in the small hours.

The important thing is to thrash out huge quantities of fairly well-
written poetry. If it doesn't last, who cares? . . . The Movement weren't
prepared to churn out a bad poem about the most important experience
of their lives. A willingness to do that seems to me the first essential of an
important poet.

The trouble with this is that whatever quality an experience may have in life,
on the page it has only the quality of the poem. In Macbeth's sequence of love
poems, it is obvious that a distinct and telling experience is being com-
municated: but the communication is markedly impaired by over-emphasis.
The compulsion to dramatise finally renders the verse turgid. For all his
temptation into neo-gothic extravaganzas, Macbeth's real gift is much
nearer home, closer to Thurber than it is to Poe or Lovecraft.

Macbeth has acknowledged the early influence of Ted Hughes, and one
can see in his work an interest in animal violence:

In the reign
of the chicken owl comes like
a god.

("Owl")

Yet Macbeth invokes the owl against a human setting

Owl is an eye
in the barn

and within the framework of its own domestic economy

                                        Six
            mouths are the seed of his
            arc in the season.

The owl is not only a bird of prey, but a force latent in the human, which breaks out by the end of the poem. As Macbeth says, a spell to become an owl. In the avowed interest in writing from the viewpoint of a child, in recording the animal movements around the human, and in elements of style, "Owl" links directly to "A Child's Garden". In this area, the invasion of the domestic by the animal, Macbeth's work has genuine vitality.

Typically, "Owl" starts very much as a literary property

                        Is a feather
            duster in leafy corners ring-a-rosying
            boles of mice.

but around it Macbeth creates a style that is at once comic, startling and sinister:

                        Who flies
            like a nothing through the night
            who-whoing . . .
                            . . . Twice
            you hear him call. Who
            is he looking for? You hear
            him hoovering over the floor
            of the wood.

The middle section is less assured: from "Cold walnut hands/on the case of the brain!" it lapses to "For a meal in the day/flew, killed, on the moor", which always reminds me of Hotspur, and "Torn meat/from the sky" is almost padding: but the final spell-binding has conviction,

            Flown wind in the skin. Fine
            rain in the bones. Owl breaks
            like the day. Am an owl, am an owl.

In "Beast", where the poet becomes a rhino, the tone is warmer—it is a humorous parable, not a spell-binding: but the style is a masterly blend of comedy and threat:

            a trundle of bulk
                on the wary stairs.

            I steam in your face,
                munching an orange.

            I can hardly see
                the way to my pen
            or feel the tiny

                    beaks of your nails
               cleaning my sides

until the final acceptance

                    or slowly roll
                         like a barrel of apples
               to have my tummy
                    thumped like a drum
                         and be your beast.

"Scissor-Man" and "Marshall" are similar successes, using domestic images
—a pair of scissors, and a broad bean—as the focus for human characteristics.
In this semi-comic treatment of themes which are basically serious and
realistic, Macbeth seems to me to be at his best: the writing is agile, surprising
and direct. The style abounds with effects, and the poems are uproarious in
performance: yet the style is used to resolve forces already latent, not to
generate them out of the void, as it too often is elsewhere.

   Animals don't feature only in spell and parable: the quality carries over
into a number of poems which celebrate animals in their own right—chiefly
in a domestic, and sometimes in a nursery setting. In "At Cruft's" the style
hasn't quite the same electric quality—the chief effect of the syllabic exercise
seems to have been to retard the writing until the stated number of syllables
have been used—but the slightly disconcerting perception is still there, and
the humour. In a similar set of exercises to describe his cat, "Fourteen Ways
of Touching the Peter", the style is alive again

                         You can shake
                         his rigid
                         chicken-leg leg,
                         scouring his
                         hind-quarters
                         with his Vim
                         tongue.

or

                         You can have
                         him shrimp
                         along you,
                         breathing,
                         whenever
                         you want
                         to compose poems.

and the writing expresses a considerable tenderness

                         At night,
                         you can hoist
                         him
                         out of his bean-stalk,

> sleepily
> clutching
> paper bags.

Peter's death is the subject of a lament, "To a Slow Drum", perhaps the most delicate and moving tribute ever paid to a household pet: the other animals gather from all over the house, toys and vermin alike,

> Gemmed with a dew
> of morning tears,
> the weeping armadillo
> has brought his shears:
> the droop-ear dog
> and the lion came,
> dipping their long waists
> to meet the drum. . . .
>
> . . . Over the red-black
> kitchen-floor,
> Jeremy the spider
> stalks to his place,
> all eight legs
> wet from the waste:
> he climbed up the drain
> to be here on time.
>
> Now, to the slow
> egg-timer's chime,
> shiny in state
> come things from the grime:
> tiny slaters
> with wings and hoods,
> beetles from the closet
> under the stairs. . . .

and they stand together on the top storey, to watch the smoke disperse from his cremation, and to chant his dirge

> Peter, salt Peter,
> fish-eating cat,
> feared by the blackbird,
> stung by the gnat,
> wooden-spider collector,
> lean as a rat,
> soon you shall fall
> to a fine grey fat.
>
> Peter, salt Peter,
> drift into the wind. . . .

There is another, rather grandiose tribute in "The Snow Leopard". It is in a reference to this death, in "A Christmas Ring", that Macbeth suggests a

possible reason why his writing on domestic themes is so much more success-
ful than his work on so-called *bigger* themes:

> Well, what if it's not true
> that a slash of cruel headlines nails you through?
> Suppose, though, a brittle corpse does, burned, and
> tossed
> across a bald earth, graved in pewter frost?

It would be interesting to know which of this cluster of poems, "To a Slow
Drum", "A Death", "The Snow Leopard", and "A Christmas Ring",
was written first. What is simple, clear and effective in "To A Slow Drum"
and "A Death" becomes blurred and over-written in "A Christmas Ring".
Or did the inchoate "Ring" crystallise into the other two? Does Macbeth, in
effect, publish his first drafts? Or has he fitted a poetic afterburner, in an
attempt on the metric speed record? I suspect the second.

The writing about animals is clearly linked to Macbeth's interest in writ-
ing "for those who, like myself, regard themselves as children". The poems
about Peter express tenderness without becoming mawkish, but in the writ-
ing which is directly for children, the balance tilts occasionally towards
whimsy. "A Child's Garden" starts well—

> Whose are these eggs? Ladybird's.
> Hard like crumbs of sleep. . . .

but ends dubiously, and "House for a Child" lapses from a very concrete
evocation of the house, full of sounds and textures, into

> I kiss my bear
> with his bashed face who keeps me safe
> and who gave his squeak
>
> to a tiny rhino . . .

There is a similar tendency in "Noah's Journey": the majority of fine verses,
like "lynx" and "lightning", are diluted by others, like "bat" and "tiger",
where sentimentality and even condescension leak into the Ark:

> We are safe,
> mewed up in our tub with a
> tiger to care for us. Tiger, look fierce.

The style has not developed markedly since the early poems. The associ-
ative choice of a noun, to create an emblematic effect, was already striking
in "the windward owl . . . in the glass of air". With adjectives, the technique
had a more active intention, to capture an elusive quality, such as the texture
of a movement: a surprising adjective is used like a grab-net;

> I lurch in a dry
> run.
> ("The Beast")

More recently this has been extended to verbs, where again the intention is
active, not to pose the language before us but to short-circuit our expectations
of it, to get a response direct from the nerves: "if love winced in then,"
("A Light in Winter"); the choice of verb is violent, but intuitively right.

This effect is particularly found in "A Light in Winter", where it is com-
bined with other effects, all similar in intention: there is compression

> As they broke the street,
> rain-lashed, with black cars shining . . .

verb-coining

> She strudged in
> clenched in her coat, stiff, man-like

oxymoron, "her powered absence" . . . "an absorbed wilting". The com-
pression extends to the syntax, which becomes almost Latinate: "oblivious
to/his laid work, he sat waiting". There are dangers in this sort of compres-
sion. In a recent poem, "In Winter", Macbeth gives one of his cats a tortuous
moment

> One leapt
> washing itself
> to the sill.

The combination of all these techniques throughout a long poem can be self-
defeating: "A Light in Winter" is battering to read at one sitting, and although
each individual effect aims at compression, the final effect is one of verbosity.
It is partly a question of pace—*A War Quartet* lacks energy, and becomes
turgid, "A Light in Winter" is all energy, insistently so—but more a question
of not overcrowding. In "A Light in Winter" absolutely everything is
heightened, so that the writing is always interesting but often verges on
excess:

> Outside, thin birds
> with breaking feathers, lifted, hurled
> oceans of muscle into bald air.

The balance in this poem is not helped by Macbeth's curious habit of
dramatising the furniture;

> In exchange, his grooved
> whirling disc drove her furies back

means, presumably, that he gave her an L.P. for Christmas, which cheered
her up. It is related to the decorative impulse in poems like "The Heir",
that I mentioned earlier: "the wheels we hired were stayed on wet stone"—
it was a taxi presumably, not a pair of unicycles. This coyness about transport
and consumer goods underlines again Macbeth's Romantic twitch, and the
limitation of his gifts to traditional strengths. Throughout this poem he
handles descriptions of the weather and the seasons well, and the scenario of
street and building site fairly well, but he is utterly daunted when he comes

to contemporary interiors and city nightlife. His description of a discotheque has a quite adolescent combination of shocked perception and naïve enhancement of style, for which "writing in character" is an insufficient plea:

> So they came, hands held,
> to a glowing room.
>   Men bowing, instruments
> of a bored thunder, lightened.
>   By the sheets
> of traced façades, pinned elevations, tricks
> and fancies of irrelevant ornament, some
> shimmered in glass, charmed, winsome.
>   Their
> willowy consorts, offered mistresses,
> pawed, shouldered, flouncing.

For a later moment in a stadium, he resorts to a vague sketch and a dash of hip-talk:

> In the glare
> of all those egos, flowered silk and sound,
> he was relaxed.

In "Owl" and "The Beast" there is a simpler and more effective technique for compression: he uses a shorter line, and leaves out unnecessary words. The poems are held together by an inspired use of assonance and internal rhyme, which is why they perform so well. The technique is there again, in a less intense form, in parts of "Noah's Ark":

> pig
>
> will need guiding with this
> boar board. He is heavy with
> acorns. Incontinent pig!
> Why did they send me a pig
> so big? . . .

There is also a crisp, sardonic style, which combines a relaxed line with a delivery of quick patter. It is the style of "Scissor-Man" and "Marshall", and has perhaps an early ancestor in "The Spider's Nest", a wry monologue spoken by the invalid Eugene Lee-Hamilton:

> After all, success in drowning
> ants in vermouth requires only time and I
> collect it like dust.

Macbeth's style was impressive from early on. In recent years it has not acquired significant new strengths: rather it has become muscle-bound. The bold use of the associative force of words, which was particularly Macbeth's achievement, has been developed into a violent element of style; odd instances are effective, but the constant use of it turns surprise into a mannerism. One

senses a restlessness here: the language has been so roughly treated that
Macbeth is now dissatisfied with it. He has pushed the subjective choice of
words so far—"racing through the savage park", is one instance among many
—that there is little reason left why he should put one word in preference to
another. The gift is still provocative—it has run to seed rather than gone to waste
—but there's little future in its development unless it is controlled. Similarly,
Macbeth's rejuvenation of blank verse has been carried to the point where it
creates only a jagged monotony.

Thus the publication of *Collected Poems* comes at a very odd time,
when the author is clearly at a transitional stage. His achievement so far,
though its virtues have been somewhat hidden beneath its ambitions, has
been real enough: there seems nothing in the section of new poems to stand
alongside it. "Painter's Model" has a certain panache, but it is quickly
predictable. "Dr. Crippen's Elimination Kit" is a dreary progress, with few
bright moments. Macbeth can be very entertaining, but he has turned enter-
tainment into a burdensome obligation. *The Orlando Poems* don't justify
themselves on any count, simply because they are neither very funny nor
very original. As a parody of *Crow*, they don't bear comparison in wit or
stylistic mockery with, say, "Charred Whitlow", Henry Reed's parody of
Four Quartets. As a disposable epic, they are shallow beside the quaint
depths of *Musrum* (Thacker and Earnshaw, Jonathan Cape, 1968).

"The Auschwitz Rag" is representative of a number of pseudo-Pop songs,
which quite overshadow Macbeth's versions of Keats as an error of taste.
They are embarrassing rather than shocking, and "Sheath Man" in particular
is more prurient than virile. Worst of all, they are unbelievably crude
specimens of their type: as actual pop songs they wouldn't make the grade,
for most pop songs, however poorly structured, have more verbal life in
them. Macbeth has another go at the hip-talk, but it is heavy and unconvin-
cing—after all, hip is a quality of mind, not a particular dialect, just as the
quality of jazz is independent of specific styles.

For the moment, "the trapeze-artist of the abyss" is definitely grounded.
In fact, he is an altogether more clownish, more pathetic figure, like the cow-
boy in the comic song—"It's been lonesome in the saddle since my horse
died".

On the other hand, in recent uncollected poems there are signs of a more
direct, personal voice, and a gentler mood, though the voice is often blurred
by stylistic ambitions, with a particular tendency to rhetoric. "In Winter"
escapes these vices: a delicate development of a small, unextraordinary
moment.

One of the current epitaphs that Macbeth likes to sport is "extraordinary
gifts arrogantly wasted". On the evidence so far, I rather think that we have
seen a distinct but limited gift, artfully deployed. He has worn the guises of
Surrealist and Expressionist, but he is by natural sympathy a neo-Romantic,
with inclinations to the sentimental. Thus his best work has, in fact, been in a

domestic setting, with tinges of humour: for in this vein the postures aren't possible, or else they're material to be debunked, but the sentiment can be real. Macbeth is clearly concerned to be "the important poet", but he has perhaps not realised where his own strengths lie. Until recently, the use of masks and devices has dissipated most of his "important" material. On present form, he may well find himself with classic status, but not on the same podium as Byron: he is more likely to be cherished as a twentieth-century descendant of Edward Lear, with a certain infusion from A. A. Milne—but that is no mean compliment.

Peter Porter

Peter Porter is an uncompromising realist, who made his terms of reference clear from the start. What was surprising initially was the strength of his statement; what has been startling since is the consistency with which this reference has expanded over an ambitious range of material, until the map of Sydney Cove has become a personal chart of Western Civilisation, with a projection across Time that would have defied Mercator. This was possible because of the particular clarity with which Porter looked at the society into which he was born. He saw the Australian background as incorporating in its very origins the stress marks, the crowsfeet and grey hairs, of the European tradition:

> In this new land the transplanted grasses root,
> waving as sulkily as through old falling soot.

In a curious way, and despite huge differences of outlook, the Australian forefathers knew by instinct what the twentieth century regards almost as its own revelation, that love is rarely disembodied, that the life of the mind cannot exist separately from the facts of economics, that the body wears like a machine. Porter is one of the few poets really to write of people as corporeal beings:

> . . . an old mother
> wastes herself for a busy cancer,
> she has always sacrificed flesh and time
> for others

He is one of the few to assign any realistic place to money:

> At the top,
> I say, there are words which feeling cannot mar,
> but here there is only money and the use of it.

He is alert to material objects, for more often than not they are the definition of spirit:

> —the stewing meat
> smells savoury past the pruned back roses
> and wafts on the street's spindly limits,
> the only fragrance of defence and love.

Death has been a presence in his work from the beginning, for in his world,

> Death's a relation,
> waiting to get in touch.

For him, it is almost axiomatic that any human enterprise ends in dis-appointment. He sees the very intention as limited in its scope:

> —they've retired in the sun
> by the seaside. All they want is to avoid pain.

This is not cynicism, but a shrewd sense of the realities. His work is striking, not simply for its honesty, but for its balance: he is honest in tone as well as in content. For instance, in the vignette of his mother, in the first section of "Ghosts", he achieves a clarity of statement which is neither tender nor bitter, but more piercing than either:

> A large woman in a kimono, her flesh
> already sweating in the poulticing heat
> of afternoon—just from her bath, she stands,
> propping her foot on a chair of faded pink,
> preparing to cut her corns. The sun
> simmers through the pimply glass—as if
> inside a light bulb, the room is lit with heat.
> . . . the clicking of her scissors
> fascinates the little feminine boy
> in striped shirt, Tootal tie, thick woollen socks,
> his garters down. . . .
> The inheritance I had, her only child,
> was her party melancholy and a body
> thickening like hers, the wide-pored flesh
> death broke into twenty years ago.

This honesty alone would have been a considerable achievement: but onto the integrity he has grafted a quality of daring, so that his range of achieve-ment has grown successively with each book. Realism has become an adventure of thought, a trading with surprise as well as a harrying of truth.

Porter's satirical sense was already alive to the Australian background, or at least to the British beginnings there:

> A box of bibles was washed up today,
> the chaplain gave them to two methodists . . .

but it found its full scope in the London Chelsea Set:

> From Heals and Harrods come her lovely bridegrooms
> (One cheque alone furnished two bedrooms).

There is a shrewd perception of the protean English social structure, still persisting:

> The colonel's daughter, in black stockings, hair

> like sash cords, face iced white, studies art,
> goes home once a month. She won't marry the men
> she sleeps with, she'll revert to type—its part
> of the side-show: Mummy and Daddy in the wings,
> the bongos fading on the road to Haslemere
> where the inheritors are inheriting still.

but already this perception is combined with a historical perspective:

> These jeans and bums and sweaters of the King's Road
> would fit Marston's stage. What's in a name,
> if Cheapside and the Marshalsea mean Eng. Lit.
> and the Fantasie, Sa Tortuga, Grisbi, Bongi-bo
> mean life? A cliché? What hurts dies on paper,
> fades to classic pain.

Even the social structure is only the contemporary expression of an ageless problem: the real constriction is the limited scope of human life:

> The same thin richness of these worlds remains—
> the flesh-packed jeans, the car-stung appetite
> volley on his stage, the cage of discontent.

And so, before Porter's satire has had time to pall, just as

> Cancer touches in the afternoon, girls in Jensens . . .

becomes a familiar element of his style, the satire broadens from the social scene to the universal human situation: we "join the historians on their frieze of pain". As Edward Lucie-Smith points out, if we consider Porter a satirist, we must place him alongside the Elizabethan "biting satirists", in the tradition of Juvenal: accurate as it is in particulars and scathing as contemporary comment, his satire is essentially timeless, its subjects the omnipresence of death:

> . . . A starlight epitaph—*Here they belong*
> *who died so young although they lived so long* . . .
>
> Eighty years dead, at last death quits the brain.

the limitations of human possibility:

> But we die in the first room we see,
> the bright locked world, the captivity.

He is markedly unindulgent as a satirist. If we compare him with Juvenal, for instance, he pays far less attention than he might to the innumerable varieties of human folly. The satires on the Chelsea Set are balanced by wry studies of the callow, vulnerable outsider, in "Metamorphosis" and "Beauty and the Beast": sympathy lies with the outsider, who is solely, yet insuperably, handicapped by lack of income and status; but he is no White Knight, he has his own vanities and naïvetes. In "Beauty and the Beast" there is a final twist

to the dénouement, and we notice again the terms in which humanity is
defined:

> So he sits alone in Libraries, hideous and hairy of soul,
> a beast again, waiting for a lustful kiss to bring
> back his human smell, the taste of woman on his tongue.

The theme of awkwardness receives its final definition in "The Bird Dream",
in which the wry humour furnishes an oblique love poem:

> You're throwing bread on the water,
>   I take a piece from your hand
> and have to waddle over gravel to do it.
>   I'm a floating furnace of love
>   but I'm not adapted to walking.
> You walk away over the pathway
>   and the statue-mounted grass.

The invocation of death as the underlying condition of life—"Eighty years
dead, at last death quits the brain"—is not a rhetorical flourish. Porter's
originality as a satirist, and his particular relevance to this century, is that he
concentrates, not on the kaleidoscope of folly, but on the monotony of human
aspirations, the mean perspectives that, increasingly, we have in common.
Every satirist has stressed that we all come to the same fate in the end:
Porter's point is that we never get away from it in the first place. The
claustrophobia is global—"When/did brushed pigskin reach this part of the
world?"—and here the reference is strictly contemporary, to the shrinking
globe, the sprawl of World City; but it is also timeless, it is the bugbear of
bodily existence; somewhere else

> in this unjust landscape a donkey takes
> two steps forward raising water in an old bucket,
>
> the wheel moves a broken spoke a perfect circle,
> the set bee moves through its archipelago,
>
> beside the A.A. box in dusty nettles
> a dog leaps a dog and finishes too soon.

And beyond this there is the final, infinite occlusion:

> . . . and if we shout
> at the gods they send us the god of death
> who is immortal and who cannot read.

In this respect, Porter's interest in Culture as a theme has broadened out,
just as the scope of his satire has broadened. There is an occasional yearning
for the optimism of the past:

> Where George Herbert would
> have seen this day the holiday

> that made natural the good
> in its six forerunners . . .

and for its breadth of credulity:

> wishing to cry as freely as they did who died
> in the Age of Faith

and a matching disdain for the bland assurance of materialism:

> man
> in heaven and God in aspic . . .

—thus the mixed feelings which conclude "The Historians Call Up Pain",
and which are the basis of "Sunday":

> and I wake up
> to Sunday in London, to comfortable words
> and the Grail filled with orange cup.

Nonetheless, there is no romancing about the past. The attraction is to its
uninhibited energy, the perfection of the human monster:

> Now back to Quantz. I like to think
> that in an afternoon of three sonatas
> a hundred regiments have marched more miles
> than lie between here and Vienna and not once
> has a man broken step. Who would be loved
> if he could be feared and hated, yet still
> enjoy his lust, eat well and play the flute?

There is a corresponding attraction to the theme of the "Last Days", the
decline of Western Civilisation, and if this produces a certain grandiloquence:

> In your last silk
> shirt by bomb light you are fingering Bach . . .

it is matched by a vigorous, down-to-earth disgust:

> we've been Europeans now for a millennium
> and where's it got us? Doing piece work
> by strip lighting in Waco, Texas.

Behind it, I think, is a genuine sense of responsibility, cultural and moral:

> . . . only a tradition
> of mind going uphill and always
> getting steeper.

> Having taken the graph of pain to the top
> of the paper, we rule new grids with love;
> why should the line ever stop? . . .
> The West is washing its dirty linen in blood.

There is a double perspective here. If, on a cyclical view of history, the West is in decline, one of the achievements of its decline has been to throw the future of the whole planet into doubt. This is a matter of contemporary concern, and Porter has stood by his contemporary perspective: hence the particular unease in his last two books, the sense that ours may be the final epilepsy on the frieze. Yet in terms of Porter's work as a whole, the intimations of the future are no more a prophetic stance than the allusions to the past are historical romance. Like the social perspective, the historical perspective ties into a deeper concern. Future and past take their place as matters of contemporary relevance, within a continuum of pain.

From the beginning, Porter's imagery has been concrete in a particularly acute sense, the material defining the spiritual, not just representing it; but at the same time these concrete images have had a slightly surreal edge to them:

> Their sophistication was only to be dead
> after drinking the sun down into the bay.
> Their gulps shake out time, their health
> is in country roses, a hard red wealth.

Here the colour attribute is almost a force in itself: "red" becomes an element, a power. As the style has moved out of description into allusion, from orderly sequences into sudden epigrams, this edge has sharpened, but the imagery has shifted towards the allegorical:

> A forgotten name bruises a girl's blood.
> The world waits for love to cast a claw.

It hasn't shifted far, though: Porter uses allegory as a bestiary rather than a shadowland of symbols:

> Evil done on the mainland
> will let down a bloody feather at your door . . .

and it relates strongly back to that corporeal definition which is still Porter's basic habitat:

> A common name for five of us,
> tap-rooted to the world's work:
> we are the unknown bearers,
> the wearers of fatty uniforms.

Two contrasting tendencies have both become stronger as his work has progressed: the first is towards an earthy, debunking common sense,

> Was there ever a man in Nazareth who was King of
>   Kings?
> There is a fat man in Rome
> to guide his people home.

which has its own kind of unease, "the boarding house of hell where meals are prompt"; the second is towards a classic finality of statement:

> To end up on a tideless shore
>   which this is the dream of, a place
>   of skulls, looking history in the face.

> Hell has no faces but many proper names.

It is a blend of these two, a sardonic classicism, which has become the distinctive voice of Porter's recent work:

> I am building my sandcastles of scar tissue
> . . .
> Faster went the Athenian boat but faster still
> went death.
> . . .
> I have found an opening into high self-love
> like a belly full of God in stained glass.

There is a new confidence in the act of writing, hinted at perhaps by the rather effective use of the grammarian's technical terms as a source of imagery:

> a sure verb to bind the vision to the rock
> . . .
>   . . . —the moon
> goes into Alcaics; at six bells
> Agamemnon comes into the bathroom to die.
> . . .
>   even syntax
> falls from the bone,
> . . .
> I am struggling with the pronouns me and my. I am happy,

A delight in twists of thought informs the language, a delight in linguistic *coups* leads on the thought; this sounds like a description of rhetoric, and certainly the technique can be showy, jaunty, unabashed—"Chemical rain in its brave green hat/drinks at a South Coast bar"—but as often as not the *coup* is simple, direct, quietly resonant:

> So much time and blue.
> . . .
> love's face peers between husband and wife,
> a cautious colour like afternoon.

Porter's two latest books are serious and uncompromising to the point of obsession—"death" and "pain" are probably the two most frequent words in his opus, "love" appears most often in the context of defeat—but the writing is filled with this sense of adventure, and the final tone is not heavy, but elusive, startling. They are very much "raids on the inarticulate", strictly guerilla performances. To an extent, the achievement is greatest where the risks are greatest, and there are two overt experiments. "The Porter Song Book" is a departure in the direction of the German Lied— "their construction is dramatic, and they do not resemble the English lyric of tradition", to be precise. "The Sanitised Sonnets" are elliptical, enigmatic, even kinetic in that the ideas are presented in a circling storm, rather than driven to a conclusion: they are rather like cut/ups of the sonnet form. Both experiments are highly successful. "The Song Book" has a freedom of movement between images and tones that produces quite uncanny effects, belonging to no known world, from between worlds, yet anything but otherworldly:

> One great soul
> saw the light go out, reached for
> the Akkadian dark: smelling a little of urine,
> he was taking one step on to the stars
> when a French engineer found him . . .

"The Sanitised Sonnets" are random, looking very much as if they were dirrected by rhyme; individual effects tend to be throwaway, but cumulatively they are substantial:

> I haven't cried for years/I could this minute

> Nasty the scrapes we get into/as Darby and Joan
> told the TV Interviewer, we've been together
> too long/death has an earphone

> He sees a mistress turn into a judge/
> marriages are made in the grave/bad weather
> in the soul for ever/the door will not budge

It is perhaps true that for full effect both experiments depend on the context of Porter's other work: "The Song Book" acts as a sharp, oblique summary of his themes; reading "The Sanitised Sonnets" is rather like playing a fruit machine programmed with them.

Porter's recent style is an act of courage. The keystone of his early work was honesty, though the expression had all the bite of rage. But the widening range of his material challenged his style. The combination of an increasing perspective, both forwards and backwards into history, with a more nervous apprehension of a fragmented moral world, made it necessary to break out of the confines of a foursquare treatment. The present style is chancy—one would call it "transitional" if there wasn't a suspicion that part of the transition is to exclude the aim of coming to rest again. Porter has always had an instinct for good lines, and there have been plenty of them lately: but they tend to come singly, driven like plugs into layers of uneven material—who would have thought that a poem that began, "It's quiet here among the haunted tenses:" could end like this?

> You cannot leave England, it turns
> a planet majestically in the mind.

There is also a measure of obscurity, and as a collection *The Last of England* is as baffling as it is exciting; but I, for one, am willing to take the uncertainties as part of the development. Peter Porter has been consistently careful not to let his gifts become predictable, and his development has been both adventurous and logical. Too often in the 'sixties, experiment was another name for whimsy, and integrity meant a conservative writing by rote: it is refreshing to find a poet whose courage is a function of his honesty.

Peter Redgrove

When the categories are drawn, Peter Redgrove is normally bracketed with Ted Hughes. It is important, however, to an understanding of Redgrove's work to perceive that the two have very different aims. Ted Hughes's work, at least in his first two books, is a celebration of elemental drives, seen chiefly in animals because they are suppressed in men:

> Each one is living the redeemed life of joy. They're continually in a state of joy which men only have when they've gone mad. . . . These spirits or powers *won't* be messed up by artificiality or arrangements. . . . Mostly these powers are just waiting while life just goes by and only find an outlet in moments of purity and crisis, because they won't enter the ordinary pace and constitution of life very easily. . . . Maybe my poems are about the split personality of modern man, the one behind the constructed, spoilt part.

(From an interview with John Horder in the *Guardian*, March 1965.)

For Peter Redgrove the poet's task is very different; it is "discovering and fashioning these intense wholenesses which he believes in". He is concerned to interpret a wider, less demonic range of powers, no less formidable but specifically integrated into the fabric of ordinary existence, at a fundamental level: ". . . certain of my work draws upon these important forces, images of time and relative time, of absolute size and relative significance, of the impingement of still unspecified and apparently personal forces on a world that was once thought by science to be entirely material". This interpretation involves a conscious act of mind, an effort of cerebration as well as an annotation of perception: "There is I think a stronger tendency to show thought in action, and to draw upon conjecture, than in my other books" (from the author's introduction to *The Force and other poems*, Poetry Book Society Bulletin, December 1966). It will be apparent from these quotations that Redgrove's task is different in kind from Hughes's: inasmuch as it is broader in scope and less well-defined, it is perhaps more difficult.

By the same token, it would seem a *prima facie* point against Redgrove that his style is readily comparable to Hughes's. The comparison is normally to Redgrove's disadvantage, and whilst I think it is true that Redgrove is a less disciplined writer than Hughes, the reasons for his shortcomings are more complex than this. He needs discipline of a different kind, a cast of thought which is subtle, protean, innovatory; not a tauter style but a more flexible one, as acute in the articulation of thought as it is sensuous in the handling of imagery. The makings of such a style exist, but in separate poems. "The Room in the Trees" has tremendous sensuous impact, but the thought is bowled along in the rush, to emerge obscured and breathless. "Lazarus and the Sea" has a perfect articulation of thought, and a controlled use of imagery, but the vision is muted, it lacks that immediacy which is normally within Redgrove's gift.

These may seem theoretical considerations, but I think that in practice the tendency of Redgrove's work to drown in its own spume is unmistakable. His essential failing is that he has attempted what is virtually a philosophical task equipped only with the procedures of lyric. He finds his truth through imagery, but his imagery is such a rich mixture that it cloys, without an astringency of mind to balance it. His work is most successful when its basic vision is braced against alternative viewpoints. For instance, the theme of "mentality", the perception of a joyful energy coursing through the universe, underlies all the poems in *The Force*, but it is most convincingly expressed in poems like "I See", "Look Out", "The Widower", and "Decreator", where it survives debunking, or is tested against sorrow, or meets stolid uniformity. Similarly with Redgrove's emotional sympathies, his whole apprehension of the tenor of life: in the nature poems this becomes a clamour of exultation, but it rings most true when focused upon a person, as in "Earth", or set against the domestic realities, as in "Foundation", "Early Morning Feed", "Old House" or "A Bedtime Story for my Son". Domestic humour, comic self-depreciation, these leaven his best work: what belies the pure, direct statement that he obviously aims for elsewhere?

It is often vitiated by a repetitive vocabulary. His diction has all the qualities that make for a firm texture, for "hard" writing; it is concrete, drawn from everyday language but often surprising in its context, rich in sound values: but it is always drawn from the same area of language, always infused with the same sort of energy. Because it is so uniform, it is limited in its scope, to the point of inaccuracy. A prime example is his description of the lake water in "Icicles":

> Currents nerve lightly along its surface.
> Gritty with life to its depths. Turfy.

"Gritty" is just the sort of word that "hard" writers love, and it is doubtless appreciated by those readers who like to pick up a poem and feel it, like a piece of moon rock. But how accurate is it? What Redgrove means, presumably, is that the lake is full of tiny plant life, algae. In what sense does this make it "gritty"? You can see the specks floating, but they are hardly substantial enough to be picked up or rubbed between your fingers. "Dusty" might be more accurate. "Turfy" is an interesting choice, which does convey certain qualities of lake water, but only in a vague sense. What exactly does it evoke? Smell? Colour? The water in a peat bog? A lawn can be turfy, and so, for that matter, can a check jacket. Hardly a precise description. One finds here a particular Redgrove failing, that the perception is accurate enough, but the expression of it is blurred, because it is forced into the dominant idiom. An orthodoxy of sensibility operates here. The words are only gestures at meaning, but ones to which the poet knows that his audience will respond, because they are the right sort of gestures. Like wrestlers' grunts, they reassure the audience of value for money. "Gritty", "gusty", "swirl", "flinch", these and such-like words are the "hard" writer's "moon-and-June", a stubbly species of schmaltz.

Of course, constant attention to this area of language does bring its results, and Redgrove is particularly felicitous in his choice of verbs:

> he watches the crows stepping . . .
> . . . how they fletch the sopping mud . . .
> ("I see")

> more apple-cup chugs from the stouted ewer.
> ("The House in the Acorn")

> birds swing on the beams, boil off the grass.
> ("Sweat")

Nonetheless, the point remains, that because a particular texture of language is invoked constantly, the language becomes finally inaccurate, glossing all surfaces over with the same pebbledash. The rare occasions when Redgrove ventures into a different area of style are successful enough to make one wish for more. This is how he ends his description of a fly, in "A Small Particle of that Former Blackness":

> Merely one of the conditions of living, but a black one,
> as the greenery is a condition, sunlit.

Redgrove is concerned to express an organic unity of being, in which no bodily function is shameful or meaningless. Urination is beneficent, a contribution to the soil's fertility; the brief energies of erection and ejaculation are increments to the world's spirit, additions of power to the source; the blood's circulation is the action of happiness, the heart beats out an anthem. The obvious generosity of this theme is somewhat marred in the expression. Sometimes the vision comes across clearly:

> Our son watering the black mud
> does this duty with a beam
> gentle, clear and strong as a sunbeam . . .
> ("A Testament")

but too often sentiment glozes it over:

Gold liquors lash away from ourselves
into deep sewers and wells . . .

("Autumn Lunch")

More damaging is an academic tendency in the language, which robs it of
immediacy:

The white castle of a man's tupping
is as long as any time, embattled
in which all future is extended, and rears
his excellent and lasting instant . . .

("The Moon")

The dark tree of the blood flexes
slender and minutely-fashioned until death,
rejoices, with the hammer-stroke at its roots,
both pump and measure of time.

("Human Beam")

There is a linguistic nostalgia apparent here, an attempt to re-vivify terms like
"rejoice" and "excellent" which belonged to a more ordered world of thought:
it is a wistfulness born of literary involvement, a hankering after some
imagined Merrie England of the sensibility. One of Redgrove's qualities is
that he rediscovers and seeks to express an order, a meaning, in the basic
conditions of existence: but rediscovering order in life doesn't mean that he
can reassume order in language. The words must be newly struck, for these
old terms of approbation have no modern currency, outside their trite
appearance in varieties of cant.

Hearty sentiments, stolid idioms: these blend into an almost throw-away
style. It is related to Redgrove's good-humoured, rather Falstaffian apprehen-
sion of life, and in the humorous poems it is successful. A poem like "Human
Beam" which begins "Hot laughter-coughing drunkard" can afford to end
"proud of their rejoiceful pumping": it is a comic apocalypse, and its humour
redeems the fulsome phrases. In *The Force* particularly, Redgrove often
writes out of that ample benignity which reigns after several pints of beer,
but the constant use of a beery perspective is monotonous, and reduces
experience to bodily heaves, feeling to "Hail Fellow! Well Met!" So, too,
the broad comic style infiltrates and dilutes the serious poems. There is a
predilection for using words like "twinkling" which no other contemporary
poet would dream of using seriously. The lack of verbal snobbery is refresh-
ing, but it is part of a conscious drive towards a homely style, which becomes,
finally, simplistic, belittling what is said:

We need only pluck up courage, and live
in a summery fashion—sun'd be out again.
. . . it's as if
the sun fed on me, and the food glad-hearted.

("Power")

since the seasons move because we shine
("Only Resting")

Cabby! the clouds rise
because the sun wants them. Each cloud is unique.
("The Contentment of an Old White Man")

To take a rather different example from "The Gamut", the matchflame is a masterly image, carelessly organised:

That pet of a matchflame
serves me clouds of calm
at my cigarette,
flips shadows about, whispers
with its tiny sting, wrings
the wood elderly, pricks at my thumb
before my breath splits and garottes it.
We hang between extremes.

The focus, which is sharp in "serves me clouds of calm/at my cigarette" and "wrings the wood elderly", is distracted by the casual phrasing of "flips shadows about"; and the phrase "whispers with its tiny sting", in itself excellent, steals the impact from "pricks at my thumb" and so confuses the dramatic progression of the image. The clear direction from "clouds of calm" through "elderly" to "garottes" is lost, and so the relevance of "We hang between extremes" is lost too.

For Redgrove, writing is "the thing with which I feel out the world, a sense organ combined of, and worth more than, all the others put together" (*P. B. S. Bulletin*): but this sense organ, like all the others, can only provide the raw material of art. Once fixed in words, sense perceptions take their quality from the quality of their verbal organisation. In Redgrove the discoveries of the verbal sense are presented in too unrefined a form. It seems to me in "Power", for instance, that "heat at the centre and fright at the fringes" has the obvious look of a beginning, a workpoint: it is too crude to satisfy as a final expression. The intellect must be at the tip of the verbal sense, as at the tip of all the other senses.

The bracket which links Redgrove with Ted Hughes also links him with David Wevill. All poets writing at the demise of a formal tradition are linked by one common problem, how to structure a poem without resorting to traditional devices. Redgrove and Wevill are linked together in their attempt to structure by using an image as a motif. In Redgrove's shorter poems this works well: in "For No Good Reason" the wasteground acts as a mirror-image of his home, its atmosphere wrecked by a quarrel; in "Foundation" the three stanzas are built on three images for the pregnant belly. The same rationale does not apply to the longer poems, for here the linking image is not the vehicle of the thought, but is reduced to the status of a refrain, stitching a variety of thoughts together. In "Power" a cluster of words, "bubbles", "flick", "centre", "fringes", are arbitrarily repeated to hold the thought sequence together—the repetition is arbitrary in that each image in the sequence could equally well, if not better, be phrased in other words. "Bedtime Story for my Son" is a different case: the refrain "the empty air" has point, but the formal procedure of the poem is too weak for it to be conclusive. The stanzas do not drive to a climax, they tail off into the refrain, and the rhythm of the last stanza is particularly awkward. These two rather different examples teach the same lesson: the retention of vestiges of traditional form only serves to underline the weakness of a poem's organisation. Form must exercise a compulsion over material. It is a mould, not a stringbag. It can be an organic form, a growth of thought through words, with no reference to stanzas or any other traditional device: but the words must be integral to the thought. To use refrain as a linkage, stringing ideas on the repetition of words, is a pretext, a palliative to the yearning for form. It may record the movement of a poet's mind, the discoveries of association, but it does not in itself create the movement of a poem.

In the lack of any intellectual or formal organisation, Redgrove's forceful and original view of human life remains a register of emotional convictions. His theme of "mentality" dwindles to the repetition of a small cluster of blunted words. Redgrove is an attractive poet, of generous sympathies and undoubted verbal power: but our response to him is limited by the narrowness of his development. He has not matched up to his own intentions. He has tried to do something quite new in English poetry, to fuse the traditional feeling for Nature with a knowledge of the biological processes and the theories of the structure of the universe. This is the material for a major work, but to its making he has so far brought only an obsession with already outworn verbal devices. If he now reads like a lyric coda to the *Book of Rugby Songs*, that is precisely because the quality of thought rarely breaks clear of the scrum of boisterous verbiage which comes milling into every poem. He should have been a poet sui generis, who created his own form; to date, he has put all his energy into dynamics, and he looks like ending up as a poetic sub-species, a rather traditional figure in the background of English Expressionism.

David Wevill

Edward Lucie-Smith's remark, in a note in *British Poetry since 1945*, that whilst Wevill's style associates him with Hughes and Redgrove, essentially he is a quieter writer than both, delineates neatly the area of Wevill's achievement. His poetry is not so much violent as unsettling. The lightest touch can be the most disturbing:

> And I am coming to you this last time
> before the spreading sun has touched your eyes,
> passed on, and left no dawn where your eyes were.
> ("Winter Homecoming")

Here the naturalness of the threat, the immanence of death within the recurrence of dawn, is characteristic: for Wevill the recognition of the order of things is the beginning of unease. Like Redgrove, he perceives a world of organic relations: the human figure is set in the midst of a living pattern in which nothing is inert. There is no dead ground, and man's mobility is only a movement among many. But where Redgrove's characteristic moment is the freshness after rain, the grass shining, a blackbird singing, in Wevill the rain is tropical, the harbinger of monsoon damp, of mould growing across the pages of a book. This isn't a question of having lived in the tropics, for the same feeling is apparent in "Body of a Rook":

> In the scenery of crushed glass, here,
> among kneading hands of mud, the scoured head lies.

Wevill's universe is less ebullient than Redgrove's, but it is more active against man. Where Redgrove strains "to pull the sun down", Wevill walks warily, lest he be pulled down:

> I cannot comfortably gaze at standing water,
> some focus seems to lie drowned there and waiting,
>
> . . . the weight of water, slimy tension of skin,
> might rise to collect me, much later,
> and suddenly, when I'm feverish or weak.
>
> ("Puddles")

Beneath the calm surface lies the threat. Wevill's poems are investigations, and this is reflected in their structure: the strongest line is often the last, when the stalking stops, and from the brink of consciousness the discovery wells up. Thus the poem "My Father Sleeps", for most of its length, isolates the living character of his father, a realistic appraisal, written in a vein of shrewd affection common enough in contemporary poetry. But the matter does not rest there; in the last line that appraisal cracks right open, into a darkness that threatens both father and poet:

> . . . And watching him thus
> sprawled like a crooked frame of clothes
> in the sleep of sixty years, jaws firm,
> breathing through the obstacle of his nose
> a stubborn air that is truth for him,
> I confront my plainest self. And feel
> in the slow hardening of my bones, a questioning
> depth that his pride could never reveal;
> that in his sleep stirs its cruel beginning.

In a much later poem, "1969", a section of *Firebreak*, Wevill uses the image of Plato's cave:

> Rimbaud
> multiplied by millions

> the inner voice
> moves out into the sun
>
> Plato's cave is empty
>
> and earth has a green
> center again—

In the second stanza, the confidence turns sour:

> and the cave is full of noise
> decibels deeper than sound—
> the inner voice crawls to the dark where
> Rimbaud
> shrinks to zero . . .

It is this area, the cavern at the back of the cave, that is the theme of most of Wevill's work.

The technique of strong endings has its doubtful uses too. Sometimes it seems suddenly to kick the poem into a deeper resonance, in a way that is effective, but perhaps arbitrary. The end of "Monsoon" is an example:

> Then after an hour the ground steamed openly.
> The rain, flickering northwards into the shallow hills
> left little puddles behind, rubies aflame
> in the fattened grasses drinking the sunset down,
> deep, through stem and root, and into the cave of stone
> where the scorpion hungers, carrying his bruise down.

Nonetheless, this specific weakness typifies an essential quality, that Wevill is very much a dramatic poet.

The matter of his poetry may be meditative, but the manner is lithe, active, compelling. The poems are often a commentary on movement, on the poet walking, as it were, into his subject—"Street Stroller" and "Spiders" are obvious examples. Less obvious but equally effective is "Boy with Cancer": the situation is static, the tone is elegiac, but the technique is dramatic. It comes far closer to its subject than a fixed portrait or a formal elegy could have done:

> But the days slumbered, and the sun stroked
> every hour as it passed the finespun curtain;
> and the whine of leaves grew to a buzz of flies,
> the hidden wall crumbled, his head
> sank like a stone into his palms—
>
> all around, the noises, the noises
> fell still.

In "Birth of a Shark" or "Groundhog" one reads as much for the mastery of suspense as for the mastery of the theme. Indeed, it is hardly possible to separate them, for in the suspense is the theme: in "Groundhog" the situation is a groundhog in the sights of the poet's gun:

> And I cannot kill, but mark him, fat
> as a neighbour safe in his rocking-chair.

The question "will he shoot?" is part of the reason why he does: "The riddle's this nerve that pecks at my hand." In the climax of the narrative comes the resolution of the theme:

> I fired because confusion made me think . . .

> One spoilt instant's enough to be conqueror.

In "Birth of a Shark" there is no observer, thinking, only the shark's action and inaction; but his action is symbolic, and the expression of this symbolism increases the suspense on the narrative level,

> He was something rising under their minds
> you could not have told them about: grey thought
> beneath the fortnight's seaside spell—
> a jagged effort to get at something painful.

The action, and the subsequent hesitation, is symbolic for the shark too, and expresses what he, in turn, symbolises: "Powerless to be a shark, a spawned insult . . ." he is outdone by others,

> Whose aim lay in their twice-his-length
> trust in the body and shadow as one
> mouthful of mastery, speed and blood—

> he learned this, when they came for him;
> the young shark found his shadow again.
> He learned his place among the weeds.

In dramatic narrative there is a strong contrast between Wevill's technique here, and the technique of Peter Redgrove. It is intelligence contrasted with skill. The casual but carefully turned "He was something rising under their minds/you could not have told them about", enhances the poem on both levels, narrative and symbolic, and draws its power from its very restraint. "I fired because confusion made me think", is the most accurate description of the action of brain and trigger finger—it is also the neatest statement of the theme. It is mimetic, yet it is simply the clarification of the thought. This is the truer expressionism of intelligent style. Wevill has a greater range than Redgrove because intelligence is one of his instruments, as much as sound-values or rhythm: it is part of his verbal texture, a shaping element in his work. His strength is in expression, not phrasing: not in the muscles of language, but in the akkido of style.

Wevill and Redgrove are similar in discovering a pattern in their surroundings, distinct in their relationship to it. In Redgrove the poet-figure is integral with the landscape, a microcosmic churn of natural forces; when he stands apart, his stance becomes humorous, a caricature asserted against mocking contrasts; and out of this burly of exaggeration comes a sharper definition of truth. In Wevill the warmth of self-mockery is replaced by a stealthy self-watching, a fascinated caution. In his earlier work the anxiety is for an identity proof against stress, which at times rises to a hectic narcissism:

> Rare cat,
> we've lit our darkness forever
> by the imagined brightest flash possible
> to earthly fire. Your beauty
>
> is power. Tell me how to contain it.
> Tell me how to prowl
> the dark of our false electric day
> in savage possession of eyes that forever see.
>
> ("Black Pantheress")

In his latest book, *Firebreak*, the egocentric questioning has widened into a determined questioning of all meaning. The anxiety and caution have dropped away, to be replaced by qualities at once leaner, starker and more generous. It is a more complete reassumption of earlier themes, in the mood of "Love-Stones" rather than "Visit of the Son": a desperately serious attempt to settle for "nothing that isn't there and the nothing that is".

For the most part, Wevill's poems do not take any traditional form, but they are elaborately organised. They tend to focus on some external object and then develop it as an image of the internal state: the parallel tends to be developed at all points of possible relevance, to turn from an image into a full-blown conceit. In the pages on Peter Redgrove, I associated Wevill with Redgrove's anxiety for structures that would match traditional forms in conviction. I do not think that Wevill makes Redgrove's mistake, of coming close to a recognised form but not quite fulfilling it: but I do think that he over-organises to an extent which weakens the particular effect that he is aiming for. In his note in *British Poetry since 1945*, Lucie-Smith quotes Wevill's recorded criticism of the New Lines group, "I think that what is often lacking is what I can only call intuition, the transforming quality of mind and the senses," and then adds, "And essentially his own poetry *is* sensuous, building itself up image by image, rather than idea by idea." This, I think, is a fair statement of what Wevill aims to do: but often he treats the images rather as if they were ideas, stressing their interlinks, and so confuses the rationale of his chosen process. An organisation of wit, as in the Metaphysical conceit, is one thing, intuition is quite another: one requires notice, an appreciation of skill, the other wishes to be unnoticed, requiring a suspension of disbelief. As soon as organisation becomes overt, there is suspicion, and a resumption of disbelief. In Wevill this suspicion is distinct, though not disabling: it is perhaps more obtrusive over several poems than in any one poem. I can best illustrate the tendency in miniature by a quotation from "Our Lady of Kovno":

> From their holes in the earth, without lights
> the red ants caught her smell, like the sea;
> they followed the threadlets of blood
> up the eyelets of air, lacing themselves
> in lines and clusters, licking wounds
> which were never theirs to fear or mourn.

In "threadlets . . . eyelets" the expression is active in the perception, it is a catching hold, a realisation of the event; in "lacing themselves in lines and clusters" it has become passive, the inert victim of its own logic—more simply, it is obvious, and therefore unnecessary. It is only fair to add that the conceit is strikingly re-assumed at the end of the poem, in an image that is both unnerving and poignant:

> ants carry her blood to their holes
> on tiny shrill bobbins.

Individual images tend to be taken to their logical conclusion, even where the decorative is thus confused with the organic. In "Petrel" there is an opposition of air and water throughout, but these lines are an odd lapse of phrase-making:

> But the shallow beak can pluck
> in a second out of a wave the air's vendetta,
> fish: a thrash of droplets fraying in the wind,
> water shaken to nothing.

There is a weakness for asides, too:

> Where ice struck, under the sun's thumbnail
> a splinter, she prowled for her own blood.

Precisely because the organisation of Wevill's poems is taut, these little indulgences are disturbing. There is also a trailing edge of Romanticism, a loose hem on the Muse's skirt, which is evident in lines like:

> And tempt, however terrible, the sun's transfixing fire.

Perhaps because his strengths were evident so early on, one senses that somewhere along the line Wevill may have escaped chastening criticism.

Firebreak is clearly under American influence, particularly from the Black Mountain school, and shares, to a small extent, in the faults characteristic of the style. There is the taste for forging wayside wisdom, and the tendency for quotidian details to receive their apocalyptic heightening—"Night of the singing roots". These both seem part of a greater assumption, which is expressed in "X4":

> Fell into a false sleep—woke up
> there were clouds smoking across the stars
> white clouds

> and a wind in the room
> the room alert, the curtains alive
> in their night-dance
>
> My northern friend, asleep by the East River
> My southern friend, asleep by the lake of mountains
> No one comes,
> no one goes

Throughout Wevill's work there has been the sense of a pattern, neutral, inexorable, as the background to human life: here the pattern is equally strong, equally inexorable, but in a very evident sense the poet has taken it to himself, claimed it as particularly his own. There is a sense of ownership of the void, peculiar to the American way of Zen, which has, with a quite sincere arrogance, colonised Nirvana, taken to the infinite spaces of Eastern thought as its spiritual home, and now waxes homely about them. For poets this has the same danger as any other set of assumptions: the Sirens croon over green tea, just as irresistible as when they whispered in absinthe, or seduced Alfred O'Shaughnessy over muffins in the Temperance Hotel.

There are hints of these dangers in *Firebreak*, but more often the poem trandcends them. The complete change of style is justified, not only by Wevill's present residence in America, but by the naturalness with which he handles the new style. The quality is of a different order from Wevill's previous work, and the difference is representative of the change of medium, from a collection of lyric poems to one uniform work, interspersed with, but not in any sense interrupted by, passages of prose. The language has less edge but a wider competence: it is less startling, less of a literary achievement, but it has the greater strengths and the greater relevance of common speech. There are fewer individual felicities, a smaller mass of worked detail; even so, some of the sections are more concise, more conclusive than anything in Wevill's earlier work,

> I visited your grave
> too often in dreams
> while you were still alive
>
> Now I do not want to touch
> the real body and the real grass
> see the real trees
>   Because
> your voice will begin to describe
> the leaves, the ladybugs
> roots as they are
>   the germ of wind
> that reaches you
> flowers, your neighbours' names

the same voice
that claimed and exclaimed so often
such things, your eyes
                    quicker than mine
                            still quicker than mine
                                    ("Memorial II")

Varied and telling as is the impact of specific sections, "Firebreak" is, quite
rightly, most impressive as a whole. There has been no compromise and no
refusal, no narrowing of vision to achieve an easier harmony, but a complete
unity welded out of all elements, a realised present in which both past and
future retain their power. It is as a whole that the book is most true to Wevill's
earlier work. The development of theme has been both consistent and chal-
lenging: one would say that the widened range was ambitious, if it was not
clearly so deadly serious, taxing all his resilience of mind.

The one extravagance is an occasional rhetorical *coup*, an uncanny, almost
surrealist extension of rhetoric, reminiscent of Peter Porter's recent style:

Lose no sleep over this dream of re-entry into the condom of
daylight and dust.

It seems to be an assumption common to both, that extreme freedom of
expression is the perquisite of extreme seriousness. It is a technique rather
like acupuncture: the outrageous jab at the sole of your foot, over your left
kidney, in your groin, hits the spot in the brain. Whilst it remains accurate,
who will grumble?

The Making of the Movement

by Ian Hamilton

WHEN the anthology *New Lines* appeared in 1956, the ground had more than been prepared; it had practically been churned into a quagmire. The advance promotion had in fact been initiated two years earlier, in the *Spectator*, with Anthony Hartley declaring to the world (in an unsigned leading article) that there existed a group of young poets who were ripe to dislodge the old Forties gang. "For better or worse," he wrote, "we are now in the presence of the only considerable movement in English poetry since the 'thirties." These young poets (few of them were named, but they included the newly famous— as novelists—Kingsley Amis and John Wain, both of them regular *Spectator* reviewers) were announced to be in concerted reaction against the tangled and pretentious neo-romanticism of the post-war years; where the old lot had been bardic, overblown and religiose, these new men were clever, cagey, scornful. They had rediscovered irony, wit and syntax, they bowed the knee to Leavis, Empson and Orwell. More than all this, though, they represented in their verse moral attitudes which were excitingly appropriate to the grey new Britain of the 'fifties. Coining the title by which the group came to be officially identified, Hartley went on to draw a swift identi-kit portrait of "The Movement":

> It is bored by the despair of the 'forties, not much interested in suffering, and extremely impatient of poetic sensibility, especially poetic sensibility about "the writer and society". So it's goodbye to all those rather sad little discussions about "how the writer ought to live", and it's goodbye to the Little Magazine and "experimental writing". The Movement, as well as being anti-phoney, is anti-wet; sceptical, robust, ironic, prepared to be as comfortable as possible in a wicked, commercial, threatened world which doesn't look, anyway, as if it's going to be changed much by a couple of handfuls of young English writers.

The odd thing about Hartley's communiqué (aside from the fact that the poets in question, though assertedly fairly numerous, had published only a few pamphlets and one or two small press hardbacks) was the transparently calculated tone in which it was delivered; the tone, pushing and unblushing, of the hard sell. Readers at the time must have felt a bit puzzled and bullied; the material itself (which Hartley obtrusively avoided discussing in any detail) seemed so thin and elusive, the claims for it so strident. And those who had not yet got round to reading *Lucky Jim* would hardly have felt tempted by the flaunted philistinism. Those who had read *Lucky Jim*, of course, might well have detected a highbrow-debunking hoax; let's show them how easy it is to start one of their phoney trends.

In the weeks following the *Spectator*'s PR job, there were some sardonic rejoinders from, as it were, the battle-front: Alan Brownjohn and Anthony Thwaite (both at the time editing Oxford poetry magazines in which some of the supposed Movementeers were often to be found) wrote deflating letters, with Thwaite ironically acknowledging that the article had "the importance of a White Paper in a field where previous remarks merely had the nature of, say, inter-departmental memoranda". But the poets actually named by Hartley held their peace, and throughout the ensuing chat they tacitly collaborated in the construction and promotion of their group identity—though at the same time quietly murmuring that the whole thing was a bit absurd. "We ridiculed and deprecated 'the Movement' even as we kept it going," Donald Davie has confessed:

> All of us in the Movement had read the articles in *Scrutiny* about how the reputations of Auden and Spender and Day Lewis were made by skilful promotion and publicity, and it was to placate *Scrutiny* readers that we pretended (and sometimes deceived ourselves as well as others) that the Movement was not being "sold" to be public in the same way; that John Wain on the BBC and later Bob Conquest with his anthology *New Lines* weren't just touching the pitch with which we others wouldn't be defiled. Again, I limit myself to my own case; I remember nothing so distastefully as the maidenly shudders with which I wished to know nothing of the machinery of publicity even as I liked publicity and profited from it.

Davie is perhaps right to feel anguished, and there is no doubt that the Movement, along with the Sitwells, has its distinctive niche in the history of publicity—it was a take-over bid and it brilliantly succeeded. Indeed, by the time *New Lines* actually came out (it had been preceded, in 1955, by D. J. Enright's *Poets of the 1950s*—but this was published in Japan and wasn't much noticed) it had evidently succeeded all too well. Almost every young university poet had become a Movementeer; the Oxford and Cambridge magazines, the Fantasy Press pamphlets, the column-ends of many of the weeklies, were brimming over with neatly tailored ironies, with feeble neo-Augustan posturings and effortful Empsonian pastiche. The talentless had been given a verse-recipe only slightly more difficult to follow than that handed out by Tambimuttu fifteen years earlier.

The task of *New Lines* was not to inaugurate a Movement, but to stop the rot by sifting the senior members from the mass of imitators and disciples. D. J. Enright's anthology had already made it clear that these seniors—Amis, Wain, Davie, John Holloway, Philip Larkin, Robert Conquest and Elizabeth Jennings—were most of them already fairly gloomy about the fashion they'd precipitated. John Wain wrote:

> I am, in fact, sometimes told that an article on the poetry of Empson which I contributed to the final issue of *Penguin New Writing* (1950) was

responsible for starting the astonishing vogue of his poetry which has produced so many diminutive Empsons in the last five years. If so, I have certainly a grave charge to answer.

The others spoke of "too much value being attached to intellectuality", of "well-constructed dry bones among the younger poets", of a verse "too limited in its scope, insufficiently various and adventurous", of the prevailing aridity, academicism and triviality. Of course, these reservations were delicately balanced by acknowledgments that, bad as it was, the new stuff was much preferable to the work it had supplanted (and it doesn't take a subtle eye to detect the essential boastfulness of Wain's self-deprecations).

One's suspicion that a principal function of *New Lines* was to annex for its participants a pigeon-hole in literary history which was beginning to get over-crowded is supported by Kingsley Amis's testimony in the Enright book. He writes: "nobody wants any more poems about philosophers or paintings or novelists or art galleries or mythology or foreign cities or other poems." I have heard this statement quoted as one of the Movement's rallying cries; in fact it is more like a death warrant. Amis accurately describes here the subject matter of most of the poems in *New Lines*—just under half the poems in the book, for instance, are to do with poetry, painting or foreign cities, and most of the others are heavily sprinkled with Merlins or Spinozas. A neat ruse, to kill off the Movement even as you are about to foster its historical significance.

Robert Conquest's introduction to the book itself adopts a similar strategy. In modest tones, it outlines the well-known virtues of clarity, honesty, intelligence and rigorous empiricism, but notes with sadness that "any forthright lead will find its followers and imitators among young writers" and that a number of young poets are "following Empsonian and similar academic principles and often producing verse of notable aridity."

Today, looking back on the poets included in *New Lines* (the Enright team, plus Thom Gunn), it seems difficult to conceive of aridity more notable than theirs. It's difficult, also, to fathom how such largely tame and awkward verses could ever have been found dazzlingly fresh and skilful. The intellectual brilliance of Elizabeth Jennings, for example, consists of a laborious obsession with "the mind". "This afternoon disturbs within the mind", "And this awareness grows upon itself, Fastens on minds", "Image and pattern combined into a whole/Pattern within the loving mind", "But when the music ends/There lie within our minds/Thoughts that refuse to fit", "As thought to unfasten from the mind/Our moods and give them outward forms", "There is so much/That separates those motionless proud horses/From minds that only move through words". And these are selected from a mere ten poems. Miss Jennings's weakly ruminative verses are stiffened with some neat travel views, but she is no more rigorous and complicated than, say, Bernard Spencer. Similarly, John Holloway's contorted cerebrations, though certainly arid and technically ingenious, are no more demanding than Roy Fuller. And neither in Holloway's work nor in the heavily abstract soliloquies of Robert

Conquest is there any sense of the poems' supposed formal skills being any more than fiddlingly external to what is being argued or thought out. Much the same could be said of Thom Gunn's contributions (in large sections much more strangulated and cumbersome than anything in the book) but here one has to concede a novelty of tone and persona; a persona, however, utterly at odds with ideals of moderation or ordinariness. One doubts that Gunn had learned anything, at this stage, from any modern poet.

An anthology including Miss Jennings, Holloway, Conquest, Enright and Thom Gunn would hardly have attracted any group label; such a volume could also have offered work by Spencer, Fuller, Henry Reed, and no one would have thought it odd. Indeed, Henry Reed would probably have been considered closer to the regulation Movementeer than any of the others. The anthology's real claim to notoriety resides, appropriately enough, in the handful of poems which self-consciously seek such notoriety; those poems, in other words, which speak directly from and about the literary milieu of the early 'fifties. They are poems-as-criticism, or as literary journalism. Amis's "Against Romanticism", "Wrong Words", "Something Nasty in the Bookshop", "Here is Where", Davie's "Rejoinder to a Critic", "Cherry Ripe", "Too Late for Satire", "Remembering the Thirties", Wain's "Reason for Not Writing Nature Poetry", "Who Speaks My Language" and "Eighth Type of Ambiguity": all are minipolemics against the standard romantic postures of the 'forties. They are prescriptions for the new poetry, and to that extent are enactments of it, but each is saturated with a strategic, blow-striking self-awareness, each inhabits an imaginative world dominated by trivial exigencies of literary warfare.

Efforts, in some of these poems, to extend a narrowly literary anti-romanticism into a general critique of what Conquest describes as "great systems of theoretical constructs" or "agglomerations of unconscious commands" now look fairly laborious and crude; the real spur, the true source of the wit, the edge, the slangy confidence of the best Movement poems, was thoroughly ephemeral. The Movement, in fact, could almost be said to have been the sum of its manifestos; its most apt footnote can be found in Anthony Hartley's *Spectator* review of *New Lines*, in which the erstwhile prophet is to be heard calling for "a reversion to dynamic romanticism".

Conspicuously absent from the foregoing "reappraisal" is any comment on the poet whose contribution to *New Lines* seems to me to have any lasting potency; at one level, it could be said that Philip Larkin's poems provide a precise model for what the Movement was supposed to be seeking. But having noted his lucidity, his debunkery, his technical accomplishment and other such "typical" attributes, one would still be left with the different and deeper task of describing the quality of his peculiar genius, the task of talking about poems rather than postures.

Cautious Vision:
Recent British Poetry by Women

by Margaret Byers

TODAY, with the publicised growth of regional literatures and the emergence of numerous rough diamonds from the Muse's mines, women poets still consistently come from middle-class backgrounds, progress through University or some form of higher education, and come to rest in metropolitan or accessibly pastoral settings. No female spawn have been reported in the swamps of Liverpool or the slow waters of Tyne. The best contemporary women poets seem to derive their energy mainly from the humdrum or lurid realities of a moderately well-to-do suburban existence, tempered by their situations (teacher, housewife, invalid). Many of them use literature and art allusively as a consistent alternative reality, giving their poetry a well-educated aesthetic quality which in some instances seems a limitation of range. The exclusively intellectual, like the exclusively emotional approach to form, image, and experience itself has weakened the achievement of many of these poets, few of whom have managed to emancipate themselves from the conditioning of education and class, to confront and resolve problems with combined emotional and intellectual intensity. A few of them transcend intellectuality by applying it with total precision, finding through traditional or original forms the areas beyond form. Their work is personal without being private, and despite their manifest differences in temperament and development they can in a real sense be grouped together. "British woman poet" is rather more than a sexual classification.

On the reading circuits and through broadcasting, a number of women poets have recently come into prominence whose work is outside the scope of this essay. They write without distinctive style—without style at all—and are tolerated as chameleons in whatever adopted skin they sport—whether Sylvia Plath's or Stevie Smith's skin or their own whim-mottled pelts. Jeni Couzyn and Libby Houston are the most notable of these—they are performers whose work is as temporary as their topical allusions, gestures, unformed and self-regarding sentiment, and their unambitious language.

But there are a number of women writing interesting poetry, and they have neither individually nor collectively been given their due. I am always disappointed to see how few women are included in anthologies as they appear. The Penguin trilogies have so far included the work of four women at most. Jeremy Robson, for his anthology, *The Young British Poets*, was unable to find even one. And in Michael Horovitz's *Children of Albion*, of the sixty three children only three were daughters. Stevie Smith, Kathleen Raine, sometimes Elizabeth Jennings—their work is available in selection and anthology. But others whose work is of similar standard, and certainly equal to that of many men writing, are excluded. A short survey of the younger or neglected writers, or those whose work is in interesting transition, reveals both the variety and variable success of the women poets.

Anne Beresford, whose volume, *The Lair*, appeared in 1968, is one of the less interesting figures. Her poems work as private fables, nostalgic or bitter gestures, occasionally successful in single images but usually unsustained. Her language is simple to the point of being drab, and her forms (which include often the use of lower case throughout despite punctuation) are arbitrary. Frances Horovitz reveals similar limitations, but her small collection, *The High Tower* (1970), reveals a poet trying to deal more directly with a private world. The phrases (punctuation is usually by dashes) often show a strong sense of language as well as image, and though most of the poems are faulty, unable to establish form, they are seldom uninteresting. If she develops a wider range of reference, a more than tritely archetypal sense of image, she will prove a fine poet in time. At present she is far better than many of the "underground" poets with whom she is usually grouped.

Rosemary Tonks is an altogether more interesting poet. She is widely ambitious. A novelist as well, she experiments with sound poems which have, nonetheless, linguistic interest on the page. She writes prose poems. Though her work to date, drawing exhaustively on contemporary urban experience and literary reference, has fallen short of satire in wit, it is keenly alive to things—buses, bottles, tins, husbands; titles like "The Ice-cream Boom Towns", and "Addiction to an Old Mattress"—things which always refuse to settle into an order. She is not in fact a surrealist and yet she cannot impose or discover structure in the mass of objects which press on her eye and her body. The result is a poetry of hysterical but random gesture, fused not very successfully by the gabbling voice, and the range for all its reference is unfortunately narrow because the voice seldom modulates out of staccato—a lady Whitman uncertain of her rhythmical pace:

> The trains come in, boiling, caked!
> The station half tames them, there's the sound of blows; the uproar!
> And I—I behave as though I've been starved for noise,
> My intestine eats up this big music
> And my new bourgeois soul promptly bursts into flames, in mid-air.
>
> ("Farewell to Kurdistan")

This is visionary only in the sense that it sees and is individually felt, but always the poet is responding and not generating a similar response in the reader. We could wish a more varied voice from her. With amusing accuracy, she places herself.

> I have lived it, and lived it,

My nervous, luxury civilization,
My sugar-loving nerves have battered me to pieces.
                              ("The Sofas, Fogs, and Cinemas")

With the work of Fleur Adcock we come upon a relatively traditional poet. A New Zealander, she seems, like the Australian Peter Porter, to have settled in England for good. She is formally accomplished, with a wide range of experiences and tones. It seems to me that her best poems are not the dream fantasies nor the Tiger poems that give the title to a recent collection, but those deft considerations with a slightly academic ring, like "Note on Propertius 1.5", or the gentle ironies which get beyond quiet satire to miniature tragedies of self-deceit and frustration, as in "The Man who X-rayed an Orange", and "Miss Hamilton in London" (a latently autobiographical poem). She has the kind of elegance, though not yet the verbal skill, of the American, Elizabeth Bishop; and though she is a person saying the poem rather than a voice giving us a particular experience, the variety is great. Transitions are her *forte*: she falls from the present, apparent security of a human relationship to a sleep where her loneliness is reaffirmed by nightmare and she wakes solitary. The present is forever undermined by the accretions of the past and the uncertainties (and the one certainty, death) of the future. "For Andrew" is a poem addressed to a child asking about death. "Will I die?" And she, "To soften my 'Yes'", offers consolations. She suggests that fulfilment will come with age, grandchildren, and the most ironic consolation, "indifference ('By then you will not care')". The child cannot believe. The poem ends with a charming false hope based on the child's incredulity, a little vision of potential which is strong for being on the *brink* of sentimentality. But it manages to clarify without simplifying.

Fleur Adcock's range is from humour (and never mere humour, always tempered by a sense of the ephemeral) to a near tragic statement of isolation. "Unexpected Visit" is witty and yet poignant—a suffering expressed not with dislocating, neurotic intensity but with complete formal deftness. She does not let form become disrupted; she intensifies form to cope with a painful experience. Form and content are in counterpoint, as it were. The poem sketches an almost allegorical visit the speaker was unwilling to make ("I do not want to be here, I can't explain"). She happens on the garden of the hostess' house, a garden of falling rain and rising damp. The poem moves through the frenzy of unwillingness and unwilledness to the final, almost impotent exertion of will:

                    I shall go

And find, somewhere among the formal hedges
Or hidden behind a trellis, a toolshed. There
I can sit on a box and wait. Whatever happens
May happen anywhere.

> And better, perhaps, among the rakes and flowerpots
> And sacks of bulbs than under this palid sky:
> Having chosen nothing else, I can at least
> Choose to be warm and dry.

The speaker escapes from form in form.

Her least successful poems so far seem to be the love poems; the strongest, those where textures, objects, things solid and present, blur into the recurrent dream, the garden, the nightmare, and re-emerge altered by the experience (as particularly in "Incident"). This fluctuation between areas of consciousness—reminiscent of Elizabeth Bishop and of Iris Murdoch, too—is seldom "cleverly" handled, and usually is convincing. The dimension of fable or the fabulous is revealed in such poems as "Regression", and "The Man who X-rayed an Orange". These poems again recall Elizabeth Bishop, with her "A Man-Moth" and her early allegorical poems. The vision of the man who x-rayed an orange, in his futility and isolation, is a virtuoso performance:

> . . . surely he had lacked nothing,
> Neither power nor insight nor imagination,
> When he knelt alone in his room, seeing before him
> Suspended in the air that golden globe,
> Visible and transparent, light-filled:
> His only fruit from the Tree of Life.

Fleur Adcock's achievement is remarkable, and her most recent book and the poems she has published in periodicals reveal various possible developments. She will hopefully continue to strengthen the varied sense of form which is her chief virtue, finding new free verse techniques to answer to her increasingly social preoccupations.

Molly Holden has published two collections, *To Make me Grieve*, and *Air and Chill Earth*. Her debt to Hardy, as recorded in the title of the first book, is more of tone and setting than a strong formal debt. She is, unlike Fleur Adcock, a rural poet, with keen sensibility but little sense of humour and a limited use of irony. The poems are personal in the same way Fleur Adcock's are, but the voice is less sympathetic because of the monotony of tone. There is a slight literariness about the poems which suits them—references to Constable, Housman, poems often about poetry, though not in the manner of, say, John Fuller, whose recent poems seem a function of his critical trade (word formulae of sorts) and not functions of a more vital imagination. Molly Holden's literariness is convincing because it is as intimately part of her rural experience as the earth itself. Her own illness is almost an illness of that earth.

> I had always a skin too few, identified
> with sun-hot blossoms on the far side of the road,
> felt beneath the warm envelope of flesh
>
> the foreign winter that calcined the delicate
> bones of the organ grinder's shuddering monkey.
> A ploughed field poiniarded my chest.

So now it seems a wry desert that youthful
ecstasies, my earthly husks of joy,
should be so turned about by this disease

that feels like a mist upon my fingers, like
a cold wind forever against my body, and
air and chill earth eternally about my bones.

("Illness")

The poem reveals some of Molly Holden's weaknesses—a rhythmical lameness elsewhere present as monotony or predictability, an over-strong first person pronoun. But the strengths are there too, a profound identification with earth and its conflicting forces which becomes in some of the poems an identification with rural characters. She uses the enjambment with skill, and her forms are by no means arbitrary.

Like Hardy, she does not idealise the past and the rural life. She realises them, revealing mis-spent potential or the facts of the present dissolution of rural traditions. Her expression, however, lacking in irony, is prescriptive rather than evocative. She lays meanings down explicitly and leaves little unsaid—a weakness, because her language can be rich with suggestion. Talking of farm boys, she says,

No romance
enhaloes those who will grow, without luck,
to inherit the tenancy of a damp cottage
or, taking their fortunes in their hands, get
digs near Austin's and make more money at the bench.

The poem ends with this effective gesture toward romance: slightly over-literary, perhaps. She sees a boy driving a tractor one morning:

So, perhaps, in his triumph, might Vercingetorix
have stood, the golden Gaul, before the world
closed round him with its sober Roman fate.

The perfect enjambment gives us the hero before the world and before the world closed round him; the end of this poem is rhythmically inevitable.

Molly Holden, perhaps because of her illness, achieves many of her best effects in recounting incidents from others' lives, or in responding to others' experience. When she does, the first person "I" becomes like Hardy's in some of the "Satires", omniscient and objective. But at the same time it is intimate with what it sees. The poems are complex interpretations of relationship: between the images or characters observed, between herself and the images or characters. Such poems as "The Dying Publican" (with its unduly portentous ending), "Seaman, 1941", and "Housman Country" have the complexities of varied relationships, contrasted time levels, and the recurrent tension between nature, art, and the artist. I feel in reading through Molly Holden's two books that, rather like her mentor, Hardy, she will continue writing fine lyrics for a long time, developing in deftness but not altering much in range, and her final achievement—a large body of good work—will be cumulative and substantial. Certainly she is one of the finest rural poets writing in England today.

Unlike Molly Holden's, Elaine Feinstein's poems are best read singly. Collected—most recently in *The Magic Apple Tree* (1971)—they do not help each other. Elaine Feinstein is one of the few poets on whom translation has had an appreciable effect. Her work on the poems of Marina Tsvetayeva enriched her with allusion and broadened her scope of formal experimentation. Unlike other poets whose experiments with form are whimsical, her attempts work often to create continuous metaphors of both an emotion and an idea without distracting us onto the mechanics. The form, being new and different for each poem, is constantly called upon to justify itself—and it *does*, unexpectedly often.

Elaine Feinstein's frame of reference includes the scientific, the cinema, the everyday, the literary—not gestured at randomly (as in the poems of Rosemary Tonks) but more or less assimilated. Her poem, "Sundance at Sawston", despite a literary cuteness which intrudes often in her work, draws together with imagistic precision, though without similar compression, the experiences of a film about the end of the Wild West, and of the very quiet English day. From the electrifying opening.

> In these corridors which are not my country
> my gait is awkward as a scorpion . . .

who would expect the sinister, almost unreal calm of the ending?

> The sun is a silver disc and this morning
> is lost in a white mist.
> It is English weather. Our thoughts sidle. Over
> there in the whiteness: apple trees float.

She uses her punctuation and her line endings with a strong, literary deftness, and elsewhere spacing helps us read the poems almost with the accuracy of musical notation. One is never in doubt of the rhythms or the tone.

Continually she discovers, in a sense like early Rilke, things in the everyday to praise, to sing—things released from their quotidian context by a jarring of associations. "The Magic Apple Tree", title poem of her most recent collection, presents a drab day. The memory of a Samuel Palmer tree, with colours of unusual brightness, fuses with an actual, apparently drab tree, suggesting the icon makers who "stilled their spirits before using gold" and created colours, like Palmer's, hyper-real, that "induced/the peculiar joy of abandoning restlessness". Back to the drab street scene, a heightening of perception occurs, and an object, more or less real, reveals the potential reality of the street:

> if we sing of
> the red and the blue and the texture of goat hair,

> there is no deceit in our prophecy:
> for even now our brackish waters can
> be sweetened by a strange tree.

"Our brackish waters"—and despite the rhythmic deadness and, unfortunately, the imprecision of the last line, something has been released and asserted. "Transfigure" is one of her favourite words. The process, repeated in a number of her poems, of associating images which release a composite image or significance—not in metaphorical terms, but by fusion or transition of images—is central to Elaine Feinstein. So, in "Mother Love", one of her best poems, the stating in wonder of what seems initially sordid has a remarkable effect. She has learned a lesson from imagism without accepting its more sterile tenets of utter compression; and though we are often let down by her poems, and many are vitiated by imprecision, her use of images and single words (though not her use of language in a more complex sense) is skilful. She lacks liveliness to internal suggestion, to semantic nuance, to the potential of undislocated syntax and rhythm. But her vision—no weaker word will do— is extraordinary. Her preoccupation with ephemerality, her fear (as expressed in "Moon", for example), her sense of suffering are strong. "For Malcolm Lowry" and "Offering: for Marina Tsvetayeva", with their effective hesitant progression, are among her best poems. Here is the ending of the Lowry poem:

> that
> enormity of remaining awake, inside
> the sick pain of your head
>
> as you went on. Choosing *words* to hold the red
> light of the heat had cracked through your
> adobe skull. So they still should carry.
> The last flow of. Your fear-sodden blood.

The sense—in intensity reminiscent of Samuel Beckett—of the mind painfully alive in the *cul-de-sac* of its determined fate could hardly be more effectively expressed. Her range is wide—a range of theme and tone as well as form. Her experiments are always, identifiably, her own, functions of a lively, humane—and feminine—imagination. Her "I" is not self-obsessed but solitary. Her poems attempt to share, to caution. This is perhaps why they are best read singly—they are each isolated, each a new attempt as single as each incident or experience is single. They do not add up to an *oeuvre*, as Molly Holden's do, since each rises out of a different mode of experience, is expressed in a different tone and a different form.

The only woman poet formally as inventive as Elaine Feinstein is Patricia Beer, and her inventiveness is less instinctive, more mechanical in nature. She works often in syllabics which force unnatural enjambments and cripple rhythm effectively—the rhythm of most of Patricia Beer's poems, because of the prescribed form, is even, tentative (not flat) like the poems themselves, progressing cautiously. Caution is the hallmark—a caution in vocabulary and "significance" as well as rhythm, and it pays off without strident effects or substantial statements—in a peculiarly *literary* way. Caution occasionally leads to contriving; forcing ambiguities or ironies of juxtaposition which the reader does not so much feel in reading but sees in study of the poems. This is something short of wit, provoking an "Oh, I see" from the reader rather than electrifying him, much as the detail of an emblem book effects this response.

This artifice, this cautious tone, while proving a limitation to the poet's range, is nonetheless consistent and—one is almost tempted to say, therefore—true to the poet. Patricia Beer's poems are recognisably hers. With her, style and voice are almost indistinguishable. She writes about many subjects—literature, stains of various sorts, fissures, "last things", cats—and all of them are incorporated into her voice so that her poems, like Molly Holden's, constitute a coherent *oeuvre*. One hesitates to quote her out of context because quotation misunderstands her poems. They *sound* ordinary in fragments; yet as entire structures, quietly dynamic, they repay study as well as reading. Her "I" does not project false vision or call attention to itself. It is the emotional, perceiving eye and the checking voice, the perception that discovers patterns and structures and presents them—coolly but effectively—as experiences:

> Being detached now seemed a skill
> He had mastered, not a windfall.
>
> ("Looking Back")

Her stark poems are often allegorical in suggestion,

> a touch
> That looks both domestic and
> Mythical.
>
> ("A Birthday Card")

Her objective description is strongly evocative with a carefully trimmed vocabulary. Here is the second stanza from the title poem of her most recent collection, *The Estuary*.

> No one can really taste or smell
> Where the salt starts but at one point
> The first buildings look out to sea
> And the two sides of the river
> Are forced apart by cold light
> And wind and different grasses.

The insertion of "really" in the compound verb suggests, and by the negative pronoun at once denies a possibility of "poetic" experience—the sea is not romanticised, it is perceived coldly, objectively—but we have glimpsed what we cannot feel or see, the taste and smell. The actual objects are literalised in terms of perception (literalising is a central process of these poems). The river does not seem water here but wind and cold light forcing a suture open; the grasses are "different" only—a word which, without detail, suggests both colour and texture. The river assumes an allegorical significance which it can bear because of the spareness, the precise imprecision, of the evocative rather than descriptive words.

The weakness of Patricia Beer's poetry is an over-literariness. But her controlled expression, her breadth of vision and reference, her so-far non-confessional sense of generality even in the personal poems, where experience is applied, rather than portrayed in its singularity, far outweigh the main weakness. There seems a danger that she is moving into confessional territory, probing her childhood relationships as private, or exclusively personal, and as a result narrowing her heretofore broad perspective. These lines from "The Cat in the Tree" embody her strong sense of perspective, the "active passivity" by which she can, through her own experience, enter without modifying alien experience, at once retaining the integrity of her own. One hopes she will not forsake this skill. The cat is on a high branch:

> I see her weight as the branch dips
> But it becomes mine too.
> I look both up at her and
> Down with her. I fear falling.

In 1967, Elizabeth Jennings' *Collected Poems* appeared. Edmund Blunden described her poetry as uniting "the deepest sensibility with a poetry of restraint and yet of great candour". Her restraint is of a different quality from Patricia Beer's, a formal restraint rather than a tentativeness of statement. Her prose poems are her most successful deviations from strict form, while the free-verse or aformal poems at the end of the *Collected* are the least successful. Miss Jennings requires traditional form, and she uses it with authority. Her temperament is not innovative in this sense. With her, form helps to discover order or disorder, rather than (as with Elaine Feinstein) order or disorder discovering form. Form is a primary poetic necessity rather than a device in Miss Jennings' poetry. Early on, she saw it, rather as Donne did, controlling the otherwise inarticulable. Here is a stanza from her early poem, "A Game of Chess":

> Is it that knight and king and small squat castle
> Store up emotion, bring it under rule,
> So that the problems now with which we wrestle
> Seem simply of the mind? Do feelings cool
> Beneath the order of an abstract school?

Her central preoccupation is not, then, with technique—something she takes for granted and uses skilfully. Nor does she worry much about "what poetry is"—she recognises that it is essential to her, and it would be solipsistic in her to tease out the reasons for this urgent necessity. If anything, poetry is a mode—perhaps the only mode—she has of reaching beyond her individual isolation and discovering relationship. When her poems are aesthetic in preoccupation, she is usually exploring the applicability of art to experience, or its vital relationship with experience. Most often her preoccupation is with suffering of various sorts, with loss, and occasionally fine celebrations of love. She is a poet of different calibre from those hitherto discussed, a poet who is still developing, within her chosen formal confines, towards a new clarity. She began as a love poet and has developed into the poet of complex relationships. Her best poems are not descriptive but exploratory of relationships. She seems at present to be putting aside rather than losing her earlier, more complex language, her aesthetic frame of reference, and her for a time obsessive mental hospital themes for direct confrontation with relationships. Some of the recent poems strike one as sentimental: simplifications rather than lucidities. But the best of them are her finest work to date, rediscovering meaning in apparently overused words, finding a linguistic spareness and clarity which render the poems direct and to the heart. The stylistic transition is almost complete.

Love, shadows, the mind, silence—all these are basic themes in her work. Time, too, obsesses her, and time rather than space is the poet's plane, through which she moves. Her images from nature are usually explicated, allegorised. The poems with plots (especially the early poems) become archetypal in her treatment, and effectively so. Thus "The Island" becomes like Arnold's island.

> Each brings an island in his heart to square
> With what he finds, and all is something strange
> And most expected . . .

We are "Seekers who are their own discovery". From this tendency to archetypes, Miss Jennings has proceeded on her course. The imagined and generalised has become realised. Intellectual preoccupation, where the mind implied thought, has become preoccupation where the mind implies perception in the widest sense—moral and human perception. There is no more hypothesis. The experiences of loss, the uncertainty of continuous identity, unfulfilled or frustrated longing, the ephemerality of landmarks and timemarks, a failure to find roots and security, to establish permanent relationships with nature or with human beings, have become the burning concerns of Miss Jennings' poetry. "It is acceptance she arranges", one of the recent poems says—perhaps this is the almost sacramental function of her art, expressed earlier in "Visit to an Artist". There the host and wine, the offering—which the experience underlies, validates, sanctifies—are most real and impart an ultimate validity to the poetic act.

"It was by negatives I learned my place. . . ." Without ever having been a genuinely confessional poet, Elizabeth Jennings has explored more territory in more depth than most poets writing today. Her recent work continues with the preoccupations of the earlier, but moves always closer and closer to

bedrock. It is strange for a poet, at the outset of a career, to foresee intellect-
ually most of the problems which will become realities for her later on. To
have kept course and cut always deeper as she went and goes is a remarkable
achievement.

All of the poets we have mentioned share certain things—background,
themes, formal preoccupations, aesthetic frames of reference, social class.
And despite their differences and the varied quality of their achievement they
constitute a sort of group—and that their successes have not been more widely
appreciated in a decade when poetry has thrived popularly is a criticism of
the critics and anthologies of the period, as well as having far wider social
implications.

The Little Magazine and the Small Press

by Harry Chambers

(Editor of *Phoenix* and *Phoenix Pamphlet Poets*)

THERE is no intrinsic virtue in longevity alone: too many centenarians have babbled their Secret of Long-Life too often. Yet the fact remains that during the twentieth century the life expectancy of a "little magazine" has been considerably less than one-tenth of that of a human being. It is in my capacity as editor of *Phoenix*, a poetry magazine which has kept going for over ten years, that I have been invited to contribute this article. The obligation is to explain oneself as phenomenon.

One reason I have *tried* to keep *Phoenix* going is because I think it is a worthwhile activity. Intentionalist Fallacy? Perhaps. But it is for others to judge the artistic credibility of what has gone into *Phoenix* and I am disinclined to attempt editorials: magazines—along with kingfishers and bells—declare what they are: "*myself* it speaks and spells,/Crying *what I do is me : for that I came.*" However, the contrived world into which the naked, good-intentioned self leaps is, as Lord Goodman reminds us: "an economic world where it is simple untruth that worthwhile activities must necessarily succeed." (*Introduction to Arts Council Report, 1970.*) I hope it will not be construed as biting the hand that now helps feed me to point out that a provincial poetry magazine must be a hardy blossom to survive up to the point of actually receiving a grant from the Arts Council: that body's bread is not cast idly upon the poetic waters unless the river happens to be the Thames. (By some process of double-think "London-based" gets to be equated with "national".)

Some editors do manage to scrape along, for two or three years even, on a diet of poverty-cum-paranoia, and the aesthetic affront afforded by the appearance of their magazines may be held by the fanciful to constitute an ethical protest, almost, against the economic facts. Other magazines manage to float awhile on an editor's private funds or manage to conceal drabness/poverty of content behind trendy psychedelic/typographic presentation and therefore "succeed"—as long as the trend lasts. But the reasons for *Phoenix* lasting/ "succeeding" (you takes your pick) are not to be found here, although I have, on occasion, had to dip into a not very deep pocket in order to meet bills.

Phoenix has kept on over the years partly because of the one editor's innate stubbornness—his literary heroes are Conrad's Captain MacWhirr and Orr from *Catch 22*—and partly because he has received steadily growing support from regular subscribers who seem satisfied that what they are getting is the real thing. What they are getting is certainly *one* man's personal taste: too many editorial cooks spoil the broth, of that I am convinced. If, taking my cue from Alan Tarling's ("pamphleteers without usura to today's poets") Poet & Printer press, I were to wear my editorial mast-head on my sleeve it would be Lord Reith's "ideal form of government", i.e., "monocracy tempered by summary execution". (I'm fond of the "tempered", though poets who have submitted manuscripts to me might quarrel with the "summary".) At any rate, it's my conviction that a committee choice is nearly always a compromise—and therefore an emasculated—choice: witness the general feel of the annual *P.E.N.* anthologies, even when the committee is composed of good poets; witness the quality of the *first* prizewinning poem(s) in relation to that of the runners-up in the Guinness and other poetry competitions. I also should mention that the simplicity/severity of presentation of *Phoenix* publications comes of a happy blend of economic necessity and aesthetic distaste for the gimmick graphics of certain magazines and poetry publications which tend to publish poems which I have (quite properly, I think) rejected.

Phoenix had anarchistic-political rather than literary roots. It came into being in February 1959 during my second term as a post-National Service student reading English at Liverpool University. It was not my own idea, rather the platform for an idealistic left-wing staff-student group of which I was a not-quite-peripheral member. The group was called *Interaction* and it talked about the "9 to 5 syndrome" and set up an *underground* (!) "Dream University". One of its leading lights was a very nice assistant lecturer in the Psychology department who got dismissed for having written a thesis on "Humour" that was funny, or for "dressing like a student", or for having mentioned The Royal Family and The Dunlop Rubber Company in the same paragraph in an attack on monopolies. Or some such reason. I discovered recently that he is now lecturing in Politics at York University. I became one of the magazine of Interaction's editorial board of eight. The first issue was roughly duplicated and stapled through the night into its utility blue serge sugar-bag cover and sold, complete with rubber-stamp art-work and sticky-label title, for 4*d.* That was in February 1959. I forget to mention that the magazine was called *Phoenix*: a committee decision that was supposed to radiate a mordant-ironical-toughly-idealistic comment on the supposed lack of literary-social-political life at the University. I had it reported later that I was thought "sound on the bomb, but no real politics: a pity". Meanwhile I was deputed sole editor for the second issue the appearance of which (price 10*d.*) in something I chose to call "Fall" 1959 coincided with the break-up of Interaction.

Phoenix 3 came out in Spring 1960, again under my sole editorship, and billed as "formerly the magazine of Interaction". Apart from one article on Apartheid, the content was literary: poems, short stories, and my own review of Larkin's *The Less Deceived*. Fittingly my editorial opposed, "those who would have literature aspire to the condition of music", and reaffirmed, "a faith in words and all that reflects ordinary human activity", asserting that, "If the music of the spheres can only be heard from the confines of the ivory tower, we prefer to go no higher than the top of a bus, where at least we may hear the human voice".

By *Phoenix* 4, I had obviously decided that a literary magazine didn't need the excuse of a political organisation to underwrite (morally) its existence. I continued editing *Phoenix* because, like the proverbial mountain, it was (as Leavis might have said) "there". I knew a bit about Lawrence by this time and the name *Phoenix* was a source of embarrassment which I endured at first with an innocence ignorant of such concepts as "tired brand-names", soon with a cavalier (Ford/Granada?) possessiveness, and now with a kind of ironical pride: after all *I* was born at Eastwood as well. With *Phoenix* 5 (Spring 1961) the drift from politics to poetry was complete, and for some years I have been convinced that this was an unconscious stumbling in what was surely the right direction, an impression not to be dinted by retrospective uneasiness at having given space to the likes of Hobsbaum, McGough, Pete Brown and Anselm Hollo in numbers 6 and 7.

After No. 7 (Spring '62), I left Liverpool to find a teaching job in Yorkshire, handing over the editorship to David Selzer and Tony Chapman; both had two years yet to serve at the University. Issues 9, 10 and 11 under their editorship represented the end of *Phoenix*'s long crawl to maturity. Wherewith being crowned, it ground to a halt for two and a half years while David Selzer grappled with his first job, a sense of his own emerging talent as a poet, and a rogue printer the equal of L. S. Caton.

In 1967 it was agreed that I should reassume the editorship from Belfast, where I had recently taken up a lecturing appointment at the local nondenominational (i.e., Protestant) Teacher Training College. *Phoenix* 1, in the optimistically labelled "new *quarterly* series", was a 60-page *Arts in Ulster* issue. What was left of a £50 grant the Arts Council had made for what should have been No. 12 helped its production. It appeared in March 1967 and carried several poems each by my new friends Michael Longley, Seamus Heaney and Derek Mahon whose dissimilar, yet fully-fledged talents, were already being misleadingly conflated by metropolitan trend and movement spotters eager to patronise with a blanket "promising". But the bland are still attempting to lead the blind, as is evidenced by the Lucie-Smith guide (!) to *British Poetry Since 1945* (Penguin, 1970): "Derek Mahon's work is close to Heaney's in style." Should one smile or stamp one's feet in rage? The three Heaney poems were (the still uncollected) "Boy Driving His Father To Confession": "What is going on/Beneath that thick grey hair? What confession/Are you preparing? Do you tell sins as I would?/Does the same hectic rage in our one blood?"; "Elegy For A Still-Born Child": "Your mother heavy with the lightness in her"; and "The Outlaw"—about an unlicensed bull: "Just the unfussy ease of a good tradesman;/Then an awkward, unexpected jump, and/His knobbled forelegs straddling her flank,/He slammed

life home, impassive as a tank." Mahon's world is light years away from the
warm dark of Heaney's (often disturbing) domestic interior. The Mahon
poems in *Phoenix* 1 included "As God Is My Judge": about the sinking of
the *Titanic*, and as good a poem as Hardy's; "Poem To The Memory of
Louis-Ferdinand Céline", and the light (and subsequently rejected) "Boise
Idaho", which I still relish for the panache of its unfair, yet not unfunny
excursion into the realms of lit crit:

> Some day when I have the time, a month
> Or so to spare and money in my pocket,
> I want to go to Boise, Idaho.
> Now, you will tell me not to be
> Ridiculous. You will say—
> "But Boise, Idaho, is the backside of
> Nowhere. In Boise, Idaho,
> They still think Eliot was a great poet."

(This poem unconsciously prefigures "No Land Is Waste", by James Sim-
mons, published in *Phoenix* 6 & 7: "The Muse has fired me, the conviction
burns/That I can justify the ways of men to Stearns".)

One other item in *Phoenix* 1—my own longish article on the novels of
Brian Moore—is worthy of note, if only for the fact that it was the last article
about something other than poetry to have appeared in *Phoenix*: *Phoenix* 2, 3,
4, 5, 6 & 7 and 8 have published exclusively poetry and reviews of poetry,
with the balance of space strongly favouring *poetry*. Even the current 84-page
Black Paper On Poetry issue carries 50 poems as against 35 pages of articles.
Phoenix is very definitely what Grigson would call "a poem periodical", and
as such—to borrow from Edna Longley's article on Ian Hamilton and *The
Review* in *Phoenix* 8—I trust that "*Phoenix* will be more remembered for the
poems it has published than will *The Review* for those it hasn't".

Looking back over the 323 poems that were published in the eight issues
of my "quarterly" to have appeared between Easter '67 and Easter '72, there
are very few that I now regret having printed. I do not apologise either for the
catholicity of my taste or for that catholicity being somewhat bounded by
what some might regard as a slavish regard for syntax, sense and the iambic
pentameter: rhythmic vitality has also been a prime consideration. As
Michael Longley ("An Inner Adventure", *Phoenix* 5) has it: "If the rhythm
is wrong the paraphrasable content will be worth absolutely nothing anyway.
Failure of rhythm is heart failure." Although I see my own political position
as being that of a radical-liberal, I have never been much persuaded of the
value of political radicalism in a poet as guarantee of winning the Muse's
favours. When someone like Adrian Mitchell asserts in a poem: "I'm talking
about/Pain man and fear man and shock man and death man,/Not the Holly-
wood kind", I feel that his message is corrupted by his medium: his language
is the Hollywood kind. When he uses the same synthetic rhythms and diction
both to celebrate love and to condemn war there ensues a sell-out of both

poetry and values.

My motives for starting the *Phoenix Pamphlet Poets* series after my move to Manchester in 1967 had much to do with growing feelings of unease about the big publishers' poetry lists. The contrast in quality between what was coming into my own hands via *Phoenix* submissions and some of what was getting published by both the established houses (e.g., Chatto, Cape Goliard, Penguin) and the nouveau-riche Anti-Establishment presses (e.g., Fulcrum, Rapp & Whiting), convinced me that what new poets got published was either a matter of random chance or wholesale intrigue. Whether it constituted an attempt to compete with the purveyors of profitable kitsch or not, many of the established houses were certainly guilty of gross dereliction of standards.

Glyn Hughes' *Love On The Moor* (November, 1968) was the first *Phoenix Pamphlet*. This edition of 1,000 sold out within a year, and my pride in this fact and in the review that described the pamphlet's appearance as being "in the worst traditions of jobbing printing" (it was!) was diminished only by the reflection that sales might have been influenced by the title affording delusive promises to the dirty mac brigade. These suspicions seemed to be bolstered by the poor sales of the second pamphlet, Michael Longley's *Secret Marriages* (the pornographic market wasn't to be fooled twice!) until it hit me that these were nine (only) *short* poems and might therefore have provoked the full scorn of the poetry buying public's quantitative philistinism: three bob, after all, was three bob!

My resolve to continue publishing young unknown poets of quality, in the company of such work by more established poets as lent itself especially to pamphlet production (e.g., Heaney's *Lough Neagh Sequence*, Massingham's *Magician* poems for children), was strengthened by the complacent enormity of the anonymous *Commentary* column in the *T.L.S.* of April 11, 1968:

> Pamphlets are a useful form of first publication for young poets who do not feel ready for a full-scale book; this is common procedure and not in any sense curiously phenomenal. But they can also provide a dumping ground for the tenth-rate (poetry that is rejected by the big publishers nowadays really does need to be tenth-rate) and there seems little point in trying to turn languishing mediocrity into evidence of splendid, scorned rebelliousness.

This is too sweeping: against it could be said that it is also an unhealthy state of affairs when a bad volume of poetry put out by an established publisher can usually command several reviews in the main literary journals while a good pamphlet collection by a press like *Phoenix* is very lucky to get even one mention. (I deliberately put that case at its most extreme, and I am aware that the reviewing situation is gradually changing for the better.) I have it in writing from one national reviewer that he did not think much of the poems in Glyn Hughes' *Love On The Moor*, yet when the same poems formed a substantial part of Hughes' first Macmillan collection that reviewer welcomed the publication with warm, though qualified, approval spread over several column inches. Again, Derek Mahon's *Ecclesiastes* has so far failed to attract the attention of more than one English reviewer; one wonders what will happen when the same poems appear in the context of Mahon's second collection, *Lives*, expected soon from O.U.P.

It seems to me that the metropolitan reviewers are guilty of the very "provincialism" tag which the *T.L.S.* imputes *indiscriminately* to the pamphlet presses. I use the word in the sense defined by Paddy Kavanagh in *Self Portrait*: "The provincial has no mind of his own. He does not trust what his eyes see until he has heard what the metropolis, towards which his eyes are turned, has to say on the subject." Kavanagh opposes "provincialism" with the positive of "parochialism": "all great civilisations are based on the parish." It is in this sense that I would be proud for *Phoenix* to be thought "parochial". Confusingly, Frederick Grubb writing on Larkin (*A Vision of Reality*, Chatto), uses the counters in reverse: "The *parochial* is the glorification of prudence, chosen through self-interest, mediocrity or fear . . . the *provincial* is the trust in roots, the refusal to be gulled, the *reservation* of respect and enthusiasm before the glamorous and the seductive." I would be happy for *Phoenix* to be judged *provincial* in the sense defined above. A typical *Phoenix* poet is, perhaps, Stanley Cook (No. 12: *Form Photograph*): "I like to feel, too, that I have been as practical and unsentimental with a poem as if I had farmed, smithed or carpentered it—that the rest of the family would think that I had done some 'real work' and not let them down."

But this does not mean that there is no room for a bravura lyricism within the series. For this the reader is advised to turn (particularly) to David Howarth's "Manchester Madness" (pamphlet 14), or to Peter Scupham's "The Small Containers" (pamphlet 16) as here from "Un Peu D'Histoire: Dordogne":

> . . . Bleached timbers lean
> By lime-washed naves, corruptible, sea-green.
> In faded reds and blacks, the names rank where
> The small brass badges tarnish. Triste, la guerre.
> Fusillé. Asphyxié par le gaz. Towns burn;
> A tufted pill-box haunts the river's turn.

Scupham, to my mind, is incontrovertibly one of the finest poets under 40 now writing in English. The fact that he has been rejected by the big publishers might persuade the *T.L.S.* (see *Commentary* April 11, 1968) that his poetry *therefore* "really does need to be tenth-rate", but anyone anxious to strike a blow for poetry against punditry is advised to write to me for details of Scupham's *The Snowing Globe*, a 48-page hardback collection, and the first in a new series (*Peterloo Poets*) that I am editing for the publisher Eric Morten of Didsbury. (Stanley Cook, John Mole and David Selzer are also appearing in the series.)

The function of the small press publisher/little magazine editor, as I see it, is to act as an *anti-Nebbish*. A *nebbish*, you will remember, is the small naked man—he does not know he is naked—who appears in the cartoons of Calman. In his most characteristic pose he is standing on top of a mountain of culture. The levels of his ascent are labelled something like this: BEET-HOVEN, IBSEN, TOLSTOY, GOETHE, KING LEAR, IAN HAMIL-TON, GOD. He is scanning the horizon and the caption reads: "On a clear day you can see something trivial." It may have been unkind of me (but not frivolous) to make a collage by teaming this up with a photograph of Dr. Leavis: it is my conviction that the supposed "minor" poetry of today becomes the "major" poetry of ten years or so hence. Why wait? The task of sorting out the good from the less good/bad, from that which lies in front of our eyes *now*, is far from trivial, and it should not offend our nostrils.

Poetry, Rhetoric and the Mass Audience: The Case of the Liverpool Poets

by Grevel Lindop

FOR the social historian, one of the more interesting features of life in Britain during the 1960s must be the growth of what is vaguely known as Pop Culture. As the phrase perhaps implies, the centre of the phenomenon was the emergence of a large, comparatively affluent and predominantly young audience for popular music, which became the focus and the symbol of a whole complex of new attitudes and patterns of behaviour. Parallel with this, though on a smaller scale, went the development of a new audience for poetry: new, in that it approached the condition of a mass audience.

A "mass" audience differs in kind from a merely "large" audience not so much in numbers as in the relationship between the audience and the art-form it supports. Where a large audience may, in the case of poetry, buy great numbers of books and even attend poetry readings in force, it does not necessarily turn the writing of poetry into anything approaching a communal activity. The mass audience, on the other hand, in poetry as in television or music or the cinema, is regarded to some extent as a "consumer" and so tends to impose its own criteria upon the artist and thereby, indirectly, participate in the creative process.

It is necessary to be clear about this from the beginning, for in tackling the phenomenon of "Underground" poetry one must remember that the audience is often of primary importance. The poet wants, and often succeeds in getting, a large audience which must be held and satisfied by performance. If the audience falls away, the poet has failed.

In this connection, of course, a good deal has been made of the links between pop music and Underground poetry. There are certain obvious similarities: when the poets use regular verse-forms they are simple and often loosely-constructed ones; many of the verbal clichés of the pop song are appropriated; the audiences of both have a good deal in common in terms of age and culture, and the conditions of performance are often alike.

But there are deeper significances in the linkage. The names of Bob Dylan and the Beatles are commonly mentioned as influences on certain poets, and as examples of the *rapprochement* between poetry and popular song. Bob Dylan certainly deserves considerable credit for having, almost single-handed, made both symbolism and verbal complexity acceptable in pop music. But that he should be considered a part of a wider *avant-garde* is merely a measure of how far popular song has lagged behind the development of literature, for his achievement consisted of introducing into the former art techniques which had been commonplace in the latter for forty years or more. If some poets find Dylan or John Lennon genuinely important influences on their own art, they are testifying only to the extent to which they have lost touch with the poetic tradition. An indication of serious defects in our society and its culture, certainly; but scarcely a fact that should lead us in itself to expect anything very new in their writing.

Critics and reviewers tend (and I have already fallen into it myself) to write glibly of "The Underground" as if there were some clearly-defined "school" of Underground poets. This is not the case: not only does no grouping exist in the manner of, say, the "Movement" or the "Group", but there has been no defining anthology comparable to *New Lines* or *A Group Anthology*. The nearest approach to this has been Michael Horovitz's *Children of Albion: Poetry of the "Underground" in Britain*,* published in 1969, a book which serves only to show how far the word *Underground* is from labelling any coherent group. The expected names (Mitchell, Cunliffe, Pickard, the two Horovitzes) are there; but so are John Arden, Gael Turnbull, Anselm Hollo, and Alexander Trocchi. The Liverpool poets are conspicuously absent, although Patten is mentioned in the "Afterwords" at the back of the book. The joint criteria for inclusion, apart of course from the editor's taste, were (apparently) revolutionary or nihilistic political attitudes, distinctively modernist verse-technique, and lack of availability in published form. Most contributors satisfied at least two of these requirements. But an attempt to follow any one of them through the anthology would be fruitless. Not that this in itself constitutes an adverse criticism: probably anthologies should be anthologies, not manifestoes. But it highlights the problem of definition.

Rather than attempt a limiting definition myself and survey a carefully marked-out area of Underground poetry, therefore, I shall centre this essay upon the Liverpool poets, who share the technical and political positions mentioned above but are distinguished from the other Underground poets by their popular success. This success may to some extent be fading now, but it has assured that their work is widely known, and that their names will always have significance for literary history. They have themselves become important influences on the Underground, and it will be seen that discussion of their purely literary qualities is relevant to an examination of the work of many writers who consciously dissociate themselves from the literary "establishment". The reasons for their success, so far as these can be discovered, have their own significance for an understanding of the relationship between poet and audience, a matter to which most of the self-consciously "anti-establishment" poets attach great importance. (Significantly, Michael Horovitz feels that Underground poetry really came of age at the first International Poetry Incarnation at the Albert Hall in 1965, when "the buds of a

* Michael Horovitz (ed.) *Children of Albion: Poetry of the "Underground" in Britain.* Harmondsworth, 1969.

spreading poetry internationale, the esperanto of the subconscious sown by Dada and the Surrealists and the beats bore fruit—a renewal of light, of 'the Holy Word/That walk'd among the ancient trees'—made flesh".)*

With this in mind, I shall continue to refer without further definition to the "Underground", inviting the reader to make what exceptions and inclusions seem proper to him. Having no better phrases to propose in their place, I shall refer without inverted commas to the Underground poets and the Liverpool poets, defining the latter as those poets (Brian Patten, Adrian Henri, and Roger McGough) whose work appeared in *The Mersey Sound* (*Penguin Modern Poets 10*).†

I should perhaps confess at this point that although I have heard both Patten and McGough read their poems, Adrian Henri's are known to me only on the page. This may conceivably have affected my estimate of his work, although by the very act of publishing in book form (rather than, say, making use exclusively of records and tapes) all three poets have implicitly affirmed that their poetry is worth reading in print. The relationship between poet and audience is one of the main topics with which I shall deal, the others being the characteristic rhetorical structures of Underground poetry and the theoretical writings of the poets themselves. Each aspect of the subject will, I hope, illuminate the others, for the three appear to be inextricably linked.

First, then, the audience. The work of the Liverpool poets, and that of many of the Underground poets, is written to be read aloud, and the extent to which the audience determines what it is going to hear should not be underestimated. In Adrian Henri's words,

> When I started doing readings I used to find sometimes that I'd written bits in older, i.e., pre-reading, poems that I couldn't say. Obviously these were altered in the reading. The interesting thing is that in every case this improved the purely literary value of the line or phrase—it was simpler, clearer, more direct. I'm never *conscious* of doing it, but I suppose now one writes with the underlying assumption "If you can't say it, don't write it".‡

It is clear that this is far more than the usual vague tributes paid by poets to "the speaking voice". Henri, later in the same statement, explains that the form of a poem, the question of which lines shall be included and which expunged, and so on, is determined ultimately by what "seems to go down well". The audience thus plays an almost direct part in the organisation of the poetry.

The composition of that audience is therefore a matter of some interest. To judge from the various readings I have attended over the past few years, readings particularly by Patten, McGough, and Adrian Mitchell, it is (pre-

---

* Horovitz, *op. cit.*, p. 337.
† *Penguin Modern Poets 10 : The Mersey Sound* (Harmondsworth) 1967.
‡ Henri, *Tonight at Noon*, London, 1968, p. 69.

dictably) a young audience: it includes few people whom one would guess to be over 25, and a mere scattering of the obviously middle-aged. In the earlier days, before and shortly after the publication of Brian Patten's first book, *Little Johnny's Confession*, the audiences of at least the Liverpool poets were rather less student-dominated than they are now, but no less predominantly young. It is clear also that people come expecting a good show: one notices the absence of a respectful pre-reading hush, and the noisy, spontaneous applause. McGough and Henri at least actively encourage the audience to see poetry as an entertainment: both read to music, and McGough reads his poems in the intervals between performing sketches and songs with The Scaffold, whose act hovers between pure music-hall comedy and sallies of an intricate verbal humour which itself often comes close to poetry. McGough's style of reading is very attractive: in the old Everyman Theatre in Liverpool, where he seems most at home, he perches on a high stool, looking like a sad, exotic bird because of both his posture and his flamboyant clothes; he reads in a tone of sprightly melancholy, periodically glancing up with an apprehensive expression to take in the audience through a pair of heavy, black-rimmed glasses. His reading—one tends almost to say, "his act"—is meticulously controlled: the moods of poems are carefully varied, McGough keeping an entirely straight face through even the most comic ones, and one suspects that the audience is constantly being observed for the smallest sign of discontent or boredom. Patten on the other hand seems both more spontaneous and less relaxed. He appears moody, even inarticulate between poems, and the audience is excited, probably, not only by the enormous passion with which he reads (or rather intones or chants) his poems but also by the suspicion that at any moment he may be going to pick a quarrel with someone. These rather unusual conditions of performance (and therefore of composition) often override the individual characters of the poets and go some way to explaining the ease with which they can be considered as a group.

The direct relevance of the audience and its attitudes to the poems themselves is less obvious, but it nonetheless seems fairly clear that many of the most obvious characteristics of Underground poetry can be explained best with reference to the audience. By this I mean not only that the poems display attitudes which are also characteristic of their audience, but that the style and rhetorical organisation of the poems are to a surprising extent socially-determined.

This assertion can perhaps be demonstrated best by an examination of what Adrian Henri, the main theorist of the Liverpool poets, calls "The revaluation of the cliché". In Henri's words,

> This seems to me one of the most interesting aspects of what the Liverpool poets and some other English poets are doing. The cliché is a living piece of language that has gone dead through overwork. At any time it can be energised or revitalised. Often by changing its context, putting it in an alien context, contradicting its apparent meaning. . . . In new English

writing perhaps the most striking example of this revitalising process is
the beginning of Pete Brown's "Slam":

> They slammed the door in my face
> I opened the door in my face . . .*

Other examples are Henri's "Liverpool Poem 3", which works not by context
but by Spoonerism:

> Liverpool I love your horny handed tons of soil

and *Morning Poem*:

> "I've just about reached
> breaking point"
> he snapped.

Consider also Roger McGough's

> Your finger sadly
> Has a familiar ring about it†

and the conclusion of Brian Patten's *Party Piece*:

> Later he caught a bus and she a train
> And all there was between them then
> was rain.

   This rhetorical device might almost be called the hallmark of the Liverpool
poets and the Underground poets in general. Henri rightly gives it prominence
in his essay, associating it with certain aspects of Dada, Surrealism and Pop
Art, as well as with Mallarmé's and Eliot's concept of the poet as purifier of
"the dialect of the tribe". But it is more relevant, I believe, to see it as a
symbolic gesture of rebellion which appeals especially to the particular type
of audience we have considered. The revived cliché is a fire-cracker under the
dead hand of time, a little rebellion against the moribund language created
by previous generations, by "officialdom", by politicians and parents and all
the other tedious stereotypes against which the young audience feels itself
to be in revolt. It is a social gesture, and it is no coincidence that it forms
almost a whole *genre* of Underground poetry.
   This may seem an exaggeration; but one remarkable feature of the work of
the Liverpool poets in particular is their tendency to construct entire poems
around a single rhetorical device, so that one figure of speech will almost
suffice to define the construction of a whole group of poems.
   Perhaps the most frequent of these sub-generic categories is what used to
be known as the "*ubi sunt*" lyric. The keynote of such poems is "Where are
they now?" and perhaps the best-known example is Adrian Mitchell's
"Nostalgia Now Threepence Off":

---

* Quoted by Henri, *op. cit.*, p. 80.
   † Quoted by Henri, ibid.

> Where are they now, the heroes of furry-paged books and comics brighter than life which packed my inklined desk in days when BOP meant Boy's Own Paper, where are they anyway?

This is obviously a theme which can be developed *ad infinitum*. Brian Patten provides several examples:

> Where are you now, Batman? Now that Aunt Heriot has reported Robin missing
> And Superman's fallen asleep in the sixpenny childhood seat? . . .
>
> ("Where are you now, Batman?")
>
> Maud, where are you Maud?
> With your long dresses and peachcream complexion;
> In what cage did you hang that black bat night?
> What took place in the garden? Maud, it is over,
> You can tell us now.
>
> ("Maud, 1965")

Such poems are to some extent a revival of an ancient and rather primitive *genre*; their basic rhetorical organisation is similar, for example, to that of the best-known passage of "The Wanderer", which was probably written during the seventh century A.D.:

> Where is that horse now? Where are those men? Where is the hoard-sharer?
> Where is the house of the feast? Where is the hall's uproar?
> Alas, bright cup! Alas, burnished fighter!
> Alas, proud prince! How time has passed,
> dark under night's helm, as though it never had been. . . .*

The obvious difference is of course in the diction, and in fact a part of the impact of this type of poem in the work of the Liverpool poets lies in their use of a rather portentous style for the treatment of comically insignificant or undignified subjects. An appreciation of the poems depends upon an instinctive understanding on the part of the audience of the way in which the poet is flouting traditional decorum. This is clearest, of course, in the case of "Maud, 1965", where Patten attains his effects by playing off his poem against Tennyson's and suggesting knowingly that Tennyson left a good part of his story unrelated. (But notice that our knowledge of Tennyson's "Maud" is assumed to be only superficial: familiarity with more of the poem than the single section to which Patten refers actually destroys what effectiveness Patten's poem possesses, by turning against Patten the charge of naïvety which he implicitly levels at Tennyson.)

As the title of Mitchell's poem suggests, however, the real basis of such poems is a somewhat debased notalgia; a sense of superiority to one's childhood self or (in the case of "Maud") to a figure from the despised Victorian era, coupled with a comfortable and specious regret for the innocence one is

* *The Earliest English Poems*, Translated by Michael Alexander, Harmondsworth (Penguin Books), 1966.

assumed to have lost. Poems of this type can be developed to any desired length, progressing normally by sets of parallel statements or questions, for the only necessity is to keep up the particular emotion which the poem evokes in the reader or hearer. Any change or development, indeed, would jeopardise this state of affairs by rendering the audience's response less direct and simple, and therefore less unanimous.

Another important *topos* among the Liverpool poets is the poem of Metamorphosis, which in modern poetry has become the simplest and most accessible form of surrealism:

> Tonight at noon
> Supermarkets will advertise 3d EXTRA on everything
> Tonight at noon
> Children from happy families will be sent to live in a home
> Elephants will tell each other human jokes
> America will declare peace on Russia
> World War I generals will sell poppies in the streets on November 11th
> The first daffodils of autumn will appear
> When the leaves fall upwards to the trees
> > (Adrian Henri, "Tonight at Noon")

> > mother the wardrobe is full of infantrymen
> > i did i asked them
> > but they snarled saying it was a mans life
>
> > mother there is a centurian tank in the parlour
> > i did i asked the officer
> > but he laughed saying "Queens regulations"
> > (piano was out of tune anyway)
> (Roger McGough, "Mother the Wardrobe is Full of Infantrymen")

> > > Please Mr Teacher, Sir,
> > > Turn round from your blackboard,
> > > The whole class has its hands up,
> > > We're in rather a hurry.
> > > The desks are returning to forests,
> > > The inkwells are overflowing,
> > > The boys in the backrow have drowned.
> > > (Brian Patten, "Little Johnny's Change of Personality")

In such poems the poet seems to be revelling in the power of words to create pictures. As Henri puts it, in his discussion of a similar poem, "It's like primitive magic—to name something is to evoke its existence". Poets and audience seem often to share an innocent delight in metaphor for its own sake, which in practice means that both are satisfied with very little else. This may account for the prevalence of "metamorphic" poems in the *oeuvre* of the Liverpool poets. It also allows the most hackneyed clichés to pass muster, as in the case of McGough's ailing busconductor who

> all the time
> deepdown in the deserted busshelter of his mind . . .
> thinks about his journey nearly done,
>> ("My Busconductor")

where the metaphors of bus shelter and journey are produced at the climax of the poem as if they constituted an incisive conceit. It is as if the poet takes a certain pride in having, however clumsily, developed a metaphor over two lines.

A less harmless form of name-magic is present, I think, in those poems where cult-figures are invoked for decorative effect. Adrian Henri is particularly given to this:

> Kurt Schwitters smiles as he picks up the 2 pink bus tickets
>> we have just thrown away.
>>> ("Manchester Poem")
> I want to paint . . .
>> Francis Bacon making the President's Speech at the Royal
>> Academy Dinner . . .
>>> ("I Want to Paint")

In "Me (if you weren't you, who would you like to be?)" the method takes over completely:

> Paul McCartney Gustav Mahler
> Alfred Jarry John Coltrane
> Charlie Mingus Claude Debussy
> Wordsworth Monet Bach and Blake . . .

The poem continues in this vein for eleven stanzas and must rank as one of the most audacious exercises in name-dropping ever perpetrated.

One of the dangers of submitting entirely to the magic of verbal associations is that the poet fails to question his own purposes and motives. The implications of such a poem as "Me . . ." are obvious: if all, or most, of the names here mean something to you, then you will easily deduce from them a certain intellectual ethos, a certain vaguely implied blend of fashionable attitudes to life and art, and you will feel flattered by the poet's assumption that you are able to do this. If, on the other hand, the names of many of these cult-figures are unknown to you, or if you dislike the juxtaposition Henri forces upon them, you are out in the cold: you don't belong to the club. The apparent innocence with which Henri constructs such a poem, whose entire effect depends upon mapping out the boundaries of a clique, is very revealing.

What it reveals is, surely, an attitude to art based firmly on that advertiser's concept, the "life-style". It is a very short distance from the crudely explicit snobbery of the advertisement that asks us whether we are the kind of person who is capable of appreciating Someone's expensive brand of cigarettes, to the implied question of Henri's poem: "Are you the kind of person who knows about Jarry, Coltrane, Debussy?".

The similarity between this type of poetry and the techniques of advertising is not, perhaps, consciously aimed at in all cases; but the basic affinities are easily discoverable, and they serve to demonstrate the dangers of an important theme in Henri's critical writing:

> Because we live in an era of communications-explosion, certain specialist uses of language seem particularly relevant [to poetry]: that of advertising (hoardings, slogans, tv ads) or newspaper headlines, where the aim is to transmit a message (or feeling) as quickly as perception allows, or that of pop songs or tv jingles where the basic aim is to establish a word/sound pattern as quickly as possible. Both demand considerable economy of means and a rethinking of ideas about syntax. In tv advertising, for example, a couple of extra words may cost hundreds of pounds.*

Henri, followed by many Underground poets, has parodied the language of advertising, trying to use its techniques to convey attitudes and insights more subtle than those for which such techniques were first developed. But here, as elsewhere, the means corrupt the end. Henri mimics the slightly ludicrous scene-setting of fashionable advertising copy in the opening lines of "I Love You":

> When listening to Bruckner in the sunlit bathroom
> When the hills and valleys of your morning body
> are hidden from my gaze by Body Mist . . .

But the resemblance is really too close for parody. Now that the copywriters have taken to setting out their text like verse (opening a women's magazine at random, I come upon this:

> Think cool breezes
> and icy drinks.
> Just relax and think of
> last winter when
> you were wishing
> for summer . . .)†

it is no longer possible to say who is parodying whom, and whether in any case parody has not faded into imitation.

The problem is that advertising is, in a certain sense, more flexible than poetry: it cares nothing about the moral or aesthetic attitudes it induces, so long as these are conducive to the single practical end of selling the product. The language of advertising will happily absorb any style of writing, whether literary or non-literary; it is happy to parody itself. In taking over the techniques of advertising, the poet is tackling an adversary without a conscience; and since even the poorest poet has some scraps of a conscience about his use of his art, the poet will lose. His attitude to his subject-matter will be cor-

---

* Henri, op. cit., p. 76.
† Tampax advertisement, *Woman's Story Magazine*, July 1970, p. 10.

rupted, whilst the copy-writer will happily imitate his opponent's work as a means of making his text more insidiously persuasive. The fact that much advertising copy is written by poets or poets *manqués*, of course, only makes the danger greater.

The self-consciously Modernist attitudes behind Henri's poems thus form an opening through which deeply damaging influences are able to move into his work. And where there is a mass-audience to be held and entertained, it is inevitable that the poet will welcome the techniques of mass-persuasion. It may be for these reasons that, in general, those Underground poets least preoccupied with theory produce the best work. Dave Cunliffe, for example, one of the better-known poets to appear in Michael Horovitz's "Children of Albion" anthology, often attains a kind of wholeness and symbolic vividness by a process of thinking in images:

> Come join in the angels naked march.
> Each bearing truly special gifts of
> precious fruit, prayer-beads, love-chimes,
> wooden dolls & brightly coloured masks.
>
> O come love these savage warring armies
> & scatter rose-petals upon their tanks.*

Conventional enough, perhaps, but the incantatory note (attained by carrying a single long sentence through a four-line stanza and ending it with the assonance of *march* and *masks*) and the hints of wide-ranging symbolism put such a poem into a different realm from Henri's playing with brand-names (which of course are the opposite of vivid particulars) and his staunch adherence to the adman's principle of one-sentence-to-the-line.

Part of the problem in Henri's case is his tendency to follow other people's manifestoes. Henri's essay "Notes on Poetry and Painting" glitters with references to the father-figures of the *avant-garde*, to Tzara, Burroughs, Duchamp, Dali, Bob Dylan, Moholy-Nagy and Stockhausen, as the writer attempts to relate his work and that of other poets whom he admires to the "tradition" of modernism. What is significant is the lack of originality, the lack of ideas stemming from the tackling of specific poetic problems. Documents such as Olson's "Projective Verse" and the "Manifesto" of the Dadaists are seen, not as emerging from and justifying a particular and limited body of work, but as contributions to a canon of scriptures which it is the duty of the right-minded modernist to study and obey. They are made to be prescriptive rather than descriptive. The one original point, where Henri perceives the importance of what he calls the "revaluation of the cliché", is fumbled and misinterpreted because Henri insists on relating it to Dada *via* Meret Oppenheim's "Fur-covered Cup, Saucer and Spoon", thereby missing the crucial features which constitute the difference between the two types of

---

* Dave Cunliffe, "O Come Love These Warring Armies" (*Children of Albion*, p. 56).

aesthetic incongruity and so failing to enlighten us in any way about his ostensible subject.

Of the Liverpool poets, Roger McGough and Brian Patten most often escape the trammels of demagogic technique and modernist theory. McGough in particular tends to keep close to a fairly strict stanzaic pattern, which enforces a certain simplicity that, coupled with his often skilful handling of rime, can occasionally lift a poem out of the morass of self-indulgence and portentousness.

When McGough's poems fail, they fail because they are damaged by the very rhetorical devices that mark them as part of a particular movement. A poem such as "Comeclose and Sleepnow" shows a good deal of playful psychological penetration:

> . . . when a policeman
> disguised as the sun
> creeps into the room
> and your mother
> disguised as birds
> calls from the trees

—but the tone is suddenly damaged by puns and near-puns which are jarringly contrived:

> you will put on a dress of guilt
> and shoes with broken high ideals

so that we feel McGough anxiously trying to jerk some extra life into the poem at the expense of the coherence of the whole: there has been no hint previously in the poem that "high ideals" are involved or broken, so that the lines stand out as pieces of non-functional cleverness afflicting the poem like a nervous twitch.

When McGough tackles a subject which involves openly the social and political attitudes of himself and his audience, the result is often total debility. A poem like "Why Patriots are a Bit Nuts in the Head" is sufficiently defined by its title. Consciously juvenile in its language, the poem is also primitive in its attitudes and its reasoning:

> when you are alive
> you can eat and drink a lot
> and go out with girls
> (sometimes if you are lucky
>   you can even go to bed with them)
> but you can't do this
> if you have your belly shot away . . .

It is hard to disagree with such a statement, but beyond that, the fact that McGough thought the poem good enough to include in a short selection of his work, and that it is deeply enjoyed by his audiences, requires further explanation. The answer must lie in the social function of the poem. It is the mirror-image of the patriotic verse of (say) Newbolt, and enjoyed for the same reason: that it flatters the unthinking assumptions of the audience, and particularly those assumptions which, underlaid by deep but unrecognised anxiety, especially need to be propped up.

This said, the judgment of McGough's poems as a whole needs to be modified by the recognition that, happily, in a very few poems the rhetoric of Underground poetry is transformed to brilliant effect. Probably McGough's best poem, and in my opinion the best poem so far written by any Liverpool poet, is "Let Me Die a Youngman's Death", from which I quote the first and last stanzas:

> Let me die a youngman's death
> not a clean & inbetween
> the sheets holywater death
> not a famous-last-words
> peaceful out of breath death . . .
>
> * * *
>
> Let me die a youngman's death
> not a free from sin tiptoe in
> candle wax and waning death
> not a curtains drawn by angels borne
> "what a nice way to go" death

The poem sags a little at the centre, but the verbal vitality of the beginning and the end carry the weight of the less accomplished passages.

Why is this poem successful? Surely because it is compressed and complex. Rejecting the usual Underground poet's reliance on a single trope or metaphor to carry the weight of a whole poem, McGough packs together internal and interlinear rime, alliteration, the revived cliché and the fruitfully mixed metaphor to produce a texture which contrasts strongly with the thinness, the poverty of invention of most of these poems. The "economy" of the television advertisement, where every word must be perceived and comprehended at a single hearing, has been abandoned.

The ghostly echo of Dylan Thomas in "candle wax & waning" is probably no accident. One suspects in other poems that McGough sometimes strives with less success for Thomas's exuberance and prodigality of language, as in his reference to the children who

> played ollies in the
> knockeruppered barefooted tripe and fishcaked streets,*

where the debt to Thomas and (for example) his "dogs in the wetnosed yards" becomes embarrassingly obvious. But even in such lines as these one applauds the attempt to escape from the kind of "simplicity" and "economy" which Henri, as we have seen, regards as the ideal. In this direction there may perhaps lie a way out of the most serious defects of Underground poetry.

---

* "Cafe Portraits" (*The Mersey Sound*, p. 65).

Moving away from these central rhetorical problems in a different direction, Brian Patten's more recent poetry, as represented by his books *Notes to the Hurrying Man* and *The Irrelevant Song*, seems to be seeking a calm lyricism in which there is, I think, an implicit realisation that the hectoring "public-poet" style of *Little Johnny's Confession* is a *cul-de-sac*, a literary manner that offers no hope of development. Surprisingly, the main influences now seem to be Graves and the early Auden. Here, for example, is a poem from "The Irrelevant Song" which presents a very sharp contrast to most of the poems in "Little Johnny's Confession":

At Four O'clock in the Morning

As all is temporary and is changeable,
So in this bed my love you lie,
Temporary beyond imaginings;
Trusting and certain, in present time you rest,
A world completed.

Yet already are the windows freaked with dawn;
Shrill song reminds
Each of a separate knowledge;
Shrill light might make of love
A weight both false and monstrous.

So hush; enough words are used:
We know how blunt can grow such phrases as
Only children use without
Awareness of their human weight.

There is no need to impose upon feelings
Yesterday's echo.
I love you true enough;
Beyond this, nothing is now expected.

The thought of the poem, and the imagined situation, strongly recall Auden's "Lullaby"; the recollection is confirmed by the line "Awareness of their human weight" which, giving considerable stress to *human* as an adjective, reminds us of Auden's similar use of the word ("Human on my faithless arm"; "Watched by every human love"). We notice also that the metrical pattern of the line, an iambic tetrameter, follows that of Auden's poem. The "windows freaked with dawn", by the occurrence of the word *freaked*, distinctly rare in modern English, send us at once to Graves's "Three Songs for the Lute", where we find

a wan winter landscape,
Hedges freaked with snow

which likewise suggests a metrical reminiscence. And in the last line of Patten's poem it may not be too far-fetched to deduce an echo of another Graves poem, "Nothing Now Astonishes". That one should even suspect such echoes demonstrates the extent to which Patten's tone has changed. More than this, it is clear that a specifically poetic diction has made its appearance, in the repeated *is* of the first line and the inversion (verb before subject) of "already are the windows freaked with dawn" and "how blunt can grow such phrases". The poem has a new weight and balance, albeit precariously achieved.

In other poems, however, another characteristic of Underground poetry emerges: in place of the falsely-naïve violence and whimsy of the earlier poems, there is a falsely-naïve gentleness, a sense that shrinking from experience or from pain is somehow admirable in itself:

> The first love's well vanished,
> or sunk at least beneath
> an ocean I made, made out
>
> the clouds I became when
> all round me bruised itself.*
>
> * * *
>
> She might have said, if words
> Were more her medium than touch:
> "Near you is one
> Frighteningly real who cannot plan;
> Whose heart's a cat from which
> Your habits dart like birds . . .†

One notices still the willingness to use clichés, and now without any attempt at "revaluing" them. "Frighteningly real", for example, is a cliché one comes across both in bad fiction and in factual journalism. And below these, a different manifestation of the cult of youthfulness, even juvenility, that invested the earlier poems: a contrived innocence, a fear of the slightest suffering, which several Underground poets (not least Dave Cunliffe and Tina Morris, whose work has been quite influential) seem to feel to be especially appropriate to poetry. And with this goes a condescension both to subject-matter and to audience. Many poems of this type have about them a curiously "Victorian" striving for prettiness, a basic sentimentality that seems odd in the work of poets who tend to regard themselves as innovators, even revolutionaries.

The problem, again, seems to lie in the poet's attitude to his audience. Fashions change. The audience which in 1967 demanded parody of the language of its elders and wry variations on the theme of a lost childhood innocence now demands a different set of values, based on the assumption that everything is pretty and melancholy, that life seems hard not because we are all cruel but because we are all vulnerable, and that this vulnerability is

---

* "Season Blown" (*The Irrelevant Song*, p. 28).
† "If Words Were More her Medium Than Touch" (ibid., p. 32).

self-justifying and requires no analysis. The tone is one of self-pity (I quote
from Patten's "The Irrelevant Song"):

> His first songs,
> The loneliest,
> The loveliest,
> Fled into an irretrievable country.
> The city hardly found him.
> Nature soon forgot him.

There is an approach to the vagueness, the blurred verbal "magic" of the
lesser poems of Shelley or Swinburne. The nervous evasion of any kind of
analysis or precision is the most conspicuous characteristic of such poetry,
and this in itself is a sign of a fundamental lack of confidence in the poet's
own perceptions, a fear that to take hold firmly of anything, even in words,
will damage or destroy it.

There seems, at least, to be more potential for development in Brian
Patten's recent work than in that of the other Liverpool poets and Under-
ground poets. By moving back to a lyric tradition which has not been
thoroughly corrupted by propaganda and mass-persuasion, a poet comes into
a region where individual perception and self-analysis are not prohibited from
the start.

But this is only to say that on present showing the experiments of the
Liverpool poets and their less famous associates have largely failed. Close
contact between the poet and the audience as *readers* of his work is perhaps a
basic necessity, but close contact between audience and *writer*, where applause
or laughter at a single hearing constitute the criteria for preferring one version
of a poem above another, seems to be a recipe for failure. It presents the
public—*any* public—with a temptation it cannot withstand, the temptation
of having its own attitudes, its concealed anxieties and its complacencies,
flattered by the poet. Not only the poet's subject matter, but his vocabulary,
his very figures of speech, will be affected for the worse, because in bowing to
his audience he is joining the whole throng of less scrupulous word-mongers
whose daily business is to breed complacency and propagate a false vision of
the world.

That other forms of poetry than Underground verse are liable to fall into
such traps is undeniable; and perhaps the only general point which needs
stressing is that where we sense something wrong in the language of a poem,
some basic lack, either of tact or of intensity, we may often be able to under-
stand it best by looking in the first instance not at the poet himself but at the
audience for which he is writing.

Poetry in the North East

by W. E. Parkinson

[*I*] HAVE *learned more* [*from Balzac about French Society*] *than from all the professional historians, economists and statisticians put together*—Friedrich Engels (letter to Margaret Harkness, April, 1888).

Today, more than ever, faced with Marshall McLuhan's Global Village culture and an increasingly dominant national culture, partially created and sustained by the mass media, it is vitally important for writers, folk-singers, critics and researchers to sustain and energise our distinctive and differing regional cultures, both written and oral. The importance of such an enterprise is slowly being recognised but, as A. L. Lloyd has said,

> So far researchers . . . have only feebly scratched the surface, several jewels have been unearthed, certainly enough to convince us that by systematic combing of archive and library materials, broadsides, printed or cyclostyled song-books, newspapers, trade union journals, workers' manuscripts and such, a rich store of folklore native to the industrial proletariat may be brought to light. Properly organised and carried out such an enterprise could produce valuable material for historians, social scientists, writers, musicians and the like, but its supreme importance is in its service to the working class itself, drawing together the scattered and hidden bits of heritage, and in stimulating the continuation of workers' creative traditions.

This begs the questions: what is a regional literature? How exactly do we define it? Normally when applied to literature the term "regional" is used pejoratively, suggesting minor poetry, written in obscure impenetrable dialects and concerned with parochial subjects of largely local and hence limited interest. Sadly, much of our regional literature, except for the oral tradition or the occasional novelist or poet like Sid Chaplin or Tony Connor, deserves the epithet so interpreted, vitiated as it is by narrow-minded chauvinism, nostalgia, self-indulgence, and characterised by a brutal and dangerous simplicity, "good old days" and "honest working folk" clichés, an unremarkable use of language and predictable, old-fashioned literary forms. In fact, a literature dead to the experience of the people.

Can we define a regional literature as that type of literature which fully reflects the writer's response to his environment? This would produce a richer strain but the definition is at once too broad and too narrow, for under it one could include Thomas Hardy, D. H. Lawrence, William Wordsworth; the list could be extended indefinitely until most of our national literature would also be regional, nor would the definition establish the unique features of different regional literatures. A vital definition seems to require other criteria. Perhaps they can be found in the tentative notion that a unique regional literature, depending on more than the writer's response to his environment, should include a regional awareness, a response to those features that make a region distinctive, and the people in it aware that it is so; its history, political struggles, economic adversities, traditions, folklore, myth, people, humour and language. Our dialects, much under-used, are richly expressive tools. David Craig in *Scottish Literature and the Scottish People* expresses this well:

> The vernacular they [the Scottish writers] draw on comes from a society with its own strong character which lives to a great degree in its language —the spoken tongue—and a tongue which is close to the movement of an alert feeling for life. Speech has its being in the mass of individuals who use it, with the run and stress, the direction and depth and the force of feeling at work as they live out their kind of life. It is a force of life in action, alternately affecting and itself being played upon by particular phases of experience.

The potential of our dialects is discovered in the oral tradition and in the many historical documents describing working class life: for example *The Children's Employment Commission Report 1842* contains the evidence of a 10-year-old pit boy, who, describing the atmosphere in the pit after an explosion at Low Fell Colliery, Co. Durham, stated that the sparks from his flint mill "tumbled doon slowly like drops of dark blood". Here the verb phrase and simile vividly catch the density of the suffocating air and the mutilations he had witnessed underground. Responding unflinchingly, as this pit lad did, to the realities of experience, grasping what is important, founded in the texture of daily life, a regional literature would give us a clearer conception of events, ourselves, our past, the present, and catch the wave of the future; such a living tradition would transcend the parochial.

This regional potential has been fully realised in the oral tradition. Since the early Industrial Revolution a strong song and dance culture has existed in the North East; created from an intensely communal life by men and women identifying with their communities and sharing common experiences. Clusters of songs of impressive technical skill emerge from the desperately hard circumstances of working class life; the crushing industrial conditions, the mass evictions of families, the 1831 and 1844 Durham Strikes, the 1872 Durham Lock-out; and with each pit-disaster a fine song sequence is maintained. The makers of these songs were above all conscious of their responsibilities to their communities. Tommy Armstrong, a pitman-poet, is recorded as having said:

> When you're a pitman's poet and looked up to for it, wey, if a disaster or a strike gans wi' oot a song from you, they say, What's wrang wi' Tommy

Armstrong? Has someone druv a spigot into him an let oot aal the inspiration!

This inspiration or "holy daftness" as he called it, was very common in the pits and frequent bardic duels were held in the villages. An old pitman has said

> Making rhymes and songs used to run through the pits like a fever. Some of them used to gan daft thinking of verses. Even us young lads used to answer back in rhyme.

Nor was this fever for making songs and poems confined to the pit-villages; keelmen and railwaymen also took part. Terry Coleman in his book *The Railway Navvies* records that resident poets and singers in the make-shift railway towns were paid 1*d*. or 2*d*. per day by the navvies to record their achievements.

The oral tradition died in the early part of this century but re-emerged vigorously with the closure of the pits and the decline of the primary industries in the 'fifties and 'sixties. Its strength lay in the close creative relationship between the individual and his community, but even as the communities fragmented the changing personal relationships were used creatively. Adrian Mitchell's maxim that "most people ignore most poetry because most poetry ignores most people" is not true of the oral tradition. However, modern poets in the North East, standing apart from their communities, have lost this creative relationship, and are prone to the self-regarding excesses of an illusory individualism.

The written tradition of the region barely exists. There are many reasons for this thin vein of talent. Most of the people's creative effort was found in the oral tradition. The high degree of literacy required was almost non-existent until after the 1870 Education Act, and the "high culture" of the privileged classes, few of whom lived in the North East, and the workers' cultures were developing in opposite directions and had few fruitful points of contact. And the patronising literature written *for* the people, which might have produced a kind of literary tradition, was largely ignored because the working class cultures were self-reliant. Tolstoy remarks on a similar phenomenon in Russia: "The only books that the people understand and like are not the false and useless books written for the people but those which come from the people." This harsh truth is not a call for simplification of "great" art nor a sneer at the people but a recognition that the style, form, and content of "high art" and people's art are different and that only with difficulty was it possible for either the privileged classes or the workers to understand each other's art forms.

There have been dribs and drabs of comparative success: Edward Chicken's "Collier's Wedding" (1776), a bawdy and humorous narrative poem; Thomas Wilson's "Pitman's Pay" (1843), a dialect poem describing the conditions of the pitmen; Joseph Skipsey's (1832–1903) poems—a small

number of which are passable. But it would be a mistake to conclude that this
is anything more than a few consolatory crumbs. When these poets were
removed from the centres of suggestion that made their small success possible
their work was ruined by a conscious literariness. This is true, most obviously,
of Skipsey after his "discovery" by Dante Gabriel Rossetti. Leaving his
region to be fêted in London and then becoming the curator of Shakespeare's
house, he shows in his work the harmful effect of his literary Grand Tour.
Worst of all, he re-wrote his early work in the light of his new found literari-
ness. For example, contrasted with any pit-disaster song the limitations of
these stanzas are starkly revealed:

> One day as I came to Jarrow
> Engirt by a crowd on a stone
> A woman sat moaning, and sorrow
> seized all who gave heed to her moan.
>
> "Nay chide not my lamentation,
> But, oh let," she said, "my tears flow—
> Nay offer me no consolation,
> I know there are dead down below."

A prolific novelist, Harold Heslop, a pitman, emerges in the three decades
1920–1950, but, with the early poets and other working class novelists like
Walter Greenwood (*Love on the Dole*), his work—including the novels
The Earth Beneath, *Last Cage Down*, *Gate of a Strange Field*, *The Journey
Beyond* and *Goaf*—was radically weakened by two assumptions which lead
to an over-conscious literariness: first, the nature of an acceptable literary
language; and secondly, the expected middle-class literary audience. His
novels are written neither in the language of the region nor for the people of
the region. It is not until the advent of Sid Chaplin, a formidable and develop-
ing novelist with a confident grasp of his own language and a mature vision
of how things really are in the region, that an embryonic written tradition is
being created. Two of Sid Chaplin's recurring themes make him a regional
and working class novelist. One is the delicate business of the writer's place *in*
working class society. The other is the very contemporary problem of the
involuntary expatriates leaving working class homes for University, College,
or middle class jobs; being unable to ignore the conditioning of childhood,
they return, or try to return, or think of returning home for acceptance.
Christopher Jacks, the narrator of *The Thin Seam*, is an embodiment of this
problem:

> I know that, in a sense, all scholarship battens on the backs of the workers
> and with a sense of horror I saw that, although the primrose path was
> open to me and that not a soul would condemn me for taking it, just the
> same I knew that all the time I would be supported on the bowed sweated
> shoulders of my father, brothers and others like them.

Like many other working class expatriates, Christopher Jacks becomes a "cultural bastard", spurned by both classes. Sid Chaplin, whose creative relationship with his community is like that of the folk-singers, has given lyrical expression to the social observations of commentators from George Orwell to B. Jackson and D. Marsden, *Education and the Working Class*.

Our literary tradition is taking root, but are the published poets of the region contributing anything to this embryo? Although there are more indigenous poets writing today than ever before, the short answer is *no*, except for a negative contribution. The work of Tom Pickard, Barry MacSweeney and Basil Bunting lacks a distinctive regional voice, but paradoxically it is in the work of the immigrants like Jon Silkin and Tony Harrison that a regional voice is heard.

Bunting's work, although not properly within the scope of this essay, must be mentioned because of its harmful influence on the work of the younger poets. His work and theirs reveals a lack of modern sensibility. *Loquitur*, a collection of poems written between 1924–35, and *Briggflatts*, a clumsy poem in the heroic mood, contained a hodge-podge of poetic styles (generally more effectively used by their originators), overworked and over-conscious literary effects, collages of literary allusions reminiscent of Pound, and a meretricious display of erudition. Present also are the clues that point to an elitist view of life and art; the Art for Art's sake doctrine, "Poetry is seeking to make not meaning but music" (a curiously anachronistic view of language); the facile rejection of modern society; contempt for modern man, present in *Briggflatts*, "Chomei at Toyoma", and "How Duke Valentine Contrived"; over-weening pessimism, proud cynicism and the dishonest use of history conjuring up a former Northumbrian Golden Age that cannot be recovered. Bunting wallows in his illusions of the past, and like T. S. Eliot, Ezra Pound, W. B. Yeats, Oswald Spengler and Ortega y Gassett, apparently considers himself an embattled intellectual engulfed and threatened by hostile events while struggling to be the bearer of real cultural values. T. S. Eliot succeeds through his linguistic skills; Bunting is windy and often turgid rhetoric.

> Where we are who knows
> of kings who sup
> while day fails? Who,
> swinging his axe,
> to fell kings, guesses
> when we go?
>
> (*Briggflatts*)

Other elitist symptoms are the bardic condescension and self-effacing sycophancy towards his mentors found in his own introductions:

> With sleights of hand learned from others [a long list is added to this self congratulatory note] and an ear open to melodic analogies I have set down words as a musician pricks his score, not to be read in silence but to trace

on the air a pattern of sounds that may sometimes, I hope, be pleasing. [After the rhetorical flourish the heavy downbeat of humility; and next the condescension]. Unabashed girls and boys may enjoy them. This book is theirs.

Another objectionable strain in his work, and in that of Pickard and MacSweeney, is the sympathetic circularity set up through poems like "What the Chairman Told Tom", and introductions in which each genuflects towards the other. This looking for comfort and approbation is symptomatic of "the man of sensitivity" living in a hostile society that hates "Art". "Chomei at Toyoma" is an extended comment on this attitude:

   (i)   One generation
         I saddened myself with idealistic philosophies

  (ii)   I know myself and mankind
         I don't want to be bothered

 (iii)   A man like me can have neither servants nor friends
         In the present state of society

 (iv)   My jackets wistaria flax
         My blankets hemp
         Berries and young greens
         My food.

  (v)   I am out of place in the capital
         As you would be in this sort of life,
         You are so—I regret it—so welded to your vulgarity

Tom Pickard's and Barry MacSweeney's collections make monotonous reading. The reader endures page after page of unrelieved tedium, sluggish and slovenly language, peacock displays of egocentricity poorly disguising a lack of self-criticism. Their work is virtually inaccessible to those unable to share the crude and simplistic emotions or tolerate the inarticulateness of the language which goes as near to using words without meaning as one can. Their claims to spontaneity and originality are also suspect; the influence of Bunting, Olson and the Black Mountaineers is evident, along with innumerable snatches of pop language, drug-culture language, and techniques and situations derived from American B. Films. Like Bunting they are caught up in their own myth; they stand permanently in awe of their own sensitivity and whatever situation they write themselves into. One is reminded of John Barthes' magnificent poetaster, Ebenezer Cooke, Gent, Pt. & Lt. of Md. (Gentleman, Poet and Laureate of Maryland). They form with Bunting a small clique of self-regarding poets in an attitude of mutual poetic back-scratching.

Pickard, who runs a poetry centre at Mordern Tower, Newcastle, has published two collections, *High on the Walls* (1967) and *The Order of Chance* (1971). Extraordinary claims for him have been made by reviewers and poets.

Bunting, who writes in an introduction to *High on the Walls* in his usual pseudo-prophetic style, "Few poems, but new and lasting, their maker" [ah, the twee primitive craftsman at work] "very young", has referred to him as one of the five great poets produced by the North, including Cowper, Wordsworth, and Swinburne; Ginsberg says he is "an original genius", "a master of natural language", who has "startled the English speaking world". On what evidence are these claims based? His limitations are glaringly obvious when he moves beyond the haiku. These short lyrical squirts themselves show limited visual perceptions, conventional use of language, and a poor ear even for his own dialect which he uses with boring crudity. The longer poems, few and *non*-lasting, lack a framework of thought, which probably accounts for his insistent use of haiku. His visual perceptions, from the evidence of Iona and Peter Opie's *Lore and Language of School Children* and the following children's poems, are severely limited. In Bunting's poem "What The Chairman Told Tom" the chairman asks:

> Who says its poetry, anyhow?
> My ten year old
> Can do it and rhyme!

Here is what some children can do.

> Twisting turning
> Clinging to the contours of the earth
> Black—black as night
> With white lines down its back
>   (Mei-Ian Law, 11-year-old)
> The bee is a merchant
> He trades among flower planets.
>   (Peter Kelso, aged 12)
> The day was dull,
> The smell of the air,
> Icy.
> The colour of the air
> Was as dark
> As a wolf's coat,
> Misty.
>   (David Hill, 8-year-old)

Here the children's poems, fresh and rhythmically vital, alive with concrete accuracy and good visual perception represent remarkable attempts to come to terms with their visual experiences. They all have what Ted Hughes calls "explosive compression". Pickard's attempts are by contrast banal, particularly "glitter like stars" and the clumsy "bucket you with water" (below), and are not nearly so compressed. He is unable to crystallise the wisps of feeling and momentary insights he does have:

> Lights from the industrial valley

Glitter like stars
And ships' horns have the mellow tones of an owl.
                                        ("Bunk")

Crumble my turrets with your toes
Wash me with your foamy sea
My starfish my towers
Whilst I bucket you with water
                                        ("Sandcastles")

Tears flower in her restless head
Waiting for sleep
                                        ("Poems")

Fingers of a hand
that whisper softly
at my nape's hair
Smoke blowing
in the winds of engines
                                        ("Factory")

MacSweeney's visual images are marginally better, but still clumsy and artificial in comparison with the children's poems

Soft, soft bark in water,
fresh as cress

The blue cattle of your eyes
grazing on the green of mine
                                        ("Pastoral")

The sun always goes down
like this between the
staithes of the High Level bridge
dragging a golden plate across
the sewage.
                                        ("To Lynn")

The lack of punctuation in his work often leads to laughable incongruities and misunderstandings (as do "yr", "i", and "&", all three varied pointlessly with their full forms); for example

Lace curtains rhapsodic
With wind our lips

Respond like
Romany
Tambourines

We are no doubt expected to pause after "wind" not "rhapsodic" since the latter would make "our lips" vibrate in a raspberry (—due to indigestion?) but the line arrangements make it appear that this is indeed the correct interpretation—a poor exploitation of the breath principles of projective verse.

Pickard, MacSweeney, and J. C. Grant, a Northumbrian poet who possesses extraordinary visual gifts, fail to move beyond the worn mode of imagistic poetry and the non-interpretative level of sensory perception to more complex modes of perception and feeling that require "the intolerable wrestle with words and meanings". Apart from J. C. Grant, the visual inadequacy of the images indicating half-buried experience is linked directly to adolescent inarticulateness. Hindered by an insecure grasp of language their perceptions become channelled and stultified, with the verbal and visual cliché emerging as a common feature of their work. Coleridge, in *Biographia Literaria*, comments trenchantly on the inadequacies of single-image poetry:

> It has been before observed that images, however beautiful, though faithfully copied from nature, and as accurately represented in words do not of themselves characterise the poet. They become proofs of original genius only as far as they are modified by a predominant passion; or by associated images or thoughts awakened by that passion; or when they have the effect of reducing multitude to unity, or succession to an instant; or lastly, when a human and intellectual life is transferred to them from the poet's own spirit.

Lacking a "predominant passion" and "associated images or thoughts" the few long poems that exist in their canon are merely concoctions of immature confetti—imagery structured to no end, strung together by verbal cliché. The lack of a language that can come to grips with experience and give expression to controlled coherent thought is perhaps their greatest handicap. Indeed there is evidence in their work to suggest that they are reluctant to use language at all:

> I was a bubble
> adrift in the wind
>
> Foolishly resorted
> to a former human
> frailty
> and spoke
> Words
> broke my circumference.
>
> (Pickard)

> All belief
> is a barricade against complete
> freedom, the language in
> this poem, restrictive of
> belief, communication.
>
> (MacSweeney)

To break away from the image poems and the instant verbal orgasm demands real mental discipline, sustained imagination, and a greater degree of poetic organisation than they have at present. Pickard's poem on the creative act is just not adequate.

> Writing poems
> (keeping rabbits)
> each day the shite
> to be cleared
> fresh straw to be laid.

Until they achieve the necessary linguistic skills, there is little hope of better poetry from them.

Pickard's love and sex poems range from the physically impossible "To my unborn child":

> Our heads met
> when both of us
> bent to kiss
> your mother's womb,

to the endearingly comic

> Caressing with my lips
> Your sensual parts
>   I felt a tear, and through the darkness
> I could feel it shatter, streaming many ways.

Once again the lack of punctuation between "parts" and "I" produces a grotesque comic effect, while "shatter" and "streaming" do not work together semantically. But the crudest love poems, "New Body"—a contemporary Protean bestiary, "Butterfly", "Rape", and "The kind of animal I am", wallow in gratuitous obscenities. MacSweeney, on the other hand, searches eagerly for the grand romantic gesture:

> I kissed you for the first time in the
> middle of the Swing Bridge in between two counties in
> order to spread the loveliness over as
> much ground as possible

This type of romantic attitude, so savagely satirised in *The Female Eunuch* by Germaine Greer, derives from the infantile Romance stories in *Marilyn*, *Mirabelle*, *Woman's Own* and other pulp magazines. There is an interesting similarity between the sex poems of Pickard, MacSweeney and Pete Bland (co-author of *Joint Effort* with MacSweeney) in their surprising use of the archaic word "seed". Perhaps it hints at a search for momentous significance in the sex-act

> I love
> & give my seed in a shower
> of dragons
>   (Peter Bland)

> To seed you, soft belly
> thin hands
> and your blonde tresses
> bleeding on the pillow
>   (MacSweeney)

Lips wet
        with my seed

(Pickard)

Unconscious of their habitual self-indulgence they wear their poetic souls on their sleeves; unaware, too, that this intrusive self-consciousness spoils some passable poems. Pickard's "Game Bird" and "Nent Head" suffer from appalling preciosity:

My hand open she dived for the heather
and vanished
I would have brought her home for you
but feared her death
and your sorrow afterwards.

("Game Bird")

and a soul
passed into me,

("Nent Head")

while "Death is an Owl" has the *cri de coeur*:

I called to my God
for food for my family
    My voice echoed in the valley
        and the chill of winter
made me shiver

This is in the worst vein of working class literature and puts him squarely in the Victorian Gas Light Tradition of such gems as

Underneath the gas light's glitter
Stands a little fragile girl . . .

while "To my friends who go" is a direct descendant of the Gilt-edged Souvenir Card Tradition:

Home—where we grumble the most
And are treated the best.

MacSweeney exhibits a similar tendency in "To Lynn at work whose surname I don't know", and "If it were Winter":

And after you had gone
I would secretly build it [*a snowman* ed.]
and hide it from you
(not wishing to hurt you),

and in "The Track, Fervour" with a sub-Bob Dylan statement:

Each friend away
from my outstretched hand
and from my reason   *Oh*
    tell me it is not so

and again in an untitled poem:

> Still, I am dewy eyed, soaring away
> in a huge loop from the rich earth.

They remind one of Belle Poitrine (Beautiful Tits), the ever so sensitive and gushing heroine of Patrick Dennis's *Little Me*.

Their political poems are clod-hopping wordy generalisations. "The Decadent Voyeurs", the melodramatic "Hunga": "on Friday aa gans an aa begs", and "The Devils destroying angels exploded", by Pickard, with the lines

> beneath jagged brows
> stooped backs
> making others rich
> with the dust which killed you,

ought to be compared with "Aa wish Pay Friday wad Cum", and "Ee Aye Aa Cud Yew", both folk songs, to reveal these "literary" poets' social ignorance and sloganising simplicity. MacSweeney once again prefers the grand gesture *a la* Whitman in his search for "manly adhesiveness".

> Oh fertile architecture that replenished my eye
> in dockland, when knotted groups
> of pickets shook me as a friend
> & grabbed my shoulders bruising me even in
> their union strength
> (from "Sealine")

There is no real sense of identification with the region, pitmen or ship-builders; nothing is grasped and held, and their excessive self-indulgence excludes the capacity for imaginative sympathy with anyone.

Jon Silkin in comparison (and it is rather like training a 16-inch naval gun on a pair of coracles) reveals a depth of feeling in *Killhope Wheel* (1971) sadly lacking in much of our native regional literature; and the complex emotions he experiences on visiting the scene of a bitter strike in 1860 are suggested by three questions in the poem "Killhope Wheel 1860":

> A board says we are free to come in.
> Why should it seem absurd to get
> Pain from such permission? Why have
>
> I to see red coat soldiers prick
> Between washed stones, and bayonets
> Tugged from the seeping flesh?
>
> Why does a board, tacked to wood
> Concerning my being free to visit
> Give my useless pain nourishment?

From the following two quotations, Pickard and MacSweeney could learn how to use the personal pronoun "I" without self-indulgence, and to build an image successfully:

> I can't fudge up a relationship, but it gladdens
> you, as the sun concentrates it, and I
> want the creature for what it is
> to live beyond me
>
> ("Tree")
>
> The water shrinks
> to its source. The wheel,
> in balance.
>
> ("Strike")

Jon Silkin has recognised that the history of the North East is the history of Killhope Wheels and has given voice to it for the first time in written poetry. His technical skill in shaping working class speech ("Platelayer" and in the simplest stanzas of "Spade"), sets an example for the next generation of poets:

> Soldiers, who do not strike,
> thrust
> their bayonets into you.

Here the isolation of "thrust", following the ironic clause "who do not strike" conveys the effect of a savage aggressive lunge; and by placing "thrust" and "strike" with the latter's ambiguity together, he achieves a rich ironic juxtaposition.

Outside the North East other equally impressive poets are working with the raw material of their environment: Tony Connor from Manchester, whose poem "An Elegy for Alfred Hubbard" illustrates how gifted he is with an eye for the important detail that makes a place or village or street come alive in depth; and Douglas Dunn living in Hull, whose first book, *Terry Street*, gives a rare sense of the quality of working class life. He records and describes with sympathy and poignancy the minutiae of daily life in the street.

> At their Sunday leisure, they are too tired
> And bored to look long at comfortably.
> It hurts to see their faces, too sad or too jovial.
> They quicken their steps at the smell of cooking
> They hold up their children and sing to them.

He is aware of the gulf between himself and the people of the street and uses this separateness to give us a sense of himself and them, while avoiding the pitfalls of nostalgia and sentimentality.

> The lonely glutton in the sunlit corner
> Of an empty Chinese restaurant;
> The coughing woman, leaning on a wall,

Her wedding ring in her son's cold hand,
In her back the invisible arch of death.
What makes them laugh, who lives with them?

I stoop to lace a shoe, and they all come back
Dull mysterious people without names or faces,
Whose lives I guess about, whose dangers tease
And not one of them has anything at all to do with me
("The Hunched")

He also has an eye for the graphic detail

I lay down
On the grass and saw the blue shards of an egg
We'd broken, its warm yolk on the grass
And pine cones like little hand grenades.
("After the War")

The simile describing the "pine cones" is drawn directly from immediate experience and is, consequently, superior to MacSweeney's derived and contrived simile about pine cones:

Slits under its mail
give it the effect & carriage
of a Samurai.

Solzhenitsyn said,

Literature which does not breathe the same air as contemporary society, which cannot communicate to society its pains and fears, which cannot give warning in time against social dangers, does not deserve the name of literature. It deserves only the name of literary make-up.

Unfortunately, much recent regional literature is literary make-up.

There is a disastrous failure in contemporary written North East poetry. It is possible that the younger poets are hampered by the absence of a strong literary tradition that would exert a positive influence and save them from the "secondhandedness" of Basil Bunting or the half-understood Black Mountaineers; but from the appalling shallowness of thought in their work it is evident that they have not faced up to their own experience, whatever its source. Faint gleams show here and there but if they are to pass beyond the adolescent stage, they will have to develop language skills, literary techniques, a historical sense, and live up to the present experience. It is as well that Jon Silkin and Tony Harrison are now living and working in the region; their presence, and the *Stand* quarterly now published in Newcastle, may well influence and encourage the next generation of poets. There are, at the moment, talents that deserve encouragement: J. Chappell, whose short story "The Girl on a Swing" is promising; and F. G. Reed—both writers of considerable accomplishment. F. G. Reed, now aged 70, began work in the pits at 14 and educated himself until he became an educational lecturer. He won the Sir Arthur Markham Memorial Prize, a poetry competition held exclusively for pitmen, and has also published a collection of poems, *An Undine Overture*. His poem "Springan" is extremely skilful in its use of dialect, visual conceits and ingenious juxtapositions. Here are three stanzas:

> Like a kibble gyen amain
> Spring cums boonding doon the lane,
> and buttercups 'nd pittleybeds
> lift thor bonny goulden heids
> aglistening wi' rain.
>
> The lambs are lowping doon the neuk
> or, dunchin yows, they thrust and suck,
> and chasin coneys in the wood
> wi neethor airt nor luck.
>
> The burn runs deep in yalla mud
> and on the bend hes kirved a jud
> them doon the swalley lowps and reels
> and blethors, froths and cowps hor creels
> se rollickin in flood.

Within a traditional stanza form his skill lies in the confident handling of pitmatic (a pit dialect) to describe natural events, and produces very humorous visual conceits. Spring is likened to a coal-tub (kibble) running loose underground, the lambs "dunch" into "yows" like coal-tubs crashing together, the stream has "kirved a jud" (a term describing how a coal-hewer cuts into the coalface with a pick), and "blethors" (talks endlessly), "lowps" (jumps), and "cowps hor creels" (somersaults). Later there is a vivid description of bees sucking flowers:

> The dronin' bumler powks his snitch
> in dusty gowld concealed

Except for poems like "Springan", which have a distinctive North Eastern voice, and the work of Jon Silkin and Tony Harrison, the state of written poetry in the North East is disappointing. Too many promising talents simply disappear or are turned into self-regarding hacks. However, there are beginnings and prospects. We can hope that the next generation of writers will find the means to express the impulse and experience of their region and produce a literature of repute, based on the best of folk tradition and continuing the high-level of achievement represented by the novels of Sid Chaplin; for, as Antonio Gramsci wrote in *Letteratura E Vita Nazionale*, "If the cultural world for which one struggles is a living and necessary fact . . . it will find its artists".

Second Flowering: Poetry in Wales

by Glyn Jones

THE first job of the writer about poetry in modern Wales is to remind his readers that the words "Welsh poet" are ambiguous. Dylan Thomas is probably the most famous poet Wales has produced in her long history, but to many of his fellow-countrymen he is not a Welsh poet at all. In 1949, a writer called T. Gwynn Jones died in Aberystwyth at the age of 78—scholar, novelist, dramatist, short story writer, but above all superb and prolific poet. Despite Gwynn Jones's towering achievement, the production of a body of verse easily as impressive as that of Dylan Thomas, his death passed unnoticed in the world's press and even today he remains unknown outside his native Wales. The reason? All his work was done in Welsh, "the old British tongue", a language with an unbroken literary tradition extending back to the sixth century, but spoken today only by about a quarter of the population of our country, not many more than half a million people. Contemporary Welsh language poets like Waldo Williams (1904–71), Euros Bowen (b. 1904), Bobi Jones (b. 1929), Gwyn Thomas (b. 1936) and others, are all in the same poetic boat as was T. Gwynn Jones. Their splendid and enduring verse can be appreciated by only a little clan. Translation? Much of the excellence of work like Gwynn Jones's lies, not in the newness of its ideas, but in its brilliant use of language, its astonishing technical mastery and the originality and intricacy of its music. These are surely the first virtues to run out of the leaky bucket of translation.

Poets like Dylan Thomas, Welshmen who write their poems in English, are usually called Anglo-Welsh poets, a designation some of them indignantly reject. But the label seems a pretty handy one and is unlikely to be superseded. Welshmen have, in fact, been writing poems in English for a long time now, at least since Tudor times, when the anglicisation of Wales began in earnest. Every century since the fifteenth has produced a few of them—gentry, clergy, Welsh-speakers—many writing their poems in both languages, Welsh and English. Some, like Henry Vaughan and George Herbert, have secured a permanent place in the canon of English poetry; others, like the Victorian Sir Lewis Morris, famous in his time, have now been forgotten. But Anglo-Welsh poetry as we understand it today is in fact a phenomenon of the twentieth century, a product of two modern factors and one traditional one, namely the spread of advanced education in Wales, the Englishness of that advanced education, and the characteristic Welsh attitude to poetry which I shall touch upon later.

Despite the fact that Anglo-Welsh poetry in an undeveloped form has been in existence for five hundred years, the first anthology did not appear until 1917. It wasn't very good, although the standard was no worse than that of many other anthologies appearing about that time. After a gap of twenty-seven years a second anthology, *Modern Welsh Poetry* (Faber) appeared, edited by Keidrych Rhys, and this collection marked a tremendous step forward in the development of Anglo-Welsh poetry. By this time, 1944, an impressive number of highly gifted Welshmen writing in English had appeared and begun to publish their work in the magazines or in volume form, so that Keidrych Rhys was able to include in his selection poems by Dylan Thomas, Vernon Watkins, Idris Davies, R. S. Thomas, Alun Lewis, and David Jones. A few years before the publication of his anthology Keidrych had founded his famous magazine, *Wales*, which had, since 1937, published the work of many of the contributors to *Modern Welsh Poetry*. In his provocative introduction to the first number of his magazine he proclaimed that "There is actually no such thing as 'English' culture. . . . The greatest of present-day poets are Kelts. . . . Though we write in English, we are rooted in Wales", and so on. These observations suggest that Keidrych edited his magazine with some sort of nationalism in mind.

Keidrych was in fact, with his magazine and his anthology, the first great impresario of the Anglo-Welsh poetic scene. He was the percipient talent spotter, the encourager and sustainer, the focal point of that "group of young Welsh writers" that aroused Yeats's interest and which he asked Vernon Watkins about. Before Keidrych's time, Anglo-Welsh poetry was a matter of a few brilliant but isolated figures like Dylan Thomas and Vernon Watkins. He helped us to see the work of Anglo-Welsh poets writing at that time, not as isolated productions however accomplished and attractive, but as part of a new literature in Wales, of Anglo-Welsh literature.

I said above that I thought Keidrych was some sort of nationalist. I don't think that politics meant much to some of the most gifted members of the group of contributors he gathered around him. The poetry of Dylan Thomas and Vernon Watkins can hardly be called political. That first flowering of Anglo-Welsh poetry, heralded by Dylan's *18 Poems* in 1934, took place in a Wales suffering from unparalleled unemployment, emigration, crippling poverty and every sort of social distress consequent upon these things. Yet these appalling conditions did not on the whole inspire the Anglo-Welsh poetry at that time, as similar conditions in England inspired some of the poetry of Auden, Day Lewis, Spender and their generation. Idris Davies, two of whose volumes of poetry deal exclusively with the Depression in South Wales, was a notable exception. But his protest was of course the socialist one against capitalism and economic exploitation, not the nationalist one against English influence and disregard of special Welsh conditions. The next step in the creation of Anglo-Welsh literature, the sense of national identity, did not take place until the poetry of this literature had entered its second flowering in the 'sixties. This article will I believe show that that flowering still continues.

In 1965 Meic Stephens (b. 1938), a Welsh speaking poet who writes mainly in English and who since 1967 has been the Welsh Arts Council's Assistant Director with special responsibility for Literature, founded his magazine, *Poetry Wales*. No magazine like it had ever existed in our country before. Keidrych's *Wales* was entirely unprecedented because it was the first Anglo-Welsh literary magazine ever to appear in Wales. But *Poetry Wales* was unique in being concerned *entirely with poetry*, largely poetry by Welshmen in English, but also by Welshmen in Welsh, together with translations into English of Welsh poetry, articles in English on Anglo-Welsh and Welsh language poets, reviews of books of Anglo-Welsh, Welsh, English and foreign poetry. Keidrych, by pioneering enterprise and his combative public advocacy, succeeded in forcing upon the attention of a frequently reluctant and even hostile Wales, the existence of his group of Anglo-Welsh poets, and helped to convince large sections of the English-speaking world of their merit. The problems confronting Meic Stephens and his *Poetry Wales* were different. By 1965 Wales, long accustomed to the presence of her own Welsh-language poets, had begun to accept within her society the existence of that other group of poets who, although Welsh by birth, blood, domicile and sometimes even by speech, nonetheless wrote their poems in English. An important aim of *Poetry Wales* has been to bridge the gap between the two groups of poets in our country, the writers of Welsh on the one hand, proud of their immensely long poetic tradition, and the Anglo-Welsh on the other, a group which, whatever their poetic achievement, has arisen only as a result of forces operating in this century. A measure of the success of this "ecumenical" attempt by *Poetry Wales* has been the creation of an English language section of *Yr Academi Gymreig*, the national association of writers in Wales, and the opening of their doors to Anglo-Welsh writers by publishers who previously confined their lists to books written in Welsh. Much of the credit for the present atmosphere of tolerance and respect between the two groups must go to the Welsh Arts Council, which has readily recognised that in a bi-lingual country like Wales, two literatures will almost inevitably exist. In the editorial to number three (Spring 1966) of his magazine, Meic Stephens says, "Our business is to publish the best available poems by young men and women who are writing now, in and about Wales. . . . Our first commitment, as our title has it, is to the craft". The next paragraph begins, "Our second is to the country", and a little later he writes, "But we protest, on our contributors' behalf, that there is more sympathy for the senior literature [i.e., Welsh language literature], among us, than there was in our first heyday, twenty years ago".

I feel sure that Meic Stephens in claiming this is right. One has to remember of course that the two Anglo-Welsh groups he has in mind, the *Wales* group and the *Poetry Wales* group, are not mutually exclusive or self-contained. Emyr Humphreys, a political Nationalist of the *Wales* era, now contributes to *Poetry Wales*. R. S. Thomas, also a Nationalist, appeared in *Modern Welsh Poetry* and now also writes for *Poetry Wales*. John Ormond, Roland Mathias and Brenda Chamberlain are all associated with both groups. But I think it is correct to see a growing consciousness of Welsh national identity, itself a feature of the 'sixties in Wales, as a distinguishing feature of the more recent group for which *Poetry Wales* is the platform.

I suppose that if Dylan was the characteristic poet of the first flowering of Anglo-Welsh poetry in the 'thirties and 'forties, R. S. Thomas occupies a similar position today. Although he was born before Dylan, his first book of poems, *The Stones of the Field*, did not appear until 1946, the year of Dylan's last before *Collected Poems*. Modern Welsh language poets, almost every one of them, are deeply concerned in their work with the future of Wales as a nation, with national identity in a world of mass communications, with the Welsh society, with the fate of the Welsh language, and with wider issues in a European context. A fine Welsh language critic, Alun Llywelyn-Williams, claims that the most sensitive analysis and the most forceful expression of this crisis of modern Welsh society is to be found, not in the work of any of the Welsh language poets, but in the poems of the Anglo-Welsh writer R. S. Thomas. There are of course excellences in R. S. Thomas other than his ability to treat effectively the situation in which Wales finds herself; but I think there are features in his work which provide pointers to what has happened and is happening to the generation of poets that arose after the non-political Dylan Thomas.

I do not claim that the whole present generation of Anglo-Welsh poets, or even all those that contribute to *Poetry Wales*, are committed political Welsh Nationalists, nor do they have to be. Some of them are—Harri Webb, Gwyn Williams, John Tripp, Anthony Conran, Raymond Garlick, Tom Earley—but the majority are not, although many are involved in various ways with Welsh affairs. But what even many of the non-political poets have come to experience now is an awareness of their own Welshness, a growing consciousness of the fact that, although for historical reasons they are using English, they are not English poets at all, any more than W. B. Yeats, or Robert Lowell, or Hugh MacDiarmid are English poets. They see themselves as the products of a society and a historical process very different from England's, a society highly democratic in its forms and also in its attitude to poetry. In his introduction to *Wales* (number one) Keidrych Rhys wrote, "Welsh literature is carried on, not by a clique of moneyed dilettantes, but by the small shopkeepers, the blacksmiths, the non-conformist ministers, by the miners, quarrymen, and the railwaymen", and this underlines an important Welsh attitude to poetry. The poet in Wales is very much part of his society, not some sort of freak, a man apart or a way-out figure. Poetry might often have meant eccentricity, but seldom aestheticism or bohemianism. And this status has been welcomed by the modern Anglo-Welsh poet also. He now turns less to London and England for publication, reputation and audience. He sees Wales as his home and starting point, and himself as part of developing Welsh history; he feels involved in the practice of his fellow Anglo-Welsh poets and he is conscious that with them he has created in Wales something entirely new and important, namely a distinctive poetic scene and a literature of immense possibilities.

In 1969 Meic Stephens and John Stuart Williams edited an anthology of poems entitled *The Lilting House* (Dent-Davies) which covered fifty years of Anglo-Welsh poetry (1917–67). This was the fourth anthology of Anglo-Welsh poetry to appear in the twenty-five years since *Modern Welsh Poetry*. [The other three were *Presenting Welsh Poetry* edited by Gwyn Williams (Faber, 1959); *The World of Wales*, edited by Gerald Morgan (University of Wales Press, 1969); and *Welsh Voices* edited by Bryn Griffiths (Dent, 1967).] The common ground of recognition of their Welshness shared by so many of the younger, or at least the newer, contributors, certainly did not produce uniformity of theme or political orthodoxy in their work. The contributions of Harri Webb, pamphleteer, balladist, political journalist, former Welsh Nationalist candidate, showed the great variety of approach and technique which characterises his work. No one could accuse him of having nothing to say, of being without a standpoint, of merely playing about with words. In his volume *The Green Desert* (Gwasg Gomer, 1969) he has deeply-felt poems of nostalgic, sometimes bitter, response to what he sees as the tragedy of modern Wales, and also political squibs like his "Ode to the Severn Bridge", the gigantic feat of engineering which joins England and Wales across the Severn.

> Two lands at last connected
> Across the waters wide
> And all the tolls collected
> On the English side.

But the elements of mockery and fluency in his work should not blind us to the genuine and profound feeling in well-worked poems like "The Stone Face" and "Gwenallt", a sort of brief elegy for the Welsh language poet of that name who died in 1968.

No greater contrast is imaginable than that between the work of Harri Webb and Roland Mathias (b. 1915). A critic of Roland Mathias's most recent volume, *Absalom in the Tree* (Gwasg Gomer, 1971), said that the poems appear to be written as a brick-layer builds a wall, they rise row solidly upon row. I think the image appropriate, and not in any pejorative sense. The slightest acquaintance with his work shows that he is not a poet of loose rhetoric or easily maintained attitudes. Poetry, like life, is difficult, and only complete honesty and integrity will suffice for both. "His poetry," John Stuart Williams says, "presents a consistent view of the world expressed in a tough and concentrated verse of considerable individuality." Roland Mathias himself (he read history at Oxford) says of his work, "I think of history still, of my stock, my parents, family love, and my own insufficiency in the line of descent. For me the old Nonconformist sense of guilt is not inhibiting and useless: it shows me a particular vision, a measurement. Out of it I write." In "Testament", he says,

> I was the child
> Of belief, aching pitifully
> In the unready hours
> At the wounds I must suffer
> When I walked out weaponless
> And grown.

And stylistically more characteristic, "A Last Respect", a poem about the funeral of his minister father—

> In this hiatus when no stolid ghost respires
> All that was left of breath suddenly ruffed the flowers
> On the bier ahead. The hearse, its guttural base,
> Ground into some declivity of gear and all
> But the elm and the brass handles had air
> About it and petals flying, impassioned as
> Wings, an arc of will prescribed, mounting
> And Sion crying, quick in the eyelash second.
>
> Who are you to say that my father, wily
> And old in the faith, had not in that windflash abandoned
> His fallen minister's face?

Ten years ago a group of Anglo-Welsh writers then living in London (John Tripp, Bryn Griffiths, Sally Roberts) used to meet regularly to read their poems and exchange news. Most of the members of that group have now returned to Wales and contribute their poems to such periodicals as *Poetry Wales* and *The Anglo-Welsh Review*. Leslie Norris, Robert Morgan, Douglas Phillips are among the diminishing number of Anglo-Welsh poets who still live in England but one suspects from the evidence of their poems that a good proportion of their emotional and imaginative life is still lived in their native land. Leslie Norris (b. 1921), former lecturer in English at Bognor Regis College of Education, but now a full-time writer, regularly visits Merthyr, where he was born, Cardiff, the literary capital of the Anglo-Welsh, and Cardiganshire. His poetic career has been an unusual one in that, after a successful start with two volumes of poetry, he was silent for fifteen years, until 1967, when his volume *Finding Gold* was published by Chatto and Windus. His subjects are childhood, nature and her creatures (dogs, owls, buzzards, curlews, nightingales, pheasants, polecats) and prize-fighting. Quotation from his work is not easy, because his best poems ("Water", "Early Frost", "A February Morning") are closely integrated structures. This, however, is how he closes "A February Morning", which describes how one early morning walk, presumably in England, recalls another, a starlit mountain walk in Wales, when a woman also sang,

But gently, and from no apparent direction,
The voice of a singing woman used the air,
Unhurried, passionate, clear, a voice of grief
Made quite impersonal by the night and hour.
For full five minutes' space along that mountain,
Not loudly nor ever fading away,
A full voice sang
Of such inhuman longing that I no more
Can say which was the song or which the fiery star.
One or the other lit the hollow road
That lay behind my clipped and winter steps
Time out of mind ago, in Wales.

This frosty morning, across the February fields
The militant bush of the sun in tawny splendour
Has not extinguished it, that song or star.

Raymond Garlick's first volume of poems appeared in 1950, and his
collected poems *A Sense of Europe* in 1968. He is a critic and literary historian
as well as a poet, and his research has brought to light much that we know
about those earlier Anglo-Welsh poets who wrote between about 1450 and
1900. Born in London in 1926 but educated in Wales, he speaks Welsh and
has thrown in his lot with that of Welsh Nationalism. For a few years he lived
in Holland and one of his best poems, "Note on the Iliad", is about that
country.

Why are epics
always about
the anti-life
of a noble lout?

I sing Lely
who burnt no tower
but brought the sea-floor
into flower.

Imagine it—
the moment when
out of the
architectured fen

the polder surfaced
sleek as a whale
and still awash.
Then the last veil

of standing water
slides away.
. . .

Now wheat ripples
where schooner and barque
thrashed down the waters
to ultimate dark—

avenued Holland
wanes over plains
which twenty years back
rocked fishing-seines.

Emyr Humphreys (b. 1919) is better known as a novelist than as a poet, but his own poetry and his translations from the work of his Welsh language contemporaries, published in *Ancestor Worship* (Gwasg Gee, 1969), are highly individual and accomplished.

There is no such thing as the image of a country
For this reason put up this flag for approval:
It is made of skin and stained with sunlight and tobacco
It speaks in pickled phrases the language of apples
And it is wide enough for a shroud.

It remembers the road as a track, pigs
In every sty, a railway running, a harbour
With ships, a quarry working, fresh fish, young people
And planting trees in holes big enough
To bury a horse.

This man is a king except
He makes his living emptying caravan bins
And uses English in the shop to avoid giving offence
To visitors who do not know where they are
Or who he is.

Emyr Humphreys, Christian, pacifist, Nationalist, sees in the old man of his poem a symbol of the decline of his country. John Tripp (b. 1927), although his methods and attitudes are very different, is also much concerned in his poetry with the condition and destiny of our country. He says that the major themes of his work are Welsh—Welsh history and people—from the point of view of one who is extremely conscious of his roots. "I have tried," he says, "to create a small document about Wales, its harsh past and its difficult present"—within a tight verse-form which makes no concessions to the expansive and "over-stating Celt" in him. The English in their sleek cars still see us and our land, John Tripp claims, like this:

A tangled image of pits and poverty,
Eisteddfodau and love on slag-heaps,
invades their haphazard minds.
Four hundred years of the king's writ
have not shaken their concept of our role:
                                        foxy, feckless,

articulate, mercurial, lyrical and wild,
we are clogged with feeling,
ranting preachers on the rebellious fronde.

The development of John Ormond (b. 1923) has been slow. Although he was writing poetry as early as 1944, when Keidrych Rhys included some of his work in his *Modern Welsh Poetry*, we were not able to see the real measure of his achievement until his *Requiem and Celebration* (Christopher Davies) appeared in 1969. He is a poet whose range of subject matter is wide. He opens "Design for a Tomb", a poem about the burial of an upper-class whore, like this,

> Dwell in this stone who once was tenant of flesh.
> Alas, lady, the phantasmagoria is over,
> Your smile must come to terms with dark for ever.
>
> Carved emblems, puff-cheeked cherubs and full vines,
> Buoy up your white memorial in the chapel
> Weightlessly over you who welcomed a little weight.
>
> Lie unprotesting who often lay in the dark,
> Once trembling switchback lady keep your stillness
> Lest marble crack, ornate devices tumble.
>
> Old melodies were loth to leave your limbs,
> Love's deft reluctances where many murmured delight
> Lost all their gay glissandi, grew thin and spare . . .

In addition to the seven poets I have mentioned briefly above, the following have all published one or more volumes of verse since 1960: Gwyn Williams, Cyril Hodges, Douglas Phillips, Alan Perry, Tom Earley, John Stuart Williams, Robert Morgan, John Idris Jones, Anthony Conran, Herbert Williams, Bryn Griffiths, Dannie Abse, Alison Bielski, Sally Roberts, Peter Gruffydd, Elwyn Davies, Peter Finch. To do justice to all this work would require a substantial volume, but it can be said that what one senses in Wales at the present time, in the field of poetry as elsewhere, is a tremendous quickening, a sense of vitality and renewal. Never has there been such widespread dedication to poetry by its Anglo-Welsh practitioners, and the value of what is produced is being recognised increasingly both inside Wales and beyond her boundaries; in particular by the Welsh Arts Council which has played a major role with its support for our magazines, anthologies, recordings, volumes of new work, and so on. The interest of libraries and research departments of universities in France, Germany, and America seem to indicate the growing stature of Anglo-Welsh poetry. As Kathleen Raine wrote in a recent issue of *Agenda*, "Much fine verse is being written in Scotland and for a like density of concentration of good poets one would have to go to Wales".

Suggested reading.

The principal anthologies:
A. G. Prys-Jones (ed.) *Welsh Poets* (Erskine Macdonald, London, 1917. Re-issued 1918 and 1922.)
Keidrych Rhys (ed.) *Modern Welsh Poetry* (Faber, London, 1944.)
Gwyn Williams (ed.) *Presenting Welsh Poetry* (Faber, 1959.)
Bryn Griffiths (ed.) *Welsh Voices* (Dent, London, 1967.)
Gerald Morgan (ed.) *This World of Wales* (University of Wales Press, Cardiff, 1968.)
Meic Stephens and John Stuart Williams (ed.) *The Lilting House* (Dent-Davies, London, 1969.)

An annual collection of the best Anglo-Welsh poems has appeared, published by Gwasg Gomer of Llandysul, Cardiganshire, Wales, since 1969.

The principal Anglo-Welsh literary magazines:
Poetry Wales, edited by Meic Stephens.
The Anglo-Welsh Review (formerly *Dock Leaves*), edited by Roland Mathias.
Planet, edited by Ned Thomas.

Discussion of contemporary Anglo-Welsh literature:
The Dragon has Two Tongues, essays on Anglo-Welsh writers and writing, Glyn Jones (Dent, 1968).
An Introduction to Anglo-Welsh Literature, Raymond Garlick (University of Wales Press, 1970).
Triskel One, edited by Sam Adams and G. R. Hughes (Christopher Davies, Ammanford, Carmarthenshire, Wales, 1971).
Literature in Celtic Countries, edited by J. E. Caerwyn Williams (University of Wales Press, 1971).

Writers in Wales, a series on the work of individual writers, including poets, is published on behalf of the Welsh Arts Council by the University of Wales Press. The editors are Meic Stephens and R. Brinley Jones. Volumes on the work of Alun Lewis, W. H. Davies and Idris Davies have appeared, and further volumes on Edward Thomas, Dylan Thomas, Richard Hughes, Vernon Watkins, Jack Jones and Glyn Jones are due out in future.

Scottish Poetry in the 1960s

by Edwin Morgan

THE difficulty is to write naturally. The Scottish air tends to be thick with advice and assertion, much of it hectoring, strident, unconsidered. Vehemence, and various sorts of fierceness, we have; but reason and thought and justice, and the stillness out of which a personality can grow to its full stretch without spikiness and shoulder-chips—these are harder come by, and much to be desired. The bad old days of Scottish education, so nicely summed up by Alexander Scott in his two-line poem on that subject—

> I tellt ye
> I tellt ye

—may be going, but they have left their mark, and now that we are struggling out from under, and looking at the world, and flexing our muscles, and whistling a bit, and even doing our own thing, there is all the confusion of release coupled with the delight of escape. The spate of recent anthologies of Scottish poetry has shown that we can claim a fairly vigorous and varied scene as we look back through the last decade, yet more than one reviewer has pointed out that vigour and variety don't guarantee a direction or consolidate an achievement. Perhaps these are worries we can leave to the youngest, or the next, generation. It seems more important at the moment to be ourselves and to let the grids catch us if they can. As Tom McGrath wrote in *Glasgow University Magazine* (editorial, June 1971):

> Recognise the life you have: recognise your flesh, recognise that this absurd conglomeration of backgrounds and social norms that are pressing in on you all the time, be they Catholic Protestant Conservative Labour or Hip, recognise that you can discard them right now, this very moment, just by seeing them in your mind, all those inhibitions and present attitudes . . . and you can see how they have no substance, they have no basis, they have no justification—you can see that and step free of it, just by deciding to—you have, after all, only this life, don't let inhibitions unlive it for you—you can say goodbye to it all and step into freedom.

But the step into freedom may be for the Scottish writer the hardest step. A residue of moral nervousness, a shying before images of joy or strangeness or abandon, can still cripple him with bonds that easily seem virtues. Obligations bark at him on all sides as he goes down the path to the gate. There is so much that he is asked to, or may legitimately want to, relate himself to. He is aware of native traditions that are distinct from English traditions—Dunbar, Lyndsay, Burns, MacDiarmid, the Gaelic poets, the Kailyaird—

and even when he turns aside to Olson and Ginsberg (Tom McGrath) or Jung and Camus (Alan Jackson) the subterranean Scottish notochord may still be tingling, and carrying messages even from a disowned past. The over-emphasis on Scottish tradition which is so tempting to the more beleaguered-feeling, nationalist-minded poet, is in the end stultifying when it is allowed to inhibit the naturalness of voice and heart in whose absence anyone aiming to address his contemporaries might as well stay in bed plucking the coverlet. Yet the shifting complexity of the situation is such that to say this is not to deny that (for example) Scots language or dialect is still perfectly viable in the right hands at the right moment. It is perhaps not so surprising to find that viability evident in the 1960s, since unashamedly non-metropolitan poetry has willingly used the accents of Newcastle and Liverpool, to say nothing of Gloucester, Mass. Poetry in Scots persists on a knife-edge: rejoicing in its expressive lexical potential, but afraid to nail its colours to the mast of real local speech-patterns. The MacDiarmid "renascence" of a general synthetic Scots fifty years ago can still be felt, and learned from, but the move should now be towards the honesty of actual speech, and in the decade which has been a decade of spoken and recorded poetry and the poetry-reading explo-sion, this is indeed what has been happening. The Edinburgh poet Robert Garioch shows that the natural vividness associated with speech is by no means incompatible with formal poetic patterns. Some of his "Edinburgh Sonnets", of which "Heard in the Cougate" is an example, are virtuoso pieces in this respect, though with none of the coldness virtuosity can bring:

'Whu's aw thae fflag-poles ffur in Princes Street?
Chwoich! Ptt! Hechyuch! Ab-boannie cairry-on.
Seez-owre the wa'er. Whu' the deevil's thon
inaidie, heh?' 'The Queen's t'meet

The King o Norway wi his royal suite.'
'His royal wh'?' 'The hale jing-bang. It's aw in
the papur. Whaur's ma speck-sh? Aye they're gaun
t' day-cor-ate the toun. It's a fair treat,

somethin ye dinnae see jist ivry day,
foun'uns in the Gairdens, muckle spates
dancin t' music, an thir's t' be nae

chairge t'gi'in, it aw comes aff the Rates.'
'Ah ddae-ken whu' the pplace is comin tae
wi aw thae, hechyuch! fforeign po'entates.'

Garioch's approach may be compared with that of a young poet from Glasgow, Tom Leonard. In his pamphlet *Six Glasgow Poems* (1969) the uncompromising spelling, which in no way exaggerates natural Glasgow dia-lect, serves as a useful reminder of how inadequate southern standard English is when it tries to extend its shaky empire into the big cities of the north. "The Good Thief", with admirable economy, unites the two Glasgow pre-

occupations of football and religion, and non-Scottish readers should not be
put off by its apparent strangeness:

> heh jimmy
> yawright ih
> stull wayz urryi
> ih
>
> heh jimmy
> ma right insane yirra pape
> ma right insane yirwanny us jimmy
> see it nyir eyes
> wanny uz
>
> heh
>
> heh jimmy
> lookslik wirgonny miss thi gemm
> gonny miss thi GEMM jimmy
> nearly three a cloke thinoo
>
> dork init
> good jobe theyve gote thi lights

Worries about language, like worries about "national identity", can be
unhelpful to writers and tiresome to readers, but one feature of the 1960s has
been the persistence of Gaelic poetry, as well as poetry in English and Scots,
even while the native-speaking strength of the language seems to be drai ing
steadily into the machair, and while bilingual Gaelic/English poets utter
their cries about its disappearance. Iain Crichton Smith's remarkable poem
"Am Faigh a' Ghàidhlig Bàs?", translated by himself as "Shall Gaelic Die?",
does not seem like an elegy despite its sharp sense of the imminent loss of one
more of the world's languages (give it a century perhaps?), and the Celtic-
Twilight tushery with which the theme would once have been larded has now
been pared away to the bleak but glittering frame of a philosophical medita-
tion on the "world" that a language uniquely embodies. And the fact that the
Gaelic here is sown with English words—"neon", "orange", "mauve",
"furniture", "barometer", "melodeon", "skeleton", "maze", "dictionary",
"spectrum"—doesn't have the effect of linguistic contamination and decline
but rather the opposite: a necessary injection of new life, hazarded against the
objections of Gaelic purists and traditionalists. Here is Section 5:

> He who loses his language
> loses his world.
> The Highlander who loses his language
> loses his world.
>
> The space ship that goes astray among planets
> loses the world.

In an orange world how would you know orange?
In a world without evil how would you know good?

Wittgenstein is in the middle of his world.
He is like a spider.
The flies come to him.
'Cuan' and 'coille' rising.*

When Wittgenstein dies,
his world dies.

The thistle bends to the earth.

The earth is tired of it.

Wittgenstein prowls round Oban Bay. A spaceship lands on Lewis. An orange world, having been imagined, exists. A Gaelic poet becomes a "Gaelic" "poet" and looks at himself from behind the mirror. The very title-question of the poem flickers on and off like a neon sign as if to mock the too plodding enquirer. This is living poetry, and its flashing, jumping, discrete quality says no to Highland mists. Iain Crichton Smith's English poetry has also advanced and matured during the 'sixties, shedding some of the decorative devices of his early work and moving into more direct confrontations with society. Both in long poem-sequences and in some very striking short poems he has emerged as a poet of great potential for Scotland: sensitive and concerned, but too intelligent to fall for easy slogans. In his sequence "The White Air of March" (1969) he wrote: "It is bitter / to dip a pen in continuous water / to write poems of exile / in a verse without honour or style." And this theme of being an "exile in one's own land", a theme that is driven about with some satire and irony as well as through occasional straight bitterness, is linked to the idea of "excellence" and its rarity and the search for it, among the rocks if need be. "The Cuillins tower high in the air—Excellence". But the man who says this should have read his Wittgenstein, his Kafka, his Dostoevsky; innocence is as culpable as fanaticism, Ossian is bones.

In the white air of March
a new mind.

Norman MacCaig, who draws much imagery and sustenance from the Highlands, and who published half a dozen collections during the 'sixties, would doubtless appreciate these ideas of Iain Crichton Smith, though his own poetry is more delicately surefooted, and less troubled and passionate, than Smith's. An extraordinary gift in observation and comparison is used by MacCaig as a lever to flype reality with, and after this metaphysical process the new reality is tried on for size, paraded a bit (but without name-dropping), and eventually returned to nature in its original shape, but touched by human hand. Short on alienation, but surprising, accurate, and well-turned, his

* "sea" and "wood".

poetry offers many pleasures. Its urbanity is by no means unable to get under the skin, though he himself has complained (in "A Sort of Blues"): "—My luck to live in a time / when to be happy / is to have no neighbours." A characteristic report on experience, which manages to be convincingly realistic while remaining sardonic and sly, is "Basking Shark":

> To stub an oar on a rock where none should be,
> To have it rise with a slounge out of the sea
> Is a thing that happened once (too often) to me.
>
> But not too often—though enough. I count as gain
> That once I met, on a sea tin-tacked with rain,
> That roomsized monster with a matchbox brain.
>
> He displaced more than water. He shoggled me
> Centuries back—this decadent townee
> Shook on a wrong branch of his family tree.
>
> Swish up the dirt and, when it settles, a spring
> Is all the clearer. I saw me, in one fling,
> Emerging from the slime of everything.
>
> So who's the monster? The thought made me grow pale
> For twenty seconds while, sail after sail,
> The tall fin slid away and then the tail.

"So who's the monster?" MacCaig's question has many echoes in the liberated and often forceful Scottish poetry of the last ten years. Iain Crichton Smith in his *From Bourgeois Land* (1969) makes a Janus-monster of Calvin and Hitler, watches "gauleiters pace by curtained windows" in tidy Scottish towns, while "distant Belsen smokes in the calm air". Sorley Maclean, master Gaelic poet of this century, finds something similar but perhaps worse, because mindless and anarchic, in the monsters of Glasgow:

> The broken bottle and the razor
> are in the fist and face of the boy
> in spite of Auschwitz and Belsen
> and the gallows in Stirling
> and the other one in Glasgow
> and the funeral of (John) MacLean . . .
> ("Am Botal Bristie", trans. by the author)

George Mackay Brown, writing lovingly of the ancient simplicities and sanctified rituals of life in Orkney, sees his disruptive twin monsters as Protestantism and Progress. "The Rackwick croft ruins are strewn with syrup tins, medicine bottles, bicycle frames, tattered novels, rubber boots, portraits of Queen Victoria." And so

> The poor and the good fires are all quenched.
> Now, cold angel, keep the valley

From the bedlam and cinders of A Black Pentecost.
("Dead Fires")

Alan Jackson, who like George Mackay Brown has emerged strongly in the
'sixties, has many monsters, beasts, and dragons in his anthropological,
antropological ("the study of the anteriors") verse; they have to be fought in
psychology as well as in history, and "the worstest beast" of all is man himself
at his present stage of responsibility and power—

> he's the worstest beast because he's won
> it's a master race and it's almost run
> ("The Worstest Beast")

D. M. Black filters through verse of clipped, staccato resourcefulness a half-
surreal brood of monstrous judges, dwarfs, hangmen, sperm donors, ants as
big as motor-bikes, "monsters at large on / every cliff: they / gather and peer
down / into a sea stiff with reptiles"—but these seem props and tryouts,
establishing tone, mask, stance, on the way to a more lucid and experiential
poetry. Really experiential monsters, on the other hand, torn lavishly and
deliberately from the historical superficies of our time, are pinned squirming
on the pages of Tom Buchan, from Heydrich to Nixon, and Scotland the
Brave becomes an American staging-post with its once holy lochs patrolled
by "obsolescent new submarines":

> Bohannan held onto a birch branch
> by yon bonny banks and looked down
> through several strata of liquid
> —there is someone somewhere
> aiming a missile at me (he thought)
> ("The Low Road")

And glacial monsters underpeer the quiet, lean, scalpelled verse of Robin
Fulton, deceptive waters washing between statement and incantation. A pro-
lific but conscientious and precise poet, he has talents that can be seen deepen-
ing during the decade as he himself moves more closely into committed
involvement with the subject. His sequence "Hung Red" (in *The Man with
the Surbahar*, 1971) is one of the striking poems of the end of this decade in
Scotland—an eye, which is also a TV eye, staring and flickering out at recent
history and horrors, caught between the desire to be effaced in the white
glare of ideal ends and the necessity of being "hung—red" on the rack of our
terrible means. Fulton, outward-looking but not unaware of native traditions,
mingles in this sequence a central image drawn from Hugh MacDiarmid's
"The Glass of Pure Water" with others that may have been suggested by
Beckett and Bacon. Here is Section 3:

> *hold a glass of pure water to the eye of the sun*
> the sun will score your retina like a merciless razor

hold up a glass of the Mekong or the Jordan
the eye of the sun will be safe now only a glimmer
in the cloudy element our substitute for daylight

the cloud preys on itself yet the cloud survives
always at the infinite cost of those who do not survive

(this is the non-miracle, repeated daily and exactly,
the putrid water struck from *the rock of capitalism*)

the water of the Ganges is also cloudy: what kind
of cleanliness justifies the wet pilgrims?
there's a scum of filth on the naked eye, don't trust the eye

Other single longish poems which in different ways are able to show, it seems to me, the sort of seriousness or awareness that Scottish poetry has been jolted into (as opposed to certain stereotypes of "entertainment" and "character" which have always been available) are Alan Bold's "A Memory of Death" (an elegy on his father, warm, imperfect, moving), Pete Morgan's "The Meat Work Saga" (a poem for performance, and one of the best examples of that genre), and Roderick Watson's "Fugue for Parker" (montage technique to relate the agony and achievement of an individual musician to the world of 1939). And if these are all poems with monsters—death, alcoholism, war, heroin, the atom—it must be remembered that Scotland in the 'sixties has also produced the tranquil, ordered, playful, and above all anti-monstrous little world ("a little world made cunningly", indeed) of Ian Hamilton Finlay. Beginning with an attractively whimsical lyrical verse in traditional form (*The Dancers Inherit the Party*, 1960), and moving out into concrete poetry, poster-poems, postcard-poems, poem-objects, and environmental or landscape poems, Finlay has proceeded impressively step by step in the search for a new lyricism which would still be basically verbal but would take into account the changes in our sensibility induced by developments in the plastic arts, design, typography, and (especially) constructivist aesthetic theory and practice. Concentration on a narrow range of familiar images, particularly those drawn from the sea—fishing-boats and nets, stars and sailors—has enabled him to explore a small field (and he claims no more) in depth and with great originality, producing a series of metaphors from one area of human experience which have been made into concrete objects for contemplation and use. Beauty—dirty word or not—is what those objects have, but it is not a wet beauty. The effects have point, often wit, usually clarity. Contrasted with (say) the hard muscular Scots of Alexander Scott's long poem on Aberdeen ("Heart of Stone"), Finlay's poetic language may seem frail, and out of phase with the supposed perfervidness of the Scottish genius. Yet the world of little things, when it is also a world of art, can stand confidently among the larger social commentaries. If Scotland seems traditionally cast as Kokoschka-country, there is surely reason to welcome a touch of Mondrian.

This essay has not attempted anything like an exhaustive survey, but has aimed merely to offer a series of pointers across and through the scene. For a fuller picture, reference may be made to the following anthologies:

The Scottish Literary Revival, ed. George Bruce (Collins-Macmillan, 1968).

The Akros Anthology of Scottish Poetry 1965–70, ed. Duncan Glen (Akros, Preston, 1970).

Contemporary Scottish Verse 1959–1969, ed. Norman MacCaig and Alexander Scott (Calder & Boyars, 1970).

Four Points of a Saltire (Reprographia, Edinburgh, 1970).

The Ring of Words, ed. Alan MacGillivray and James Rankin (Oliver & Boyd, Edinburgh, 1970).

Twelve Modern Scottish Poets, ed. Charles King (University of London Press, 1971).

Voices of Our Kind (Saltire Society, Edinburgh, 1971).

Scottish Poetry 1–6, ed. George Bruce, Maurice Lindsay, and Edwin Morgan (Edinburgh University Press, 1966–1972).

FIGURES

The Poetry of Geoffrey Hill

by Jon Silkin

i

THE word "formal" in criticism often associates with ideas concerning metrical iambic, strict stanzaic form and rhyme, and the containment by these devices of whatever the poet has to say. It may be used approvingly, or, since the current has recently run more the other way, as a means of implying that a poet using these forms has little to say, and that his sensibility and imagination are insensitive, that the courage a poet needs in order to articulate what ought essentially to be his way of exploring life is absent. As corollary to this, it is implied that only what is new in structure can sensitively and honestly engage this, since, it is argued, we are in the midst of such changes that only those forms originated by the poet in co-operation with his constantly changing environment can adequately express the new (as well as the past and hidden) in the tormenting life so many are forced to live.

The second position is persuasive, providing one keeps in mind the counter-balancing caveat that every more-or-less defined position provides the grounds for much bad work; and that even if the second position seems to account for a greater share of low-tension poetry, it is arguable that the position has helped into existence poetry that might not otherwise have got written (*vide* Alvarez writing of Plath and citing Lowell*). On the other hand one might ask what there is in such a position for Hill, whose work contrasts so strongly with, say, Ginsberg, and the Hughes of *Crow*.

There is, however, another way of defining "formal", which involves the origination of constraints and tensions with those forms themselves evolved by the concerns of the writer and his sensibility, as he or she worked these. One might say that a co-existing condition of the material evolving its forms involved, for this kind of formal writer, a productive impediment, a compacting of certain forms of speech, refracting the material into a mode of compression and close conjunction not normally found in speech, and which, probably, could not be found there. Such a definition, however, would imply that the mode of response, which could be brought to conscious active thought, was habitual to such a writer. The question of conjunction is especially important to such a poet as Hill, and in making these definitions, I have been trying to illustrate both a general type and identify a particular writer.

* A. Alvarez, "Sylvia Plath: A Memoir" in *New American Review* 12, New York, 1971, pp. 26–27.

Such formality bears with its own problems. The payments on such a premium are continuous, and one way of apprehending this condition in Hill's work is to consider the variety of forms; to consider the restlessness within the variety. Formality of the first sort occurs with Hill's early poem "Genesis",* although here it seems that the formal iambic line, stanza, and section, are used to *express* that already stylised conception of earth's creation; and that the formality while representing such stylisation is already at odds with the central theme of the poem

> There is no bloodless myth will hold

and to a lesser extent with the sub-theme's concession

> And by Christ's blood are men made free.

Hill's "argument with himself" over formal means and expressiveness is already embryonically visible in the poem, but, for the moment, one might consider the difference in form between say this poem (and "In memory of Jane Fraser"—a poem he has had trouble with) and "September Song";† between that, and the unrhymed sonnets of "Funeral Music"‡ and between all these and the prose hymns (canticles) of *Mercian Hymns*.

Restlessness of forms is not something one would normally associate with Hill's work, but this is probably because the voice is unusually present and distinct. Sometimes it becomes over-distinctive, and this is usually the result of the formal means degenerating into mannerisms. Even so, a voice cannot itself provide more than a spurious unity, and to put on it work that is beyond its proper capacity produces the strain that exists in a fraction of Hill's work. This "mannered" and "mild humility", however, is more often disrupted by the variety of forms. Is it imaginative experimentation, or an inability to find one embracing and therefore controlling mode? It could be argued that such unity is undesirable, but I am suggesting that for a poet such as Hill, unity of form, as of thought and response, are important. This is why we have such apparently absolute control within each poem (or form) but such variety of form over the spread of his work so far. Each fragment of absoluteness represents a pragmatic concession to the intractable nature of the matter and response to it in each poem. One is glad that it is so, and it reflects the ongoing struggle between form, expressiveness, and the scrupulous attention Hill usually gives to his material, even when it is struggling against that oppressive attention so as to return an existence (in life) independent of his own.

---

* *For the Unfallen*, London, 1959; also Nos. 3, 11.
† *King Log*, London, 1968.
‡ *King Log*.

ii

Hill's use of language, and choice of words, has been noticed, often, one feels, to the detriment of his themes. One sympathises with the reviewers. The compressed language is intimately bound up with what it is conveying. This is true of many poets, but true to an unusual degree with Hill. It is true in another sense. The language itself is unlike most other writing current, and coupled with this is an unusually self-conscious pointing on the part of the poet to the language. This is not because he wishes to draw attention to it for its own sake, but because the language both posits his concerns, and is itself, in the way it is used, an instance of them. Moreover, his use of language is both itself an instance of his (moral) concerns, and the sensuous gesture that defines them. It is therefore difficult to speak of his themes without coming first into necessary contact with the language.

Hill's use of irony is ubiquitous, but is not, usually, of the non-participatory and mandarin sort. It articulates the collision of events, or brings them together out of concern, and for this a more or less regular and simple use of syntax is needed, and used.

> Undesirable you may have been, untouchable
> you were not.

A concentration camp victim.* Even the "play" in the subtitle "born 19.6.32 —deported 24.9.42" where the natural event of birth is placed, simply, beside the human and murderous "deported" as if the latter were of the same order and inevitability for the victim; which, in some senses, it was—even here, the zeugmatic wit is fully employed. The irony of conjuncted meanings between "undesirable" (touching on both sexual desire and racism) and "untouchable", which exploits a similar ambiguity but reverses the emphases, is unusually dense *and* simple. The confrontation is direct and unavoidable, and this directness is brought to bear on the reader not only by the vocabulary, but by the balancing directness of the syntax. This stanza contains one of Hill's dangerous words—dangerous because of its too-frequent use, and because these words sometimes unleash (though not here) a too evident irony:

> Not forgotten
> or passed over at the proper time.

"Proper" brings together the idea of bureaucratically correct "as calculated" by the logistics of the "final solution" and the particular camp's timetable; it also contrasts the idea of the mathematically "correct" with the morally intolerable. It touches, too, on the distinction between what is morally right, and what is conventionally acceptable, and incidentally brings to bear on the whole the way in which the conventionally acceptable is often used to cloak

---

* "September Song" (*King Log*).

the morally unacceptable. One of Hill's grim jokes, deployed in such a way
that the laughter is precisely proportionate to the needs of ironic exposure.
It is when the irony is in excess of the situation that the wit becomes man-
nered. But here it does not. So the poem continues, remorselessly.

> As estimated, you died. Things marched,
> sufficient, to that end.

One feels the little quibbling movement in

> As estimated, you died.

as, without wishing to verbalise it, Hill points to the disturbing contrast
between the well-functioning time-table and what it achieved. "Things
marched" has the tread of pompous authority, immediately, in the next line,
qualified by the painfully accurate recognition that just so much energy was
needed, and released, for the extermination. "Sufficient" implies economy,
but it also implies a conscious qualification of the heavy, pompous tread of
authority. The quiet function of unpretentious machinery fulfilled its pro-
gramme, perhaps more lethally. One also notices here how the lineation
gauges, exactly, the flow and retraction of meaning and impulse, and how
this exact rhythmical flow is so much a part of the sensuous delivery of res-
ponse and evaluation. It is speech articulated, but the lineation provides, via
the convention of verse line-ending, a formal control of rhythm, and of sense
emphasis, by locking with, or breaking, the syntactical flow. Thus in the third
stanza the syntax is broken by the lineation exactly at those parts at which the
confession, as it were, of the poem's (partial) source is most painful:

> (I have made
> an elegy for myself it
> is true)

The slightly awkward break after "it" not only forces the reading speed down
to a word-by-word pace, in itself an approximation to the pain of the confes-
sion, but emphasises the whole idea. By placing emphasis on the unspecifying
pronoun, Hill is able to say two things: that the elegy was made for himself
(at least, in part) since in mourning another one is also commiserating with
one's own condition.*

> When we chant
> "Ora, ora pro nobis" it is not
> Seraphs who descend to pity but ourselves.

But "it" may also refer to the whole event; I have made an elegy for myself,
as we all do, but I have also made an elegy on a "true" event. True imagin-
atively, true in detailed fact; both for someone other than myself. Thus he is
able to point to the difficulty of the poet, who wishes, for a variety of reasons,
to approach the monstrousness of such events, but has compunction about

* See also No. 5 of "Funeral Music", a variation of this idea.

doing so. He tactfully touches for instance on the overweening ambition of the poet who hitches his talent to this powerful subject, thereby giving his work an impetus it *may* not be fully entitled to, since, only the victim, herself, would be entitled to derive this kind of "benefit". But he also modestly pleads, I think, with "it/is true" that whatever the reasons for his writing such an elegy, a proper regard for the victim, a true and unambitious feeling, was present and used. I hope enough has been said here to point to Hill's use of irony at its best, and to indicate that the tact with which he uses language is not a convention of manners which he is inertly content to remain immersed in, but an active employment of the convention as it co-operates with his scrupulousness. The scrupulousness, like the pity, is in the language. The theme permeates it.

iii

In pointing to the importance of the Imagist movement as it has affected English and American poetry, one is of course considering how central the image has become both in the writing, and for the considering, of twentieth-century poetry. What is strange about this is that apparently unrelated movements and poets apparently ignorant of each other were writing in modes which had certain formal elements in common. The hermetic poems of Ungaretti's earlier period as well as certain of Pound's and Eliot's earlier poems use the hard, clear image, seemingly as an instrument considered valuable for its own sake. In the expressionist poetry of Stramm, the images are used, as Michael Hamburger has indicated,* as the only needful flesh of the poem; the poem disdains the use of syntactical connections, thereby placing upon the image the whole burden of expressive meaning and impulse. To a lesser extent one finds this preoccupation with the image in Lorca; although even here one feels that sometimes the syntactical connections are used to lay stress on the image thereby placing on it a similar labour. The image becomes that point at which an ignition of all the elements of meaning and response takes place; that is, not only do the meanings and their impulses get expressed, but at that point are given their principal impetus. Even with the hard clear image calmly delivered this occurs. Hill has been both the innocent partaker and victim in this. He has used and been used. This is partly because of course the age as it were reeks of such practice. But with Hill one also feels that the choice has been made because he has come to recognise that the use of the image can properly communicate the intensity he wishes to express. Through it he can express the intensity, but fix it in such a way that it will evaluate the concerns of the poem it is embedded in without its intensity overruling the other parts. The intensity finds in its own kind of formality its own controlling expression. At the same time, the image as artefact has a perhaps satisfactory and not unmodest existence. It can be regarded, but it is also use-

* Michael Hamburger, *Reason and Energy*, London, 1957, pp. 219–22.

ful. Curiously enough, although the impression of imagery in Hill is, in my mind at least, strong, checking through the poetry, one is surprised at how controlled is the frequency of the kind of imagery I am thinking of. There are many instances of images used to represent objects, creatures, events. But it is as though the image whereby one object is enriched by the verbal presence of another, combined with it, and a third thing made—as though such a creation were recognised as so potentially powerful, and so open to abuse, that he was especially careful to use it sparingly. And he is, rightly, suspicious of offering confection to readers who enjoy the local richness without taking to them the full meaning of the poem, which is only susceptible to patience and a care for what it is as a whole thing. He says as much:

> Anguish bloated by the replete scream. . . .
>   I could cry "Death! Death!" as though
> To exacerbate that suave power;
>
> But refrain. For I am circumspect,
> Lifting the spicy lid of my tact
> To sniff at the myrrh.*

The images have a richness, but here he is not so much reproaching himself for that, although he implies such a possibility, but rather for the perhaps evasive caution which is characterised by "tact". The self-questioning exposes further recessions of self-doubts and questions, themselves seen to be faintly absurd. There are other examples, however, of the kind of image I am describing:

> Bland vistas milky with Jehovah's calm—†

and

>   cleanly
>   maggots churning spleen
>   to milk‡

from a poem for another concentration camp victim, Robert Desnos; and

>   we are dying
>   to satisfy fat Caritas, those
>   Wiped jaws of stone**

and from the earlier Dr. Faustus:

> A way of many ways: a god
> Spirals in the pure steam of blood.††

---

* "Three Baroque Meditations" (2) (*King Log*).
† "Locust Songs" (3) (*King Log*).
‡ "Domaine Public" (*King Log*).
** "Funeral Music" (2) (*King Log*).
†† "Dr. Faustus" (1) (*For the Unfallen*).

What is noticeable about these images, chosen for the way in which they combine disparate elements, is their ferocity. Their expressiveness occurs at its fullest in the moment of sudden expansion, when the elements combine in often intolerable antipathy and produce judgements issuing from a disgust that has behind it a sense of outrage at this or that situation.

More often the images are "abstract", combinations of adjectives and nouns, whose conjunction is ironically disruptive, but with a similar moral evaluation intended. Thus in one of Hill's best shorter poems, "Ovid in the Third Reich", we again confront his justly obsessive concern with innocence, and its mutilation, or impossibility, within the context of human barbarism:

> Too near the ancient troughs of blood
> Innocence is no earthly weapon.*

The notion of innocence as a defence against earthly corruption has an ancient lineage; but here it is linked with the more combative "weapon", and in such a way as to suggest weapon in a very literal sense. Of what use is innocence in such a context? And: if it is of no use on earth, what is its use? Are we right to think of a condition as useless because inoperative on earth. And if thus inoperative, can it be so valued in a "heavenly" context? Hovering near the phrase "earthly weapon" is the phrase (no) "earthly good" with its worn-through substance, a little restored by Hill's regenerative irony. In these two lines Hill returns of course to the consideration of "Genesis"

> There is no bloodless myth will hold.

(The "Ovid" poem suggests *to me* an Eichmann-like figure—not Eichmann—with whom the reader in his ordinariness and banality is invited to identify, thus being asked to make the connection with that other aspect of Eichmann, his evil. Ovid's exile may be seen to parallel our inability, or reluctance, to associate with guilt—in case we sully an innocence—already sullied.)

There are many examples of these "abstract" combinations, often zeugmatic in form (the device which has built into it a moral judgement). Thus

> fastidious trumpets
> Shrilling into the ruck†

and

> my justice, wounds, love
> Derisive light, bread, filth‡

and, at the funeral of King Offa, the punning zeugma where the successive adjective suffers qualification by the former:

> He was defunct. They were perfunctory.**

* From *King Log*.
† "Funeral Music" (2) (*King Log*).
‡ "Men are a Mockery of Angels" (*King Log*).
** No. 27 (*Mercian Hymns*).

And again from *Mercian Hymns*, the man who has imagined, with ambiguous relish, a scene of torture

> wiped his lips and hands. He strolled back to the
> car, with discreet souvenirs for consolation. . . .

"Discreet" is not an image precisely, but it produces an image of a man hiddenly guilty, voyeur upon his own imagination, which is, however, discreet in that it is secret. It has not tortured another's flesh.

In these instances, where Hill's intensity is released, I have tried to show that it is through images, of several kinds, that the sudden evaluative expansion occurs. Hill has more recently been concerned to accumulate meaning and response in a more gradual way. But, in the earlier work especially, the intense evaluation, response, judgement—all are released at that sudden moment of expansion which is the moment of visualisation. Hill's poetry has more often consisted of, not continuous narrative, but a conjunction of imagistic impulses. A conjunction of intensities, sometimes sensuously rich, and nearly always scrupulously evaluative.

iv

The imagistic impulse in Hill's work, as both imagistic and image-making, is of course related to the question of narrative and discursiveness. Imagism, considered as a reaction, developed out of an antipathy for the discursive nature of Victorian poetry. That was not the sum of its antipathies, but it is clear, from the principles and the practice, that Imagism constituted, among other things, an attempt to enact, rather than assert, a response. It wanted to cut from it those dilutions of response which had rendered a verse that was vaguely descriptive of states of feelings, and it found a method. It found in the image a pure answer. That is, it found in the image something that could not be adulterated. An image did not attempt to explain; it rendered the verbal equivalent of what was seen, and the more it rendered exactly what it saw, the better. Clearly this kind of antidote was needed in English poetry and we are still receiving its benefits. Yet the difficulty lay in that by nature, the hard, clear image, untroubled by a discursive reflectiveness, had little or no valency. It could only accommodate other images, perhaps of different intensities and implications, and it could not accommodate the syntax of argument or narrative. And despite what its claims implied, it could hardly accommodate connections of any kind; Imagism had to select very carefully indeed, and its methods could not easily be used without its being diluted. And at that stage in its development, to dilute its purity would have been to have annulled its impetus. What it gained in intensity it lost in its capacity to cope with a range of experience.

This is immediately apparent when we consider Imagism in relation to the war. This is not the place to speak in detail of, for instance, Aldington and

Herbert Read, but, briefly, I should like to instance two very different poems by Read—"The Happy Warrior" and "The End of a War".* In the first, Read manages to make of his war experience an imagist poem. That is, he manages to make the "syntax" of Imagism render a particular set of very careful responses to combat, and to render, by implication, a set of arguments. But this is one instance, which, once done, could not be repeated. Moreover, the poem relies, for its deepest reading, on its being correlated with Wordsworth's poem "The Character of the Happy Warrior" of which it is also a criticism. But the fact that it needs, finally, this correlation with a poem that is anything but imagistic places Read's poem in a special relation to Imagism. Nothing like this that I know of in Imagist poetry had been done before, and one suspects that Read found his necessities out of what he called war's "terrorful and inhuman events".

In his autobiography, *The Contrary Experience*, Read wrote:

> I criticised [the Imagists] because in their manifestoes they had renounced the decorative word, but their sea-violets and wild hyacinths tend to become as decorative as the beryls and jades of Oscar Wilde. I also accused them of lacking that aesthetic selection which is the artist's most peculiar duty. . . . We were trying to maintain an abstract aesthetic ideal in the midst of terrorful and inhuman events.†

There is of course a skeletal narrative structure in "The Happy Warrior" but poems could hardly be written like that of any length and complexity. In his subsequent "war poems", those composing *Naked Warriors* (1919), we see Read introducing narrative, but the imagistic elements are much diluted by it, and in such a way as to enervate the poetry. In other words, Read had relied, as he had to, upon the imagistic elements to render intensity and expressiveness, but the collision of the two modes produced compromise. By the time Read came to write *The End of a War* (published 1933) he had worked out a solution; he pushed the narrative outside the poem, setting the scene and describing the events of the episode in a prefacing prose argument which, though essential to the reading of the poem, is in ambiguous relationship to it, and without any relationship to it structurally.

Hill is clearly a poet having little in common with Read, but he has, I think, similar problems engaging him. "Genesis" for instance is held together by using days of the week as a means of tabulating impulses in sequence. The sequence of days is important to the poem structurally, and through it Hill tries to initiate an image of growing consciousness. Yet it is only a proper sequence as it refers back to God's six days of work. The poem itself does not have narrative coherence so much as a sequence of formulisations; in his subsequent work, Hill abandoned this kind of stylisation, and to a lesser extent, the incipient narrative structure.

---

* Herbert Read, *Collected Poems*.
† Herbert Read, *The Contrary Experience*, London, 1963, p. 176.

With "Funeral Music", the prose note that at one time preceded the
poem stands in similar elucidatory relation to it as Read's "Argument" does
to "The End of a War". Less, perhaps, or perhaps less in Hill's mind, for the
note has, in *King Log* itself, been placed at the end of the book, and separate
from the poems, as though Hill were determined, with such a gesture, to
make "Funeral Music" un-needful of any elucidatory material. The poems
do not form a narrative sequence, although they lead through the battle (of
Towton) into some deliberately incomplete attempts at evaluating the cost in
both physical and spiritual excoriation. Evaluation is made partly by reference
to a supposed, or possibly supposed, after-life, in which the ideals of an
exemplary spiritual life would if anywhere be found; partly by reference to
this, or to eternity, yet into which no sense of human evaluation can be
extended with the certainty of finding corroborative "echoes". (Compare
the following with the first stanza of "Ovid in the Third Reich".)

> If it is without
> Consequence when we vaunt and suffer, or
> If it is not, all echoes are the same
> In such eternity. Then tell me, love,
> How that should comfort us—*

Even supposed *notions* of an after-life, with its spiritual absolutes, are in-
sufficient here since the first of the unrhymed sonnets opens in platonic
supposition; that is, the platonic structure throws into ambiguity the question
of whether we are to suppose an after-life is to be believed in—does this by
supplanting the idea of an after-life with its own metaphysical scheme. I am
indicating here that in Hill's longer poems, sequences and extended work
that demand some correspondingly developed structure, he meets the prob-
lem without conceding to narrative a function it might usefully fulfil in his
work. Fearful of sacrificing the imagistic purity of his work, of sullying that
compression, of impairing a dramatic enactment, or mimesis of psychological
impulsions, he prefers to accumulate intensities than involve them in
accumulating and continuous action. This may partly be due to the preference
Hill shows for writing that, by dramatic mimesis, introduces to the reader
internal impulsions rather than dramatic action. Thus in "Funeral Music",
the battle of Towton, and its murderousness, is not encapsulated as dramatic
action, but brooded on after the event, thereby allowing the external state of
the field and the state of the mind experiencing and responding to it to meet.
It is the self-questioning, the doubts, the beliefs half-held with a conviction
of personal honesty, the motives and the state of the spirit, that interest Hill,
rather than the shaping action of narrative. Nevertheless, these things too
have their form of collision with other minds, and through action, alter and
are altered. And they could also, I feel, build a narrative unity that Hill has
only tentatively, if at all, used.

* "Funeral Music" (8) (*King Log*).

One of the most interesting and moving aspects of "Funeral Music" is its plainness. The images in the following passage do not fabricate either a local richness to colour-up the passage, nor is there an over-arching image employed supposedly to enlarge or make more significant the events and the responses to these of the observer-participant:

> "At noon,
> As the armies met, each mirrored the other;
> Neither was outshone. So they flashed and vanished
> And all that survived them was the stark ground
> Of this pain. I made no sound, but once
> I stiffened as though a remote cry
> Had heralded my name. It was nothing . . ."
> Reddish ice tinged the reeds; dislodged, a few
> Feathers drifted across; carrion birds
> Strutted upon the armour of the dead.*

An Ecclesiastes-like consideration of vanity moves in these first lines, located in the ironic flashing of the armies mirrored in each other's armour. But they do not see themselves; they see only the flash of their *own* pride by which they are, each of them, dazzled. Yet with an honesty that compels a grudging kind of admission, we are also told that theirs was a kind of sad "glory": "Neither was outshone". But this is also qualified by the other idea inherent in the phrase—that neither had more pride, nor was more capable of victory; what is impending is not the surfeiting of pride but its extinction in the futility of combat. If they mirror each other's pride they also mirror each other's destruction. The strutting carrion birds confirm this judgement.

Yet impressive as this is as narration implicated with judgement, and pity, there is also a turning inwards and sealing off from the outward visible of all this in the ambiguous "the stark ground/Of this pain". The ground is at once the actual ground where soldiers inflicted pain on each other; it is also, because of the disposition of the syntax, a kind of personification where the ground itself becomes absorbed in the huge lingering tremor of pain. This serves to incarcerate the reader, and perhaps the writer also, in an inescapable response, but it also fails, I think, to release him from a pre-occupation where the event has been so internalised that there results more response than event itself. The passage seems to recognise this by resuming its re-creation of the desolate battlefield. The sense of the pentameter, in these lines, and throughout the sequence, serves not merely a unifying function but as a framework within and around which Hill can make his supple impulses and retractions of rhythm:

> ". . . as though a remote cry
> Had heralded my name. It was nothing . . ."
> Reddish ice tinged the reeds; dislodged, a few
> Feathers drifted across.

* "Funeral Music" (7) (*King Log*).

The second line begins with a slow, regular pentameter; after the word "name", the expectations of the pentameter are reduced in the foreshortened remainder of the line, reducing exactly the expectations of the person in the *poem* as his feelings are disappointed. In the next line the pentameter is extended. The other speaking voice is describing minute events on the surface of the battle-field. "Dislodged", in its participial form, is syntactically isolated, and mirrors the disconnectedness of the feathers, from a bird, or some martial plume, but reflects also the disconnectedness of the dead from the living. In the little halting movement at the end of the line, which the line-break emphasises, the temporary emphasis falls on "few" and thus serves to re-create sensuously the stillness of the battle-field which is

> its own sound
> Which is like nothing on earth, but is earth.*

These lines, from No. 3 of the sequence, serve to pre-resonate the irony of the situation, where the dead are unearthly (because of the possibility of the dead having an after-life) but are for us no more than the earth they have been reduced to by human action. Seen in this way, "Funeral Music" is, among other things, a consideration of war where "war", to use Clausewitz's strategy "is a continuation of state policy by other means". The sequence is at once an elegy of pity, an examination of pride, a self-examination of the responses appropriate to this apparent constant in human living. It is all these in relation to the question of whether suffering has any meaning in earthly life; and whether there exists some ideal platonic and/or spiritual system in which suffering, which is perhaps the only state during which we are innocent, can have a meaningful and positive place.

V

Sebastian Arrurruz ("The Songbook of Sebastian Arrurruz") was, as we now know, not an actual poet (1868–1922) who has bewilderedly survived into the twentieth century, but an invention that may have perplexed critics searching for the original work.

The poem makes use of the necessary "silence" surrounding the "original". The lack of information on the poet may obliquely refer to Arrurruz's own apprehension regarding the oblivion both of himself and his work, and is thus a wry part of the poems themselves. The poems composed by Arrurruz are also records of certain attitudes towards both the (discontinued) relationship with his mistress and to poetry. In a sense the poem, or group, is Hill's *Mauberley*. But where Pound is using himself, both for what he feels himself to be kin to as a poet, and for what the figure stands in contradistinction to in the effete and vulgar English culture, Hill's Sebastian (the saint pierced with arrows) is more separate from the poet who has shaped him.

* "Funeral Music" (3) (*King Log*).

Arrurruz (arrowroot) is a man pierced by the arrow (another's predation upon his relinquished mistress); the arrow remains rooted in him. He is also a man, the root of an arrow, himself equipped, organically, and with the incising gift of the poet. Both these, though, in the poem, are laconically expressed, and survive increasingly on the wryly self-regretful memory of what once obtained. But this double image, of potency, and the quite powerful if intermittent observation of it, serves to illustrate, among other things, the fate of The Poet surviving through two eras. The original potency may have had a bardic vigour unimpeded by a self-conscious and mocking observation of its impulses; but the later work of Arrurruz that we are offered presents a considerable shift in temper and emphasis. In these poems we have, initially, not so much a man expressing passion as recollecting it:

> Ten years without you. For so it happens. . . .
>
> The long-lost words of choice and valediction.*

The energy is not in the passion itself, but re-located in the stare that re-collects it, and which is itself observed. Arrurruz's writing is at once more complex than it was, and, significantly, more difficult to achieve. Whatever the auto-biographical references may amount to, Hill is clearly defining the poet's difficulties as he encounters an environment that is at once more self-conscious and less bardic. The attention is scrupulous and modern.

Arrurruz is of course a middle-ageing man, and knows it. Yet his struggles are not those of a defeated one.

> "One cannot lose what one has not possessed."
> So much for that abrasive gem.
> I can lose what I want. I want you.†

The first line is between inverted commas because it is a line from a poem he is writing or has perhaps recently completed. Either way the line is embedded in commentary by an older, more self-conscious, part of the man. "Coplas"— this is the first of four that constitute the poem—are "songs", perhaps somewhat lyrically un-selfregarding and unironic poems. They are also popular poems, often used to serenade the beloved. Some measure of Hill's irony here may be obtained by contrasting these simple definitions with the stance of the present Arrurruz' coplas which form neither a serenade, nor are popular, but unlyrical, allusive, and complex. The form is of course traditional and it has therefore accumulated to itself the energy of those poems which have earlier filled the form. But like so much else in the twentieth century, the traditional form has broken down. Or rather, not so much broken as become inappropriate; and not this, entirely, but that we have lost the ability to use the form. We have lost spontaneity.

---

* "The Songbook of Sebastian Arrurruz" (1) (*King Log*).
† "The Songbook" (2) (*King Log*).

Much of this centres in the phrase "abrasive gem". It is abrasive because it is a reminder of what he has lost. It is a gem because it is a lyrical utterance faceted and cut like a jewel. Hill however uses "gem" to bring in other, colloquial meanings. Thus gem can mean a real beauty, but the poet can also, and certainly here does, mean it ironically and self-contemptuously. The self-contempt arises not only from his awareness of having lost his wife to another, but also of how his line of poetry untruthfully renders in lyrical terms a considerably unlyrical event. Arrurruz brings to his and our awareness the discontinuity between the two ways of looking at such an event, and the two ways of writing about it. There is no elegising or consolatory sweetness to be got; the paradox of Arrurruz's poem is still-born; and is replaced by the unparadoxical and unironical lack of consolation:

> I can lose what I want. I want you.

But in the second of the coplas there is already a modification of the harsh tone:

> Oh my dear one, I shall grieve for you
> For the rest of my life with slightly
> Varying cadence, oh my dear one.

The tone of this first line softens that of the previous copla's ending. He is, it seems, back in the convention of elegising the lost one. But the phrase "with slightly/varying cadence" tinges the whole with mockery. Is the irony conscious on Arrurruz's part, or is it reserved for the reader's inspection only? It hardly matters. The absurd monotony of such poetics is rendered, and we understand how the irony qualifies into clarity the whole situation. He is perhaps even beginning to write a poetry that feeds on such ironic awareness. Yet the irony cannot dissolve the passion, a crucial point for the poems that follow: "Half-mocking the half-truth." Michael Hamburger wrote of Hölderlin in *Reason and Energy* (pp. 17–18):

> Even before his enforced separation from Susette Gontard he had felt that his fate would be a tragic one. . . . Now he was to lose his last support against the sense of personal tragedy. As he had foretold in 1798, all that remained was his art and the quite impersonal faith that sustained his art. . . . What Hölderlin did not know when he wrote this poem is that long after his heart had indeed died, as he says, his "mellow song" would continue; that the music of his strings *would* escort him down.

So with Arrurruz, in a way. Abandoned by his wife, musing with increasing, dilapidating irony on his loss, seeing that the earlier way of writing will fit neither the age, nor the event in his life, nor now his temperament, nothing it seems can prevent his gentle decline into oblivion. One might therefore expect the poems to degenerate, by mimesis, placing at the reader's disposal an irreversible picture of disintegration, among a flickering irony. This does not occur. What Arrurruz could not have foreseen, since he was engaged in it, was that his ironically truthful examination of the events in his life, including his poetry, would revitalise his art. For I take it that the succeeding poems of the "Songbook" are not only made of Arrurruz speaking but of his writing. If so, there is no failure, but rather, regeneration. In poem 5, Arrurruz can respond to, or write, a poem of genuine deprivation:

> I find myself
> Devouring verses of stranger passion
> And exile. The exact words
>
> Are fed into my blank hunger for you.*

A hunger that may not be fed; therefore blank. The crucial word, however, for the poet is "exact". The gaze has caught its truth. The reward is exactness, and its pain. Similarly in "A Song from Armenia":

> Why do I have to relive, even now,
> Your mouth, and your hand running over me
> Deft as a lizard, like a sinew of water?†

The emphatic, simplified movement of the song has returned, but this time filled with rich, *painful* memories, constantly reawakened, and admitted into his consciousness by the wry ironic truthfulness with which the mind regards such experience. It is not the distancing irony of the man who can afford irony because he is detached, but an irony created in pain. The relationship may have ceased, but the pain does not get subsumed in distance. There are two final twists to the "life", both occurring in the second of the prose poems which conclude the sequence:

> Scarcely speaking: it becomes as a
> Coolness between neighbours. Often
> There is this orgy of sleep. I wake
> To caress propriety with odd words
> And enjoy abstinence in a vocation
> Of now-almost-meaningless despair.‡

"Orgy of sleep" oddly reverses the ironic vitality I have noticed, suggesting a dying inwards of life. The sexuality gets transcribed in a caressed "propriety". Yet the last word is despair. The registration is in the end one of feeling. Is there a further irony in that Arrurruz, caught up with an exact sense of it, can no longer make poems out of his pain because his equipment belongs to an earlier more rhetorical mode? I think not; although one can imagine that for Arrurruz this might often seem to have been the threat. As a latter-day saint, he experiences two temptations. One is to succumb to his earlier inexact rhetoric, as both an expression of and a response to his experience. The other is to create a distant and neutered irony from his pain. This latter gets suggested in "Postures". As it happens, Arrurruz succumbs to neither temptation.

* "The Songbook" (5) (*King Log*).
† "The Songbook" (9) (*King Log*).
‡ "The Songbook" (11) (*King Log*).

vi

As with the Arrurruz sequence, the thirty prose poems that make up *Mercian Hymns* have a central figure from whom the poems depend, in this instance King Offa. Historically, as Hill tells us, Offa reigned over Mercia . . . in the years A.D. 757–796. During earlier medieval times he was already becoming a creature of legend. However the gloss is not entirely helpful in that the reader does not find a historical reconstruction of the King and his domain. Interleaved with a reconstruction of some of the King's acts are passages and whole poems concerned with the contemporary and representative figure Hill makes of himself. Why not? Additionally, the poem deliberately thwarts any attempt by the reader to keep his or her imagination safe in the past. The King himself, although rooted in the past, is to be "most usefully . . . regarded as the presiding genius of the West Midlands", and thus threads "his" way in and out of his past and our present. Hill makes quite sure we get this by offering, in the first Hymn, a description of the figure as

> King of the perennial holly-groves, the riven sand-
> stone: overlord of the M5: architect of the his-
> toric rampart and ditch. . . .*

Nevertheless the historic facts of Offa the King are relevant, if tangled, and we should look at them. Entangled with them, however, are Hill's references themselves: (i) *Sweet's Anglo-Saxon Reader* (1950, pp. 170–80) and (ii) The Latin prose hymns or canticles of the early Christian Church; *The Penguin Book of Latin Verse* (1962, pp. xvii, lv).

The interested reader will not be glad to discover that although there is a group of Hymns in Anglo-Saxon, quoted by Sweet, these texts are interlineally placed with the Latin taken from the *Vulgate*, of which these are literal and apparently not always accurate translations. Moreover it has been suggested that these translations embody no sense of the haecceity of the Mercian domain, or of the Anglo-Saxon world at large. That is, they were probably intended as instructional texts for the teaching of Latin. Moreover the two Vulgates are themselves of course translations from the Hebrew, the relevant Biblical references being made by Sweet at the head of each Anglo-Saxon translation (from the Latin). The first reference then suggests that, apart from some elaborate, heavy-witted joke, Hill's pointing to the Mercian Hymns indicates no more, as far as the Anglo-Saxon is concerned, than a homogeneity sanctioned by the Mercian dialect, a homogeneity that stems of course from a geographical area over which King Offa did rule, whose reign may or may not have witnessed these translations.

The second reference is as apparently oblique: "The 'Te Deum', a canticle in rhythmical prose, has been used in Christian worship from the fourth century to the present day. . . . As the Jewish psalter was the sole hymn-

* *Mercian, Hymns* (1) London, 1971.

book of the early Church, it is not surprising that the 'Te Deum' is character-
ised throughout by the parallelism which is the basis of ancient Hebrew
poetry."* As it happens, there appears to be no use of Hebrew parallelism in
Hill's poems other than those traces which, through contact with the Bible,
have crept into our speech and left there residually a few emphatic forms. Yet
checking, in fact, through the relevant Biblical passages in Isaiah, Deutero-
nomy, Habakkuk, and Luke (which are the original texts for Sweet's Mercian
Hymns) I found, almost by accident, and by linking my apprehension of
rhythm in these English passages with the phrase quoted earlier—the "Te
Deum", a canticle in rhythmical prose—I began to follow the point of the
references, and even to give grudging assent to their obliquity.

It is helpful to remember that much of the *Old Testament* is, in the Hebrew,
poetry, and that in rendering these translations in English of the Authorised
Version, what is offered us is, precisely, "rhythmical prose". Moreover it is
not merely rhythmical prose, but prose versions of poetry, although rendered,
one feels, partly through the repetitions of parallelism, with emphatic *and*
subtle rhythms. It is as if the exterior device of line ending, and all those
devices contingent on this convention, have been discarded (not *entirely* true
of *Mercian Hymns*); what is left, in the main, however, is the inherent struc-
ture itself, depending more than ever upon the rhythmical arrangement of the
words. Greater stress may get laid on word-choice, and a closer attention is
charged, perhaps, upon the meaning. These hopeful attempts at describing
a prose poem, but in particular Hill's canticles, now offer the point of the
references, since, without falling back on a description of his own method of
writing, they allow the reader to pick up, in the best possible way, through
example, the kind of poetry he is writing in *Mercian Hymns*. Moreover,
although the Mercian dialect and the Anglo-Saxon language have little to do
with the structure of the Hymns, and no comparison with the Anglo-Saxon
will profitably help us in a reading of Hill's poems, I suggest that the Anglo-
Saxon *Mercian Hymns* act as a historical filter for Hill. That is, they remind us
that the Biblical transmissions which reach us additionally passed, for whatever
reason, through the Mercian dialect, and that however indistinct the locality
is now, and however restricted King Offa's jurisdiction may have been,
Biblical contact was made via Mercia, which is also Offa's and Hill's locality.

As for the relevance of the Bible to King Offa, and both these to the
character of Offa in Hill's poems, verse 21 from *Deuteronomy* 32 may help:

> They have moved me to jealousy with that which is not God; they have
> provoked me to anger with their vanities: and I will move them to
> jealousy with those which are not a people; I will provoke them to anger
> with a foolish nation.

In Hill's eighth poem:

* Edited by Frederick Brittain, *The Penguin Book of Latin Verse*, Harmondsworth, 1962,
pp. xvi–xvii.

> The mad are predators. Too often lately they harbour
> against us. A novel heresy exculpates all maimed
> souls. Abjure it! I am the King of Mercia, and
> I know. . . .

> Today I name them; tomorrow I shall express the new
> law. I dedicate my awakening to this matter.

It is useful to remember that while all of chapter 32 of *Deuteronomy* consists of God's words, Moses speaks them. They have the backing of God, but are vested in Moses' temporal authority. Of course, Moses the prime leader of Israel in a tight situation, had much to cope with, not least of all the comically frequent backsliding of the Israelites. But we recall that Moses was an autocratic ruler and, in this, had adequate sanction from the God of the *Old Testament*, who was jealous and wrathful. Curiously, those passages of the Bible translated into Anglo-Saxon stress, perhaps by accident, this aspect of God: provided we obey Him we shall find Him loving and protective: but should we not, we shall discover his wrath and punishments. The autocratic nature of such a God was perhaps a useful reminder, in that probably more anarchic period, that the nature and power of the Anglo-Saxon King was not unlike that of the Hebrew God.

R. W. Chambers in *Beowulf: an Introduction** interestingly examines the character of King Offa II as well as the legends surrounding his supposed ancestor Offa I. He points to the shuffling of the deeds of the King onto his Queen by the monks of St. Alban's as a way of exonerating their benefactor of crime. Chambers speaks explicitly of "the deeds of murder which, as a matter of history, did characterise [King Offa II's] reign". History helps us to link the autocratic nature of God with King Offa, and see too what Hill has done with this in his *Mercian Hymns*.

Finally, I should quote from C. H. Sisson's Epigraph for *Mercian Hymns*:

> The conduct of government rests upon the same foundation and en-
> counters the same difficulties as the conduct of private persons.

The quotation goes on to suggest that the technical aspects of government are frequently used to evade those moral laws which apply alike to individuals and governments.

The question of the private man and his public actions is one that Hill has already worked in "Ovid in the Third Reich". With such a figure as a king the question multiplies in direct ratio to the power of the king and his abuse of it. History suggests that Offa was a tyrant. In No. 7 ("The Kingdom of Offa"), a part of Offa's childhood, we have

> Ceolred was his friend and remained so, even after
>   the day of the lost fighter. . . .
>   Ceolred let it spin through a hole
> in the classroom-floorboards. . . .

---

* R. W. Chambers, *Beowulf: an Introduction*, Cambridge, 1932, see pp. 31–40.

> After school he lured Ceolred, who was sniggering
>   with fright, down to the old quarries, and flayed
>   him.

Then he continues with his play, alone. One cannot mistake the ferocity, or the egocentric peace of mind following it. Hill does not set out to establish the figure of a tyrant, since the sequence does not have that kind of narrative structure or intention. Yet in Offa's adult life the poems produce a similar ruthlessness to that of the child. Thus in dealing (in No. 11) with forgers of the realm's coinage:

> [the King's "moneyers"] struck with account-
>   able tact. They could alter the king's face.
>
> Exactness of design to deter imitation; mutil-
>   ation if that failed. . . .
>
> Swathed bodies in the long ditch; one eye upstaring.
>   It is safe to presume, here, the king's anger.

"Safe" underlies the irony and helps us to refer back to his "moneyers" who, alone, were free to alter, that is, flatter, the face. One is reminded of the monks rewriting the *Life* of King Offa their benefactor, by putting on his Queen the murder of his vassal, King Aethelbert. But the flattery tactfully (via Hill) points to the King's severity, if not cruelty. Of course we see here the attempt to establish in the kingdom the idea of money available only through productive work, and an attempt to establish a concept of lawfulness. Yet one is also aware of the naked word "moneyers", as opposed to the more neutral words available, with the suggestion that the King is, out of "good substance", making money. There are many qualifications here, and if the judgement is finally against Offa in the poem, there are mitigations. In poem 14, Offa assumes the role of powerful businessman:

> Dismissing reports and men, he put pressure on the
>   wax, blistered it to a crest. He threatened male-
>   factors with ash from his noon cigar.

The effect is one of humour, and opulence. The ritual "noon" cigar suggests the power of a minor potentate. The power has its reserves; yet in the obvious sense the vulgarity is miniature; he threatens with "ash". But ash, we recall, is what the concentration camp victims were reduced to. One notices the zeugma, with the built-in moral device. Men are dismissed as easily and thoughtlessly as reports (the line-split, male/factor, emphasises this by means of the pun). The touch is light and has humour; but it engages the reader only to repel him.

There are other touches of opulence, of a more private kind, connected even more with the contemporary man than the king. He has been driving (in No. 17) through the beautiful "hushed Vosges". Some accident occurs with or between cyclists. It is unclear to me if it involves himself, as an adult, with these cyclists, or himself as a child with another cyclist, or whether Hill is merging both possibilities. In a sense it hardly matters. What is more important is the implied lack of compunction, whoever was to blame for the accident. The car "heartlessly" overtakes all this and

> He lavished on
> the high valleys its *haleine*.

By using, it would seem, the more delicate if exotic French for "breath", Hill is able to draw attention to the discrepancy between the beauty of the country he travels through, and the linked "heartlessness" of the pollution and lack of concern for the accident. The French word is beautiful, but cold, and lacks compunction in its erasure of concern.

Again in No. 18, we return to the problems of cruelty, with the contingent problem of the enjoyment of it:

> At Pavia, a visitation of some sorrow. Boethius'
> dungeon. He shut his eyes. . . .
> He willed the instruments of
> violence to break upon his meditation. Iron buckles
> gagged; flesh leaked rennet over them; the men
> stooped, disentangled the body.
>
> He wiped his lips and hands. He strolled back to the
> car, with discreet souvenirs for consolation and
> philosophy.

The irony emerges. Boethius wrote his *De Consolatione Philosophiae* while imprisoned at Pavia. Still the tourist of the previous poem, the man visits Pavia with the conscious, formal intention of commiserating with Boethius' obscene death, and of wondering at the man who could console himself with philosophy at such a stage in his life. He wills himself to imagine the philosopher tortured, perhaps out of a dutiful compunction, but finds that, secretly, a part of him relishes the scene. "He wiped his lips and his hands". Both relish and guilt are here. The souvenirs are discreet because secret. He practises his enjoyment on no man's flesh. Yet there is a sense in which he is guilty, certainly, of unclean thoughts. The contrast between the cerebral and touristic appreciation of philosophy, and the voyeur's appreciation of cruelty is notable. Rather, he is not only voyeur, but, in his relish, participator. "Flesh leaked rennet over them" is horrifying; the blood curdles under the extremity of the suffering; the blood is said to leak, uncontrollably, as if itself incontinent. The wracked body becomes truly pitiful. The buckles restrain the victim, and perhaps muffle his cries; they also choke. What is remarkable here, however, is that the scene and its relishing are admitted to. Admitted to, but hardly confessed. It is not so much a release from guilt as a judgement on the thought and its stimulation. And this judgement is as valid for the tourist as for the king:

> I have learned one thing: not to look down
> So much upon the damned.*

One should be careful to avoid the impression that there is relish in Hill's re-creation of cruelty. The pity is not punctured carelessly over the Hymns, as some kind of reward to the reader, but it is present, and, in particular, in the finely intimate and tender No. 25:

> I speak this in memory of my grandmother, whose
> childhood and prime womanhood were spent in the
> nailer's darg.

And

> It is one
> thing to celebrate the "quick forge", another
> to cradle a face hare-lipped by the searing wire.

The insight is crucial to the tender pity. It is one thing to celebrate the dignity of labour, another to endure it in one's first maturity, especially when the work itself has caused the mutilation. Even the sound of the phrase "nailer's darg", the phrase isolated on a line of its own and following a rather rapid syllabic flow—the long-drawn vowel of "darg" expresses the reductive nature of the experience. The poem does not indulge in melancholy. It consistently touches on the harshness of the experience. The man is said to "brood" on Ruskin's text concerning labour. Ruskin's letter, which begins with reflections on a Worcestershire nail factory, is concerned with the immorality and hypocrisy of usury. Hill is suggesting, I imagine, that his grandmother's labour, with that of others, borrows money from her employer, and his profit on that represents his interest.

One has to finish. Offa dies and one is left with not so much the figure of a man, but an area, changing, and filled, on balance, with more distress than comfort, and "presided over" by a ruler and an ethos more cruel, more harsh, than severely just. Capricious, light, but capable of some consistent authority. One may feel that the work as a whole is perhaps too inconclusive. On the other hand, as Lawrence abjured the novelist, Hill finally refuses to tip the balance by putting his own thumb on the scales. He is concerned with how things are (and an evaluation of that), not firstly upon how they ought to be; although that perhaps also emerges.

Number 27 is not the last of the Hymns but I should like to indicate its diverse elements, and to suggest how the entire set of poems, as they draw to their end, contrive to echo their diversity within this one poem. At the funeral of King Offa an absurd composition of mourners, from all ages, attends:

> He was defunct. They were perfunctory.

---

* "Ovid in the Third Reich" (*King Log*).

The contrast is not only between the finality of death and the continuity of the living. There is an absurdity contingent on death, but this is not entirely it either. The comic element here mediates between the two and both eases and recognises the sharpness of the dividing line. Additionally, as Hill suggests, the more public and dignified the man who has died, the more absurd the situation, and the more susceptible to hypocrisy, since those intimate, mourning connections, do not, properly, exist. The pun joins the living recognitions with the dead man, only to distinguish finally, and for good. Then follows a last stanza of extraordinary beauty, in which nature mirrors the uprooting of the man. But even in the largeness of the event, death is seen to touch every creature. It is the leveller:

> Earth lay for a while, the ghost-bride of livid
> Thor, butcher of strawberries, and the shire-tree
> dripped red in the arena of its uprooting.

"Butcher of strawberries" carries the right amount of pathos. The innocent fruits are remarked on.

Alone in a Mine of Reality:
A Matrix in the Poetry of Jon Silkin

by Anne Cluysenaar

The Portrait and Other Poems, published in 1950 when Silkin was nineteen, contains a poem, "Night", which in several ways points the direction of his later development.

> In the unthinkable dark we walk. In there
> We move all ways to anywhere, nowhere
> Is any place nor up nor down nor slope
> House, church, stream, tree nor any known landmark
> Yet still in the darkness of eternity,
> But utterly alone in a mine of reality,
> Of this place, that place, there, here, nowhere, somewhere,
> Where is, was, has been, will be, an infinite
> Number of perpetual combinations and
> Permutations. Your voice goes ringing ringing
> To that other place through a series of doors
> And dark corridors. This is the zero mark.

The notion that man walks in the dark, recurs in the "Prologue" and "Epilogue" to *The Peaceable Kingdom* (1954) and elsewhere. It seems to represent a fundamental impression, but is always coupled, as in "Night", with a strong sense of life as quest, as a constant probing of its own conditions. And the probing tends to take on religious connotations, as here with the reference to "that other place": in other poems, to God. These references are not, perhaps, to be taken dogmatically, but they indicate the seriousness with which Silkin views what he is undertaking to do. He often speaks for others ("we"), or of his own experiences, however intimate, as a model of man's experience, of what our reactions (including his own) should be rather than of what his happened to be once. And, finally, his rendering of experience is intricate: he is above all aware of "a mine of reality", of "perpetual combinations and permutations", and his poems generally convey this on a formal as well as a semantic level, by means of elaborate syntax and a diction devoted to teasing out nuances. Silkin's poetry from 1950–71 is a process of reformulation and development, constantly more relevant to social issues and more precise with regard to inner contradictions. In what follows, I want to discuss a central cluster of ideas and images which seem to form the matrix within which this process takes place. It would be possible and interesting to do this at greater length, taking into account permutations and transformations which I shall have to ignore. But those I consider do show, I think, an increasingly consistent articulation of the relationships between life's positive and negative forces.

In crude terms, it can be said that the destructive forces become more and more internalised, are recognised as intertwined with the sources of growth and therefore not to be treated within any simple dualistic framework. In *The Peaceable Kingdom* (1954) there is still a clear distinction, and *separation*, between good and evil, innocence and the predator. The fox of "The Cunning of an Age" and "This Dreaming Everywhere", the man-fox of "No Land Like It" and "First it was Singing", might, it seems, have lived peaceably were it not for a fortuitous threat, something not endemic to life itself—perhaps even imposed by an all-powerful condemnatory decree. The lost kingdom is described in the past tense, and with such tenderness that the earth which "curved away in a style he knew to be home" seems threatened as soon as it is described, even before the

> spot
> Of red spat up at his eyes

and the hunt is on. In fact, the wind that joins the hunters was always there, though its blackness streamed "over the top of the hill" harmlessly. The difference to the fox, though, is radical. Things look the same but are forever changed. And the change comes from outside. In the companion poem, *This Dreaming Everywhere*, it is therefore natural for the fox to feel

> unrepentant anger
> The hate of hate the moist smell
> Of blood running
>
> Through the riders' red coats.

(I quote the poet's final version, which shows incidentally the greater inwardness of Silkin's mature style.)

The tender and angry vision of *The Peaceable Kingdom*, relatively simple in its articulation, allows for loving incantation: not mere wishful thinking, but the will to cherish (and to *will* that will) of a heart still innocent of its own guilt. I am thinking of "A Space in Air", "Death of a Son", "Never any Dying", "For David Emmanuel".

The Two Freedoms (1958) has moved, in the main, beyond such possibilities. It is stylistically less assured. The poet seems to be casting about for a mode of statement that will distance and give general significance to radical changes of attitude. His appeals to the Bible, to Milton and Eliot, are particularly clear, though there is no question of mere imitation—the pressure of individual needs is too strong. Typical are "The Third Death", "And I turned from the Inner Heart", "Hymn to the Solid World": the titles alone tell part of the story. Here the peaceable kingdom is implicitly contrasted with "the actual kingdom" (a phrase from the last-mentioned poem).

And I turned from the inner heart having no further cause
To look there, to pursue what lay inside,
And moved to the world not as I would have world
But as it lay before me . . .

The relevance of this to the matter and manner of the previous book is clear.
The Two Freedoms is the least intrinsically successful of Silkin's collections,
but it is not a wrong step. In it, he begins to deal openly with the Jewish
experience ("Light", "The Victims"); and even more significantly perhaps,
for his future development, begins to elaborate the cluster of images to which
I have referred. Certain features, of course, anticipate these from the begin-
ning. But it is in *The Two Freedoms* that close *analogous* relationships are
insistently suggested between man and the natural world (for instance in
"The Return", "Bronze Noon", "From . . . the Animal Dark" and "Poem").
There is also an early attempt to formulate the relationship of man and woman
in terms of natural processes, processes treated not as decorations or expres-
sions but as literal parallels. A woman's eyes on a man are like the "steady
main"

> Which through the texturing earth
> Is always working its queer alchemy.

There is a certain clumsiness of over-precision in the eye being described as
"curved scalding" (with connotations of the sea's curve and its saltness, and
of the saltness of human tears). But this neo–Metaphysical touch, not unique
in Silkin's work, is a mere excrescence on a deeper purpose. "The Breaking
of Rock", in the next volume, reverses the image so that the man is the ocean
and the woman rock, a reversal which lays the ground for the much more
adequate imagery of a poem like "Something has been Teased from Me", in
Nature with Man. The significant features are: the notion of rock breaking
down into particles, the association of woman with rock *and* soil and of man
with the agency capable of bringing about the transformation from one to the
other (for rock, stone, brick are themselves associated, as early as "Death of a
Son", with death, inertness, lack of consciousness, sterility). The terminology
in which Silkin handles both civilisation and the human body under the
threat of death is also revealing. The first passage comes from "Light", the
second from "Poem".

> the Germans found
>
> > Civilisation to be
> > Fragile, a chandelier-like lilac, nor hard
> > > Such multiplicity of
> > Singular petals to dash in the might of the wind.
>
> *
>
> And now we speak of death
> Each stress of life trembles, disintegrate of
> Experience, several-branched, forming one tree though,

Multitudinously branched inside
My head.

It is clear from these passages and others that the poet's view of life involves
already a highly complex, articulated, "multitudinous" structure, and that
this conception allows him to englobe, without smudging, the veins of con-
tradiction to which he is agonisingly sensitive. This is the point of "Depths"
in *The Re-Ordering of the Stones*.

This later volume (1961) is indeed a "re-ordering". In some respects, it
amounts to a devastation, though temporary, of the poet's normal approach
to his subjects and forms. Before and after this volume his manner tends to be
tentative and, simultaneously, ruthlessly insistent. In *The Re-Ordering of the
Stones* (in terms of the imagery we are discussing, a significant title) he becomes
explicit, even forthright, and the forms show an immediate and obvious
change, from complex syntax and stanzas to short phrases, short lines and an
absence of stanza-divisions. This description does not cover all the poems,
but characterises the most striking differences between this book and those
which precede it. The re-ordering clearly involved an attempt at sorting out,
and to some extent mastering in *intellectual* terms, personal and social themes
which had so far remained partially latent. Jewish experience is taken up
again, in relation to atrocities committed against the Jews of York in 1190 and
of Europe in our own time. Silkin tends, as one might anticipate, to see these,
and the traces they leave behind in individuals and in societies, as perversions
of natural functions, as tumours or growths, as the desire to procreate

Changed into a labyrinth of cruelties.

Similarly, reverting to the soil-image, a man deprived of love by a barren
society and forced to resort to pornography offers to other men "the purchase
of loose sands", so that

those following
Fell on the clambering grains and gave
To a dry planet drier loves
Eviscerated of the desire
To create anything
But the compositions of death.

Here the rôle of Silkin's frequent references to the natural liquids of life, to
the secretions of living things—saliva, tears, the "milk of pulped grass",
semen, "micturating roots", blood, the vaginal flow, the breast's milk—
becomes evident. All are signs of that life, they oppose the sterility of the
desert, their poisoning or cessation signals death. And any revulsion they
arouse is therefore profoundly ambivalent.

The image of stone broken to make soil is treated from a slightly different
angle in the first of two beautiful complementary poems that conclude this
volume, "The Possibility" and "The Wholeness".

> Tiny stones
> Have misery
> Unforfeited though bound with
> Good roots.

(Compare these lines with the last eleven of "Savings".) And yet, later on,

> the mental
> Forces billow, and joy
> If it is joy, as we are torn
> Quickens you to grow;

> And then
> The billowings of
> The entire meadow of curved stem.

The "billow" of growth counters the billows of the storm in "The Possibility". The relevance of these images needs no commentary. But perhaps the control of language can be quickly noticed: the poignant choice of *quickens* and *entire*, the plural *wheats* and the singular *stem* which, with their abnormality, draw attention to an almost overwhelming process of fecundity, such that

> Silent in

> The stirring
> Crop, the predator
> Is dismayed, and takes flight.

But the dominant if not final impression left by *The Re-Ordering of the Stones* is, intellectually at least, rendered in "Asleep?" and "The Measure". The latter sees man as "formed to love", but appallingly

> Man's love disintegrates
> In the spaces void of him.

The feeling is similar to that recorded in Tony Connor's "Names in Stone" (quoted elsewhere in these pages). And

> that shape
> Or measure, in awareness
> Through love of what we are,
> Is that measure of space death is.

"Asleep?" in turn insists that

> everything that is
> Is agony, in this sense:
> That things war to survive.
> Pain is complex, something akin
> To a stone with veins of colour
> In it, that cross and cross
> But never reconcile

Into one swab of colour
Or the stone that contains them.

Silkin's poetry aims at an embodiment of

intellect
Coupled to the embraces,
The convictions, of feeling.

The image is relevantly sexual. The relationship of man and woman is a fundamental emblem of separateness and relationship. *Nature with Man* (1965), asserting mankind's relationship to and difference from the unconscious natures from which he grew (in the poem "Nature with Man"), contains a near perfect paradigm of symbiosis: "Something has been Teased from Me" is too long to quote entire, and since partial quotation would fail to show the interpenetration of the themes we have been discussing, I hope the reader may be able to turn to it. The poem presents a man, a woman, and the child about to be born of their union. That union has since failed and the adults must now grow "unnaturally", through separation. But the original relationship is handled in terms of the dependence of grass (man) on soil (woman), and of soil on grass for its firmness, its "composure". And the child, too, grows in the mother

persisting as grass, a blade of bone and flesh
Lifting to consciousness,

a part of the man fastened in the woman despite her later rejection of him. The terms of that rejection, again, have social implications, since it arises from the woman's intolerance of something which, though dependent on her, is utterly different. She cannot accept, that is, a symbiotic relationship, but seeks to impose identity. (Comparable issues reappear in the flower poems—the poet's own commentary on these, at the end of the volume, needs no expansion.) The poem gathers together and interrelates at least four central themes: man's relatedness to nature and its processes; his difference; the dual though not dualistic root of love and growth (woman is soil to the man who can grow in her—when, that is, she is "a woman to a man", as she longs and fails to be in "Amana Grass"—but soil was once stone and, therefore, it would seem, represents a metamorphosis of destructive forces, perhaps even retains particles of death: suffering is comparably ambivalent); and the wider social implications of any division or community between individual lovers.

Amana Grass (1971) cannot pass undiscussed. It continues the exploration of the matrix. Referring himself now to Israel and to America, Silkin writes poem-sequences more explicitly social than all but a few of his earlier poems. (A similar orientation is evident in *Killhope Wheel* of the same year.) The title poem attempts what amounts to a summary. It is enough to point to the title itself, to the "filaments of root, everything" that tangle under the earth, to the woman's legs

> Stockinged, their tan rushes to compare with the net's colour
>
> (a detail of more than visual significance), to the grass that
>
> > tightens fierce roots on fractions of soil
> while
> > The soil, from stone, in passivity, grins; is to ingest all.

These lines, near the beginning of the poem, cast a foreboding dread over the lovers' relationship, especially if they are understood in the context I have been outlining. Further on, we find that the angels' "sapphired and webbed flesh" is no longer to be seen in the sky. The train has been described as linking "points in which the human crouches". To grow means to fight amid natures whose "egotisms conflict", and the man requires his woman to pay out

> > the veined, the thin, lines
> > Of your shape in durable contour.

It is beyond the scope of this discussion to do more than point to the ubiquity, in *Amana Grass*, of such references to a webbed, veined, filamented, inter-linked world—though here these images are deeply infected. I do not believe the poem to be successful. It attempts to carry more weight than its mode permits, and the poet has not solved the problems raised by his introduction of dialogue. But this is a growing-point: a long narrative poem on which Silkin has recently been engaged tackles the problems of dialogue and of social scope much more convincingly. My point is, simply, that the matrix is still, in this latest book, a viable basis for further development.

It would be wrong to follow such a short discussion with any overall judgement. Silkin is a genuine artist: an explorer, never a reproducer of his own or of other writers' acquisitions. He is often felicitous, and often clumsy or archaic; at times crystalline (in the fullest sense), at others difficult, even matted. He has, indeed, the faults of his qualities. It is as easy to point to awkwardness in such a writer as it is foolish to stop at it. His work embodies vital impulses and these are bound not to be self-protectingly tidy: they are about other business. The "open" overall form of the best poems, together with the complex internal controls that operate on syntax, word-choice and imagery, convey on a stylistic level a dominant onward thematic process, together with a minute hold on the "perpetual combinations and permuta-tions" which that process must not sacrifice or brutalise. There is, I think, something of crucial value for the 'seventies in a poet who can conceive, utterly without mere fancifulness, of a world of "mind and matter" whose various elements conflict and yet enter into (generally symbiotic) relation-ships that effect both personal and social realities.

On Charles Tomlinson

by Calvin Bedient

CHARLES Tomlinson is the most considerable English poet to have made his way since the Second World War. There is more to see along that way, more to meditate, more solidity of achievement, more distinction of phrase, more success as, deftly turning, hand and mind execute the difficult knot that makes the poem complete, than in the work of any of Tomlinson's contemporaries. It is true that the way is strait; but Tomlinson would have it so. For his is a holding action: he is out to save the world for the curious and caring mind. And if he is narrow, he is only so narrow as a searching human eye and a mind that feeds and reflects on vision—an eye that to everything textured, spatial, neighbouring, encompassing, humanly customary, and endlessly and beautifully modulated by light, dusk, weather, the slow chemistry of years, comes like a cleansing rain—as also like a preserving amber. The quality everywhere present in Tomlinson's poetry is a peculiarly astringent, almost dry, but deeply meditated love; this is true whether his subject is human beings, houses, lamplight, chestnuts, lakes, or glass. Tomlinson is a poet of exteriority and its human correlatives: the traditional, the universal, the unchangeable, the transparencies of reflection. And he is thus the opposite of a lyric or "confessional" poet. Yet what a mistake it would be to confuse this outwardness with superficiality. To read Tomlinson is continually to *sound*: to meet with what lies outside the self in a simultaneous grace of vision and love. Tomlinson's chief theme is, in his own phrase, "the fineness of relationships". And though his poetry is in great measure restricted to this theme, the theme itself is an opening and a wideness.

Tomlinson's theme, or his strict relation to it, is one with his originality; and this originality is most salient in his poems on the world's appearances. We have been asked to admire so many poets of "nature" that we can but sigh, or look blank, to hear it announced that still another one has come along; and we will greet with scepticism any claims to originality. But Tomlinson is unmistakably an original poet. There is in him, it is true, a measure of Wordsworth: the at-homeness in *being* as against *doing*, the wise passivity, the love of customariness, and what Pater spoke of as Wordsworth's "very fine apprehension of the limits within which alone philosophical imaginings have any place in true poetry". Both poets awaken, moreover, in Shelley's phrase, "a sort of thought in sense". But how different in each is the relation of sense to thought. In Wordsworth, sense fails into thought. Nature strikes Wordsworth like a bolt; it is the charred trunk that he reflects upon. His thought looks back to sense and its elation, hungering. In Tomlinson, by contrast, the mind hovers over what the eye observes; the two are coterminus. Together, they surprise a sufficiency in the present; and if passion informs them, it is a passion for objectivity. For the most part, Wordsworth discovers himself in nature—it is this, of course, that makes him a Romantic poet. Tomlinson, on the other hand, discovers the nature of nature: a classical artist, he is all taut, responsive detachment.

The sufficiency (or something very near it) of the spatial world to Tomlinson's eye, mind, and heart, the gratefulness of appearances to a sensibility so unusual as his, at once radically receptive and restrained, separates him from such poets as D. H. Lawrence and Wallace Stevens—though the latter, indeed, exerted a strong early influence. This marked spiritual contentment —which makes up the message and quiet power and healing effluence of Tomlinson's work—may be conveniently illustrated by one of his shorter poems, "The Gossamers".

> Autumn. A haze is gold
> By definition. This one lit
> The thread of gossamers
> That webbed across it
> Out of shadow and again
> Through rocking spaces which the sun
> Claimed in the leafage. Now
> I saw for what they were
> These glitterings in grass, on air,
> Of certainties that ride and plot
> The currents in their tenuous stride
> And, as they flow, must touch
> Each blade and, touching, know
> Its green resistance. Undefined
> The haze of autumn in the mind
> Is gold, is glaze.

This poem is in part a parable on the propriety of the self-forgetting mind. The mind—it seems to hint—is in itself a wealth, like a gold haze; the mind turned outward, however, is wealth piled upon wealth, a glaze upon particular things—a haze lighting up glittering gossamers. This reflection, which encloses the poem, forms part of its own wealth; and yet it is to the poem only what the enclosing haze is to the gossamers: an abstract richness outdone by and subservient to the vivid interest of the concrete. The poem is as good as its word: proclaiming the supremacy of the particular, it stands and delivers. To the tenuous intellect, it presents a living, green resistance. Tomlinson's poem discovers gossamers as a scientist might discover a new chemical; indeed, Tomlinson himself has quoted with covetous interest from Lévi-Strauss's *The Savage Mind* a phrase applicable to his own cast of thought: "the science of the concrete". Of course the phrase omits the grateful quality of Tomlinson's attention: a scientist observes, Tomlinson regards, has regard. The gossamers are his host, he their thankful guest. And as a consequence of this humble gratitude, of this self-abnegating attention, Tomlinson brings into the human record—as nothing else has ever done—the look and being of gossamers, an obscure yet precious portion of articulated space. Impossible, now, not to know how gossamers plot currents, ride air, tenuously stride, connect and resist. Modest as it is, the poem is as good as a front row, a microscope, the opening of a long-buried treasure.

With this example before us, we may perhaps approach to a sharper view of Tomlinson's originality as a poet of nature. Among such poets, he is the anchorite of appearances. To poetry about them he brings an unexpected, an unparalleled, selflessness and objectivity. An ascetic of the eye, Tomlinson pushes poetry closer to natural philosophy than it has ever been before—and at the same time proselytises for fine relationships with space, writes and persuades in earnestness, if not in zeal. Into an area crowded with hedonists, mystics, rapturous aesthetes, he comes equipped with a chaste eye and a mind intent upon exactitude. Nature may indeed be a book; but not until now, say the chaste eye, the intent mind, has the book been more than scanned. The fine print, the difficult clauses, the subtle transitions, the unfamiliar words— Tomlinson will pore over them all. And his language will be as learned and meticulous, his dedication as passionate, his ego as subdued, as that of the true scholar—though mercifully he will also exercise, what few scholars possess, a deft and graceful feeling for form.

The clue to Tomlinson's originality lies in the apparent incongruity between his chosen subject and his temperament. In part, the subject is all the opulence of the visual world—jewelled glass, golden gossamers, fiery clouds. The temperament, by contrast, is strict and chaste, not far from sternness, flourishing only in an atmosphere of "fecund chill", of "temperate sharpness". It is akin to that grain of wheat which, unless it die, cannot bring forth fruit. Ordinarily, of course, men of such temperament turn to God, to the State, to the poor, to science, to learning. They would no sooner turn to the sensual earth than the pious would turn to the Devil. Or if they did, they would bring a scourge, not a strict curiosity indistinguishable from the most discrete and delicate love. A nature of which there is no "point" to seize, as the first of the "Four Kantian Lyrics" suggests, exists, after all, only to the senses; and the senses are notorious panders to the self, tributary streams of the torrential Ego. And yet what the chaste temperament desires is, precisely, to be selfless. Men of such mould would fall to the ground and emerge— something else, something richer. An anti-hedonist who cultivates his senses, an ascetic of

> the steady roar of evening,
> Withdrawing in slow ripples of orange,
> Like the retreat of water from sea-caves . . .

—these are patent contradictions in terms. Tomlinson, politely denying the contradiction, steps in among the hullabalooers and coolly and dedicatedly clears serious ground of his own in the region of the senses, in the forests and "further fields" of nontranscendent space. The result is a nature poetry as unique in its classical temperateness as in its consecration to the Being of Space, to the face and actions of our natural environment.

Tomlinson looks outward, and what he sees becomes, not himself exactly, but his content. Seeing discovers his limits—but they are the limits of a vase or a window, not of a prison. Indeed, to Tomlinson it is a happy circumstance that the world is "other"; were it identical with the self, there would be no refuge from solitude, nothing to touch as one reaches out.

> Out of the shut cell of that solitude there is
>   One egress, past point of interrogation.
> Sun is, because it is not you; you are
>   Since you are self, and self delimited
> Regarding sun.

Observer and observed stand apart, then, as the necessary poles of a substantiated being. The eye is the first of philosophers; seeing turns up the soil of ontology. Beholding thus applies to the spirit a metaphysical balm. The "central calm" of appearances, their very thereness, gives a floor to the world. So Tomlinson walks and looks, and he finds it enough. Philosophically, he begins in nakedness—in nakedness, not in disinheritance; for the scrutinising eye detects no twilight of past dreams of transcendence, only a present wealth of finite particulars, an ever shifting but sharply focused spectacle. In Tomlinson, the spirit, as if ignorant of what once sustained it—Platonic forms, Jehovah, the Life Force, the whole pantheon of the metaphysical mind—finds bliss in trees and stones that are merely trees and stones. And doubtless this implies an especially fine, not a particularly crude, capacity for wonder. Tomlinson is one of the purest instances in literature of the contemplative, as distinct from the speculative, mind. No poet has ever before regarded the intricate tapestry of Space with such patient and musing pleasure, with so little dread or anxiety to retreat through a human doorway or under the vaulted roof of a church. On the other hand, neither has any poet been less inclined to eat of the apples in his Eden. Tomlinson holds up to the tapestry a magnifying glass: he is all absorption, but, courteously, he keeps his place. And evidently his reward is a sense of answered or multiplied being. Let others—Dylan Thomas, D. H. Lawrence, E. E. Cummings—mount nature in ecstatic egoism. They will not really see her, except distortedly, through the heat waves of their own desire for union; they will not be companioned. Let still others—Thomas Hardy, Robert Frost, Philip Larkin—suspect the worst of her, dread her, hint at wrinkled flesh beneath the flowered dress. They, too, will be left with only themselves. Tomlinson, putting himself by, will gain the world.

What Tomlinson values in human beings is a similar facing-away from the self, a rock-like, disciplined submergence in *being*. For the most part, the people in his poems are either models of subservience to task or tradition, as in "Return to Hinton", "The Farmer's Wife", "The Hand at Callow Hill Farm", "Oxen", "Geneva Restored", "Maillol"—or examples of the discontent of desiring: the ambitious castellan of "The Castle", the Symbolists of "Antecedents", the "Black Nude" who is sullen until she learns the "truce" of the eye, the restless poet in "Up at La Serra", and "Mr. Brodsky", the American "whose professed and long / pondered-on passion / was to become a Scot". Like the hills and seas of his poems, Tomlinson is conservative through and through. If he could, one feels, he would bring all the world to a halt: to the "luminous stasis" of contemplation. The dread he conveys is not of nature, nor even of human nature, but of the "rational" future and its present busy machines—of what is happening to the earth, our host, and to the distinctively human source of our contentment, the filaments of custom that hold us lovingly to place. Better a contented poverty, he believes, than a standardised prosperity:

> No hawk at wrist, but blessed by sudden sun
>   And with a single, flaring hen that tops the chair
> Blooming beside her where she knits. Before the door
>   And in the rainsoaked air, she sits as leisurely
> As spaces are with hillshapes in them. Yet she is small—
>   If she arrests the scene, it is her concentration
> That commands it, the three centuries and more
>   That live in her, the eyes that frown against the sun
> Yet leave intact the features' kindliness, the anonymous
>   Composure of the settled act. Sufficient to her day
> Is her day's good, and her sufficiency's the refutation
>   Of that future where there'll be what there already is—
> Prosperity and ennui, and none without the privilege
>   To enjoy them both . . .
>
>   ("Portrait of Mrs. Spaxton")

No doubt this leaves much to be said; but there is wisdom, passion, and sting in it, as well as beauty. In Tomlinson, the present as the latest and brimming moment of the past has both a first-rate poet and an able defender. "Farm-bred certainties", "ancestral certitude", or, as here, "three centuries and more"—these, to him, have the same sanctifying use as a beech tree or a mood of light: all are alike, for human beings, the conditions of an "anonymous/ Composure". All conduce to, all are food for, a contemplative life.

The Tomlinson of these portrait poems beholds not so much his subjects' individuality as their fine or fumbled relation to time and place: he beholds, in other words, their beholding. He is thus himself once removed—though, in another sense, also himself twice over. In his other poems he beholds natural objects directly and minutely—standing back only so far as will allow him to reflect on the virtue of the eye. In either case, he is the poet of contemplation. It is this that gives him his strong and peculiar identity. The atmosphere of his work is that of a calm and cherishing attention. It is an atmosphere in which the objects of this world suddenly stand forth as part of the beautiful mystery of the founded. Whatever can be apprehended as the locus of a fine relation, dwelt on with intent devotion—whether gossamers slung in a haze, or a woman knitting in the rain-soaked air—becomes, to this poet, an "Eden image"; at once pristine and permanent, it radiates being. Tomlinson's sensibility homes to everything well established, and alights, and broods. And though it comes for grace, it comes also like a grace. It consecrates. This rare and valuable quality, never in excess but always temperate and chaste, is the essence of almost every Tomlinson poem.

It is this patient intention to consecrate that saves Tomlinson from the rapids of the senses. Indeed, it is doubtless a fear of the sensual and gluttonous Ego that gives thrust to the intention to consecrate. Accordingly—at least until lately—beholding in Tomlinson has seemed as much a discipline as a delight. In such recent poems as "Clouds" and "In the Fullness of Time", Tomlinson comes through as impressively equal to what he contemplates—a large, gracious, and answering stability. In many of his early poems, by contrast, he seems a trifle *determined* to see chastely and feel calmly. Indeed, so little excitement, so little spontaneous joy do these poems convey that their seeing seems rather more a discipline than a delight. The description never blurs, but neither does it glow with enthusiasm; no sentiment ever spills over the detail into a general, joyful reference. Not that Tomlinson's sensibility appears ever to have been in great need of restraint. Though exquisite, it is far from being abundant. But disciplined it nonetheless is. Adding its own kind of intensity to Tomlinson's poems is the reactive force of a self-rejection. Here contemplation is, in Tomlinson's own word, a shriving. Light, this poet says in "Something: A Direction", is split by human need: accept the light, and you heal both the light and your need. At each dawn the sun is recovered

> in a shriven light
> And you, returning, may to a shriven self
> As from the scene, your self withdraws.

So it is that Tomlinson would make of beholding an *ascesis*, a chaste, chill atmosphere to cool the hot and clouding Ego.

In consequence, Tomlinson's poems have something of the severity of a religious cell. Whitewashed of the self, chill, close-packed as stone walls, they are rooms for intense and selfless meditation. Austerity marks both their language and their movement. The diction has the dryness of exposure to mental weather—though the dryness of living bark, not of stones. Learned and exact, it joins the concrete with academic abstraction: in "Gossamers", for example, the sun is said to *claim* the spaces that *rock* in the leafage; and if the gossamers *ride* and *plot*, they are *certainties* that do so. Tomlinson's

descriptions, accordingly, both feed and ration the eye. Seeing passes some-
what difficultly into thought and stops just short of an easy clarity. At the
same time, the depictions give out only so much emotional warmth as they
counter with the chill of a rational diction. Even when almost entirely
concrete, this poet's delineations remain anatomy:

> A trailed and lagging grass, a pin-point island
> Drags the clear current's face it leans across
> In ripple-wrinkles. At a touch
> It has ravelled the imaged sky till it could be
> A perplexity of metal, spun
> Round a vortex, the sun flung off it
> Veining the eye like a migraine—it could
> Scarcely be sky . . .

Like a window that allows vision through only one side, this looks out lucidly
toward surfaces, is blind and indifferent to the inner life. Concrete with
respect to spatial things, it is abstract to feeling. Not that it fails to touch feel-
ing; for there is delight here—the delight of detected resemblance and, deeper
still, the pleasure that comes from perceiving that a thing has escaped being
simply itself—"it could / Scarcely be sky. . . ." And this is to say that there
is considerable imaginative life in the description—an aspect of the poetry
that we must return to. All the same, Tomlinson analyses and photographs
the current as one who stands over against it, alien though not estranged. He
neither attempts to become the water, as any number of poets might have
done, nor leaves chinks in his description for sentiment. With Robbe-Grillet,
his passage declares that "to describe things . . . is deliberately to place
onself outside them, facing them", and also that "there is in existence in the
world something that is not man, that takes no notice of him". So the stream
is itself, and the words merely serve its being. While Tomlinson stands over
against the water, his language, as it were, stands over against him and on the
side of what faces him. Indeed, until recently, it has even turned a deaf ear to
itself, avoiding all but the most discrete self-echoing—as here, for instance,
the tucked-away rhyme of "lagging" and "drag".

Metre is also, of course, a self-reference of sound, and Tomlinson's verse
logically eschews it, is "free". It is not, however, free as the verse of D. H.
Lawrence or William Carlos Williams is free: it is not free to empathise with
its subjects. Empathic rhythm, like metre, awakens feeling: the difference, of
course, is that where metre is emotionally introverted, empathic *vers libre* is
extroverted. So the metre of Christina Rossetti's

> My heart is like a singing bird
>   Whose nest is in a water'd shoot;
> My heart is like an apple-tree
>   Whose boughs are bent with thick-set fruit . . .

turns feeling around and around, like a dancer in a music box, while the rhythm of Lawrence's "Fish",

> Aqueous, subaqueous
> Submerged
> And wave-thrilled . . .

or Williams' "Rain",

> the trees
> are become
> beasts fresh risen
> from
>   the sea—
> water
>
> trickles
> from the crevices of
> their hides . . .

sends feeling outward into objects. Tomlinson's rhythm, by contrast, is neither extroverted nor introverted, but emotionally suspended, stilled and poised in meditation. It springs free of the hypnotic spin of metre, but holds itself back from the emotional free-lancing of *vers libre*. It is free, not to dance new steps to the music of a vital happening, but free, precisely, from the tug and engulfing tide of feeling. Just as a rational element checks emotional participation in Tomlinson's descriptions, so an approximate accentual balance and a kind of sanity of isochronism reins in feeling in Tomlinson's rhythm—a rhythm that moves narrowly between the mind-lulling security of metre and the mind-dissolving fluidity of free verse:

> Two stand
> admiring morning.
> A third, unseen as yet
> approaches across upland
> that a hill and a hill's wood
> hide. The two
> halving a mutual good,
> both watch a sun
> entering sideways
> the slope of birches . . .

Here the first two lines have an approximate quantity or length; they also balance in beat. The next three add a beat and balance one another. The sixth, though it drops an accent, keeps the length with its two long vowels and caesura. And in the last two lines, the rhythm quickens back to its initial measure. Reading Tomlinson, one comes instinctively to look for this sort of rough yet reliable recurrence. Like the next bead in a rosary, the accentual repetition provides a necessary sense of stability. On the other hand, shifting and uncertain as it is, it discourages complicities of the pulse. It leaves the mind strung, alert, and waiting.

This condition is heightened by the frequent breakage of the lines *against* phrasal expectations and unities. The lines end long or short, in mid air; and thus left jutting and jagged, they spur the mind to attention. So of the swan in "Canal" we read:

> . . . Sinuously
> both the live
> bird and the bird
> the water bends
> into a white and wandering
> reflection of itself,
> go by in grace
> a world of objects . . .

Obviously the lines here work against any sharing of the swans' sinuous motion. The swans may be all grace, but the lines, as such, are all stiff angles. Typically fragmenting sentences down to phrases, then further fragmenting some of the phrases, omitting expected and interjecting unexpected commas, Tomlinson's lines retard and brake the mind, suspend and distance its grasp, so that when full comprehension finally comes, it arrives, as it were, soundless and clear, unaccompanied by the resonant surge of an affective rhythm.

Altogether, then, there is in Tomlinson's slow, inorganic rhythm of stops and starts and precarious, uncertain balances no wave for imagination to surf on, no independence and autonomy of accent. And yet, for all that, it has character and charm; one acquires a taste for it. Toughly flexile, it introduces a new quality into verse, as if after centuries of beating the drum of the blood, a rhythm had at last been found for the mind. Anything more fluent and facile—so one feels while reading him—would be intolerably flaccid. Whether in short lines, as in "Canal", or in medium lines like these,

> It happened like this: I heard
> from the farm beyond, a grounded
> churn go down. The sound
> chimed for the wedding of the mind
> with what one could not see,
> the further fields, the seamless
> spread of space . . .

or in the longer lines he has favoured of late,

> Cloudshapes are destinies, and they
>   Charging the atmosphere of a common day,
> Make it the place of confrontation where
>   The dreamer wakes to the categorical call
> And clear cerulean trumpet of the air . . .

the movement serves as a kind of stiffening, not only standing the lines up to the mind but constituting in its own right an aesthetic value, a virility like starch in a formal shirt.

So it is that, in both his relation to his subject and his poetic manner, Tomlinson is an original—and what is more, with an originality that counts, that comes to seem, while we read him, and the more we read him, the very intelligence of the eye, the very rhythm of a chaste beholding. And the main-spring of this originality, it has been suggested, lies in the singleness of Tomlinson's contemplative purpose, the rigour of his attempt to make of the observation of nature through the medium of poetry a shriving of the self— a naked, though not unthoughtful, encounter with appearances.

What makes Tomlinson an important poet is partly his originality; but of course it is not his originality that makes him a poet. If his poetry contained observation alone, it would be of no more interest—though of no less interest, either—than a camera set rolling in a snowy field or by the sea. Tomlinson is a poet, in part, because of a consistent, masculine elegance of language, and also in part because of his feeling for rhythm. But mostly he is a poet because he uses, and excites, imagination, and because this imagination is not of a light or gratuitous kind, but steeped in feeling, organic, pregnant with a response to life. Deeply and richly conceived, Tomlinson's poems are neither the mere notations of a stenographic eye, nor cold slabs of reflection; they begin, they vault, and they conclude in feeling. "That art is selective," writes Dewey in *Art as Experience*, "is a fact universally recognised. It is so because of the role of emotion in the act of expression. Any predominant mood auto-matically exludes all that is uncongenial with it." And the unity of Tomlinson's poems is fundamentally the unity of a magisterial and imaginative mood.

To be sure, no magistrate was ever more humble or amenable while still retaining and exercising his proper powers. Tomlinson's imagination *attends* to observable reality with almost the patience that characterises and gives distinction to his eye. Like a fine atmosphere, it can be gentle to the point of invisibility, so that objects and places, and not the poet himself, seem to be communicants of feeling. And when it does grow dense, it thickens as light thickens, making its objects as well as itself more vivid. Impossible to imagine a closer co-operation between the conceiving mind and the receiving eye. Tomlinson's imagination takes its cues, its colours, its composure, from the Persian carpet of the visual world itself.

From what has already been said, it will be seen at once that this delicate co-operation is a matter of strict principle. Indeed, it is largely the imagina-tion—that genie and temptress of the self—that the straps of *seeing* are intended to confine. If Tomlinson's poems are imaginative, it is almost in their own despite. They are imaginative, so to speak, only because they must be in order to qualify as poetry. Granted their way, so it seems, they would be, instead, only a wondering silence. Nor does this principle of imaginative containment—so jealously adhered to—remain implicit. Several of the poems give a sharp rap to the skull of Romanticism, consistently conceived as an egoistic imagination bringing to birth frenzied and false worlds of its own. For example, "Distinctions" chides Pater for indicating that the blue of the sea gives way to "pinks, golds, or mauves", "Farewell to Van Gogh" patronises that painter's "instructive frenzy", and "Maillol" glances at the "flickering frenzy of Rodin". Indeed, it is the fault of these, as well as of two or three other poems, that they seem to exist chiefly for the sake of their doctrine. Of course, all of Tomlinson is doctrinal—the bias toward passivity, receptivity, and self-effacement being as overwhelming as it is avowed, determined, and morally aggressive. But for the most part this doctrine proves unobjectionable, for the simple reason that poetry takes it over. In the anti-Romantic poems, however, the doctrine tends to tread the poetry down. And, left alone on the field, Tomlinson's vigilance against the self's excesses itself emerges as excessive. His strictures are too tight, they hold their breath in prim disapproval. "To emulate such confusion," he writes of a scuffle between wind and trees,

> One must impoverish the resources of folly,
> But to taste it is medicinal.

And just as the first line, here, drops a demolition ball on the point, so the tasting in the second seems a trifle too fastidious. Similarly, "The Jam Trap", which glances at harmful egoistic hedonism in its picture of flies immersed "Slackly in sweetness", comes through as so unfairly and extremely reductive that it makes Tomlinson, and not Romanticism, seem wrong-headed.

And yet, unobtrusive and stopped down as it is, Tomlinson's imagination is, as was suggested, precisely the gift and power that makes his poetry poetic. Though obviously far from being ample, headlong, or richly empowering, neither, on the other hand, is it faint or apologetic. It is as active as it is attentive, as forceful as it is discrete. As procreative mood, it is the tension and coherence that keeps the poems brimming, and the still depth that moves the detail toward us, magnified. As subjective transmutation, moreover, it is the gold, the glaze, that makes the detail glitter. Subtract it from the poems, and only sorry fragments would remain. Of course, the farther Tomlinson stands off from objects, the more conspicuous the mediation of his emotional and imaginative presence becomes, increasing like the green of deepening waters. Thus bare lines like these from "The Hill",

> Do not call to her there,
> but let her go
> bearing our question
> in her climb: what does she
> confer on the hill, the hill on her?

are obviously tense with imaginative concentration: with the conceived drama of contemplation, and the conceived mystery of relationship. Yet, whether noticed or not, this controlling and conceiving element is nonetheless almost always present and always felt in Tomlinson's poems. Even the largely "factual" poems resonate under imagination's bow. Consider, for example, even so unambitious a poem as "Letter from Costa Brava":

> Its crisp sheets, unfolded,
> Give on to a grove, where
> Citrons conduct the eye
> Past the gloom of foliage
> Towards the glow of stone. They write
> Of a mesmeric clarity
> In the fissures of those walls
> And of the unseizable lizards, jewelled
> Upon them. But let them envy
> What they cannot see:
> This sodden, variable green
> Igniting against the gray.

In the knock and juxtaposition of these two glowing and gloomy landscapes, the one dryly sensual, the other soggily spiritual, what a fine effect is produced by the unexpected, proud, and loving preference—so deftly made understandable—for the puritanically passionate English scene. It was imagination that caught and conveyed both the similarity and the deep polarity of these scenes, their different registers in the life of the spirit. And of course it was imagination that produced here and there the fillip of metaphor, adding local intensities to the shaping tension of the whole: a stimulation felt most strongly in the adjectives and in the verbid *igniting*, so boldly yet so rightly qualifying the suggestion of *sodden*. And elsewhere in Tomlinson one finds equal felicities of the imaginative power of augmenting and interpreting appearances without denying them—for example, the rose in "Frondes Agrestes", seen

> Gathered up into its own translucence
> Where there is no shade save colour . . .

or, in "Prometheus", the trees that

> Continue raining though the rain has ceased
> In a cooled world of incessant codas . . .

However adverse Tomlinson may be to imagination, clearly there is no lack of it in his poetry.

By now it will have become apparent that Tomlinson is something less of the simple observer and something more of a poet than he himself seems inclined to believe. The view that he encourages of himself, through his poems, is neither accurate nor fully just. Listen to the poems and you will conclude that Tomlinson is but the servant or the guest of appearances. Experience the poems, on the other hand, and you will know that he is something more, and more difficult—namely, their abettor, their harvest, their fulfilment. And this is to say that there is a notable discrepancy, widening at times into a contradiction, between what the poems declare and what they are and do. They speak, as it were, in ignorance of themselves. Thus, though they recommend passivity, it is through their own activity. Though they would teach us to conserve, they themselves are creative and therefore innovative. As they urge us to silence before the multiple voices of space, they impress us with a distinctively human voice. And as they praise nature as our replenishment, they replenish us. So it is that what the right hand gives, the left hand takes away. In "Observation of Fact", to cite a specific instance, Tomlinson cautions:

> Style speaks what was seen,
> Or it conceals the observation
> Behind the observer: a voice
> Wearing a ruff . . .

and meanwhile delights us, in the concluding image, by speaking what has never been and never will be seen.

> I leave you
> To your one meaning, yourself alone . . .

he says of an upended tree in "Poem"; but what his vehemently anthropomorphic description actually leaves in the memory is not a tree but a creature crouching "on broken limbs / About to run forward". "Only we / Are inert," Tomlinson writes in "In Defence of Metaphysics"—and then, in observing that "Stones are like deaths. / They uncover limits", himself shows admirably more than inertia of mind. In "Chateau de Muzot", he says of the stone mass,

> A shriven self
> Looks out at it. You cannot
> Add to this. Footholds for foison
> There are none. Across stoneface
> Only the moss, flattened, tightly-rosetted
> Which, ignorant of who gives
> Accepts from all weathers
> What it receives, possessed
> By the nature of stone . . .

Yet in so describing it, Tomlinson obviously and wonderfully adds to it, finding footholds not only for the imaginative "foison" of rosetted moss but for the whole parable-conceit of gift, acceptance, and possession. Examples could be mutliplied.

Altogether, then, there is in Tomlinson a rebuke to the active, creative self that, coming from a poet, seems untutored. It is as if a Catholic priest were to celebrate, from the pulpit, with both passion and eloquence, the inward light: there is professional suicide in the sermon. What other poet is so insistently and recklessly forgetful of his own gift and its prerogatives? Virtually taking a giant erasure to his work, Tomlinson will write:

> Those facets of copiousness which I proposed
> Exist, do so when we have silenced ourselves.

Indeed, Tomlinson would thus erase more than his gift; he would erase human consciousness itself. For of course the only truly silenced human being is a dead one. Dewey is again to the point: as he observes, "nothing takes root in the mind when there is no balance between doing and receiving"; for "perception is an act of the going-out of energy in order to receive, not a withholding of energy," and though "the esthetic or undergoing phase of experience is receptive," an "adequate yielding of the self is possible only through a controlled activity that may well be intense". Though Tomlinson again and again salutes the "yielding", the "activity", as a rule, he leaves out of account. So in "A Given Grace" he commences:

> Two cups,
> a given grace,
> afloat and white
> on the mahogany pool
> of table. They unclench
> the mind, filling it
> with themselves . . .

And several lines later he concludes:

> you would not wish
> them other than they are—
> you, who are challenged
> and replenished by
> those empty vessels.

This is true, but only half true. For it is just as reasonable, and just as partial, to say that it is the empty vessels that have been filled, and filled by mind. Sophisticated poet though he is, Tomlinson yet falls into what Husserl calls "the natural unsophisticated standpoint" of consciousness, which assumes "an empty looking of an empty 'Ego'". Consciousness can indeed be invested, but only in so far as it invests; as Husserl observes, it is the ego that invests "the being of the world . . . with existential validity". Apart from consciousness, after all, the world is but a sweep and waste of energy unseen, unfelt, unheard, and untasted. Of poets, moreover, it may be said that they invest appearances doubly—not only with their mind and senses but with their imagination as well. Thus in "A Given Grace", while it is Tomlinson's eye that perceives and invests the two cups, it is his imagination that sees them floating in a mahogany pool, making them something other than they are. Facets of copiousness do indeed exist, but only in a dialectic between the self and the objective world.

It should be noted, however, that though Tomlinson has emphasized and done more than justice to the passive aspect of the self's liaison with space, he has managed to strike other notes of his theme as well. In fact, however unequally these may be pressed, the chord of his theme stands complete. Thus

in a fairly recent poem, "The Hill", Tomlinson celebrates at last—quite as if
he had never doubted it (as perhaps he had not)—consciousness as itself a
grace, a grace of giving. The female figure climbing the hill named in the title
is a type of the being-investing consciousness:

> She
> alone, unnamed (as it were),
> in making her thought's theme
> that thrust and rise,
> is bestowing a name . . .

A still more recent poem, "Adam", provides a partial gloss:

> We bring
> To a kind of birth all we can name . . .

So the hill stands forth, rounds out into being, through the generosity of the
girl's attention. The grace of consciousness consists in its active intentionality:
the girl *makes* her thought's theme that thrust and rise. It is, after all then,
stones that are inert. Indeed, a recoiling spring, Tomlinson perhaps goes too
far when, in "The Hill", he adds:

> . . . do not call to her there:
> let her go on,
> whom the early sun
> is climbing up with to the hill's crown—
> she, who did not make it, yet can make
> the sun go down by coming down.

In this instance, of course, the "making" is only a manner of speaking. And
yet here Tomlinson, for one rare and indulgent moment, encourages a
solipsistic illusion. Putting by the domestic uniform it usually wears in his
poems, the mind steps forward as almost a demi-urge, capable of making, by
a simple withdrawal of attention, a heavenly body slide out of the sky.

Of course the true grace of any and every relationship is neither a giving
nor a receiving, but an interchange and balance of the two. And toward this
inclusive reciprocity, Tomlinson may be said to have ripened. His early
attempts to render it do not quite come off, and are, perhaps, not quite
sincere, the self having been made too hollow a counter-weight to space. For
example, in "Reflections" Tomlinson writes:

> When we perceive, as keen
> As the bridge itself, a bridge inlaying the darkness
> Of smooth water, our delight acknowledges our debt—
> To nature, from whom we choose . . .

But this would seem, rather, an instance of being chosen, and the declaration
of self-determination does not convince. In some of the more recent poems,

by contrast, the self seems genuinely erect before the world it experiences. Perhaps no statement and evocation—for the poem is both—of a pristine and yet not unsophisticated encounter with environment, the mind and space meeting as two equal and mysterious realities, could be at once more justly delicate and soberly beautiful than "Swimming Chenango Lake". Here, as in "The Hill", the anonymous human figure is a type of consciousness—not, in this case, however, of consciousness as the only proud Climber of Creation, but as Creation's Swimmer, active in a dense, merciless element that "yet shows a kind of mercy sustaining him":

> . . . he has looked long enough, and now
> Body must recall the eye to its dependence
>   As he scissors the waterscape apart
> And sways it to tatters. Its coldness
>   Holding him to itself, he grants the grasp,
> For to swim is also to take hold
>   On water's meaning, to move in its embrace
> And to be, between grasp and grasping free.

Not only the mutuality of two alien orders of being, but the simultaneous doing and undergoing in human experience, finds in this poem a crystal paradigm.

So it is that, here and there in Tomlinson, the self has come into its own. And still more is this true in a few of the poems addressed to art. Despite his animadversions against Romanticism, Tomlinson has shown himself quite ready to think of art—especially music—as a spiritual flowering beyond anything offered by reality. Thus in "Flute Music" he notes:

> Seeing and speaking we are two men:
> The eye encloses as a window—a flute
> Governs the land, its winter and its silence.

An early poem, "Flute Music", may perhaps be written off as an accident of ventriloquism—the result of a saturation in Wallace Stevens. But in a later and more impressive poem, "Ode to Arnold Schoenberg", the same theme sounds again. "Natural" meaning, according to the ode, does not suffice: art satisfies by pursuing "a more than common meaning". The "unfolded word" not only renews "the wintered tree" of previous art, but creates and cradles space, filling it with verdure.

Is space ordinarily, then, a winter and a silence? Decisively, persuasively, the other poems answer "No". And yet the very fact that they were written bespeaks a painful and reluctant "Yes". The truth is that, beyond the discrepancy between what the poems say and what they are, yawns the still greater discrepancy between what they say and the fact that they are. Let them set nature before us as a sufficient spiritual end; still, their very existence as poetry, their very excess over nature, suggests that it is art, and not nature, that cures the ache of being. As both the beholder and the poet of nature,

Tomlinson is the contemplative twice over; and just in that apparent superfluity, it seems, lies the fullness that the spirit requires. The poems confess that "those empty vessels" of space whet as much as they replenish; and what nature prompts, art concludes. Not so humble or subservient after all, the spirit relives its experiences, but re-creates them from itself alone— positing, retrospectively, the space that once had nourished it. The hill it climbs becomes a subjective space, memory worked over by imagination. The essential confession of Tomlinson's art is, I believe, the essential confession of all art: that man is forced to be, and also needs to be, his own replenishment, perpetually renewed out of himself. So it is that, merely by existing, Tomlinson's poetry completes the real but limited truth—namely, the gratefulness of the world to the senses—whose thousand faces the poems seek out and draw.

Tomlinson, born in 1927, is still, it may be hoped, in mid-career. It is likely that he will deepen—indeed, he has already begun to do so; it is also likely that he will diversify his canon by throwing out more "sports", such as his recent, delightful poem on a personified "Rumour"; but it is not at all likely that he will alter his course. Nor, I think, is it desirable that he should; for Tomlinson strikes one as a poet who has finally won through to himself, and were he now to become someone else, it would seem almost an act of violence.

It was in his third volume, *Seeing is Believing* (1960), that Tomlinson first became both the distinct and the distinguished poet that he is today. His first volume, *Relations and Contraries* (1951), is haunted by Yeats and Blake, and though brilliant in patches, is not of much consequence. Tomlinson next moved a good deal nearer to himself in *The Necklace* (1955), which ranks, at the least, as a prologue to his real achievement. It zeroes in on the great Tomlinson theme, but vitiates it by a kind of enamelled elegance; it has Stevens's epicurean quality, but not his saving gusto and bravura. Precious in both senses of the word, *The Necklace* is a book to be valued, but—too beautiful, too exquisite—not to feel at home in: you must park your muddy shoes at the door. The very title of the third volume, *Seeing is Believing*, suggests a homely improvement over *The Necklace*. Here the earth takes on some of the earthiness that, after all, becomes it; and the manner is more gritty, rubs more familiarly with the world. In the subsequent two volumes, *A Peopled Landscape* (1962) and *American Scenes* (1966), the same manner— at once meticulous, prosaic, and refined (for Tomlinson's early elegance is roughened rather than lost)—is extended, as the titles indicate, to new subjects if not exactly to new themes. It is largely to the Tomlinson of these three volumes and of a fourth, *The Way of a World*, that I have addressed my remarks, and it is this Tomlinson who, as I began by declaring, has produced the most considerable body of poetry, to date, of any postwar English poet.

With the exception of Donald Davie—who, however, turns out more verse than poetry—no other English poet of Tomlinson's generation so strongly gives the impression of being an artist modestly but seriously at work—a poet equally intense about his message and his craft. Tomlinson's dedication is deep and unmistakable; and joined with his rare if quiet talent, it has created not only poetry of the highest quality, but success after success, in a period when the successes of more striking and seductive poets—Ted Hughes, R. S. Thomas, Philip Larkin—have seemed haphazard. Of all these gifted poets, it is Tomlinson who best survives the rub and wear of repeated readings; indeed, only Tomlinson's poetry improves under such treatment, like a fine wood under polish.

Part of the reason that Tomlinson tells slowly is that he has gone farther than any of his contemporaries—though Ted Hughes and Thomas Kinsella follow close—in outstaring and outmanoeuvring facility. He waits in advance, as it were, of his readers, who, burdened with ageing notions of what makes up poetic appeal, must labour to come abreast. In consequence, until Tomlinson is admired, he must be tolerated. His meticulous descriptions, so often hard to seize with the eye, his laconic meditations, his uncertain, demanding rhythms, his frustrations of expectations of various kinds—these one must struggle through as if through scrub, until one emerges, pleased and surprised, into the clearings that, in reality, the poems usually are. Because of both an increased dynamic clarity and a more definite music, Tomlinson's latest poems are probably his most readily accessible; they still, however, constitute a language to be learned, a flavour to be found, and to care about Tomlinson is to approve of this difficulty. Just as the later Yeats makes the early Yeats seem somewhat facile and obvious, so Tomlinson, asceticising poetry as he has, gives one a new sense of what the art can be. His is the sort of modification of poetry that ultimately makes it incumbent on other poets to change, to make it new, to work passionately at their craft.

As for the sensibility that Tomlinson's poetry expresses, its value, I think, should be self-evident. The truth it has seized upon, indeed the truth that seems native to it, is the lesson implicit in art itself—that contemplation is the fulfilment of being. Of course we have always to know what needs to be changed; but we also do well to praise and reverence what is sufficient for the day and the vast design that, though it impinges on us, ultimately lies beyond our human agency. For without this reverence we can scarcely be committed to the value of being; it is the secret of what Pasternak called "the talent for life". Tomlinson is certainly out of season to recall us to the life of the moment conceived as an end in itself; and yet it is just this unseasonableness that puts him in harmony with what is lasting in our relations with the world.

CONVERSATIONS

The Small Magazine since 1960

—a recorded conversation with Jon Silkin

(JON SILKIN began editing the magazine *Stand* in 1952. Since then it has expanded in readership, format, and scope. At present it is among the more widely read literary magazines in England.)

How has *Stand* developed as a magazine, Mr. Silkin?
It started as a poetry magazine and has diversified. This is one of the things I both wanted it to do and was acutely uneasy about. I feel each issue should have a unity—and the danger of diversification is that unity can be destroyed.
Do you aim at any particular audience—and how do you reach your public?
We have both a static and a varied readership. Right from the start, when I was living in London, *Stand* was sold in the pubs and coffee houses there, so that the audience was both regular and drifting. We also placed the magazine in bookshops. We still use the direct method of selling, but we have also built up a subscription list which is, thank God, a reasonably permanent one, with not too massive a turnover.
Does your readership respond at all to the magazine?
I am always surprised and delighted how people write in—sometimes prompted by a renewal notice, and sometimes quite spontaneously saying *I liked this* or *I didn't like that*. However brief the response, it's good to have, isn't it.
You are, then, one of the rare editors who personally creates an audience, taking *Stand* into the streets. You still don't manage on sales alone to make ends meet, do you?
No—or we do with a grant. That's what you're implying, isn't it?
Yes. I wondered if you would comment generally on the principle of subsidies to little magazines. As you know, the Arts Council recently ceased its direct subsidies to various magazines, opting to subsidise five magazines more substantially. These were magazines with a critical or translations bias. If one has to choose, do you agree that substantial subsidies to a few magazines are preferable to a more encouragingly widespread subsidy on which editors could not so entirely depend for solvency—where they would have, as you do, to make contact with their audience more imaginatively—since their goods would certainly sell. At present—in terms of sales—some of the best editors seem to be waiting for the mountain to come to Mohamet.
This question is difficult, phrased in a general way. I'm bound to answer it in

two ways. One is biased because I am acutely thinking of *Stand* and my own position with it. In terms of *Stand*, we couldn't do without a subsidy. It's about one third of our total running cost for each issue, and without it we would have to do a number of terrible cuts, like paying practically nothing to our contributors (not that we pay much now). We'd also have to skimp on the number of pages. I don't know how we'd manage. But about spreading subsidy more thinly—what can one say about that? It depends from editor to editor. If one of the arguments against subsidy is that it's going to make an editor lazy, my answer would be that he's going to be lazy anyway, with or without a subsidy. I can think of one or two editors currently who, whether out of laziness or reticence, would make no more effort to sell their magazine if they were without subsidy.

> Let us look at it this way. A magazine is produced for an audience. If the editors haven't much interest in their readership, but only in the well-being of their contributors and in the critical stance of their magazine, do you think their magazine deserves a public subsidy?

Yes, it does deserve—a magazine that is producing interesting work always deserves a subsidy. If the editor is uninterested in his public, this seem to me irrelevant to the issue of a subsidy. But I would say that I deplore any editor's lack of interest in his audience.

> With *Stand*, one feels that your critical pages have tended to spawn critics of a non-conformist style—for example Marxian critics, or critics using linguistic methods. Does this reflect a political bias in your editorial policy? Is that one of the types of coherence you like to give the magazine?

Well, it is—but I feel you are putting the emphases in the wrong order. I'd suggest that the primary interest of our two regular reviewers—Terry Eagleton and Anne Cluysenaar—is first of all an interest in the text, the poem itself. Now, interwoven with that emphasis, or perhaps woven on top of it— it is difficult to use the correct image—is the particular bias of each critic. But it seems to me that the poem is their first concern. But, given those biases, I would say that they in fact reflect the twin preoccupations of the magazine —that is to say, a social orientation, and at the same time an awareness that social orientation on its own is insufficient for the purposes of writing.

> *Stand* is, then, unusual in this respect. Not only do you take an interest in generating an audience; you also try to place poetry and the poem being criticised into some social context—and your critics try to do this. I felt an interesting feature of *Stand*—related to this concern—was its publishing of work from other areas—fiction and drama, for example, selected with the same critical eye—placing the poetry in a wider literary context. Is part of your scheme to *keep* poetry in a wider context, unlike some editors who seem to derive their critical biases from the symbolist practice, ignoring audience and the social or wider literary context altogether?

Since I write poetry, it *has* to be the case that my first interest, or my first and last interest, is poetry. But I've become more and more concerned with the whole question of what fiction is, what it really can do, what it *does* do, and the relation of prose to poetry. So this is really what has happened with the magazine. The contributions have forced me to some extent to redefine my whole approach, and the contributors are in a way running the magazine. This is the way I look at it. It isn't just a poetry magazine with some fiction, but a magazine where the poetry and fiction are—I won't say exactly competing with each other, but they are in a sense refracting certain of each others' impulsions. They're striking upon each other. Take Isaac Babel as a case. Here is a writer who undeniably writes in prose, yet the effect of Babel's fiction is to my mind that of poetry. This puts any poems that appear alongside Babel's fiction in a very curious context.

> Speaking of Babel, you do have a predilection in *Stand* not only for work by new writers, but also for bringing certain foreign writers in translation for a first time before a British audience. This has been a feature of your policy?

This is a question that I'll have to answer personally, if I may—more than personally, almost privately. I am a Jew, and, I think, largely because of this, being a European Jew, I have for better or for worse got something of this rootless cosmopolitan or European attitude. Some people say that they feel my work is extremely English—and maybe it is in some ways. But the attitudes behind the work are not specifically English. I've always been interested in the question of different ethnic, different kinds of writing rubbing shoulders—and right from the start, if you look at the first issue of the magazine, you see translations.

> You put the point personally—you are in the diaspora situation, with all the richness and variety of source that this implies. Often the translations you publish relate to your ethnic experience. Do you see the magazine as an extension of your own personal expression, as well as a forum for others?

Knowing that, in fact, there's bound to be a hideous amount of personal directiveness, I try to balance it the other way—to, if anything, broaden and make more catholic the choice of work . . . because there is a tendency I'm aware of, in the choice of work—to be too monolithic. I had this same discussion with Ian [Hamilton]. I was depressed at the time. I said to him I felt the magazine was too narrow and that we needed a broader, more catholic approach to it. Ian's response, roughly, was that one had to publish what one liked and what one thought was good. But there is a point at which one can say that X's poem is not the kind of poem I'd go out of my way to publish, but it *is* good and I *do* like it. It is on the peripheries of one's beliefs and one's openness that one is really tested.

> A ramification of the translations question, beyond ethnic or poetic preferences—you had a correspondence dialogue in *Stand* about

translation. Do you feel personally that there is possibly a strong, negative influence from translations on contemporary British poetry? There is a tendency, perhaps, among some British poets to imitate an idiom or an image idiom which has been produced by a certain environmental experience (like the turbulence of Eastern Europe, for example) totally alien from the British poet—which is untrue in his use. He is taking a linguistic experience at one remove (translation), an experience produced by—to him—a set of circumstances beyond his possibilities (the Nazi holocaust, or the totalitarian regime); then he is attempting to turn this into something specifically English.

If I said yes and began to erode my assent . . . I'd like to reply that way. Firstly, one of the arguments about the environment of, say, Eastern Europe, being different from, say, England (which never had occupation from the Nazis)—one of the assumptions this argument rests on is that the environment is *totally* responsible for the work. Now, surely it isn't the environment that writes the poem—it is the individual within the environment. It may be that some British writer—and reader (whom we never seem to talk about)—it's possible that somebody in both rôles may have a temperamental, emotional kinship with these writers, regardless of the fact that the environmental experiences are totally different. I'm asking, why should a British or American poet who has not experienced the holocaust or holocaustlike conditions, therefore feel that this area of moral entrapment or whatever should be denied him as a writer? It doesn't seem to me either logical or just.

When the experience of—to use your example—holocaust has produced an idiom like that of, say, Vasco Popa, the idiom is a correlative for a very personal response, a fable or surreal nightmare idiom. Then you get a poet like, perhaps, Ted Hughes attempting the same effects with a similar idiom, but without a similar depth or generality of experience, producing the staccato, almost comical ends of *Crow*.

Yes, but you are granting me my argument. What we are talking about here is not so much the abusing of the difference between the environments, but the abuse of one individual trying to imitate another.

Or another individual's set of conditions—

All right, but we're talking not about Popa's conditions but about his *response* to those conditions. And any kind of personal idiom is, I would have thought, inimitable. And that's really what one's talking about. It seems to me that in raising the issue of the different environments, you mount upon one *issue* another issue which is really only marginally related to it. We know the environment is important, but what is crucial is the way the individual deeply and truthfully responds to it.

From a different angle, do you think that the language of many popular translations—translations particularly from languages unrelated or only remotely related to English in their construction—can produce in English a sort of poetic esperanto, affecting poets to write a sort of non-

English English, a sinewless language?

The linguistic point is inseparable from all the other points. You press me to say yes again, and clearly there *is* a danger. It seems to me to be paranoid, however, to suggest that because there is a danger we must not therefore be interested in translation, or translate, or use translated work, or in any way feel that we may be influenced by the perhaps very different skills (I use this in the widest possible sense) of poets coming from a very different environment. After all, the whole imaginative act, when one thinks about it, is based upon the assumption that a writer can communicate to a reader an experience either may have had emotionally but may not have had in fact. Shakespeare writes of murder—is the suggestion that he must have been a murderer before he could write about it?

> No, but I think the point is that a writer writes for a reader; a translator translates the writer for another reader *in another language*.

But is a translator not a creator? One can argue he is on perhaps a rather different level. But you suggest he is just a multiple adding machine of sorts, or a computer who, as it were, transposes the letters into another order to make a kind of English construct . . .

> I think you will agree, though, that the bulk of translations published in the last eight or nine years of proliferation has been not of a quality one would call high—and most certainly, one would hope, not remotely near the quality of the original being translated.

One guesses this is the case—but since I have no other language except a bit of French, I'm incapable of either assent or dissent. What are you saying— is this a qualification against *translating*, or against an original writer using translation to enrich his own writing?

> I am suggesting, as you did, that translation is a difficult art, not a linguistic craft, and that the proliferation of translations from— particularly—an exceptionally anguished generation of Eastern Europeans and an exaggeratedly self-indulgent generation of French and Latin American surrealists—has produced in some of the poets most involved with the translations as readers or translators (though certainly not all) a debasing of the quality which makes their language English— not a debasing of the Englishness of their experience (I don't suppose there is an essentially English experience). But—again to use the example of Ted Hughes' *Crow*—the change linguistically from *Hawk in the Rain* and earlier collections to *Crow* is astounding. The language has lost almost all but rhetorical reverberativeness.

I'm not terribly happy with *Crow*, by any means—but do you mean to suggest that all Hughes' sins are to be laid at the feet of this translatese?

> I'm suggesting that translatese has had its ill effect on Hughes, both linguistically and thematically—and on some of his followers. You perhaps receive submissions for *Stand* of this post-surrealist fable poetry . . .

Your very term post-surrealist gives away your argument. We've passed through, for better or for worse, the experience of surrealism and symbolism, neither of which originated in English writing.

Well, neither of which were *conceptualised* first by English critics, but which obviously have played a part in English writing.

Well, have they?

Surely—you can see for example Arthur Hallam's influence on Tennyson's early writing—encouraging Tennyson to cut out discursive passages and leave the symbols to do their work—is very similar to, say, the effect Mallarmé, more conceptually, had on his circle. Hallam's effect on Tennyson was the encouragement of a symbolist idiom (which Tennyson later forsook) before the term *symbolist* had been formulated. The word may not have been an English coining, but the sense of symbolism was present without the term.

All I'm trying to suggest is that there are certain cultural peculiarities (I use that word in a decent sense) which can be and are grafted more or less successfully onto British writing. We're dealing here with a very delicate thing. Clearly there is a *lot* of bad writing—some of which may be attributed to the translation "epidemic". But any fashionable mode permits a good deal of bad writing. We're not concerned, surely, with the bad writing, but with whether anything can be gained, as I believe it can, through the transposing of another sensibility into English.

On a different subject, Mr. Silkin—you've lived in the North for how many years now?

In Leeds for eight, and in Newcastle for another six.

I wondered if, in your time here, you have perceived the development of anything we might call a genuinely regional literature? In Newcastle you still have a widely used and richly expressive dialect, for example. Is it the case that many Newcastle poets have been hatched recently before our eyes and that none of them writes with a convincingly Northern idiom?

To go to the easiest point first—the dialect. There are some poems by Tom Pickard—I think perhaps not his best ones—which are in dialect. I think you're right—on the whole this expresses for me the situation. Dialect is in a very ambiguous situation, even in this part of the world where it is quite a strong part of some people's speech. It's very difficult to use today when it is not part of a regularly used and understood living English speech.

I wondered if the *experience*, then, of Newcastle, or of the North generally, as a complex industrial entity with all its implications, was being assimilated into poetry?

That's the real nub of the question now—is there such a thing as a Northern experience that makes it distinguishable from, say, experience in London, Wales, or the West Country? I've lived over different parts of this country and I would think that there was, actually—that there is an abrasive vitality in the North which makes this experience very different from, say, living in London. The culture in the broadest possible sense reflects this. The abrasiveness is integral to it. There are writers, even writers who do not belong to the area, who have, I think, used this. I think, for example—one can't tell if Geoffrey Hill would have been the same writer if he hadn't moved from Worcester and Oxford to Leeds but had gone to London (though with hindsight one might say that it was inevitable that Hill wouldn't have gone to London)—but it seems to me Leeds is his place, and that he will stay there. And thinking of his sequence, "Funeral Music"—which, as you know, we published—there is that harsh, unremitting quality, a sense of the tragic nature of human conflict, of the way in which human beings seem to have to excoriate one another. That kind of abrasive quality is essentially a part of "Funeral Music"—not necessarily the central quality, but almost; and, in many ways, a northern experience.

> What seems sad to readers living in the South is that—whereas Scotland is producing something like a Scots literature, creating a distinctive and to some degree a rich tradition—the North, with its various qualities so different from those of other regions, has not produced anything comparable in volume or quality.

Well, I'm one of those people who prefer Tom Pickard's *High on the Walls* to *The Order of Chance*. In that first book there are some poems with a sort of stubbornness and recalcitrance that I would associate with the Northern experience. Although the first poem in *The Order of Chance*, which we published, "The Devils Destroying Angels", seems to me to be a Northern poem. But if we have to talk this way it is difficult. But in this context there's a point about *Stand* which I feel I have to get in—that is, that when I came to Newcastle from Leeds at the instigation of the Northern Arts, one thing which we made clear to each other, was that the editorial would in no way be interfered with. We both said this to each other, knowing that there is an even stronger local patriotism in this area than, say, in Yorkshire, and it was said advisedly, because there were people at the beginning and there are people who still argue strongly that since *Stand* receives money from the North East, it ought therefore to turn into a regional magazine, a platform exclusively or mainly for North Eastern writers. I've always said no to this. So one is in the position of wanting to see a Northern *cultural* experience develop more, and at the same time not wanting to be parochial as opposed to regional. Here's a distinction it might be useful to draw.

> What about the other small magazines that have been running alongside *Stand* for the last ten years or so? Are they performing a different sort of task from *Stand* or achieving a different end?

Oh yes. There's no question about that. Even a casual reader would note the great difference. First, to take the *London Magazine*. Until recently it was a monthly magazine, and it still retains, as it were, elements of that earlier periodicity. It is in many ways a review rather than a magazine. That is to say, it sets out to chronicle, especially being in London, the current cultural events. It's much more on top of what is immediately happening than we are or want to be. It pays its price. One of the prices that it does pay is that the editor, Alan Ross, seems to be—I don't use this necessarily as a value judgement—seems to be more willing to mirror what he thinks best rather than to help shape that. The result is both a certain over-flexibility *and* inflexibility, because he won't, in the process, be shaped and at the same time he does mirror. This sounds contradictory, but I think there is a truth in it.

This possibly accounts for the fact that many of the contributors to this magazine—as to *The Review*—are *regular* contributors, doesn't it? There are occasional forays into new areas, but there is a core of eight or ten contributors?

—Although Ross would argue two things, I think. He would say there are a lot of new writers in the *London Magazine*. He could probably argue this credibly. He could also point out that in *Stand* there are a number of writers that appear very regularly—Geoffrey Hill, Roy Fisher, Michael Hamburger, and our two regular reviewers, for a start. Nevertheless, I think it's true that we do—perhaps because of our periodicity—have more writers new to *Stand* than the *London Magazine* has to its pages. I haven't been into it numerically. This is an impression. *The Review* is another matter. We seem to be in the middle, with Ross on the one side and Hamilton on the other. Hamilton seems to be much more, on the whole, if you say it unkindly, directive . . . or, to put it differently, very determined and positive, knowing what he wants and sticking to his choices very clearly, too. I think there is a very recognisable *Review* review and *Review* poem; a certain kind of—perhaps hard to define and pin down—refined and delicate and, at the same time, tight-lipped lyric poem he seems to like; incidentally (I have talked to Ian about this) I've not tremendously liked the poems in the magazine. But there are some things I have liked enormously—for example Alan Page's translations of Ritsos, and Michael Hamburger's anthology of East German poetry which I envied Ian for; and on the critical side that interesting dialogue between Alvarez and Davie—numerous things in *The Review* are marvellous.

You've only mentioned two magazines. Are there any others making individual and valuable contributions?

I'm interested in *Modern Poetry in Translation*, though I feel it is perhaps more culpable than we are in admitting translations which aren't good pieces of English writing—the editors might agree—but which introduce writers otherwise not available in any form. *Ambit* I'm not crazy about at all. I don't like it. It seems to me very modish. *Agenda* I think has produced some very interesting work, but very often I feel that—I've written to Cookson about this—the sometimes almost slavish admiration of Pound is very damaging in fact *to* Pound, and his readers.

It seems that you sense a lack of good small magazines—ones pulling their weight in a real literary sense.

Yes. I feel *The Review* is pulling its weight. And regardless of what I feel about the complexion of the *London Magazine*, it is a very positive asset.

Since there are so few, do you feel that the torch of the little magazine has to some degree in the last six or seven years been passed to the little presses, where a writer can reveal more of his scope to a smaller but perhaps a more intense readership than a magazine could offer?

Yes, obviously, if we are considering the word "intense"—though there are some poets who are better drastically selected. The other thing is, you are putting a set of alternatives which seem to be either/or, and really in fact it isn't the case. One can read both a magazine and a collection of someone's work.

Do you feel that the work of some of the small presses is maintaining a standard perhaps not being maintained by the small magazine? I am thinking of Anvil, particularly—or Fulcrum, Northern House itself, Trigram.

Well; there's some pretty mixed work in most of those presses. The danger of any publisher of books, as opposed to a magazine (I say this advisedly, to you) is that he'll be caught on the hook of *having* to publish or cease to exist as a publisher. A little magazine can afford to reject much more than a publisher, and does. In other words, we can afford to be more selective. Although this sounds superior, in the end that's what it comes to. In the little magazine, too, unlike a small press, the writer finds, at least in theory, a sort of pacing ground for his work. He sees it in the context of other work by other writers—and so does the reader, of course. That sort of forcing comparison is very bracing, maybe actually rather hurtful at times. But it's there.

I would have thought that a single poem by a poet, set in the context of other single poems by other poets would hardly be very revealing to a reader of the poet's range of achievement—or to the poet himself.

You're absolutely right—in *Stand* we try to achieve a sort of density of selection—more than one poem by a poet, at a time. But there is that danger.

Can you forecast any new or changing rôle for the little magazine in the 'seventies?

I can't forecast a direction. I can't see a change in pattern. But—to change the question—I've always hoped that our magazine was a co-operative thing—not only between the several editors, but also a co-operative instrument between the editors and the contributors. I'm struggling to say that the magazine is changed by the contributions we receive—so that's the answer, isn't it? The future is determined by the contributors, and these are very various.

The Poet in the 'Sixties: Vices and Virtues

—a recorded conversation with Peter Porter

(PETER PORTER is an Australian-born poet living in London. Recently he has made a living from his free-lance reviewing, editing, and broadcasting.)

Mr. Porter, as an Australian immigrant in English poetry, you have somewhat different views from your contemporaries, some of them rather contentious views. We hoped you would talk to us about the various opportunities open to the British poet since 1960, the dangers to him in his changing rôle, and insofar as you are a visionary, his future. About the teaching of poetry in England first. Martin Dodsworth, in his book, *The Survival of Poetry*, suggests a tendency to teach poetry in schools with primary stress on its present-ness, unrelated to its tradition or its social and historical context. Is this true, do you think? What implications does it have for the poets?

Basically the interesting thing about poetry is who writes it, not who teaches it or how it is taught. Teaching of poetry really is of no significance. On the whole poets are more influenced by what they read than what they're taught. This is a good thing. What Dodsworth says may well be true. But if we're talking now about poets, rather than the general student, they teach themselves, and they teach themselves by reading other poets. And one thing that people overestimate in talking about contemporary poetry is the degree to which poetry is influenced by its contemporaries, rather than the past. If you look at poets who suddenly burst on the scene with considerable new force, like Ted Hughes—the biggest single influence on Hughes' first book was Shakespeare. This seems to me to be the case, and no amount of what his tutor said, or what the prevailing fashion at Cambridge was, or what was said in exegesis of Eliot, or whether he went for Pound—none of these things really influenced him. What really influenced him in his first book was his reading of William Shakespeare. Always what poets will do will be to go through what has happened in the past—and in the present—and they will just choose, as you would in a record shop. You're not really conditioned by current practices of teaching or current theories. You're influenced by what will go. To be too much interested in the teaching of poetry is to overestimate the rôle of the University and schooling in the creation of art.

What will happen, though, in terms of a growing audience educated in the way Dodsworth suggests? Isn't it the case that the audience, a more and more potent factor in some poets' writing, will become essentially uncritical, passive, without having any sense of the structure of their tradition or any discretion of response?

Well, far more dangerous is the audience becoming, not uncritical, but joining a critical orthodoxy and looking for certain things which that criticism has taught them to look for, which may not be present. In other words this is a conditioned response rather than a completely valid one. I'd rather have an audience that was uninformed than one ruthlessly informed in one direction.

> Isn't Dodsworth's point that the audience educated in this way is as conditioned as an audience adhering to a critical orthodoxy?

Well, students of poetry aren't usually passive—they're galloping along in a certain direction. When I was up in Hull I talked to students. I felt it wasn't that students were hostile to the idea of poetry in general or even in particular—they had made up their minds on certain things on a very inadequate basis, and they were following that. There's a great deal of thought today, especially among students, that the world is full of phoneys. There's been far too much propaganda about getting rid of the phoneys and coming to "the truth". Auden says somewhere that if you had to isolate the most phoney of figures it would probably be some great truth teller like Stendhal; the man who really tells the truth is the man who goes to elaborate lengths to conceal it from himself—like Boswell. This is a dangerous paradox. But I found a lot of people saying to me in Hull things like, "Why doesn't he say what he means? Why is he going through this elaborate process?" Well, if you just say what you mean, what you mean may be so banal there's no point in saying it. Maybe you should say something a bit more interesting than what you mean. So, audience responses don't really matter or aren't bad except when they're a conditioned reaction. That's why I think it's bad to go about continually giving poetry readings which are preachings to the converted. They've come just to have their tyres pumped up, and they're not hearing anything new. I maintain that all left-wing poetry readers like Adrian Mitchell should be confined to reading to Primrose League gatherings and Tory fêtes, whereas all right-wing poetry readers like Auden should be made to read to Maoist students—so that you don't have an audience conditioned to respond in each case to your throwaway cracks.

> Along with the apathetic extremism on the one hand, and the political on the other, in poetry audiences, a problem in critical writing seems to have developed too. You have the almost entirely descriptive criticism as one extreme, and then you have the very judicial and partisan criticism of some writers—like Ian Hamilton or Geoffrey Grigson—on the other. I wondered if you sensed this critical polarisation, this failure in criticism to find any solid middle ground?

The middle ground is the ground where you get run over. It's like being in the middle of the road. It's always better to be on one extreme or the other. I think this is an inevitable difficulty. If a man has powerful convictions in one direction, then he's hardly likely to see much good in people who don't share them. So once you've got a vigorous and intelligent critic, he's bound to seem unfair. I only protest at it when he begins to believe his criticism to such an extent that he begins to think, not that he's expressing his own point of view or establishing a background for his own feeling, but that what he thinks is a divine inspiration or revelation, and that he's bringing the wisdom down from the top of the mountain on tablets. When that happens I think he does become dangerous. There are very few powerful critics who are utterly responsible.

But of course a critic like Randall Jarrell is at once very catholic and highly critical.

That is something marvellous—devoutly to be wished and not to be commonly expected. That's ideal criticism, and it's why I've always greatly admired Jarrell as a critic. He belongs to the same school as Edmund Wilson, except Edmund Wilson didn't know very much about poetry. Jarrell applies the principles of Wilson to poetry and does it brilliantly. He is the ideal critic. But you don't get more than one of those every fifty years. Otherwise, you have the sort of critic (or reviewer, as I'd prefer to call him) who is dismissed by the embattled critics as just vapid and tasteless, or you are embattled, in which case you're grossly unfair to lots of people. I just can't make up my mind. If I was full of passionate conviction, I would purvey it passionately. But I'm not. Nothing is worse than the man who pretends to be a ferocious Savanorola when really underneath he's just a fun-loving monk.

Another aspect of this critical question is the effect critics—some of them—have had on actual writing. In the last ten years, we saw for example Alvarez formulating his "gentility principle" and later his extremist school, actually affecting poets in their choice of themes and language. And recently we have had George Steiner's theories of linguistic pollution affecting poets in different ways. . . .

I can't imagine Steiner's views affecting anybody at all. I honestly don't believe a single poet has been changed by that theory about the decay of language. Because the English language *hasn't* decayed anyway. It has suffered a tremendous buffeting from commercial sources, but to my mind it's emerged to some degree stronger for it. A language which is kept entirely for proper and important concerns is half-way to being dead. Witness the way the Latin language died once it was put into the liturgy. Most critical work, no matter how brilliant it is, is tidying up after the event. I doubt very much whether poets actively keep in mind any of the injunctions or obiter dicta of critics when they are writing their poems, because—you know this well enough yourself—the necessities and pressures on a poem may be influenced by a critical climate, but are seldom influenced by a specific critical injunction— particularly when you're writing. I don't think these things are as influential as they're made out to be.

Possibly in Alvarez' case it was tidying up before the event, in fact stressing certain aspects of certain poets' work which they might not themselves naturally have come to stress, and which their not having stressed might have been virtuous rather than vicious. I'm thinking particularly of Ted Hughes' recent work.

I think one of the reasons Alvarez was influential was that he codified what a lot of people had been thinking anyway. I'm not so sure he led in any particular direction. He might have led the eyes of other critics in a direction in which they hadn't yet strayed, but I don't think it had very much influence on what was being done, because, oddly enough, when Ted Hughes appeared on the scene as a man changing the direction of English poetry, the people of a generation younger than Hughes's were throwing over the whole idea of *English* poetry as such and welcoming the United States and experimental forms from Europe. So the Hughes's palace revolution was very short-lived. What Alvarez wrote in *New Poetry* has been influential largely among teachers of English and not amongst poets.

It might be a comfortable provincial delusion, but it's widely felt that in London—where the mass media and the weeklies have their centre—there are groups of poets working to benefit their own partisans, only a few (like the loosely associated *Review* poets) with any dominant critical bias. Does this in fact obtain?

This is another department of the conspiracy theory. There may be some truth in it. I know that when I first came to London in 1951 I didn't know a single person, and I had a staggering lack of success continually for the next six or seven years and never got anywhere with anything. I didn't have my first poem published till I was 28, and then only in an undergraduate magazine in Cambridge. I suppose that there was then an orthodoxy. I seem to remember names being established and apparently appearing all over the place. But I don't think I felt there was any particular conspiracy going on—except the internal conspiracy that I was conspiring against myself or that I wasn't any good. One's self-doubt built up quite considerably. When I did meet, finally, some of the people from the literary world, the first were some that used to go to George Fraser's Wednesday evenings over at Beaufort Street. I didn't seem to me there was anything very metropolitan or smart about this. Most of the people there seemed to be drunk all the time, and one couldn't get any sense out of them. George was an influential man. He was publishing and so forth. But I don't think we felt kept out, except in the sense that every young man feels the people who are there are keeping him out. It never occurred to us at this time to think that London was conspiratorial, and that if one retreated to the provinces one would suddenly gain a great influx of virtue. If people do see a metropolitan conspiracy, I don't know where it's centred or what it is, because when it comes to the power centres of London, they overlap so much, and nobody has much power. Of course an editor has the power to choose what will go in his journal, a producer or broadcaster will choose what's to go out—this seems to me the only power.

Some editors, however, and other people too, might seem to have their thumb in more than one pie.

Well, some *have*. It doesn't matter much. It happens everywhere—a man only has to have a position of authority and he'll be asked to other things by people who have to be sure he knows his job. I don't think there's any kind of conspiracy. There's *preference*, and there always will be, and a lot of people are prejudiced—those that see conspiracies as much as those that apparently maintain them. You can't avoid prejudice. Only Jesus Christ loves everybody.

Does the provincial poet have—in his relative isolation—some advantage over the metropolitan poet who is tangled up in literary politics and so forth? Perhaps an advantage of clear perspective?

How can anyone be isolated in a country of this size? The *Daily Express* comes thudding onto your doorstep even if you're in the fastnesses of Wales. How isolated is the provincial man in England? If he were living half way up the Yucatan Peninsula, or in Sydney he'd be isolated.

You can be literarily isolated or personally isolated in England, aware of what's going on without being bound up in groups of admirers or detractors, out of the area of quotidian literary contamination. . . .

Yes—but I can't imagine any homogeneity in London itself.

Wouldn't you say, though, that these last ten years the major literary achievements in English poetry have been made by individuals living outside London?

I don't think it has anything to do with the provinces. The major literary achievements have always been by individuals. The English, for all that they may be clubable, are not very given to signing manifestoes or subscribing to creeds. You'd never get a bunch of English poets so much in agreement as, say, the French *Tel Quel* group. Orthodoxies aren't established in that fashion. Even the famous 'thirties poets, if you'd taken away the central figure of W. H. Auden, would have been a bunch of people so dissimilar that they would have immediately split up. There is no real link between them except the presence of Auden.

It quotes you on the back of George Macbeth's *Collected Poems* as saying that Macbeth had a seminal influence comparable to Auden's influence.

Well—yes, of course that's taken out of context. I said a lot of other things as well. It was in a piece of 600 words about Macbeth in which I went on to explain what the context was. I don't think he's as influential as Auden or as gifted as Auden. What he did have for us at that time was an excitement, because he was a man who was doing things and experimenting in ways which to us were new and interesting. It didn't seem to us to be something imported from America, the reason being that Macbeth still remains faithful to a lot of the old fashioned principles of English poetry, such as ways to structure and organise a poem. He is a rules man. The rules are surprisingly close to those you might have learned if you had read classics at Oxford. And it's that sort of interest, the desire to use the new material but the old structuring that made him, I think, a fascinating figure. This is also true of Auden, I think. Auden seemed the great prophet in the 'thirties, but if you look back at those poems, even the ones that made his reputation, you discover they were structured in a very traditional way. I felt Macbeth was influential in the same way. I can't think of another modern English poet who has such a remarkable technical achievement. He's influenced people by showing them the way to do things. People may not imitate him the way they imitate Plath and Hughes, but there's nothing in Plath and Hughes that gives anybody else a chance to go anywhere. Macbeth's style is far more detachable from the Macbeth subject matter or the Macbeth persona. There are ways in which Macbeth can help another poet because he is so chameleon-like himself. He is a great teacher, but a teacher by heuristic principles, as Stravinsky says, principles of doing things rather than analysing things.

> While you were in Hull as Poetry Fellow, you must have come in contact with a number of aspiring poets. Were there any dominant trends or distinctive characteristics which you perceived in their work?

I didn't see a great deal of the poetry of students at Hull. I think the poets on the campus were surprisingly reticent. Nor was there very strong interest in poetry that I could gauge. It would be difficult to tell what the tendencies were. I would gauge it less from my experiences at Hull than my experiences of going around schools and universities giving readings and talking to people afterwards, and having judged a number of competitions where thousands of poems were submitted. Of course competition is not a very good thing because 90% of what's submitted is written in complete ignorance of anything after Keats—and of anything earlier than Keats as well. The majority of poems are written by people profoundly ignorant of the fact that Eliot ever existed— and this is not improper. These are the productions of amateur poets. But taking people who are aware of what's going on, I've found that the only really popular style of poetry (I mean popular now on a purely demographic basis of how many people like it) is the pop poetry, the Liverpool cabaret type poetry—you couldn't really dignify it with the name "cabaret", more the underground shelter sort of poetry. That goes down pretty well. There's a tremendous fondness for anything soft and squashy—and the result is that of all those poets everybody laughs at McGough and Henri, but they think that Patten is for real, because he's got that little touch of moonlight on the page. This is exactly what I can't stand about it. It's all marshmallow to me. I'd rather have the crude, jokey, knockabout stuff with Henri on the guitar than the moonlight. I find a lot of people go for San Francisco styles—there's a great fondness for the work of Michael McClure (the Lord knows why). People tend, really, to be influenced honestly by what moves them, and you can't anticipate what this will be. It's the thing that gets them at the moment. I came across a man who thought the best living poet was Harold Norse. People are still idiosyncratic enough to go for what they go for, irrespective of what the tendency may be.

> You have expressed elsewhere some rather controversial ideas about

translation. Do you feel the tendency among poets directly under the influence of translation might be to write a sort of denatured English, a poetic esperanto of sorts?

It's only one of the dangers. What worries me about translation is quite simply this: that it is burdened with so much good will. And good will is what gets in the way of anything being properly realised. We also feel, in these days of awareness of each other and the responsibilities of One World, that we ought to be able to respond to other people's languages. But really it's extremely difficult. It's this atmosphere of, "If all the poets in the world got together what a wonderful new world they could make". As opposed to all the politicians. I reckon they'd make an even worse world than the politicians. They're not in any respect people who can see eye to eye with each other, even when they're writing in one language. This is notable too in, say, jamborees, when poets of different nationalities get together—every other nation in the world gangs up to stop the French from walking all over them. There's this kind of natural imperialism in many languages. The English language is rather like the American imperialism. It works without having to use armies. It works because it is a highly effective language. And you find this with American capitalist expansion—a sort of cocacolonisation without having to resort to invasion.

I think we are very conscious in our country that we ought to be taking notice of what's going on in other countries. I would welcome this if only we all had the gift of languages, the Pentecostal gift, and would learn the languages well enough to appreciate the poems in the original. I'm suspicious of the way all this Eastern European poetry, for example, has been launched on the English market, because we have a bad conscience. We haven't suffered what they've suffered, we haven't lived the dictatorships they live under, and we're not able to write such forceful fables. And the one thing that usually does translate well is a fable, because it doesn't depend on idiosyncracies of language, since its masks or its shapes are the important thing. Consequently, the fabulous way of writing which is the only way to express yourself under a mental dictatorship (what Alvarez describes as "under pressure") translates well into our language. And also it upstages us a little. It makes us feel that we are not serious people because they are very serious, being under constant threat of death and destruction, which we aren't except in terms of the bomb. So I think all our victories in translation are too easily and too readily won. I think translation gives us a spurious sense that we are in touch, that we are really coping with major art when we are in fact getting only the shadow of that art, since really to know it you have to know it in depth, and you can't really know a poem in depth when it's taken into another language. It's rather different in the case of the classics. There, they've been around so long you won't necessarily do them any harm by doing modern versions of them. And also there are still quite a few people around who can read them in the original, although they're not living languages.

Your own versions of Martial seem to be not so much translations as recastings in a modern mold.

Oh, yes—they're not translations at all but more—in musical terms—realisations, though there you're just given a skeletal thing which you then elaborate. They are done to give me the pleasure of reading his poems—in a very brutal and egotistical way. The only way I could enjoy his writing was to rewrite it myself.

This sort of activity has literary validity?

Perhaps, but if Martial were alive at this moment in Bucharest it would be very wrong.

What about a poet like Corbière, then, or some of the great Russian formalists who have had such a seminal influence on the new linguistic criticism in Europe?

It doesn't matter so much in the case of Corbière or Laforgue or Rimbaud or Baudelaire who are well-known in French, and French is a language which is reasonably accessible to most people. But in Russian—I think it matters a lot there. Few of us read Russian. And a version of, say, Pasternak, or Mayakovsky, or Blok, which isn't *very* accurate is I think dangerous—and how to make a very accurate version which isn't at the same time flat is equally difficult.

These are, though, poets who have had such influence on structuralist and linguistic criticism—

Well, have they? I know nothing about linguistic criticism . . .

Well, critics like Jakobson . . .

I haven't even heard of him.

It seems that the critical importance of these poets has been great on the Continent, on new techniques which are only now creeping into English criticism. For example, in some of the provincial Universities you have schools of linguistic criticism.

Yes, I know. I've come across these.

They are doing exciting new work. But the sources of this new work are in Eastern European poetry, particularly Russian.

Well, presumably these new critics are perfectly able to read the poems their theories are based on in the original?

The formulators of the techniques obviously are, but some of their English followers are not. They are, however, applying the techniques profitably to English poetry, deriving their knowledge through translations.

We're getting away from poetry again and back on to translation. As far as I'm concerned, the main influence of translation has been to remind a lot of English poets that the slightly narrow course of English poetry in the twentieth century, if you exclude Americans like Eliot and Pound, is not all of the story. And not only that, but one can write completely within one's tradition and still be excited by things outside it.

I've always been interested in the way misunderstanding, as well as understanding, can be an influence on how poets write. It's always the influence of poetry on *poets*, rather than its influence on society or the critics, that interests me. The good thing about the present situation is that, even if you belong to the old reactionary school of English poetry, you still have a wider range of references.

Misunderstanding can have very original influence.

Yes—the French have a very rich tradition of misunderstanding, ever since Baudelaire on Poe.

Also, of course, the influence of the surrealists on Hart Crane—he misunderstood them, yet managed to produce a very rich and original concoction.

Oh, yes—I'm a great believer in misunderstanding. After all, it's so much easier to achieve than understanding.

Back to the poet then. The poet's opportunities seem to have changed radically since about 1963 in England, in that he can make a living, or almost a living, out of his identity as a poet, if not out of the poems themselves—by the spin-off from his poetry . . .

Pollution, you mean.

He can get fellowships, review, speak his poems aloud, get them published more easily than before. He can get bursaries and grants.

Still, it's a pretty small waterhole compared with the number of animals standing about with their tongues hanging out.

But you, for example, have been able to give up advertising and copywriting recently, and are surviving on your earnings as a poet and the implications of that identity.

I haven't been able to do it. It happened. I was simply given the sack. I could either have gone back into the wretched trade again or try to survive. So I tried to survive. Whether I'll continue to survive is another matter.

But you are making a living . . .

Yes, I'm making a better living than I was before. But the enemies of the free-lance writer are prodigious. Not only the enemies to his talent, but the enemies to his very subsistence. For a start, he can't afford to be sick, even with the National Health system, because he won't be able to do the work that brings in the money. You see, you have no further expectancy at all.

I would have thought, though, that at least fifty poets in the 'sixties became able to live off their writing or their identities as poets.

It's true this identity as a poet tends to support people's views of themselves. I disapprove of it very much; thinking of themselves as poets as though they were different from other people. I suppose this isn't too unlike the Shelley idea of the poet as a person distinguished from the rest of humanity by certain gifts for which he's supposed to pay a high price. This is also the wound and the bow theory. I suppose there is a sense in which everybody believes it. I think it begs too many questions. If I am a poet, and therefore everything I write is poetry, then the obvious corollary is that some poems will be good poetry and some will be bad. But of course the idea of this distinction between good and bad poetry is anathema to the literary revolution. It's élitist, they'd say, and all the other dirty words of that kind. It's not élitist at all, really. You're right, though, that a man who sees himself as a poet can get added income these days. A good example of this is the attitude of people quite uninterested in poetry. I used to share a flat with a friend who was a statistical psychologist. If I was ever writing and he came into the room, he would never say, "Writing a poem?" but "Being a poet?" This is clearly the attitude of the public which, taking little interest in *poetry*, confirms the *poet* in his rôle. It's prepared even to pay him in his rôle of impotent jester or impotent early-warning system. I disapprove of this, because a good poet writing a bad poem is, after all, less the poet than a bad poet writing a good poem. Your rôle as a poet never guarantees a single bit of your currency. You can't, because you are a poet, guarantee to honour every stock and bond that you issue.

It's true that in the United States, the fact of achieving the "poetic identity" has, in poets like Bly, Creeley, and to some degree Lowell, and Berryman, and to a painful degree in recent Merwin, led to a poet's either going off rapidly after his acceptance, or losing a large measure of his faculty of self-criticism. The temptation to say, "I am a poet and therefore what I write is poetry" must be overpoweringly strong when the poet has a publisher for whatever he turns out and an adulating undiscriminating audience, and a failure of major critics to check his arrogance.

I think, you see, arrogance is very attractive. It gives me a pain, actually, but a lot of people are attracted by it. I got into a lot of trouble with Donald Davie for putting forward the idea that poetry is a modest art. What I meant by that was that poetry is an art conceived on a modest scale. But the very word "modest" to Davie—I couldn't have used a filthier word. He attacked me violently for this. He was more or less saying, what American poet would think of this—all American poets go around in this great cloud of arrogance, because this gives them their authority. The reason for this is that American society, for all its great wealth and despite the fact that it supports the arts far more than England does, doesn't really think there is any place for poets, and therefore they've got to be given special monster status. They're expected to be arrogant. Of course, poets have been seen in the past as having this sort of thaumaturgical, sacerdotal quality. When Augustus was trying to prop up his arriviste Empire, he got Virgil to do him a bogus epic about how noble it was to be descended from Aeneas. Here's the poet in main rôle as propagandist. And of course the Russians see it this way too. Russian poets are supposed to supply the people with major myths. The poet as a sort of supreme lie-teller in these cases is very influential. But in modern twentieth-century democracies, a poet can only tell lies in what one might call the private area. So the poet is seen now as important only in a sort of Freudian sub-world rather than in a world of actual affairs.

You don't believe then that the British poet's opportunities have altered radically in the 'sixties?

Oh, yes—they have. But in far more orthodox areas. More books are being published, there's a wider dissemination of books at cheaper prices, in popular editions.

In the 'sixties, has the poet's relationship to other poets, and to his audience and his social context not begun to alter a little?

I think the poet has come out from cover a bit more. He no longer apologises for being a poet to all his friends who are something more respectable. To that extent he's emerged. I suppose the poet is no longer such a figure from the higher culture. He's no longer educated necessarily at the best Universities, nor is he necessarily a middle-class figure as he always was. (Even Dylan Thomas was a middle-class figure, you know.) It's now accepted that the poetic calling is open to anyone who, as it were, can get the call. This is an improvement—but, mind you, the old principle of exclusiveness kept out a lot of what they might have called "creeps", and now an awful lot of creeps get in, because all you've got to do is set up your plate.

DIRECTIONS

Post-culture: Pre-culture?

by Anne Cluysenaar

I am myself a part of what is real, and that is my own speech and the strength of it, this only, that I hear and ever shall.

These words may very well be an inscription above the portal of what lies ahead.

Wallace Stevens, *The Necessary Angel.*

IT must have struck many readers of poetry that the most powerful if not always the most attractive British work in the 'sixties tended to suggest a world-picture in which destructive elements predominate, whether in the inner or the outer world. The "gentility principle" had certainly, in these poets, been overcome, as Alvarez anticipated. But even if "suicide is an art" why should art be so suicidal? In his recent broadcasts on "the Savage God", Alvarez describes the background of these tendencies in twentieth-century art. I believe, however, that he over-emphasises their ubiquity and pre-dominance in European art as a whole. Certainly they are of minimal import-ance in writers such as Pasternak, Holub, Solzhenitsyn, Popa, Voznesensky, Herbert or Hikmet—all, but for the last, admittedly *East*-European. Alvarez is, of course, aware of these writers, and treats some of them with sympathy in *Under Pressure*. But I think it possible that his close acquaintance with British poetry in the 'fifties and 'sixties leads him to overstress certain features of modern writing in general—perhaps with a justifiable tactical intention. In this respect, his interview with Donald Davie, printed in *The Review* not long after the appearance of *The New Poetry*, is revealing: as in the preface to his anthology, Alvarez is at pains to emphasise that

> . . . the forceable recognition of a mass evil outside us has developed precisely parallel with psychoanalysis; that is, with our recognition of the ways in which the same forces are at work within us.

British poetry, still insulated from the full continental shock, did need shaking up ten years ago, not because poets like Davie were unaware of the horrors of the war (or, in due course, of Stalinism); on the contrary, the moderate tone and scope of their poetry was consciously connected with suspicion of irration-ally extreme impulses—but because they were, I believe, still suffering from a more or less severe form of psychic numbing. In any case, however aware they may have been, and Davie certainly was, their poetry of restraint was quite unable to act as "an axe for the frozen sea" within their readers or, probably, within themselves.

These considerations are related to my title through the work of George

Steiner and C. P. Snow, especially as this appears in *Language and Silence*, *In Bluebeard's Castle* and *The Two Cultures and A Second Look*. Steiner's notion that we live in a "post-culture" is based partly on the suspicion that a confident culture is impossible after the last war, because the barbarism, in his view, arose at the centre of (perhaps even caused by the *ennui* at the heart of) high culture; and partly on the view that natural languages are in their decadence, having been politically exploited on the one hand and having given away their subject-matter to the specialised languages of science on the other. There are minor oddities about his exposition of the first point, notably his emphasis on Fascist propaganda and lack of reference for example to American terms such as free-fire zone, terminate with extreme prejudice, Vietnamisation, strategic hamlet, defoliation: it is as though he does not fully accept that language can *always* be misused, that it is *not* an organism with a life of its own which decays once and for all. I shall return to this later on. The point at the moment is that although Steiner does foresee an attempt on man's part to open the last door in Bluebeard's castle, the terms in which he phrases that expectation are tellingly macabre.

> We shall, I expect, open the last door in the castle even if it leads, perhaps *because* it leads, on to realities which are beyond the reach of human comprehension and control. We shall do so with that desolate clairvoyance, so marvellously rendered in Bartok's music, because opening doors is the tragic merit of our identity.

And yet, in what Steiner calls a few sentences later "this cruel late stage in Western affairs", Snow finds it possible to adopt a quite different tone. Like Trotsky in the last chapter of *Literature and Revolution*, Snow foresees an unprecedented opening-up of man's capabilities, always provided that we can overcome considerable practical and psychological difficulties in the way of an equitable world-wide distribution of material and educational resources. On our ability or inability to do this depends what will be found behind Steiner's last door, whether merely the end of an old culture (followed probably by total destruction) or an end which is also a beginning.

In what follows I shall argue, sometimes indirectly, for the validity of Snow's views, but with an eye to the sensitive if sometimes unconvincing attitudes taken by Steiner. The poetry of the British 'sixties, in its most extreme representatives, Sylvia Plath and Ted Hughes, shows the influence of a dual crisis: an emotional crisis following the war and the revelations of psychology, and an intellectual crisis dating back, probably, to the second half of the nineteenth century (see also Robert Langbaum's study of *The Poetry of Experience*). For the purposes of this discussion we can assume, at any rate, that the late nineteenth century was crucial, for it is to that period that, as Erwin Schrödinger notes, expressions such as "model" or "picture" for the conceptual constructs of science go back. The non-scientist, at least, considering developments in modern linguistics, science and sociology, and in philosophy too, may easily begin to feel himself afloat amongst systems of communication, description and value whose relationship to any "reality" have become increasingly provisional and problematic. ("How is it possible for light to be both wave and particle ?") The appalling effects some of these notations could in practice have on the real world—as in the splitting of the atom—only increases, for many, the feeling of helplessness. The response of many literary people to the scientific revolution still seems to be expressible in its essentials in the terms used by James Thompson in 1874. They see with horror a universe

> Which never had for man a special clause
> Of cruelty or kindness, love or hate:

in which

> All substance lives and struggles evermore
>   Through countless shapes continually at war,
> By countless interactions interknit:
> If one is born a certain day on earth,
> All times and forces tended to that birth,
>   Not all the world could change or hinder it.
>
> I find no hint throughout the Universe
> Of good or ill, of blessing or of curse;
>   I find alone Necessity Supreme;
> With infinite Mystery, abysmal, dark,
> Unlighted ever by the faintest spark
>   For us the flitting shadows of a dream.

These thoughts seem to lead Thompson, with a naturalness which is only too familiar, towards the possibility of suicide, as a means of escape from the consciousness of a destruction ready to engulf all that is humanly precious. The truth is, of course, that human life is intrinsically neither worse nor better when we understand it in this way. God is not dead, he never existed. But by bringing up children within a framework of ancient pieties, whose basic message may be valuable but whose terms are outworn, we allow the traumatic shock to reproduce itself again and again even in the later part of the twentieth century. Ted Hughes is surely right to say, in his introduction to the poems of Vasko Popa, that East-European poets are better able than we to avoid the disappointment of "impossible and unreal expectations".

> Their poetic themes revolve around the living suffering spirit, capable of happiness, much deluded, too frail, with doubtful and provisional senses, so undefinable as to be almost silly, but palpably existing, and wanting to go on existing—and this is not, as in Beckett's world, absurd. It is the only precious thing, and designed in accord with the whole universe. Designed, indeed, by the whole universe. They are not the spoiled brats of civilization disappointed of impossible and unreal expectations and deprived of the revelations of necessity.

This is, I think, a very beautiful statement of an alternative response to the modern view of man and of his systems of value and communication. It goes, however, beyond the world-view presented in *Crow*, which satisfies in a quite startling way (as I have argued elsewhere) the description of modern poetry given by Roland Barthes in *Writing Degree Zero*.

> The interrupted flow of the new poetic language initiates a discontinuous Nature, which is revealed only piecemeal. . . . In it, Nature becomes a fragmented space, made up of objects solitary and terrible, because the links between them are only potential. . . . This . . . discourse is full of terror, that is to say, it relates man not to other men, but to the most inhuman images in Nature: heaven, hell, holiness, childhood, madness, pure matter, etc.

The difference is one of attitude rather than of diagnosis.

> Burning
>   burning
>   burning
>   there was finally something
> The sun could not burn, that it had rendered
> Everything down to—a final obstacle
> Against which it raged and charred
>
> And rages and chars
>
> Limpid among the glaring furnace clinkers
> The pulsing blue tongues and the red and the yellow
> The green lickings of the conflagration
>
> Limpid and black—
>
> Crow's eye-pupil, in the tower of its scorched fort.

"Crow's Last Stand" hints at many themes I want to explore, and I shall let phrases from it introduce sections of my argument. The title itself, of course, brings it into relation with Steiner's "last door" in Bluebeard's castle, and the first half-line inevitably reminds one of Eliot's lament for a decadent society, of his elitist view of the "young man carbuncular" who comes, inevitably, from the lower classes (a fact which always sets up an ironic echo in my mind with Dryden's notorious elegy "Upon the Death of the Lord Hastings") and of ancient religious sanctions through its derivation from the Buddha's Fire Sermon. My point is not, of course, that Hughes is aligning himself with Eliot. It is simply that we are at once led to imagine an end-of-the-world situation, especially when we come next to an apparent allusion to the sun's expansion and the reduction of this planet to "clinkers'. In this crisis, Crow makes a last stand which, in several respects, anticipates my own argument in everything but emotional tone.

AMONG THE GLARING FURNACE CLINKERS

The removal of the "gentility principle" could not of itself account for the *direction* of the change, towards the creative exploration of breakdown. The direction of the new poetry was towards man's "suffering spirit" rather than his capability of "happiness". The cause, surely, is that emotional crisis which explicitly and implicitly haunts Alvarez' programmatic statements and, indeed, much of the poetry itself, especially that of Sylvia Plath. She appears in her poems as a typical "survivor" in the psychiatric sense. Her work shows many traits which are recognised as marking the psychology of those who have, in some bodily or psychic sense, survived an experience of death. These are described by Robert Jay Lifton, for example, in his analysis of *Death in Life: The Survivors of Hiroshima*. They can be summarised as extreme vulnerability to danger, a sense of being bound to the dead and of guilt at having survived them, an attraction towards a masochistic life-pattern and a liability to suffer from bodily complaints. End-of-the-world imagery is frequent, as is a tendency to assert mastery over death (and assuage guilt) by repeating the process of dying in an imaginative form so that its outcome is a miraculous survival. Impressions of a "monstrous alteration of the body substance" (inner dissolution) and of "a breakdown . . . in the larger human matrix" (dissolution of the outside universe) are widespread, too, amongst survivors. Sylvia Plath's poems, especially in the three main books published after her death, show all these traits to be central rather than peripheral. They are the source not only of single images but of the strategy of whole poems. Since any sensitive comment on the embodiment of these traits in the poems is impossible here, I would refer the reader for example to "Lady Lazarus", "Tulips", "Cut", "Elm", "Medusa", "A Birthday Present", "Daddy", "Fever 103°", "The Bee Meeting" in *Ariel*; "Wuthering Heights", "Crossing the Water", "Face Lift", "Insomniac", "In Plaster", "Event", "Love Letter", "A Life", "Apprehension", "Last Words" in *Crossing the Water*; and "Childless Woman", "By Candlelight", "Thalidomide", "Mary's Song", and "Three Women" in *Winter Trees*. As an element in this complex of emotions, imagining death has a life-enhancing function. To "do it so it feels like hell" and then rise "out of the ash" still "the same, identical woman" (that emphasis is revealing) is not only a gesture of solidarity with the dead, other women and the Jews—

> My face a featureless, fine
> Jew linen

or, in another poem,

> I began to talk like a Jew.
> I think I may well be a Jew.

It is an assertion of power, over death but also (less attractive but psychologically authentic) over other human beings.

> Out of the ash

> I rise with my red hair
> And I eat men like air.

Many poems are by no means so explicit, but nevertheless refer to the same complex of emotions.

Of course subject-matter which has a restorative rôle for the survivor may appear morbid to others. Lifton concludes his study of the creative response to Hiroshima with this suggestion.

> For the world at large A-bomb creativity becomes part of a wider art and literature of survival which, through directing itself both to holocausts already experienced and those feared in the future, becomes a possible source of wisdom about man's increasingly troubled relationship to the kinds of death which face him.

For this wider significance to be present there has, I feel, to be an effort at "formulation", at re-establishing contact with the general human matrix. It is here that Sylvia Plath stops short. Leaving aside the lack of any general statement of a philosophical kind, it is still true that the human figures in her poems tend to be torturers, victims, the already dead, a threatened child. The infant's gaze will be met not by the traditional charms of existence but by

> this troublous
> Wringing of hands, this dark
> Ceiling without a star.

It seems that she could not honestly formulate a positive vision of life which would be consistent with her experience of death. But Eliot's redemption of "the waste sad time", in terms of the significance of those moments between which it stretches, availed itself of concepts and attitudes (and images) irremediably out of date. To turn from the *Four Quartets* to modern astronomy is to receive an irreversible mental jolt.

A FINAL OBSTACLE

Sylvia Plath herself, in "Candles" (*Crossing the Water*), says that

> This is no time for the private point of view
> . . .
> In twenty years I shall be retrograde.

Perhaps this is not entirely ironical. Perhaps she foresaw the possibility of a passage beyond the trauma. I hope, at any rate, that what I have said does not seem to suggest that psychological explanations can ever "explain away" creative achievement. Sylvia Plath's extravagant metaphors and flashy verbal limping are, where they occur, often a form of implicit communication, a witty acknowledgment both of the reader's relative calm and of her own (in the circumstances preposterous) artistic intention. Only an exceptional person would be able to "cool it" by using vulgarity to puncture vulgarity, to retain a sense of decorum at the centre of an ontological whirlpool. And that is the crux of her message—the retention of discrimination and the will to speak, the will to communicate. Her determination not to accept relief from any ready-made dogma is admirable. As Fred Hoyle says,

> Here we are in this wholly fantastic universe with scarcely a clue as to whether our existence has any real significance. No wonder then that many people feel the need for some belief that gives them a sense of security, and no wonder that they become very angry with people like me who say that this security is illusory. But I do not like the situation any better than they do. The difference is that I cannot see how the smallest advantage is to be gained from deceiving myself.

(Many will recall the different attitude taken to similar issues in Erich Heller's *The Disinherited Mind*.) Even so, it seems that a tentative contrast might still be drawn between Sylvia Plath and, say, Nelly Sachs. There is perhaps something in the thought that the worse and more direct the experience, the more right one may feel one has, if one recovers, to take horror for granted and to construct something positive—to feel that the dead impose a duty to live rather than a duty to mourn.

THERE WAS FINALLY SOMETHING
THE SUN COULD NOT BURN, THAT IT HAD RENDERED
EVERYTHING DOWN TO

It is at this point that reference to what I have called the intellectual crisis becomes necessary, because one obstacle in the way of any attempt at formulating a life-view (given the collapse of traditional dogma) must be a general lack of confidence, at least amongst literary people, in synoptic thought. And the intellectual crisis does, indeed, run deeper than any crisis in religious thought alone could do. It affects, as I have already suggested, all man's symbolic systems (using "system" as before in its widest sense). And here I differ somewhat from Steiner.* He sees the crisis as relating to a take-over by science of territories previously thought to lie within the grasp of natural language and therefore within the boundaries of Parnassus. But this is something of a misconception. Our intellectual disturbance runs so deep because we now know that even the languages of science are only hypothetically related to "reality"—and we have not yet quite realised that the old opposition of poetry's "lies" to science's "truth" is far too unsophisticated. We are suffering simultaneously, as it were, from two incompatible attacks on our confidence. One used to tell us that science was objective—that *it* saw the rainbow while *we* (and poetry) did not—Steiner's is merely a contemporary version of that old bugbear. The other tells us that all systems, those of science

---

* This essay was written before Steiner's *Imagining Science* appeared (*The Listener*, November 18 1971).

as well as those of ordinary language, are no more than tentative—what the rainbow "really is" (if it is at all) we shall never know. The true situation, as I see it, is that since we cannot *contrast* our systems with an independent reality, the whole force of our disappointment with them is illogical—what we *do* see we see thanks to and not in spite of them. And on the other hand, the scientific and non-scientific modes of seeing the rainbow are just that— different modes, not truth versus a lie.

It is interesting to find Schrödinger (in *Mind and Matter*, 1956) discussing the same issues with reference to Eddington's two desks: the piece of furniture established by his senses and the whirl of electrons and nuclei, always separated by spaces at least 100,000 times their own size, presented to him by his scientific knowledge. Schrödinger argues that although scientific work is based on and brought back for evaluation to human perceptions and judgement, it does not account for such introspectively known impressions as those of colour, sound, taste and the rest, let alone for emotions. The world of science is colourless, soundless, tasteless and, if it even makes sense to say so, emotionless. That was what so horrified Thompson, even in 1874. But Schrödinger is surely right. The fact that the scientific world is of this nature leaves something important unaccounted for, something upon which all the rest is based. I shall not pursue Schrödinger's more ambitious line of philosophical argument. My own is, simply, that only natural language *can* deal with this central area. As Schrödinger shows, the sciences cannot. And yet if the wisdom we derive from science is to be of any value, it must be of value *to us*, and our values and perceptions form the privileged subject-matter of natural languages.

It seems, then, that these languages and their creative use, far from making a "last stand", can at last be understood for what they are—the only means we have of talking about a central area of all life-experience. Our familiarity with them has almost made us unaware of their presence, of all that we could not do or articulate without them. We no longer imagine the earth to be the centre of the Universe. But our presence is central in a far more important sense. Poetry has only to accustom itself to its true nature (about which, no doubt, we have still much to discover). *Via* the system of physics we see, as Eddington said,

> . . . a shadowgraph performance of familiar life. The shadow of my elbow rests on the shadow table as the shadow ink flows over the shadow paper . . . The frank realisation that physical science is concerned with a world of shadows is one of the most significant of recent advances.

Commenting on this passage, Schrödinger points out that the world has not suddenly acquired this shadowy character. It has always had it, only "we were not aware of it". The realisation that science's own constructs are "shadowy", are models, only completes our liberation from Thompson's and Eddington's shadows. Shakespeare, too, and Beethoven, lived in this world. We have only to accustom ourselves to "what is the case" without jumping to unwarrantably pessimistic conclusions. The result should be, ultimately, to release our imaginations from pedestrian domestic verse and equally pedestrian mythologies, for example from the literalities (as opposed to the insights) of religion and from crude notions of space and time.

IN THE TOWER OF ITS SCORCHED FORT

Although *Crow* is sophisticated enough to evolve its myth within a modern universe of hypothesis, it does not embody (as do its author's comments in his discussion of Vasko Popa) that lack of panic, that gay attitude towards the universe which one tends to find, as Steiner remarks, in scientists and mathematicians—I would think of Schrödinger, Lanczos, Hoyle, Feynman. The truth is that the literary world (or that part of it which is at all aware of such matters) is like an adolescent struggling with a first intimate sense of death—unable to function maturely in the new existential context. In this respect at least, the scientist is fortunate to have early contact with a different culture. The shock is less severe and the terms are at hand with which to handle it.

Two poets of the 'sixties do, however, appear to move in their very different ways towards a mature acceptance of the dual crisis. Burns Singer, who died at the age of 36, seven years ago, is the more intellectual of the two in the sense that his poetry explicitly handles scientific insights. His *Collected Poems* (published posthumously in 1971), his review articles for *Encounter*, *The Times Literary Supplement*, and elsewhere, and his unpublished papers, show a mind capable of moving comfortably amongst abstract ideas, whether philosophical or scientific (he was a research biologist). That such thinking did not draw him away from the main task of poetry as I have described it is evident from the following, previously unpublished, jotting:

> When a poet presents a series of logical thoughts in a poem, it is not to express the logic of these thoughts and thus to allow the reader to draw their logical corollaries in other mnemonics—rather, it is to force the reader through the thinking of these thoughts, since that process of thinking them is an essential part of the experience which he wishes to recreate in his reader. It does not matter therefore if one logical series is placed alongside another with which it is logically irreconcileable, provided that both series properly belong to the experience in which they are involved. This explains many apparent inconsistencies in the work of major writers.

He makes a similar point in a poem when he says that

> Thought is always and only thought:
> The thinking's different: thinking's in the blood.
> ("Oracle Engraved on the Back of a Mirror", 1960.)

Singer's early development was greatly influenced by W. S. Graham, and it is interesting that much later, in *Malcolm Mooney's Land* (1970), Graham interprets language as a means of making space for human contacts. "The Constructed Space" is very explicitly concerned with the relationship between public (intersubjective) language and the private (unique) meanings it may acquire in a relationship.

> I say this silence or, better, construct this space
> So that somehow something may move across
> The caught habits of language to you and me.

In another poem he insists that

> This is no other place
> Than where I am, between
> This word and the next.

And in the fine concluding poem, "Clusters Travelling Out", Graham takes the image of a man in solitary confinement tapping messages "along the plumbing of the world".

> I tap
> And tap to interrupt silence into
> Manmade durations making for this
> A dialect for our purpose.
> TAPTAP. Are you reading that taptap
> I send out to you along
> My element? O watch. Here they come
> Opening and shutting Communication's
> Gates as they approach, History's
> Princes with canisters of gas
> Crystals to tip and snuff me out
> Strangled and knotted with my kind . . .

Here, as in Singer's most powerful poems (written between the early 'fifties and his death), there is a sense of human connectedness, of the value as well as fragility of communication. In Singer, connectedness often takes a form which must owe much to his biological interests, as in this passage from "The Gentle Engineer", a poem written in 1951–2.

> It is my own blood nips at every pore
> And I myself the calcified treadmark of
> Process towards me:
> All of a million delicate engines whisper
> Warm now, to go now
> Through dragnets of tunnels forwards as my life.
> I carry that which I am carried by.

This sense of being part of the universe, not lost in it, allows for a more positive formulation than does "wodwoism". I mean by wodwoism the impression both Ted Hughes' *Wodwo* and *Crow* give, though on a different scale, of a creature dissociated from its environment, "dropped out of nothing casually" and unable, therefore, to define itself in terms of its environment. Wodwo asks, "What am I?", "Why do I . . .?", but can formulate only hypothetical answers which have not even any basis in scientific speculation and leave the questioner with nothing to resort to but tenacity: "very queer but I'll go on looking". Hughes' transposed mythical terms may have the drawback that they do not of themselves draw his imagination or ours towards any supports the natural world can give. Thinking over the difference of orientation between these two poets, Hughes and Singer, what Keats said in the letter to Reynolds of May 1818 occurred to me.

> Every department of Knowledge we see excellent and calculated towards a great whole. I am so convinced of this, that I am glad at not having given away my medical Books, which I shall again look over to keep alive the little I knew thitherwards . . . An extensive knowledge is needful to thinking people—it takes away the heat and fever; and helps, by widening speculation, to ease the Burden of the Mystery . . . The difference of high Sensations with and without knowledge appears to me this—in the latter case we are falling continually ten thousand fathoms deep and being blown up again without wings and with all the horror of a bare shouldered creature—in the former case, our shoulders are fledge, and we got thro' the same air and space without fear.

Since, however, "the axioms of philosophy are not axioms until they are proved upon our pulses", the poet is left with his task undiminished, as Singer clearly knew when he made those jottings about logical series. He strikes a fine balance between world-sorrow—analogous to Thompson's— and joy in the luck of living.

LIMPID AND BLACK

Tony Connor, on the other hand, develops his formulations on a less abstract level but with powerful and confident intelligence. To hear him discuss his poetry with an audience is to realise the extent to which it is supported by a subtle awareness of the issues I have been discussing. His admiration for Wallace Stevens, otherwise a very different kind of writer, is based on sympathy for his handling of these issues (I shall return to Stevens later on). Although Connor has been seen by some as a "local" poet, one concerned with cataloguing the features of his district (Manchester), even his first three books ('62, '65, '68) contain no poems which do not explore, sometimes in terms of rich material detail, themes of crucial importance. The first poem in the first book strikes a note which is heard throughout his work. It is called "End of the World".

> The world had gone
> and everyone on it, except the lives
> all of us had to live: the wives,
> children, clocks which ticked on,

> unpaid bills, enormous power-blocks
> chock-full of arms demanding peace . . .

Throughout his poetry, Connor is clearly a survivor, but one looking for a vision which might also "survive the silent uproar"; though in *With Love Somehow*—a significant title—he sees himself most intensely as

> bright bits of words staining a black gurgle.

A poem in the next volume, *Lodgers*, traces the source of doubt very explicitly. The poet has been trying to unblock a waste-pipe.

> Using the plunger, I began to feel jaded
> and disillusioned; something more was needed
>
> than mere poems to right the world.
> My hands were numb; I remembered the millions killed
> in God's name; I remembered bombs, gas-chambers, famine, poverty,
> and my greying hair. I could not write poetry.

The humour is self-critical, knowing that these disasters *do* affect us in such trivial ways and can be made to serve as excuses for trivial failures, but nevertheless form a deadly background to much of our thinking. *Kon in Springtime* takes its title from a poem which faces this knowledge yet again. Kon is a Russian emigré living next door to the poet.

> I like sharing
> the area with him; revolutions,
> pogroms, years in a concentration
> camp, haven't made him despair
> of human nature.

The relationship between the poet attempting to write and the Russian is rendered by implication rather than statement.

> May I survive a barbarous age
> as well! Muttering and miming punches,
> under a clear blue sky he crunches
> back to the door across the spillage
> of cinders from his pail. I watch
> from the kitchen table, where I've sat
> all night, struggling to be a poet . . .

Elsewhere, Connor speaks of the "stunned survivor's sense of guilt", of

> . . . the bleak dead
> the battle-stained dead
> lapping the black blood;
> what can I say at the world's end?

The complex of reactions which Sylvia Plath explored is present in Connor's work, though differently approached. And in the 1971 volume, *In the Happy Valley*, it is treated more intellectually than before, with a more overt determination to achieve explicit formulations of ideas and responses (if not anything so final as a "vision"). The greater clarity may have something to do with the fact that survival is now related to actual experiences of near-death, to an "attack" and to a car-accident. The latter is referred to in "Convalescence".

> The usual silent commotion in space
> shines on my multi-lacerated scalp,
>   beneath which
> I trim my expectations.

(There is a relevant echo between "silent commotion" and "silent uproar".) The worst fears are now impersonal, as in "Names on Stone".

> In old graveyards
> I could wonder what matters.
> All those particular names
> affect me like a starry sky.

Again, Pascal's silent spaces seem to be the cause of fear.

> If you go back far enough
> even the most stubborn accumulations
> lose all meaning.
> Stones hold names
>
> like stars. You look,
> and around you
> the emptiness deepens
> with everything named that no one knows.

The notion that there is a destruction beyond normal disasters, a total destruction of *meaning*, dogs these poems and is ultimately kept at bay only by the ironic knowledge that we have "inherited the earth" and that not to speak is not, either, to achieve innocence. We must not refuse

> the clumsy confusing act
> of breaking the perfect-making silence.

The concern is not with poetry, though that is often the disguise it wears, but with being human. As I wrote elsewhere, the cunningly disreputable and burlesque, the comically tricky, which appeared as subject-matter in earlier poems, now surface in rapid feints of diction, in the teasings of a deeply serious and comradely hocus-pocus. The sense of direct communication is very strong—it does not surprise me that Tony Connor is now writing plays which though they may be tragic are not despairing, and set up an extra-ordinary warmth of contact between actors and audience, an atmosphere more typical of farce than of "straight" theatre. The importance of this is obvious. Though a poet of outlived disaster, Connor has been able to retain a human vitality which has survived the blackest necessities of the "scorched fort".

CROW'S EYE-PUPIL

I have not attempted any overall assessment of the four poets whose responses to certain key topics I have been exploring. To do that, I should have had to consider their work in much greater detail and in other dimensions. Literature cannot be judged by paraphraseable content alone, thought that is not irrelevant, and modern linguistics has made us increasingly aware that meaning in the fullest sense arises from an interaction of formal and semantic structures. I have, though, kept my closer readings in mind while discussing these poets within a general framework. It is clear that they have gone beyond the "gentility principle" in very different ways. But they are all closer to George Barker and W. S. Graham, and the later "romantics", than they are to the Movement. Those who think that *Crow* is kitsch will, however, enjoy the following lines from Dylan Thomas's "A Letter to My Aunt Discussing the Correct Approach to Modern Poetry".

> Remember, too, that life is hell
> And even heaven has a smell
> Of putrefying angels who
> Make deadly whoopee in the blue.
> These things remembered, what can stop
> A poet going to the top?

My own view is that poetry needed to take seriously the notion that "life is hell" and neither healthy pooh-poohing nor a poetic doctrine of individual salvation could stand up to the pressure of that need. Both forms of psychic numbing had to be overcome. *Crow* is probably the extreme point of that overcoming, and also a formulation of it in more general terms: the embodiment, in fact, of an end which is also a beginning. The intimations of a new direction are still more striking in Hughes' discussion of Vasko Popa.

Which brings me to translation. J. M. Cohen's description of "where we are now", in his six-language study of the *Poetry of This Age* up to 1965, paints a picture of the "resolute insularity" of British poetry which was surely out of date even six years ago. However that may be, there is now no doubt of the massive adaptation of many British poets to the continental and East-European experience. Translation is indeed a symbol of the basic activities of sympathy and metamorphosis involved in creative writing. Steiner's fine "Introduction" to *World Poetry in Modern Verse Translation* makes this clear. The activities of Middleton and Hamburger, of Singer (*Five Centuries of Polish Poetry*, with Jerzy Peterkiewicz), of Davie (*The Forests of Lithuania* and *Zhivago Poems*), the translations published in *Stand* and in *Modern Poetry in Translation*, the *Poetry Europe* series started by Donald Carroll in 1966, the *Penguin* translations—all these show a growing and practical interest on the part of poets in what is going on abroad, and it is now obvious to what an extent this interest has affected not only poetic strategy but also ideas about language and reality. It is now unlikely that any poet would disagree with the linguists Whorf or Sapir, whose respective views are typically expressed in the following passages.

> Every language is a vast pattern system, different from others, in which are culturally ordained the forms and categories by which the personality not only communicates, but also analyses nature, notices or neglects types of relationship and phenomena, channels his reasoning, and builds the house of his consciousness.

> The literary artist may never be quite conscious of just how he is hindered or helped or otherwise guided by the matrix, but when it is a question of translating his work into another language, the nature of the original matrix manifests itself at once.

It is obvious that, if the linguists are right (and they echo so many poets), natural language occupies a position of central human interest. They are supported by linguistic philosophy which, as David Pears points out in his analysis of Wittgenstein, is anthropocentric. (Similar points have been made about the visual arts by Geidion and Gombrich.) The conclusion must be, that the fancies of Rimbaud and Rilke were not altogether fanciful. There is a sense in which poets are engaged in transmuting reality into language, though it would be truer to say that they are collaborating in its creation. Tennyson's parable of the mirror which "cracked from side to side" at the direct revelation of reality cannot be translated into modern terms, simply because such a revelation cannot occur (the experience of horror, even, is never received raw). The web we weave is not necessarily doomed by its flimsiness in relation to *ding an sich*, though I hope it is clear that I am not constructing a defence of mere fancifulness. In Wallace Stevens' words,

> It is not only that the imagination adheres to reality, but, also, that reality adheres to the imagination and that the interdependence is essential.

Robinson Jeffers is fundamentally mistaken when he suggests that we can abandon the poor approximations of language for a direct look at the wild swan of the world. So silence, Tony Connor's "wordless poems of winter walks", will not, as he knows, answer the challenge of reality. And the tragic "accumulation of silence" demanded by Elie Wiesel (and which seems to haunt Steiner) is of significance only as a mourning sacrifice of what is most significant and most precious. Its own significance is, in fact, *contrastive*.

It might be well to pause briefly here before concluding. Is the poetic orientation I am suggesting fundamentally elitist? I believe not. It can accommodate simple human emotions—in fact it returns to them their value —quite as well as it can more sophisticated speculation: Tony Connor and Burns Singer show this clearly. Like Snow's preference for a unified literary-scientific culture, it is an orientation which necessarily anticipates the possibility of such a culture really becoming established. Steiner's enthusiasm for science seems to me to be vitiated by the elitism of his concept of the "masses" for there is no hint, in his treatment of them, that he realises how much a decent educational system could do. Here his attitude is in marked contrast to that of Snow.

> What save half-truths, gross oversimplifications or trivia can, in fact, be communicated to that semi-literate mass audience which consumer democracy has summoned into the marketplace? Only in a diminished or corrupted language can most such communication be effective.

Even Steiner's own language, here, suffers from a most unpleasant strain of cliché. One must at least comment that the English used in these media is often an interlingua, a kind of dialectal esperanto with none of the subtlety of any of the dialects from which it is drawn. To assume, as Steiner apparently does, that it reflects the standards of speech of the individual members of the "mass audience" would be ignorant prejudice. Certainly it no more reflects working-class than it does middle-class or intellectual speech, each of which have their own riches. A similar crudity of approach, surprising in view of Steiner's generally subtler approach to language, is evident in his acceptance of vocabulary-counts as a satisfactory index of linguistic value in speech. Jackson and Marsden's comments on such partial tests are entirely to the point and are worth quoting here, although they should be read in their context in *Education and the Working Class* for their full import to become clear.

> Glancing at the difference in speech between working-class parent and middle-class child on these pages, one is reminded again of what it is in language that speaks for quality of feeling, for sharpness of mind informed by generosity of response. It is not necessarily that which can be measured easily. It is not size of vocabulary. It is not number of abstract words to concrete words. (We hardly measure language under the pressure of genius in this way.)

That over half the children leaving school before sixth-form are as talented as those who stay on (*Crowther Report*) must surely suggest to anyone concerned with the true state of affairs that amongst the "masses" there are highly intelligent men and women whose educational opportunities have remained unfulfilled. This Snow assumes. And indeed no one should need the *Crowther Report* to point out what is so obvious from everyday contacts. If I may again use the shorthand argumentation of reference, B. T. Bottomore's study of *Elites and Society* is one easily available argument for a social recognition of the fact that, as he puts it,

> . . . for all their individual idiosyncrasies, human beings are remarkably alike in some fundamental respects: they have similar physical, emotional and intellectual needs. That is why there can be a science of nutrition, and

in a less exact way, sciences of mental health and healing, and of the educa-
tion of children. Furthermore, the range of variation in the qualities of
individuals is relatively narrow, and there is a clustering about the middle
range.

A great deal therefore depends on education and on social environment in
general. One of Roland Barthes' more tenable ideas in *Writing Degree Zero*
is that the mode of writing one adopts is an implicit indication of his or her
social commitment—not only towards the present but towards the future.
Precisely because language is not, of course, an organism with its own autono-
mous life (not, that is, in Steiner's sense) but an institution modified though
not created from scratch by those who use it, the writer has a duty to use it in
a way that reflects, to the best of his ability, both his fullest and most honest
view of "man" (hence no "writing down") and the most generous attitude
he can justify towards the potentialities of "men". On both counts, Snow is
attractive and convincing in *The Two Cultures* (if not in some later work).
What he urges on us with tenable good sense is essentially that we should see
ourselves as a pre-culture. It may be after all that some of Steiner's attitudes
are to be traced back to a survivor's inability to conceive of "the next world
. . . the next spring".

I CARRY THAT WHICH I AM CARRIED BY

Singer's sense of himself, of man, as a part of reality—as reality become con-
scious, able to speak of itself—is a radically different conception from that of
a creature in a hostile world into which it has somehow been dropped. Our
minds may, by long habit, seem to us to be "over against" reality but in fact
they are certainly part of it. *I am a part of what is real, and that is my speech,
and the strength of it, this only, that I hear and ever shall.* Man is a means for
the forces he wishes to understand to understand themselves. In Singer's
words,

> . . . I meet in my least, impoverished impulse
> Enormous autonomies I come to dread,
> And then accept . . .

In this context he finds it possible (in another poem, "The Corner Boy's
Farewell", 1962) to envisage with acceptance also

> . . . my lifelong voyage
> Of seeing what has always been most loved grow dim and disappear
> Into perfection's prodigies of peace.
>
> Into the sacrifice bitterly endless of all that man means
> In terms of bones, breath, skin and brain,
> Of his achievements, even the love humility achieved.
> Love he can only like a beggar take
> From the kind hand of passage hidden in his heart,

> The hand that could be merciless as he,
> Deny as he denies.

To speak of "the kind hand of passage" so naturally in this context certainly indicates a love achieved by a very special kind of humility. Now that we have become sensitive not only to the spaces in the sky but those in the solidity of wood and stone and in the structure of our own flesh, we cannot afford to be afraid of them. They are no longer "out there" but "here" and "in here" too, where I am doing this thinking and you this reading. But let Wallace Stevens, the prophet of a viable philosophy of poetry, have his last word inscribed over the portal. Without comment, certain lines from "The Man with the Blue Guitar":

> They said, "You have a blue guitar,
> You do not play things as they are."
>
> The man replied, "Things as they are
> Are changed upon the blue guitar."
>
> And they said then, "But play, you must,
> A tune beyond us, yet ourselves,
>
> A tune upon the blue guitar
> Of things exactly as they are."
> . . .
>
> And I am merely a shadow hunched
>
> Above the arrowy, still strings,
> The maker of a thing yet to be made . . .
> . . .
>
> Things as they are have been destroyed.
> Have I?
> . . .
>
> That I may reduce the monster to
> Myself, and then may be myself
>
> In face of the monster . . .

These lines trace the paradigm of an experience to which poetry as a whole must grow up in order to achieve again a genuine confidence. If it can, it will know that Stevens was right:

> It was when I said
> There is no such thing as the truth
> That the grapes grew fatter,
> The fox ran out of his hole.

It will have matured as a poetry of hypothesis.

Myth and History in Recent Poetry

by Terry Eagleton

IN one of his *Essex Poems*, Donald Davie casts a wistful glance at a mute, inscrutable image of transcendence:

> Resignation, oh winter tree
> At peace, at peace . . .
> Read it what way you will,
> A wish that fathers. In a field between
> The Sokens, Thorpe and Kirby, stands
> A bare Epiphany.

The desire for transcendence of some kind is, clearly enough, a major impulse for the poet of *Essex Poems*—a poet who, he tells us with fine distaste, has "spun on the greasy axis/Of business and sociometrics", manoeuvring and negotiating with radical students in the heartlands of industrial Essex. Yet there's surely something notable about the blank disjunction between those placed local details of The Sokens, Thorpe and Kirby, and the cryptic epiphany which alludes beyond them. The place-names are there to localise but not domesticate the epiphany: they are needed to lend it substantial existence, to rescue it from the vagueness of closing poetic gesture, but at the same time must be made to keep their distance, so that a faintly ironic gap can be opened up between topography and the transcendent. The epiphanic tree is the mystical which can be shown but not spoken of; it comes at the end of the poem, as an ambivalently troubled and finalised note, so that the poem itself is unable to follow the symbol into the dimension to which it gestures. The poet remains stranded firmly on this side of the divide which separates greasy, empirical Essex from the dumb absolutes of peace, nature and death; he might even, one is tempted to guess, have seen the tree from a car.

Davie, one might go on to say, didn't remain stranded there long: he left for the United States.

> Pacific is the end of the world,
> Pacific, peaceful.

America, in fact, as a mode of transcendence: a passing from the constrictions of Colchester to a place which seems to unite the peace of a deathly withdrawal with the excitement of expansive frontiers. The next volume which Davie produced was his *Six Epistles to Eva Hesse*: epistles which crystallise an ambivalently critical and admiring response to Black Mountain ideology. The poet of this book is caught "in a bind" between two possibilities. On the one hand lie the attractions of the mythologising geographers

(Olson, Dorn) who, by knotting, conflating and spatialising historical time, achieve a kind of global liberation won at the possible cost of a reverence for routine causality. On the other hand lies an adherence to that temporal causality ("linear" aesthetics, the poem as process, a sense of the irreducibly historical) which can involve the equally dangerous corollary of fetishising history, so squeezing out humble contingency or historically fruitless heroics.

Out of this running battle between mythological free-wheeling and a more sober, evolutionary empiricism, emerges a tentative solution: comedy. Comedy is concerned with ends, and so linear, but also takes up an ironically tolerant stance towards historical failure:

> So we must make the Comic Muse,
> If reluctantly, infuse
> The homelier, more homespun virtues
> With some quality of *eclat*,
> A *Je ne sais* (exactly) *quoi* . . .

An equable comic poise, however, also has its limits: it can't adequately cope with the recalcitrant facts of unflamboyant misery or struggling heroism. As a posture, it preserves its equipoise only by fending off disruptive experience which would undermine it. Yet if the choice is between full-blooded historical engagement and the compassionate ironies of an aerial view, Davie will plump for the latter, weaving the threads of history into a comforting cat's-cradle into which he can relax:

> No, England, if I have to choose,
> There are some myths too good to lose;
> And if my choice must lie between
> Barbara Castle and Christine
> Brooke-Rose, I have no wish to flatter
> In plumping firmly for the latter . . .

The problem confronting Davie, then, is how to balance the liberating transcendence attainable through myth with a need to stay alertly sympathetic to the humbly particular and historical. And it seems an inevitable problem for an art and ideology which have ceased to find the possibility of transcendence within history itself—in which history has been frozen (to use a telling phrase from another of the *Essex Poems*) into a static range of "bleak equal centuries". Yet—to follow that same poem further—this blank de-historicising releases its own sense of freedom: once it is recognised that there's no trust to be placed in history as any kind of absolute, the indifferent centuries may file past the poet to receive an equable benediction:

> Goodbye to all the centuries. There is
> No home in them, much as the dip and turn
> Of an honest alley charmingly deceives us.
>
> And yet not quite goodbye. Instead almost

> Welcome, I said. Bleak equal centuries
> Crowded the porch to be deflowered, crowned.

Loss in one direction (the poem tells of Davie's disillusioning return to his Yorkshire sources) is gain in another: as the centuries lapse into a level horizon they free the poet into a wider, apparently wiser perspective. Knotting history into a single, omnipresent dimension, to revert to the imagery of the *Epistles*, is to string together a trampoline which can toss the poet into the heady realms of mythologising freedom:

> Olson in a magazine
> Explains what his cat's-cradles mean:
> Each is, he says, a *trampoline* . . .
> His knots in history he intends
> That we should take as means towards ends.
> The strings of Time are to be plaited
> Like woven canvas, bound or matted
> Into (these are Olson's glosses)
> A vibrant standing-place to toss us
> Into who knows what upper air?

Other English poets beside Davie seem to have taken a recent turn towards myth. Gunn's *Moly*, Hughes's *Crow*, Geoffrey Hill's *Mercian Hymns*, Patrick Creagh's *To Abel and others*, Stuart Montgomery's *Circe*, George Mackay Brown's Orkney sagas, Christopher Logue's experiments with Homer: slight as some of these volumes are, and loose as the term "myth" needs to be to cover that assortment, it may still be true that, taken together, they add up to a significant new phenomenon. Alongside this tendency to myth has run a concern with what might more precisely be termed "legend": Hill and Mackay Brown fall partly into this category, but the most obvious example, perhaps, is Jon Silkin's explorations of life in a nineteenth-century Durham mining community. "Myth" and "legend" suggest rather different emphases: examining modern experience through myth, in the case of poets like Gunn, Creagh and Montgomery, takes the form of timeless universalisations achieved through symbol and archetype; "legend" works in an opposite direction, excavating the substance of a specific time and place remote from ours, salvaging it for re-inhabitation. Variations of style and technique have reflected these alternative approaches: the frail, elusive, weightless diction of Creagh or Montgomery, as against the gnarled, myopically particular materialism of Silkin or the tough, burnished language of Hill's *Mercian Hymns*. The first mode threatens to evaporate, the second to bury, its subject out of sight. But the important difference is that legend is still able to accommodate a sense of historicity, in ways which myth isn't. Legend, at least in the hands of Silkin, excavates the past, explores the concept and substance of community, as a way, hopefully, of renewing the present. For myth, that historical tension is obviously difficult to sustain.

Thom Gunn's development seems particularly important here. In a fairly loose sense of the term, Gunn has been equipped with a myth from the outset —that of Sartrian existentialism. Its advantage, as in Sartre's early philosophical work, has been its ability to bring the contingencies of personal and social history into some kind of relation with an underlying ontology. That relation has rarely been an easy one in Gunn's actual poetry: the specific action of a poem too often merely stiffly bodied out (a recurrent Gunn verb) an *a priori* metaphysic. But the Sartrian myth did allow a limited kind of transaction to take place between the variable texture of experience and a framing vision. At the same time, however, that transaction was often of a negative sort: the poetry centred on a nameless *néant* which intervened between a watchful consciousness aware of its large general meanings, and the swarming bits of specific reality within which it moved. In the earlier volumes, the tactic of a particular poem was then either to dramatise that sickening sense of disparity, or, as in a poem like "Waking in a Newly-Built House", to rest satisfied with the alien self-possession of things, strictly curbing the turbulent, subversive questions which consciousness addressed to them.

In one or two of the final poems of *My Sad Captains*, however, another sort of myth began to emerge—one almost antithetical in tendency to the existentialist dilemma. It is there, for instance, in the closing lines of *Loot*:

> I am herald to tawny
>
> warriors, woken from sleep, who
> ride precipitantly down
> with the blood towards my hands, through
> me to retain possession.

It is the fusion, not the disparity, between man, nature, and history which is central here: a sub-Lawrentian myth of the individual as passive transmitter of primordial forces which fill and possess him with their own richness. If Gunn is, notably, the poet of emptiness and lack, it is also true that he is the poet of fullness: cramming, blooding, bodying are recurrent images. Consciousness either stands impotently apart from its object, fending off the invasions of chaos, or allows its vigilance to be sensually dissolved into a moment of mindless surrender to an impersonal natural force. This can only be risked, of course, if the force is somehow friendly, as the dog in "The Vigil of Corpus Christi", whose tongue licks a stiff sentry into "unsoldierly joy", is friendly. If the Sartrian myth stresses alienation, this primitivistic vision emphasises man's rootedness in the cosmos: it offers—in my view, in a mystifying and merely assertive way—a natural solution to social breakdown.

This second mythology seems to have grown stronger in Gunn's recent poetry—grown, indeed, to the point where, in a discussion of *Moly*, he can talk gravely and explicitly of certain "powers" friendly to man, in whom trust can be placed. In *Touch*, the impulse towards an edgy, defensive hardening of the self underwent some sardonic questioning, as images of melting, dissolution and momentary merging began to creep in; and that tendency becomes even more affirmative in *Moly*. One reason for this is that Gunn's sense of what sustaining "poise" involves seems to have been modified. The surf-riders in San Francisco bay keep their balance, but they do so by moving with, not against, natural forces:

> Their pale feet curl, they poise their weight
> With a learn'd skill.
> It is the wave they imitate
> Keeps them so still.

The sharp disjunctions between controlling mind and chaotic matter of the earlier books seem superseded here: it's by rooting himself responsively in the flow of natural forces, not by fending them off, that man can master them. And so, whereas Gunn's previous use of werewolf imagery sometimes suggested a potentially tragic discontinuity between man and nature, the imagery of man-beast metamorphosis in *Moly* seems to express a sense of some organic, ecological *rapport* between man and the forces he moves among. The Circe myth to which the book's title refers still underlines the need for an alert self-awareness which allows man to master the bestial; but a number of "centaur" poems in the volume view the frontier between man and beast as blurred and indefinite, a merging rather than sharp dividing. In a similar way, the mind must acknowledge the dependency of its sharpened perceptions on an amorphous undertow of mindless natural merging:

> On the stream at full
> A flurry, where the mind rides separate!
> But this brief cresting, sharpened and exact,
> Is fluid too, is open to the pull
> And on the underside twined deep with it.

It seems fanciful to relate *Moly* to Davie's *Epistles to Eva Hesse*; yet a relation of an indirect kind can be asserted. Davie, comfortably ensconced in his Californian cat's-cradle, and Gunn confidently poised on a Pacific wave, have a more than geographical contiguity: they share a tentative trust, reached through different uses of myth, that man can be at home in the universe. Man can be at home because entwined with the present in which he lives are threads or forces from elsewhere, buoying him up, binding him to Nature or geography, history or space. And because this is so, the individual can, once again, become *representative*. This is the condition of Gunn's lonely survivor in "Misanthropos":

> If he preserves himself in nature,
> it is as a lived caricature
> of the race he happens to survive.
> He is clothed in dirt. He lacks motive.
> He is wholly representative.

Myth strips the individual of his social specificity, but also, therefore, of his contingency, his social nullity. The individual—whether Creagh's Abel, Hughes's Crow, Dorn's Gunslinger, Hill's Mercian king Offa or Gunn's primitive survivor—is invested with a freshly representative significance, as the node in which natural forces, historical strands, metaphysical pre-occupations converge. Myth allows for that centripetal unity centred in a single figure, but also (and this is surely its true attraction) for a free-ranging liberty, spanning diverse dimensions of time and space. The trampoline formed by knotting the frayed threads of reality into a single structure tosses you free of temporal constrictions into an upper air from whence you can effect a leisurely re-entry into time on your own terms. From this crow's-eye-view the whole of history, suitably spatialised by the force of myth, becomes your kingdom.

The transcendental freedom to which the myths of Olson, Gunn and Hughes lay claim is clearly a considerably more ambitious affair than the orthodox freedoms of social democracy and its accompanying poetics. It represents, indeed, one reaction to the crisis of that liberal bourgeois tradition, to the increasing non-availability of its limited freedoms as the social demo-cratic centreground continues to crumble. Davie's relation to social demo-cracy has obviously been a good deal more oblique and ambiguous than that of Gunn or Hughes, who were never men of the so-called centre: but his firm option for Christine Brooke-Rose rather than Barbara Castle in the *Epistles* is a telling gesture. The recourse to art on the one hand, and to "the elemental power-circuit of the universe" (Hughes' phrase) on the other, have been paired off before, as reactions to a history which seems to have lost its capacity for self-transcendence. But if myth reacts critically to the reduction of history to sociometrics, its own lack of historicity paradoxically reproduces that condition at a higher level. There is an odd analogy between this situation and the poetics of the "underground", whose demand for an instant simultaneity of experience both challenges the bourgeois ethic of deferred satisfaction and mirrors the ideology of consumer capitalism.

It would be unfair to Donald Davie, as I've indicated already, to suggest that his rejection of history is complete: the *Epistles* struggle to grant history its autonomy within a totalising, contemplative perspective. The cost of comic equipoise is reckoned, as it isn't in the very different comedy of *Crow*. Crow's triumph over the alienating causalities of history seems too cheaply bought: the inviolable security of myth has replaced, rather than confronted, the contingencies of history, as simple compensation. The poem's cartoon-like quality has been well-noted, and this is significant: the cartoon-hero, battered and flattened by the full force of a sinister technology yet stubbornly unkillable, can plausibly be seen as one fantasy response to the actual dilemmas of oppression and insecurity in contemporary society. That kind of com-pensatory myth may work as art when it takes serious measure of the recalci-trant material it confronts; and indeed Jonathan Raban has argued persuasively for *Crow*'s value in roughly these terms—that it keeps a self-conscious eye on the real world it subverts.* My own impression is that this, while true, isn't enough: it doesn't sufficiently qualify the seriousness of Hughes's commitment to a world-view in which history can have value only in negative and caricatured form.

The compensatory aspect of myth seems to me of major importance in most of the poets discussed here. Myth provides a measure of freedom, transcendence, representativeness, a sense of totality; and it seems no accident that it is serving these purposes in a society where those qualities are largely lacking. The values which social democratic pragmatism attempts to banish from history re-appear, sometimes in assertive and exaggerated form, in myth. Comedy or cosmic forces provide the experiences of balance and security which society fails to supply; if man is rootless and estranged in the realm of culture, he can discover symbolic resolutions to real alienations in the realms of nature and art. As Frank Kermode has pointed out in *The Sense of an Ending*, it is when those symbolic resolutions cease to recognise themselves as heuristic fictions, with complex relations to a real history outside them, that they become, in the truest sense, myths: worlds to be inhabited as a refuge from reality itself. Gunn's primitive forces, Hughes's elemental power-circuits and Olson's trampolines seem to run this risk. *Crow*, *Moly* and the *Epistles to Eva Hesse* pose contrasts, implicitly or explicitly, between myth and history; but there are, in addition, alternative *histories*. History, as Louis Althusser has reminded us, is a complex rather than a monistic reality: we should talk of *histories*, and of the conflicting unities they form. If the histories of Mercia or Durham seem to have been cancelled and appropriated by sociometrics, there may still be a task to be done in salvaging them to see what they have to offer the present. History is not just now and Colchester. There are other alternatives to Barbara Castle besides Christine Brooke-Rose.

* *The Society of the Poem*, London 1971, p. 170.

A View of English Poetry in the Early 'Seventies

by Alan Brownjohn

ENGLISH poets at the moment are under increasing pressure to accept a state of demoralised inferiority by comparison with their American colleagues. A crisis of purpose has been devised for them, and if they do not willingly accept their prescribed role—one of self-doubt and apprehension for the future—it is suggested that they may only feel, as an alternative, complacently provincial. Fortunately there are not many signs, as yet, that poets are kissing this rod; indeed, as they become aware of the pressure, healthy and indignant resistance is growing to any suggestion that English poetry ought to know its (insignificant) place. But the talk goes around and the pressures will almost certainly build up, so it might help a bit to work out where such assertions originated and see if we really need fear them.

The principal symptoms of the neurosis wished on us are: a general lack of scale and ambition; a timid refusal to whip up some experimental vigour; a failure to seize chances, tackle the big themes, and face up to brute realities. English poetry, it is alleged, is at present altogether minor and unenterprising (though chapter-and-verse is not often given). English poets are worthy and honest in their own way, but sadly polite and inoffensive—"endlessly qualifying, mournfully poised and quizzical, making ruinous and rueful concessions" (Donald Davie). And the meat of the matter is the strident, irreverent confidence of the American scene, which goes boldly on breaking new ground.

It is well to be aware of a disease if one has it; but it seems rather urgent to sort out the origins and the justice of a few of these generalisations before one pleads guilty to suffering. Because any wide admission of the truth and relevance of the case against the British poets and for the Americans—things *are* getting as crude as this—could result in a very disabling situation indeed for the English. There is a general, cultural argument which allies supremacy in the arts to military and economic power, and thus establishes the predominance of the United States in poetry as in these other ways. This is a sort of vulgarity which does not require a serious response. A more genuine part of the anti-English campaign builds the weakness back into literary history and suggests that English verse as a whole in the twentieth century has only proved lively when injections of transatlantic influence have revived it. Another argument implies that certain characteristics inherent in the English national character itself may account for the trouble.

We are by nature too respectable and polite; the language we speak, with its characteristic understatements, is too reticent and genteel. It is, therefore, the viability of a whole tradition, the serviceableness of the entire mode of language, which is being brought into doubt. So it really is desirable at this moment *not* to accept without overwhelming reasons the inferiority we are being offered. Because we might thereby be accepting a chronic, even an incurable complaint which would seem to derive from unavoidable background circumstances. It would all be in our stars, and not ourselves; and therefore beyond rectification.

I do not personally believe, for a moment, in the operative existence of the English poet's failure of nerve. Nor do I feel it necessary, for any good reasons I have heard, to *start* believing in it. I sometimes feel suspicious about attempts to prove it exists—very occasionally the talk comes from poets whose success in working their native English seams has not been spectacular. But it's possible to see how the defeatist case has gained ground. And tracing the development of the theory might help to reduce the fear of it.

One strand of the argument is derived, obviously and reasonably, from the correct impression that the best individual poet of the post-war years is an American, Robert Lowell. Then it goes on—and you may extend the list as far as you wish, according to preference—the next best are Sylvia Plath, and possibly John Berryman, and perhaps X and Y, and *they* are Americans. This is certainly the most substantial part of the case because it talks lucidly in terms of proven achievement, the discussable value of bodies of work rather than the hazy merits and the dubious relevance of certain outlooks and methods of writing. It involves a reasonably mature consideration of what is good, instead of looking to see what makes most impact, seems most bizarrely ambitious, or just shouts the loudest. But then it is argued—by a large jump—because the best one or two poets may be American, clearly the conditions for a major poetry somehow cannot exist in Britain any more, perhaps haven't for a long time—the initiative, the talent, or something more intangible, must have passed to the United States. English poetry is played out.

The arguments against this attitude are very ordinary, but sometimes one has to labour the obvious to answer a simplification. Going down the charts with the names of poets seems an unpleasant procedure, but it would be a stronger reason for persuading the English into a sense of inferiority if the list (which must, on any reading, agreed, put Lowell and Plath first) really *could* be extended for any convincing distance, if it could be maintained that this situation exists because of obviously limiting cultural or political or economic circumstances, and if it is pretty certain to continue—to prove, in fact, that there is from now on likely to be an inevitable and irreversible provinciality about English poetry. And this is precisely what one cannot do. One can no more do it for English literature on the grounds offered than one could do it, presumptuously, for American literature on the basis of one's favourite definition of decadence, or for Soviet literature on the grounds that a restrictive atmosphere must now prove permanently stifling. New talents tend to appear, literatures have a way of changing and developing in unexpected ways. Was there anything inherently and irreversibly provincial about Ireland in 1904 which prevented Yeats from getting beyond *In the Seven Woods*? There is, in fact, no reason at all for accepting the label of a minor status on the basis of anything that has happened so far; and since little interesting work is likely to come from a feeling that one is either invalid or unimportant, it would be best to forget it. This would not be the strongest rejoinder, admittedly, if, by any intelligent and objective standards, all the best poets were Americans in A.D. 2000.

A second argument for feeling inferior has been built up out of a very well-intended attempt to encourage poets to be courageous. This was A. Alvarez's famous "gentility" piece, the introduction for his Penguin *New Poetry* anthology in 1962. Alvarez, as everyone remembers, was ingeniously deploring a series of "negative feedbacks" which, he argued, had stopped most of the English poetry of our time connecting with the harshest features of modern existence. In the end, the English trait of "gentility", the belief

> that life is always more or less orderly, people always more or less polite, their emotions and habits more or less decent or more or less controllable

was simply inadequate to comprehend the final horror of a Dachau or a Hiroshima. Nobody much at the time bothered to question whether this was *really* what the English character was all about. Because the kernel of Alvarez's argument was really a hope that English poets might simply write better by acquiring more of that kind of seriousness which consisted in the poet "facing the full range of his experience with his full intelligence". This was excellent, overdue advice; but one feature of Alvarez's case provided a springboard for the demoralisers to leap—by another considerable jump—on to rather different ground. Since the "gentility" in his definition was an in-born English habit, an unavoidable attribute of the national character (Alvarez's statement of the English temperament really *should* have been scrutinised), and as England was unaffected by the very worst horrors of the Second World War, *therefore* English poets suffered an inbuilt disadvantage: by virtue of their national experience, or inexperience, they would have less to say, and would say even that less urgently. By this not altogether fair extension, the Alvarez Gentility Argument became a kind of trap, a net for English poets who worried about it—the more they worried the more enmeshed they became in introspection and insularity. It was a chance for the more destructive and opportunist of their critics. Very simply, it enabled them to supplement the first argument, that most English poets are inferior to the Americans, with the additional argument that the English posture is doomed to be inherently inadequate and the English experience (Suez was no Vietnam) *cannot* support important poetry. Altogether, it begins to be more than a little to the credit of the English poets that they still find enough energy and room for manoeuvre to write poems like Roy Fuller's "Heredity", Silkin's

"Flower Poems", Porter's "The Sadness of the Creatures", Geoffrey Hill's "Funeral Music" and Hughes's "The Smile". But perhaps these poets are not tuned in enough to all the defeatism in the air. There is another important consideration about this line of argument, one which would apply to poetry, or any of the arts, anywhere. This is the possibility that in aiming to confront the harshest forms of experience, most poetry other than the most extreme and unsparing will tend to retire, or even to disappear, altogether. The critical influence of F. R. Leavis has been important in two respects, neither of which necessarily pleases him nor reflects very faithfully the directions of his thinking. In one way, it has helped to create an entire new area of cultural concerns, a powerful critique of society, its institutions and its language: education and unofficial left-wing politics have received its impact. In another way, in other hands, the pursuit of excellence and the rejection of any compromise with an inferior product has—filtered, perhaps, through Bruno Bettelheim and Hannah Arendt—fathered an attitude of "harshness is all": the criterion is the degree to which poetry can absorb modern horror while still remaining a conscious and intelligent art. This is the critical attitude behind Alvarez' plea for "facing the full range of experience". But when poetry is required to take almost exclusive cognisance of, indeed incorporate, the most brutal forms of human experience ("the bastardy of being human" —Alvarez), something essentially derogatory to the entire process of poetry occurs. What happens is that the art itself seems increasingly marginal alongside the violent things it seeks to describe with ever greater veracity. So most poetry, with all its variety of roles and guises—and most ways of writing poetry, most tones—become literally uninteresting to those critics who find it legitimate only when it deals in images of extremity, when it can be seen to represent an unquestionable personal anguish (the Plath syndrome). And most practice of the art becomes futile and marginal, even reprehensible, because lesser emotions and attitudes than anguish and stoicism begin to seem either faked or trivial.

There are some ways of accepting—or partly accepting—this particular position and still finding a way through the impasse to which it so inevitably leads. The verse of some of the younger English poets sometimes loosely brought together as the *Review* group—Ian Hamilton, David Harsent, Hugo Williams, Peter Dale, Colin Falck, and others—charts out a territory which is within some of the limits prescribed by the Alvarez philosophy; yet makes a virtue out of that confinement by an especially frank and sensitive exploration of intimately personal themes. It is more than interesting that the poem Alvarez wrote after visiting Auschwitz (mentioned by him in his celebrated dialogue with Donald Davie in No. 1 of *The Review*) was a "personal poem about loss", that the whole topic is intimately paralleled for him (in the same dialogue) by calamities in human sexual relations. At this point, where you assert the continuing importance—more than that, the primacy—of intimate, small-scale personal concerns as a subject for poetry, the *Review* group begins; but without having, or trying to bring in, the stimulus of the death camps. The smallest, most acutely personal things are what we know best and feel most. In Ian Hamilton's verse, in particular, alarm, tragedy, pathos, the unanswerable irony of situations in which you can perceive and not help, are suggested by the smallest, subtlest human actions, not the most overtly violent. The repetition, in his book *The Visit*, of images—of hands, hair, shadows, breath, snow—serves, with great fineness and integrity, to assert the relevance and dignity of the detail of purely personal living; as if to say "It is a matter of *this*". Such living is enjoyed or suffered without any extremity of paraded anguish: the anguish is inescapably there in the most basic and unalterable facts of human relationship. If there is a risk of a kind of clipped, attenuated sensitiveness about the writings of this group (sometimes a menacing sensitiveness which seems to say, "Be more histrionic or sentimental *if you dare*") they are at least helping to keep certain crucial areas of human experience open, and valid as subjects for poetry. This may be important where there is a pressure on poets to adopt one of several kinds of crudity and boredom, ranging from popular versifying to the international style to the anti-art enthusiasm for being deliberately bad. An early remark of Colin Falck's about a "New Lyricism" now seems inappropriate: the *Review* poets are committed, in fact, to a form of starkness. But what they are managing to reject is the necessity of nightmare. They have chosen a limited area, but what they can do in it may be more interesting to watch than much current activity in verse.

But the third, most refined and powerful plank in the platform of the would-be pessimists is that supplied by M. L. Rosenthal, probably the most informed and sympathetic American critic of current English verse but also a most subtle apologist for an utterly American kind of newness. Extending the arguments implicit in *The New Poets* (1967) in an article called "Poetry of the Main Chance" (*T.L.S.*, January 29, 1970), Professor Rosenthal sets the aims and methods of the new American poetry generally against the atmosphere of the English, and finds the latter wanting. It is not so much a matter of what has actually been achieved, or is of acknowledged value (Lowell, he implies, is better than the lot of them on this count), but a question of those approaches to poetry which seem to *promise* most, or will manage to defend or extend the position of the art. And something in the attitudes and methods of the English, Rosenthal argues, is necessarily, intrinsically limiting, not destined to assert the vigour of poetry. A "humane articulateness" (Larkin *et alia*) is somehow bound to offer less scope than a poetry which grasps the "main chance" and is thereby involved (often in experimental modes which extend and alter the concept of form itself) in a "bitter grappling with the gross, the anti-human, the inarticulable" (the terms used subtly advance the case). This is really an adaptation—a convincing adaptation—of the Gentility Argument; and the gist of Rosenthal's advice to English poets is that they should go to school to poets of the "main chance" like Duncan and Olson (who else!)

who offer "useful clues towards the kind of poetry that is now possible for us in the English language".

By this point the argument has begun to assume that English poets already feel queasy enough to be casting around for nostrums. At least, Donald Davie's broadcast of last summer, "The Failure of a Dialogue" (*The Listener*, August 27, 1970), with its amusing, but essentially crude and tendentious stereotypes of the "reverent and disjointed rumble" of the Americans and the "clipped British murmur", makes such an assumption. In Davie's analysis the failure of nerve is already an accomplished fact (no better way to make something so than to speak as if no one denies it): the English poet stands meekly and apologetically outside the roaring edifice of American poetry, too timid and genteel to go in. Davie's final view, agreed, is that the two poetries should restart their dialogue and develop some respect for each other; that the English lash out a bit and the Americans test their assumptions about poetry against the strength of the English tradition (and his own *Six Epistles to Eva Hesse* states the case for English attitudes with great wit and verve). But already some valuable ground has been lost to the pessimists.

By such a succession of stages has a defeatist case been built up. And the suggested remedies are: go concrete; go to the U.S.A. (Davie and Tarn); stay at home but write like the Americans; or absorb the work of the big international names who work in the accepted international style—at any rate, leave current English verse and the English tradition out of account, pull up all your roots and look for the grand, revealing gestures in some other place.

If English poets did feel themselves so demoralised as to seek these desperate courses, they would need to convince themselves that American projectivism or European post-surrealism has assembled enough substance to command their deference and emulation, and also that England is no longer a workable hypothesis. Such a way out—of an artificial dilemma—would be a disaster and a capitulation to modishness and irrationality. It would mean taking on trust, in the American case at least, a body of work which no intelligent and coherent critical approach has yet managed to grasp and appraise (but one writes this waiting for the philistine howls against criticism). Criticism in fact recoils from the cheer-leading, coterie tone of the new Americans and their English followers, whose verse functions in a curious, mesmerised, self-absorbed enclave where utterance is its own justification, time and space ultimately dissolve, and nothing is ever either fully worked out or sceptically questioned. If it did sally in with a little more courage, criticism might help people to admit that to read the *Maximus Poems* is to watch some genuine talent (see "In Cold Hell", "In Thicket" for proof) trickling out through the holes in an ever-expanding grid. Or that Dorn's verse runs the risk of dissipating its resonance and bite in making jokes, narcissistically, about its own jokes. Or that most of Duncan's poetry talks itself to death in a redious welter of derivation or pretentiousness. Or that Creeley's is in real danger of dwindling tensely to the point where all that is left to stand for a poem is half a syllable implying an implication.

But enough of the subtle and persistent reasons for feeling left behind by the big brass band. While making no claims for greatness, isn't the English verse of the post-war years really much more open, complex and intelligent than all this suggests? If we stop and listen, for once, in a way that gets increasingly difficult, to what is actually being said in this poetry, might we not hear more cogent and revealing intimations of, and comments upon, the point our civilisation has reached than in some other work? More latent energy than is ever exposed in fashionable sorts of exhibitionistic excitement? The strengths of current English verse are admittedly not those of rhetoric (but what does Ginsberg achieve in *poetry*, as distinct from enshrining in his performance, voluminously and pretentiously, the confusions of a disaffiliated generation?) Or of sheer nakedness (but would you rather have Snodgrass's *After Experience* than Larkin's *Whitsun Weddings*?) It is perfectly possible to write in a way that faces, understands and assumes the extremities of experience without parading the process (Muir, Graves, Geoffrey Hill). And it is possible to sense that modern experience asks language and form to burst its bounds to grasp it—but to regard the exhibition of incoherence and inarticulateness as an illustration of the problem rather than a definite solution. Reticence need not be a prim, a squeamish, a genteel refusal to look, but a way of saying one is *certainly* aware—and reluctant to devalue either the experience or the words by gushing out whatever first comes to mind with a confessional completeness of detail. Similarly, a disinclination to go out to the open spaces and the expanding horizons may stem from an understandable feeling that somewhere there is a point where the horizon can expand no farther in any meaningful direction—and one is back lying down where all the journeys started.

The point about reticence versus confessional could perhaps be illustrated with two well-known poems by two poets just mentioned. Both W. D. Snodgrass and Philip Larkin wrote poems about sickness and emergency: "The Operation" and "Ambulances". In "The Operation", Snodgrass places himself (as we all admittedly would, at the time) at the centre of dramatic attention:

> From stainless steel basins of water
> They brought warm cloths and they washed me,
> From spun aluminum bowls, cold Zephiran sponges, fuming;
> Gripped in the dead yellow glove, a bright straight razor
> Inched on my stomach, down my groin,
> Paring the brown hair off. They left me
> White as a child, not frightened.

No martyr—the poet is adopting the posture of a martyr to drastic experience—*ought* to be frightened. But the camera certainly homes with melodramatic vividness on that razor and its initially ambiguous journey: our squeamishness is not anticipated. Next, the narrator is clothed, for his operation,

> In the thin, loose, light, white garments,
> The delicate sandals of poor Pierrot,
> A schoolgirl first offering her sacrament.

The melodrama is turning self-pitying. The quest for acceptable images of pathos and vulnerability has pushed the poem into the purest sentimentality. Attendants tow his body on a "cart"

> Down corridors of the diseased, thronging:
> The scrofulous faces, contagious grim boys,
> The huddled families, weeping, a staring woman
> Arched to her gnarled stick

And the dramatic effect here intended turns out merely Dickensian, a caricaturist's crudity of effect. After the operation, agreed, the sense of relief at remaining alive is effectively conveyed:

> Into flowers, into women, I have awakened.
> Too weak to think of strength, I have thought all day,
> Or dozed among standing friends. I lie in night, now,
> A small mound under linen like the drifted snow,
> Only by nurses visited, in radiance, saying, Rest.

We are still requested to admire his own central importance in this hospital ward, as the "blank hero" of the preceding stanza; but there is a real serenity and a sense of life valued through minute particulars which one is thankfully conscious of, coming out of the anaesthetic:

> It is very still. In my brandy bowl
> Of sweet peas at the window, the crystal world
> Is inverted, slow and gay.

Snodgrass achieves with this ending an effect of glad, dazed ("inverted"), exhausted relief which finally just saves the poem after the indulgences of the first two stanzas.

Larkin's "Ambulances" works quite differently: with a reticence that manages an infinite, and infinitely disquieting, suggestiveness:

> Closed like confessionals, they thread
> Loud noons of cities, giving back
> None of the glances they absorb.
> Light glossy grey, arms on a plaque,
> They come to rest at any kerb:
> All streets in time are visited.

Reticence, as a quality, is about at the same time possessing, yet withholding, the features of extremity. Avoiding the obviously dramatic, but not from any attitude of shocked gentility (at the very idea, for example, of razors near groins) Larkin touches the theme of mortality in a grave, fine, genuinely understood way. Daily living and ordinary social detail ("arms on a plaque", "smells of different dinners") are quietly, yet completely, interrupted by the presence of death—

> the solving emptiness
> That lies just under all we do.

Such understanding then radiates out from the image of the "wild white face that overtops/Red stretcher-blankets" (where is Snodgrass' tumbril?) to a fuller sympathy for, and insight into, the onlookers:

> *Poor soul*,
> They whisper at their own distress;

The true isolation, the shattering of self, in the experience of sudden and grave sickness simply does not exist in the outwardly more naked and revealing patient in the Snodgrass poem. What it *is* all about is there in Larkin, uncompromised by extreme gestures. It is about

> the sudden shut of loss
> Round something nearly at an end,
> And what cohered in it across
> The years, the unique random blend
> Of families and fashions . . .

In Larkin, the sight of the ambulance, all the connotations of mortality it carries,

> Brings closer what is left to come,
> And dulls to distance all we are.

The implications of the moment of seeing it have been felt, and thought, through. The language is inviting a careful, thorough understanding of what is really too frightening to think about long:

> the solving emptiness
> That lies just under all we do.

It is not asking us to agree simply how ghastly an operation is, and how marvellous it is to be alive after it, and what a hero the poet has been—and to do all this with an uncritical reverence for the manifest excitement of the experience described.

Empirical, critical attitudes *are* the English tradition. The new American verse—and such English poetry as follows its example—tends to exist in an atmosphere where the validity and interest of any utterance made with sufficient loudness, wryness or charisma, is accepted without question. Response is immediate, intuitive, without forethought or preparation; the poetry just *is*. (The English edition of the *Maximus Poems* says nothing at all about Olson, except on a losable insert, nothing about the poems, doesn't date them, doesn't bother to number the pages.) Somewhere, in ways it would be fascinating to trace, all this links up with the new culture of dissent—its refusal of the old, institutionalised protest-forms, its engaging but ineffectual informality, its attractive and yet enfeebling forbearance. It is a culture which has more justice in its cause and less sense and coherence in furthering it than any previous, comparable movement. The new American verse faces the world with something like this mixture of the brave and the wet. By such a process, perhaps, linking up curiously with strains of stubborn dissent in some English provincial writing, has it come to invade the English campuses and there become something like an inflexible, in-group orthodoxy. But one peculiar and excellent strength of the English creative intellect is its insistence that, in the end, everything has to establish a basis of *some* kind of reasonable utterance, and be defensible (in a way the good-hearted American atmosphere is not) against the bluntest kind of attack. You are encouraged to doubt. You ask questions at readings. It is an admirable asset in a crazy, despairing age. English poets should be resolved to avoid the temptation (the more mediocre and unacclaimed the talent the stronger it will be) to jettison their native rationality and scepticism; because it might be needed.

We move daily deeper into a complex and alarming kind of technical, late capitalist civilisation where the surfaces get smoother and the realities ever more violent, irrational and ruthless. One's first, instinctive response is to resort to the counter-irrationality of a counter-culture. But the only effective response, in the long term, will come from a rational, sceptical temperament which will calmly and wisely dismantle the machinery of horror and organise the commonwealth of decency.

None of this is intended as a recipe for a reactionary, or Augustan, or even Fabian poetic outlook; simply a plea that English poets should decline the plausible reasons offered for choosing modes which could prove both irrelevant and transitory and denying the strengths of their own position. What they have to offer may prove valuable. What they can best do, while gritting their teeth and hanging on, is things like the following: be, for once, a little chauvinistic on their own account about the variety, resourcefulness and potential of the new English poetry; have faith in that language which arrives to them naturally from their background and upbringing, and beware of self-conscious transatlantic borrowing; grasp, and absorb into their verse, the nature of their own society, its changes and compromises, its peculiar variations on the arrogant debility of Western society in general; worry about *what* they are saying first, only *how* they are saying it as an afterthought; spurn any manifestation of willing irrationality or near-religious enthusiasm in the *ambiance* of poetry; take in the *energies* of the best foreign verse, including the American, not its forms (or lack of them) and its mannerisms. And lastly, experiment, ceaselessly, confidently; in their own way.

APPENDICES

Awards

compiled by Judith Higgens

ACKNOWLEDGMENTS are due to the many organisations and individuals consulted during the compiling of this chapter, and in particular to the National Book League and the Arts Council Poetry Library. The lists do not attempt to be fully comprehensive; nevertheless, apologies are extended for any omissions and errors which may inadvertently have occurred.

A LIST OF AWARDS, PRIZES, ETC. WON BY BRITISH POETS DURING THE 1960s

Poet Laureateship

(1930–68)	John Masefield
1968–72	C. Day Lewis

The Queen's Gold Medal for Poetry

1960	John Betjeman	1965	Philip Larkin
1961	(No award)	1966	(No award)
1962	Christopher Fry	1967	Charles Causley
1963	William Plomer	1968	Robert Graves
1964	R. S. Thomas	1969	Stevie Smith

Poetry Society
Alice Hunt Bartlett Prize

1966	Gavin Bantock Paul Roche	} joint winners
1967	Ted Walker	
1968	Gael Turnbull	
1969	Tom Raworth	

Royal Society of Literature
W. H. Heinemann Bequest

1961 (for 1960)	Vernon Scannell	*The Masks of Love*	Putnam
1966 (for 1965)	Derek Walcott	*The Castaway*	Cape
1967 (for 1966)	Norman MacCaig	*Surroundings*	Chatto/Hogarth

Society of Authors
Cholmondeley Award for Poets

1966	Stevie Smith Ted Walker	1968	Harold Massingham Edwin Morgan
1967	Seamus Heaney Brian Jones Norman Nicholson	1969	Tony Harrison Derek Walcott

Eric Gregory Award

1960	Christopher Levenson		Norman Talbot
1961	Adrian Mitchell	1966	Robin Fulton
	Geoffrey Hill		Seamus Heaney
1962	Brian Johnson		Hugo Williams
	Jenny Joseph	1967	Angus Calder
	James Simmons		Marcus Cumberlege
	Donald Thomas		David Harsent
1963	Stewart Conn		Brian Patten
	Peter Griffith		David Selzer
	Ian Hamilton	1968	James Aitchison
	David Wevill		Douglas Dunn
1964	Robert Nye		Brian Jones
	Ken Smith	1969	Gavin Bantock
	Jean Symons		Jeremy Hooker
	Ted Walker		Jenny King
1965	John Fuller		Neil Powell
	Michael Longley		Landeg E. White
	Derek Mahon		

Somerset Maugham Award

1960	Ted Hughes
1968	Seamus Heaney

Travelling Scholarship

1961	David Jones	1966	Charles Causley
1963	Norman MacCaig	1967	George Mackay Brown
	R. S. Thomas		Stevie Smith

The Duff Cooper Memorial Prize

1960	Andrew Young	*Collected Poems*	Hart-Davis
1968	Roy Fuller	*New Poems*	Deutsch

The Geoffrey Faber Memorial Prize

1964	Christopher Middleton	*Torse Three*	Longmans
	George MacBeth	*The Broken Places*	Scorpion Press
1966	Jon Silkin	*Nature with Man*	Chatto/Hogarth
1968	Seamus Heaney	*Death of a Naturalist*	Faber
1970	Geoffrey Hill	*King Log*	Deutsch (1968)

The William Foyle Poetry Prize

1960	Robert Graves	*Collected Poems*	Cassell (1959)
1961	George Seferis	*Poems*, translated by Rex Warner	Bodley Head
1962	John Masefield	*The Bluebells and other verse*	Heinemann
1963	Hugh MacDiarmid	*Collected Poems*	Oliver & Boyd
1964	John Lehmann	*Collected Poems*	Eyre & Spottiswoode

Hawthornden Prize

1961	Ted Hughes	*Lupercal*	Faber

The Richard Hillary Memorial Prize

1965	David Wevill	*Birth of a Shark*	Macmillan
1966	Elizabeth Jennings	*The Mind has Mountains*	Macmillan
1967	Anthony Thwaite	*The Stones of Emptiness*	O.U.P.

Sir Roger Newdigate Prize for English Verse

1960	J. L. Fuller	*A Dialogue between Caliban and Ariel*
1961	(No award)	
1962	S. P. Johnson	*May Morning*
1963	(No award)	
1964	J. D. Hamilton Paterson	*Disease*
1965	P. A. C. Jay	*Fear*
1966	(No award)	
1967	(No award)	
1968	James Fenton	*Japan Opened, 1853–4*

Pernod Poetry Award

1967	Brian Patten	*Little Johnny's Confession*	Allen & Unwin
1969	Brian Patten	*Notes to the Hurrying Man*	Allen & Unwin

John Llewelyn Rhys Memorial Prize

1962	Edward Lucie-Smith	*A Tropical Childhood*	O.U.P.
1969	Brian Patten	*Notes to the Hurrying Man*	Allen & Unwin
	David Sutton	*Out on a Limb*	Rapp & Whiting

Arts Council Awards

Categories of award by the Arts Council vary during this period, and only poetry awards as such have been listed. Maintenance grants have not been included. From 1968 or so onwards differentiated awards disappear in the general category of "Grants to Writers", and these have not been included either.

Triennial Poetry Prizes

1959–62	Robert Graves	*More Poems 1961*	Cassell
	Edward Lucie-Smith	*A Tropical Childhood*	O.U.P.
1962–5	Philip Larkin	*The Whitsun Weddings*	Faber
	David Wevill	*Birth of a Shark*	Macmillan
	Special Awards		
	Austin Clarke	*Flight to Africa*	Dolmen
	A. D. Hope	*Selected Poems*	Angus & Robertson
1965–7	Sylvia Plath	*Ariel*	Faber

Bursaries

1964–5	Martin Bell	1967	Edward Brathwaite
1965	Elizabeth Jennings		Karen Gershon
	John Heath-Stubbs		Zulfikar Ghose
1966	Basil Bunting		Patrick Kavanagh
	Jack Beeching		Richard Murphy
	Frederick Grubb	1968–9	George Barker
	David Wevill		Elizabeth Jennings
	Hugo Williams		D. M. Black
	Harry Fainlight		Leslie Norris

Other Awards

1965   Basil Bunting
                Harold Massingham
                David Wevill
                Andrew Young
1965–6   Harry Fainlight
                John Horder

Arts Council Prize for Literature (Poetry)
1966   Edgell Rickword

Best volume of English translation in poetry
1966–8   Michael Hamburger   *Poems and Fragments of* Routledge
                                       Hölderlin

Irish Arts Council Awards
The Denis Devlin Memorial Award

1964   Austin Clarke
1967   Thomas Kinsella

Special Prize
1962   Thomas Kinsella

Macaulay Fellowship in Literature
1968   Eavan Boland

Scottish Arts Council Awards

1966–7   Ian Hamilton Finlay   Tom McGrath
                Norman MacCaig   1968–9   Ian Hamilton Finlay
                Ian Crichton Smith   Robert Garioch
1967–8   Alan Bold   Charles Senior
                Ian Hamilton Finlay   1969–70   Hugh MacDiarmid
                Alan Jackson   Pete Morgan

Poetry Prize
1968   Ian Crichton Smith
                Stewart Conn
                D. M. Black
                Alan Riddell

Publication Awards

Autumn 1968   George Bruce   *Landscape with Figures*   Akros
                Stewart Conn   *Stoats in the Sunlight*   Hutchinson
                Helen Cruikshank   *The Ponnage Pool*   Macdonald
Spring 1969   Alexander Scott   *Cantrips*   Akros
                Edwin Morgan   *The Second Life*   Edinburgh U.P.
Autumn 1969   D. M. Black   *The Educators*   Barrie & Jenkins
                Tom Buchan   *Dolphins at Cochin*   Barrie & Jenkins
                Ian Crichton Smith   *From Bourgeois Land*   Gollancz

Welsh Arts Council Awards (Anglo-Welsh writers only)
Honours
1968   R. S. Thomas
1969   David Jones

Prizes

1969 (for 1968)	Raymond Garlick	*A Sense of Europe*	Gomer
1970 (for 1969)	John Ormond	*Requiem and Celebration*	Christopher Davies
	Harri Webb	*The Green Desert*	Gomer
	Sally Roberts	*Turning Away*	Gomer

Bursaries

1968–9	Peter Finch
	Leslie Norris
	Roland Mathias
1969–70	John Tripp

University Fellowships
Oxford Professor of Poetry

| 1956–61 | W. H. Auden | 1966–68 | Edmund Blunden |
| 1961–66 | Robert Graves | 1968–73 | Roy Fuller |

Compton Lectureship, University of Hull (in association with the Arts Council)

| 1968 | C. Day Lewis |
| 1969 | Richard Murphy |

Northern Arts Minor Awards

| 1965–6 | Jon Silkin |
| | Tom Pickard |

Creative Writing Fellowship, Edinburgh University (in association with the Scottish Arts Council)

| 1968–70 | Norman MacCaig |

E. C. Gregory Fellowship, University of Leeds

1959–61	Jon Silkin	1965–67	David Wright
1961–63	W. Price Turner	1967–69	Martin Bell
1963–65	Peter Redgrove	1969–71	Kevin Crossley-Holland

Granada Fellowship for Creative Artists, University of York

| 1966–67 | George Barker |

Poetry Fellowship at Durham and Newcastle Universities (in association with Northern Arts)

| 1968–70 | Basil Bunting |

Poetry Book Society Choices and Recommendations

1960	*Choices*		
	Peter Levi, S. J.	The Gravel Ponds	Deutsch
	Patrick Kavanagh	Come Dance with Kitty Stobling	Longmans
	Dom Moraes	Poems	Eyre & Spottiswoode
	John Betjeman	Summoned by Bells	John Murray
	Recommendations		
	William Plomer	Collected Poems	Cape
	James Reeves	Collected Poems	Heinemann
1961	*Choices*		
	David Holbrook	Imaginings	Putnam
	Elizabeth Jennings	Song for a Birth or a Death	Deutsch
	R. S. Thomas	Tares	Hart-Davis
	Peter Redgrove	The Nature of Cold Weather	Routledge

Recommendations

Louis MacNeice	Solstices	Faber
John Wain	Weep before God	Macmillan
Thomas Blackburn	A Smell of Burning	Putnam
Alan Brownjohn	The Railings	Digby Press
Edward Lucie-Smith	A Tropical Childhood	O.U.P.
Richard Kell	Control Tower	Chatto
Jon Silkin	The Re-Ordering of the Stones	Chatto

1962 *Choices*

Patrick Creagh	A Row of Pharaohs	Heinemann
Dannie Abse	Poems, Golders Green	Hutchinson
Thomas Kinsella	Downstream	Dolmen
Michael Baldwin	Death on a Live Wire	Longmans

Recommendations

George Barker	The View from a Blind I	Faber
Vernon Scannell	A Sense of Danger	Putnam
Roy Fuller	Collected Poems	Deutsch
Robert Graves	New Poems, 1962	Cassell

1963 *Choices*

Richard Murphy	Sailing to an Island	Faber
Alexander Baird	Poems	Chatto
Louis MacNeice	The Burning Perch	Faber
Patricia Beer	The Survivors	Longmans

Recommendations

George MacBeth	The Broken Places	Scorpion
Rosemary Tonks	Notes on Cafes and Bedrooms	Putnam
Bernard Spencer	With Luck Lasting	Hodder
Charles Tomlinson	A Peopled Landscape	O.U.P.
Austin Clarke	Flight to Africa	Dolmen
Geoffrey Grigson	Collected Poems	Phoenix House
Brian Higgins	Notes while Travelling	Longmans

1964 *Choices*

Philip Larkin	The Whitsun Weddings	Faber
Donald Davie	Events and Wisdoms	Routledge
C. A. Trypanis	Pompeian Dog	Faber
Patric Dickinson	This Cold Universe	Chatto

Recommendations

Thomas Blackburn	A Breathing Space	Putnam
James Reeves	The Questioning Tiger	Heinemann
Anne Sexton	Selected Poems	O.U.P.
Edward Lucie-Smith	Confessions and Histories	O.U.P.
Frank Prewett	Collected Poems	Cassell

1965 *Choices*

Sylvia Plath	Ariel	Faber
Roy Fuller	Buff	Deutsch
John Holloway	Wood and Windfall	Routledge
Kathleen Raine	The Hollow Hill	Hamish Hamilton

Recommendations

David Gascoyne	Collected Poems	O.U.P.
Norman MacCaig	Measures	Chatto
David Wright	Adam at Evening	Hodder

George Barker	The True Confession of George Barker	MacGibbon & Kee
D. J. Enright	The Old Adam	Chatto
George MacBeth	A Doomsday Book	Scorpion
Paul Dehn	The Fern on the Rock	Hamish Hamilton
John Heath-Stubbs	Selected Poems	O.U.P.
John Smith	A Discreet Immorality	Hart-Davis
C. Day Lewis	The Room	Cape
Christopher Middleton	Nonsequences	Longmans

1966 *Choices*

Charles Tomlinson	American Scenes and other Poems	O.U.P.
Brian Higgins	The Northern Fiddler	Methuen
Norman MacCaig	Surroundings	Chatto
Peter Redgrove	The Force and other Poems	Routledge

Recommendations

Ruth Pitter	Still by Choice	Cresset
A. K. Ramanujan	The Striders	O.U.P.
Anne Halley	Between Wars	O.U.P.
James K. Baxter	Pig Island Letters	O.U.P.
Edward Brathwaite	Rights of Passage	O.U.P.
Louis Zukofsky	"A" 1–12	Cape

1967 *Choices*

Austin Clarke	Old-fashioned Pilgrimage	Dolmen
John Fuller	The Tree that Walked	Chatto
Thom Gunn	Touch	Faber
Anthony Hecht	The Hard Hours	O.U.P.

Recommendations

Geoffrey Grigson	A Skull in Salop	Macmillan
Elizabeth Jennings	Collected Poems	Macmillan
Thomas Kinsella	Nightwalker	Dolmen

1968 *Choices*

Charles Causley	Underneath the Water	Macmillan
Roy Fuller	New Poems	Deutsch
Derek Mahon	Night-crossing	O.U.P.
R. S. Thomas	Not that he brought Flowers	Hart-Davis

Recommendations

Tony Connor	Kon in Springtime	O.U.P.
Austin Clarke	The Echo at Coole	Dolmen
Geoffrey Hill	King Log	Deutsch
Richard Murphy	The Battle of Aughrim	Faber
Barry Cole	Moonsearch	Methuen

1969 *Choices*

Peter Whigham	The Blue-winged Bee	Anvil
Seamus Heaney	Door into the Dark	Faber
Douglas Dunn	Terry Street	Faber
David Holbrook	Old World, New World	Rapp & Whiting

Recommendations

| Geoffrey Grigson | Ingestion of Ice-Cream | Macmillan |
| David Harsent | A Violent Country | O.U.P. |

Publishers' Appendix

compiled by Barbara Atkinson

The following bibliography, taken from the catalogue of the Arts Council Poetry Library, was compiled by Barbara Atkinson, Poetry Librarian.

Abse, Dannie. *Walking Under Water*. Hutchinson, 1952. *Tenants of the House*. Hutchinson, 1957. *Poems, Golders Green*. Hutchinson, 1962. *Dannie Abse*. Vista Books, 1963. *A Small Desperation*. Hutchinson, 1968.

Adcock, Fleur. *Tigers*. Oxford University Press, 1967. *High Tide in the Garden*. Oxford University Press, 1971.

Amis, Kingsley. *A Frame of Mind*. University of Reading, School of Art. 1953. *A Case of Samples*. Gollancz, 1956. *A Look Round the Estate*. Cape, 1968.

Auden, W. H. *Poems*. Faber, 1934 (f.p. 1930). *The Orators*. Faber, 1966 (f.p. 1932). *The Dance of Death*. Faber, 1945 (f.p. 1933). *Another Time*. Faber, 1940. *New Year Letter*. Faber, 1946 (f.p. 1941). *For the Time Being*. Faber, 1966 (f.p. 1945). *The Age of Anxiety*. Faber, 1949 (f.p. 1948). *Collected Shorter Poems 1930–1944*. Faber, 1950. *Nones*. Faber, 1952. *A Selection by the Author*. Penguin, 1970 (f.p. 1958). *About the House*. Faber, 1966. *Collected Shorter Poems 1927–1957*. Faber, 1966. *Selected Poems*, Faber, 1968. *Collected Longer Poems*. Faber, 1968. *City Without Walls and Other Poems*. Faber, 1969. *Academic Graffiti*. Faber, 1971.

Baird, Alexander. *Poems*. Chatto & Windus/Hogarth Press, 1963.

Bantock, Gavin. *Juggernaut*. Anvil Press, 1968. *A New Thing Breathing*. Anvil Press, 1969.

Barker, George. *Calamiterror*. Faber, 1937. *Sacred and Secular Elegies*. New Directions, 1943. *Eros in Dogma*. Faber, 1946 (f.p. 1944). *News of The World*. Faber, 1950. *A Vision of Beasts and Gods*. Faber, 1954. *Collected Poems 1930–1955*. Faber, 1957. *The True Confession of George Barker*. Parton Press, 1957. *The View From a Blind I*. Faber, 1962. *Dreams of a Summer Night*. Faber, 1966. *The Golden Chains*. Faber, 1968. *At Thurgarton Church*. Trigram, 1969. *Poems of Places and People*. Faber, 1971.

Baxter, James K. *The Fallen House*. Caxton Press, 1953. *In Fires of No Return*. Oxford University Press, 1958. *Howrah Bridge and Other Poems*. Oxford University Press, 1961. *Pig Island Letters*. Oxford University Press, 1966.

Beckett, Samuel. *Poems in English*. John Calder, 1961.

Beer, Patricia. *The Loss of the Magyar*. Longmans, 1959. *The Survivors*. Longmans, 1963. *Just Like the Resurrection*. Macmillan, 1967. *The Estuary*. Macmillan, 1971.

Bell, Martin. *Collected Poems 1937–1966*. Macmillan, 1967.

Beresford, Anne, *Walking Without Moving*. Turret Books, 1967. *The Lair*. Rapp & Whiting, 1968.

Berry, Francis. *The Galloping Centaur : Poems 1933–1951*. Methuen, 1952. *Morant Bay and Other Poems*. Routledge & Kegan Paul, 1961.

Betjeman, John. *Selected Poems*. John Murray, 1952 (f.p. 1948). *A Few Late Chrysanthemums*. John Murray, 1954. *Collected Poems*. John Murray, 1959 (f.p. 1958). *Summoned by Bells*. John Murray, 1960. *A Ring of Bells*. John Murray, 1962. *High and Low*. John Murray, 1966. *Collected Poems*. John Murray, 1970.

Black, D. M. *Theory of Diet*. Turret Books, 1966. *With Decorum*. Scorpion Press, 1967. *A Dozen Short Poems*. Turret Books, 1968. *The Educators*. Cresset Press, 1969.

SOME OXFORD POETS

Fleur Adcock	Douglas Livingstone
Anna Akhmatova	Edward Lucie-Smith
James Baxter	Derek Mahon
Edward Brathwaite	Robert Mezey
Austin Clarke	Peter Porter
Tony Connor	A. K. Ramanujan
Hart Crane	W. R. Rodgers
J. S. Cunningham	Tom Scott
Allen Curnow	Léopold Senghor
David Gascoyne	Anne Sexton
Grey Gowrie	Louis Simpson
David Harsent	W. D. Snodgrass
John Heath-Stubbs	Allen Tate
Anthony Hecht	Anthony Thwaite
X. J. Kennedy	Charles Tomlinson
Thomas Kinsella	Andrei Voznesensky

Hugo Williams

OXFORD UNIVERSITY PRESS

Blackburn, Thomas. *The Outer Darkness.* Hand & Flower Press, 1951. *The Holy Stone.* Hand & Flower Press, 1954. *In the Fire.* Putnam, 1956. *The Next Word.* Putnam, 1958. *A Smell of Burning.* Putnam, 1961. *A Breathing Space.* Putnam, 1964. *The Fourth Man.* MacGibbon & Kee, 1971.

Bland, Peter. *Passing Gods.* Ferry Press, 1970.

Bold, Alan. *To Find the New.* Chatto & Windus/Hogarth Press, 1968 (f.p. 1967). *A Perpetual Motion Machine.* Chatto & Windus/Hogarth Press, 1969. *The State of the Nation.* Chatto & Windus/Hogarth Press, 1969. *A Pint of Bitter.* Chatto & Windus/Hogarth Press, 1971.

Bosley, Keith. *The Possibility of Angels.* Macmillan, 1969.

Bowden, R. H. *Poems from Italy.* Chatto & Windus/Hogarth Press, 1970.

Brathwaite, Edward. *Rights of Passage.* Oxford University Press, 1967. *Masks.* Oxford University Press, 1970 (f.p. 1968). *Islands.* Oxford University Press, 1969.

Broadie, Frederick. *My Findings.* Chatto & Windus/Hogarth Press, 1970.

Brock, Edwin. *With Love From Judas.* Scorpion Press, 1963. *A Cold Day at the Zoo.* Rapp & Whiting, 1970.

Brown, George Mackay. *Loaves and Fishes.* Hogarth, 1959. *Fishermen with Ploughs.* Hogarth Press, 1971.

Brown, Pete. *Let 'em Roll Kafka.* Fulcrum Press, 1969.

Browne, Michael Dennis. *The Wife of Winter.* Rapp & Whiting, 1970.

Brownjohn, Alan. *The Railings.* Digby Press, 1961. *The Lions' Mouths.* Macmillan, 1967. *Sandgrains on a Tray.* Macmillan, 1969. *Warrior's Career.* Macmillan, 1972.

Bruce, George. *Collected Poems 1939–1970.* Edinburgh University Press, 1970.

Buchan, Tom. *Dolphins at Cochin.* Barrie & Rockliff, The Cresset Press, 1969.

Buchanan, George. *Annotations.* Carcanet Press, 1970. *Minute-Book of a City.* Carcanet Press, 1972. *Conversation with Strangers.* Gaberbocchus, 1961.

Bunting, Basil. *The Spoils.* Mordern Tower Book Room, Newcastle upon Tyne, 1965. *Loquitur.* Fulcrum Press, 1965. *Briggflatts.* Fulcrum Press, 1966. *Collected Poems.* Fulcrum Press, 1968.

Burns, Jim. *Cells.* Grosseteste Press, 1967. *The Store of Things.* Phoenix Pamphlet Poets, 1969. *Types.* Second Aeon, 1970.

Burrows, Miles. *A Vulture's Egg.* Cape, 1966.

Causley, Charles. *Farewell, Aggie Weston.* Hand & Flower Press, 1951. *Survivor's Leave.* Hand & Flower Press, 1953. *Union Street.* Hart-Davis, 1960 (f.p. 1957). *Johnny Alleluia.* Hart-Davis, 1961. *Underneath the Water.* Macmillan, 1968. *Figure of 8.* Macmillan, 1969. *Figgie Hobbin: Poems for Children.* Macmillan, 1970.

Cayley, Michael. *Moorings.* Carcanet Press, 1971.

Chamberlain, Brenda. *The Green Heart.* Oxford University Press. 1958.

Clarke, Austin, *Later Poems.* Dolmen Press, 1961. *Flight to Africa.* Dolmen Press, 1963. *Old-fashioned Pilgrimage.* Dolmen Press, 1967. *The Echo at Coole.* Dolmen Press, 1968.

Clemo, Jack. *The Clay Verge.* Chatto & Windus. 1951. *The Map of Clay.* Methuen, 1961. *Cactus on Carmel.* Methuen, 1967. *The Echoing Tip.* Methuen, 1971.

Cole, Barry. *Blood Ties.* Turret Books, 1967. *Moonsearch.* Methuen, 1968. *The Visitors.* Methuen, 1970. *Vanessa in the City.* Trigram, 1971.

Conn, Stewart. *Stoats in the Sunlight.* Hutchinson, 1968.

Connor, Tony. *With Love Somehow.* Oxford University Press, 1968 (f.p. 1962). *Lodgers.* Oxford University Press, 1965. *Kon in Springtime.* Oxford University Press, 1968. *In the Happy Valley.* Oxford University Press, 1971.

Conquest, Robert, *Poems.* Macmillan, 1955. *Between Mars and Venus.* Hutchinson, 1962.

Corke, Hilary. *The Early Drowned.* Secker & Warburg, 1961.

Cotton, John. *Outside the Gates of Eden.* Taurus Press, 1969. *Old Movies.* Chatto & Windus/Hogarth Press, 1971.

Couroucli, Jennifer. *On This Athenian Hill.* Chatto & Windus/Hogarth Press, 1969.

Faber Poets

W. H. Auden
George Barker
John Berryman
Rupert Brooke
e. e. cummings
J. V. Cunningham
Walter de la Mare
Emily Dickinson
Keith Douglas
Alan Dugan
Douglas Dunn
Lawrence Durrell
T. S. Eliot
W. S. Graham
Thom Gunn
Ian Hamilton
Seamus Heaney
Ted Hughes
Randall Jarrell
David Jones

Philip Larkin
Robert Lowell
Louis MacNeice
Marianne Moore
Edwin Muir
Richard Murphy
Norman Nicholson
Mervyn Peake
Sylvia Plath
Ezra Pound
Herbert Read
Laura Riding
Anne Ridler
Theodore Roethke
Siegfried Sassoon
Stephen Spender
Wallace Stevens
Edward Thomas
Vernon Watkins
Richard Wilbur

FABER & FABER 3 QUEEN SQUARE LONDON WC1

Couzyn, Jeni, *Flying*. Workshop Press, 1970.

Creagh, Patrick. *A Row of Pharaohs*. Heinemann, 1962. *To Abel and Others*. Bodley Head, 1970.

Crichton Smith, Ian. *Thistles and Roses*. Eyre & Spottiswoode, 1961. *From Bourgeois Land*. Gollancz, 1969. *Selected Poems*. Gollancz, 1970. *Love Poems and Elegies*. Gollancz, 1972.

Cronin, Anthony. *Poems*. The Cresset Press, 1957.

Crossley-Holland, Kevin. *Norfolk Poems*. Academy Editions, 1970.

Crozier, Andrew. *Walking on Grass*. Ferry Press, 1969. *In One Side and Out the Other*. (With John James and Tom Phillips.) Ferry Press, 1970.

Cumberlege, Marcus. *Oases*. Anvil Press, 1968. *Poems for Quena and Tabla*. Carcanet Press, 1970.

Daryush, Elizabeth. *Verses : Seventh Book*. Carcanet Press, 1971. *Selected Poems*. Carcanet Press, 1971.

Davie, Donald. *Fantasy Poets No. 19*. Fantasy Press, 1954. *Bridges of Reason*. Fantasy Press, 1955. *A Winter Talent*. Routledge & Kegan Paul, 1957. *The Forests of Lithuania*. Marvell Press, 1959. *New and Selected Poems*. Wesleyan University Press, 1961. *Events and Wisdoms : Poems 1957–1963*. Routledge & Kegan Paul, 1964. *Essex Poems 1963–1967*. Routledge & Kegan Paul, 1969. *Six Epistles to Eva Hesse*. London Magazine Editions, 1970.

Day Lewis, C. *A Time to Dance and Other Poems*. Hogarth Press. 1935. *Collected Poems 1929–1933*. Hogarth Press, 1936 (f.p. 1935). *Overtures to Death and Other Poems*. Cape, 1938. *Word over All*. Cape, 1943. *Poems 1943–1947*. Cape, 1948. *Collected Poems 1929–1936*. Hogarth Press, 1948. *An Italian Visit*. Cape, 1953. *Collected Poems, 1954*. Cape/Hogarth Press, 1954. *Pegasus and Other Poems*. Cape, 1957. *The Gate and Other Poems*. Cape, 1962. *The Room and Other Poems*. Cape, 1965. *The Whispering Roots*. Cape, 1970.

Dennis, Nigel. *Exotics*. Weidenfeld & Nicolson, 1970.

Devlin, Dennis. *Collected Poems*. Dolmen Press, 1964. *The Heavenly Foreigner*. Dolmen Press, 1967.

Dickinson, Patric. *Theseus and the Minotaur*. Cape, 1946. *Stone in the Midst*. Methuen, 1948. *The Sailing Race*. Chatto & Windus, 1952. *The Scale of Things*. Chatto & Windus, 1955. *The World I See*. Chatto & Windus/Hogarth Press, 1960. *This Cold Universe*. Chatto & Windus/Hogarth Press, 1964. *More Than Time*. Chatto & Windus/Hogarth Press, 1970.

Dunn, Douglas. *Terry Street*. Faber, 1969. *Backwaters*. The Review, 1971. *The Happier Life*. Faber, 1972.

Durrell, Lawrence. *A Private Country*. Faber, 1944. *Cities, Plains and People*. Faber, 1946. *On Seeming to Presume*. Faber, 1948. *The Tree of Idleness*. Faber, 1955. *Collected Poems*. Faber, 1960. *The Ikons and Other Poems*. Faber, 1966. *Red Limbo Lingo*. Faber, 1970.

Dyment, Clifford. *Poems 1935–1948*. Dent, 1949. *Experiences and Places*. Dent, 1955. *Collected Poems*. Dent, 1970.

Earley, Tom. *The Sad Mountain*. Chatto & Windus/Hogarth Press, 1970.

Enright, D. J. *The Laughing Hyena and Other Poems*. Routledge & Kegan Paul, 1953. *Bread rather than Blossoms*. Secker & Warburg, 1956. *Some Men are Brothers*. Chatto & Windus/Hogarth Press, 1960. *The Old Adam*. Chatto & Windus/Hogarth Press, 1965. *Selected Poems*. Chatto & Windus/Hogarth Press, 1968. *Unlawful Assembly*. Chatto & Windus/Hogarth Press, 1968. *Daughters of Earth*. Chatto & Windus/Hogarth Press, 1972.

Ewart, Gavin. *Pleasures of the Flesh*. Alan Ross, 1966. *The Deceptive Grin of the Gravel Porters*. London Magazine Editions, 1968. *Twelve Apostles*. An Ulsterman Publication, 1970. *The Gavin Ewart Show*. Trigram, 1971.

Fainlight, Ruth. *18 Poems from 1966*. Turret Books, 1967. *To See the Matter Clearly*. Macmillan, 1968.

Fainlight, Harry, *Sussicran*. Turret Books, 1965.

Elizabeth Bishop
COMPLETE POEMS

This volume gathers the poetry—work of three decades—by one of the master poets of the age.

'I am sure no living poet is as curious and observant as Miss Bishop. She has a humorous, commanding genius for picking up the unnoticed, now making something sprightly and right, and now a great monument. Once her poems, each shining, were too few. Now they are many. When we read her, we enter the classical serenity of a new country.' *Robert Lowell*   £2·25

Jon Silkin
AMANA GRASS

'In these new poems—his first book-length collection in six years —Jon Silkin has turned from his 'holy island' and is exposing himself to the more violent aspects of contemporary experience. Where else but Israel and America ? . . . As a stone, as an artifact, Amana Grass is full of irreconcilable veins of colour.' *Iowa Review*

'This is socially committed poetry of a deeply complex kind. It is part of Silkin's achievement that he is able to make good poetry out of his material, that he is able to fuse the atheistic with the moralistic.' *Guardian*   £1·05 cloth £0·50 paper

Molly Holden
AIR AND CHILL EARTH

In this new book of verse Mrs Holden's empathy in the poems about nature is indeed remarkable, producing work which contains beautiful seriousness and sobriety.

'Mrs Holden can produce some admirably clear-sighted Nature poetry, deftly precise in the description of its object.' *Times Literary Supplement*   £1·25

Alan Bold
A PINT OF BITTER

With admirable translations from Baudelaire, Mallarmé, Verhaeren and others, Alan Bold's new volume contains some of his most vigorous and disciplined work—sardonic, romantic, visionary or down-to-earth.   £1·05

Chatto & Windus

Fairfax, John. *The Fifth Horseman of the Apocalypse*. Phoenix Press, 1969.

Farrington, Brian. *The Emigrant of a Hundred Townlands*. Dolmen Press, 1969.

Fedden, Robin. *The White Country*. Turret Books, 1968.

Feinstein, Elaine, *The Magic Apple Tree*. Hutchinson, 1971.

Fenton, James. *Our Western Furniture*. Sycamore Press, 1968. *Terminal Moraine*. Secker & Warburg, 1972.

Fetherston, Patrick. *Three Days after Blasphemies*. Gaberbocchus Press, 1967.

Fiacc, Padraic. *By the Black Stream*. Dolmen Press, 1969.

Finch, Peter. *The End of the Vision*. John Jones, 1971.

Finlay, Ian Hamilton. *Glasgow Beasts*. Fulcrum Press, 1965 (f.p. Wild Flounder Press, 1961). *Cythera*. Wild Hawthorn Press, 1965. *Autumn Poem*. Wild Hawthorn Press, 1966. *Stonechats*. Wild Hawthorn Press, 1967. *Canal Game*. Fulcrum Press, 1967. *Air Letters*. Tarasque Press, 1968. *The Dancers Inherit the Party*. Fulcrum Press, 1969.

Fisher, Roy. *The Memorial Fountain*. Northern House, 1966. *The Ship's Orchestra*. Fulcrum Press, 1966. *Collected Poems 1968*. Fulcrum Press, 1969. *The Cut Pages*. Fulcrum Press, 1971. *Matrix*. Fulcrum Press, 1971.

Fraser, G. S. *The Traveller has Regrets*. Harvill Press and Editions Poetry, 1948. *Conditions*. Byron Press, 1969.

Fuller, John. *Fairground Music*. Chatto & Windus/Hogarth Press, 1961. *The Tree that Walked*. Chatto & Windus/Hogarth Press, 1967. *Cannibals and Missionaries*. Secker & Warburg, 1972.

Fuller, Roy. *The Middle of a War*. The Hogarth Press, 1942. *A Lost Season*. The Hogarth Press, 1944. *Epitaphs and Occasions*. John Lehmann, 1949. *Counterparts*. Verschoyle, 1954. *Brutus's Orchard*. Deutsch, 1957. *Collected Poems 1936–1961*. Deutsch, 1962. *Buff*. Deutsch, 1965. *New Poems*. Deutsch, 1968.

Fulton, Robin. *Inventories*. Caithness Books. 1969.

Gardner, Donald. *Peace Feelers*. Cafe Books, 1969.

Garfitt, Roger, *Caught on Blue*. Carcanet, 1970.

Gascoyne, David. *Poems 1937–1942*. PL Editions Poetry, 1948 (f.p. 1943). *A Vagrant and Other Poems*. John Lehmann, 1950. *Collected Poems*. Oxford University Press, 1966 (f.p. 1965). *Collected Verse Translations*. Oxford University Press, 1970.

Garlick, Raymond. *A Sense of Europe : Collected Poems 1954–1968*. Gwasg Gomer, 1968.

Gershon, Karen. *Selected Poems*. Gollancz, 1966.

Gibson, Miles. *The Guilty Bystander*. Methuen, 1970.

Gill, David, *The Pagoda and Other Poems*. Chatto & Windus/Hogarth Press, 1969.

Glen, Duncan. *In Appearances*. Akros Publications, 1971.

Gordon, Giles. *Two Elegies*. Turret Books, 1968.

Graham, Henry. *Good Luck to You Kafka/You'll Need it Boss*. Rapp & Whiting, 1969. *Passport to Earth*. Rapp & Whiting/Deutsch, 1971.

Graham, W. S. *The Seven Journeys*. William MacLennan, 1944. *The White Threshold*. Faber, 1949. *The Nightfishing*. Faber, 1955. *Malcolm Mooney's Land*. Faber, 1970.

Graves, Robert. *Poems 1914–1926*. Heinemann, 1927. *Poems 1938–1945*. Cassell, 1946. *Collected Poems 1914–1947*. Cassell, 1948. *Poems and Satires*, 1951. Cassell, 1951. *Poems 1953*. Cassell, 1953. *Collected Poems 1959*. Cassell, 1959. *More Poems 1961*. Cassell, 1961. *New Poems 1962*. Cassell, 1963 (f.p. 1962). *Man Does, Woman Is*. Cassell, 1964. *Poems 1965–1968*. Cassell, 1968. *Poems 1968–1970*. Cassell, 1970.

Griffiths, Bryn. *The Stones Remember*. Dent, 1967. *Scars*. Dent, 1969. *The Survivors*. Dent, 1971.

Grigson, Geoffrey. *Several Observations*. Cresset Press, 1939. *Under the Cliff*. Routledge & Kegan Paul, 1943. *The Isles of Scilly*. Routledge & Kegan Paul, 1946. *The Collected Poems of Geoffrey Grigson 1924–1962*. Phoenix House, 1963. *A Skull in Salop*. Macmillan, 1967. *Ingestion of Ice-cream*. Macmillan, 1969. *Discoveries of Bones and Stones*. Macmillan, 1971.

MODERN POETS

1: *Lawrence Durrell, Elizabeth Jennings, R. S. Thomas*   20p
2: *Kingsley Amis, Dom Moraes, Peter Porter*   20p
3: *George Barker, Martin Bell, Charles Causley*   20p
4: *David Holbrook, Christopher Middleton, David Wevill*   20p
5: *Gregory Corso, Lawrence Ferlinghetti, Allen Ginsberg*   25p
6: *Jack Clemo, Edward Lucie-Smith, George MacBeth*   20p
7: *Richard Murphy, Jon Silkin, Nathaniel Tarn*   20p
8: *Edwin Brock, Geoffrey Hill, Stevie Smith*   20p
9: *Denise Levertov, Kenneth Rexroth, William Carlos Williams*   25p
10: The Mersey Sound *Adrian Henri, Roger McGough, Brian Patten*   25p
11: *D. M. Black, Peter Redgrove, D. M. Thomas*   20p
12: *Alan Jackson, Jeff Nuttall, William Wantling*   20p
13: *Charles Bukowski, Philip Lamantia, Harold Norse*   25p
14: *Alan Brownjohn, Michael Hamburger, Charles Tomlinson*   30p
15: *Alan Bold, Edward Brathwaite, Edwin Morgan*   25p
16: *Jack Beeching, Harry Guest, Matthew Mead*   25p
17: *W. S. Graham, Kathleen Raine, David Gascoyne*   25p
18: *A. Alvarez, Roy Fuller, Anthony Thwaite*   25p
19: *John Ashbery, Lee Harwood, Tom Raworth*   30p
20: *John Heath-Stubbs, F. T. Prince, Stephen Spender*   30p
21: *Iain Crichton Smith, Norman MacCaig, George Mackay Brown*   35p

(SOME RECENT TITLES)

Penguin Modern European Poets *In an English verse translation*

Amichai, Yehuda *Ted Hughes, Assai Gutman and Harold Schimmel*   25p
Bobrowski, Johannes and Horst Bienek *Ruth and Matthew Mead*   30p
Ekelöf, Gunnar *W. H. Auden and Leif Sjoberg*   30p
Holan, Vladimir *Jarmila and Ian Milner*   30p
Kovner, Abba and Nelly Sachs *Shirley Kaufman, Nurit Orcham, Michael Hamburger, Christopher Holme, Ruth and Matthew Mead and Michael Roloff*   30p
Pavese, Cesare *Margaret Crosland*   35p
Three Czech Poets: Vitezslav Nezval, Antonín Bartusek and Josef Hanzlík *Ewald Osers and George Theiner*   25p
Ungaretti, Giuseppe *Patrick Creagh*   30p
Weores, Sándor and Ferenc Juhász *Edwin Morgan and David Wevill*   25p

These titles are available from your bookseller or, in case of difficulty, from J. Barnicoat, P.O. Box 11, Falmouth, Cornwall, enclosing the price of books required plus 6p per volume postage.

NORTHERN HOUSE PAMPHLET POETS

The Northern House Pamphlet Poets are small collections of work by either new or established poets. Each pamphlet contains ten to sixteen poems, often a group of poems written to one theme. Each pamphlet appears in the same format, inexpensive and printed in longer runs than is usual for poetry of the kind normally published in hard covers. The series is published by the editors of STAND.

The pamphlets cost 15p each (except nos. 1–5).
Nos. 1–5 are editors' copies which are now only available at £1·25 ($3.30) each.
A set of 8 pamphlets costs £1·20 ($4), a set of 4 is 60p ($2).
Orders should be sent to Northern House, 58 Queen's Road, Newcastle-on-Tyne NE2 2PR.

LONDON MAGAZINE EDITIONS
30 Thurloe Place
London SW7

"Whatever garlands the Muses bestow on publishers will have been delivered to Alan Ross for his cheap, elegant London Magazine editions." *New Statesman*

Grubb, Frederick. *Title Deeds*. Longmans, 1961.

Guest, Harry. *Arrangements*. Anvil Press, 1968. *The Cutting Room*. Anvil Press, 1970.

Gunn, Thom. *Fighting Terms*. Fantasy Press, 1954. *The Sense of Movement*. Faber, 1957. *My Sad Captains*. Faber, 1961. *Touch*. Faber, 1967. *The Fair in the Woods*. Sycamore Press, 1969. *Poems 1950–1966*. Faber, 1969. *Moly*. Faber, 1971.

Hamburger, Michael. *Flowering Cactus: Poems 1942–1949*. Hand & Flower, 1950. *Poems 1950–1951*. Hand & Flower, 1952. *The Dual Site*. Routledge & Kegan Paul, 1958. *Weather and Season*. Longmans, 1963. *Travelling: Poems 1963–1968*. Fulcrum Press, 1969.

Hamilton, Ian. *The Visit*. Faber, 1970.

Harrison, Keith, *Points in a Journey*. Macmillan, 1966. *Two Variations on a Ground*. Turret Books, 1967.

Harrison, Tony. *The Loiners*. London Magazine Editions, 1970.

Harsent, David. *A Violent Country*. Oxford University Press, 1969.

Harwood, Lee. *The White Room*. Fulcrum Press, 1969. *Landscapes*. Fulcrum Press, 1969. *The Sinking Colony*. Fulcrum Press, 1970.

Hawkins, Spike. *The Lost Fire Brigade*. Fulcrum Press, 1968.

Heaney, Seamus. *Eleven Poems*. Festival Publications, n.d. *Death of a Naturalist*. Faber, 1966. *A Lough Neagh Sequence*. Phoenix Pamphlet Poets, 1969. *Door Into the Dark*. Faber, 1969.

Heath-Stubbs, John. *Wounded Thammuz*. Routledge & Kegan Paul, 1942. *Beauty and the Beast*. Routledge & Kegan Paul, 1943. *The Divided Ways*. Routledge & Kegan Paul, 1946. *The Swarming of the Bees*. Eyre & Spottiswoode, 1950. *A Charm Against the Toothache*. Methuen, 1954. *The Triumph of the Muse*. Oxford University Press, 1958. *The Blue-Fly in His Head*. Oxford University Press, 1962. *Selected Poems*. Oxford University Press, 1965.

Henri, Adrian. *Tonight at Noon*. Rapp & Whiting, 1968. *City*. Rapp & Whiting, 1969. *Poems for Wales* and *Six Landscapes for Susan*. Arc Publications, 1970. *Autobiography*. Cape, 1971.

Hewitt, John. *No Rebel Word*. Muller, 1948. *Collected Poems 1932–1967*. MacGibbon & Kee, 1968.

Higgins, Brian. *The Only Need*. Abelard Schumann, 1960. *Notes While Travelling*. Longmans, 1964. *The Northern Fiddler*. Methuen, 1966.

Hill, Geoffrey. *For the Unfallen*. Deutsch, 1959. *King Log*. Deutsch, 1968. *Mercian Hymns*. Deutsch, 1971.

Hobsbaum, Philip. *The Place's Fault and Other Poems*. Macmillan, 1964. *In Retreat*. Macmillan, 1966. *Coming Out Fighting*. Macmillan, 1969.

Hogg, Quintin. *The Devil's Own Song and Other Verses*. Hodder & Stoughton, 1968.

Holbrook, David. *Imaginings*. Putnam, 1961 (f.p. 1960). *Against the Cruel Frost*. Putnam, 1963. *Object Relations*. Methuen, 1967. *Old Man New World*. Rapp & Whiting, 1969.

Holden, Molly. *To Make Me Grieve*. Chatto & Windus/Hogarth Press, 1968. *Air and Chill Earth*. Chatto & Windus/Hogarth Press, 1971.

Hollo, Anselm. *And It Is a Song*. Migrant Press, 1965. *Faces and Forms*. Ambit, 1965. *The Coherences*. Trigram, 1968. *Maya*. Cape Goliard, 1970.

Holloway, John. *Fantasy Poet No. 26*. Fantasy Press, 1954. *The Minute and Shorter Poems*. Marvell Press, 1956. *The Fugue and Shorter Pieces*. Routledge & Kegan Paul, 1960. *The Landfallers*. Routledge & Kegan Paul, 1962. *Wood and Windfall*. Routledge & Kegan Paul, 1965.

Holmes, Richard. *One for Sorrow, Two for Joy*. Cafe Books, 1970.

Horder, John. *A Sense of Being*. Chatto & Windus/Hogarth Press, 1968.

Horovitz, Frances. *The High Tower*. New Departures, 1970.

Horovitz, Michael. *Love Poems*. New Departures, 1971. *The Wolverhampton Wanderer*. Latimer New Dimensions, 1971.

Hough, Graham. *Legends and Pastorals*. Duckworth, 1961.

the Review

Editor: Ian Hamilton

A magazine of poetry and criticism

"Of all the English little magazines now appearing regularly, *the Review* seems to be by far the most worthwhile."

New Statesman

"*the Review* has a fine record both of sensitive appreciation and unflinching recognition of the limitations of contemporary English and American poetry."

The Times Literary Supplement

"The best poetry magazine we have."

The Observer

"At last what we want from a little magazine."

Encounter

"By far the best of the British little magazines."

New York Times

the Review has now established itself as Britain's leading "little magazine" of poetry and criticism, and these are just a few of the admiring comments that have greeted the magazine since it first appeared in 1962. Contributors include: A. Alvarez, John Bayley, Russell Davies, Colin Falck, Michael Fried, John Fuller, Roy Fuller, Martin Dodsworth, Donald Davie, Sylvia Plath, Robert Lowell, Peter Porter, Alan Brownjohn, Stephen Spender, David Harsent, Donald Hall, Philip Larkin, Douglas Dunn, Hugo Williams, Martin Seymour-Smith, Alan Ross, Karl Miller, Clive James, Geoffrey Grigson, James Reeves, Julian Symons, Louis Simpson, Edward Pygge, James Fenton, G. S. Fraser, Gabriel Pearson, Stephen Wall, John Carey, Jonathan Raban, Francis Hope.

**Subscription: £1·50 for 4 issues from:
11 Greek Street, London W1**

Houston, Libby. *A Stained Glass Raree Show*. Allison & Busby, 1967. *Plain Clothes*. Allison & Busby, 1971.

Howell, Anthony. *Sergei de Diaghileff (1929)*. Turret Books, 1968. *Inside the Castle*. Cresset Press, 1969. *Imruil*. Barrie & Jenkins, 1970.

Hughes, Glyn. *Almost-Love Poems*. Sycamore Press, 1968. *Love on the Moor : Poems 1965– 1968*. Phoenix Pamphlet Poets, 1968. *Neighbours*. Macmillan, 1970.

Hughes, Pennethorne. *Thirty Eight Poems*. John Baker, 1970.

Hughes, Ted. *The Hawk in the Rain*. Faber, 1957. *Lupercal*. Faber, 1960. *Meet My Folks!* Faber, 1967 (f.p. 1961). *The Earth Owl and Other Moon People*. Faber, 1963. *Nessie the Mannerless Monster*. Faber, 1964. *Wodwo*. Faber, 1967. *Crow*. Faber, 1970.

Hutchinson, Pearse. *Expansions*. Dolmen Press, 1969.

Jackson, Alan. *The Grim Wayfarer*. Fulcrum Press, 1969.

Jennings, Elizabeth. *Poems*. Fantasy Press, 1953. *A Way of Looking*. Deutsch, 1955. *A Sense of the World*. Deutsch, 1958. *Song for a Birth or a Death*. Deutsch, 1961. *Recoveries*. Deutsch, 1964. *The Mind has Mountains*. Macmillan, 1966. *Collected Poems*. Macmillan, 1967. *The Animals' Arrival*. Macmillan, 1969. *Lucidities*. Macmillan, 1970. *Relationships*. Macmillan, 1972.

Jones, Brian. *Poems*. Alan Ross, 1966. *Interior*. Alan Ross, 1969. *The Mantis Hand*. Arc Publications, 1970.

Jones, David. *In Parenthesis*. Faber, 1955 (f.p. 1937). *The Anathemata*. Faber, 1955 (f.p. 1952). *The Tribune's Visitation*. Fulcrum Press, 1969.

Jones, Glyn. *The Dream of Jake Hopkins*. Fortune Press, 1954.

Jones, John Idris. *Barry Island and Other Poems*. John Jones, 1970.

Jones, Peter. *Rain*. Carcanet Press, 1969. *Seagarden for Julius*. Carcanet Press, 1970. *The Peace & the Hook*. Carcanet Press, 1972.

Jones, R. Gerallt. *Jamaican Landscape*. Christopher Davies, 1969.

Kapur, Ishan. *Tomorrow's Dark Sun*. Carcanet Press, 1969.

Kavanagh, P. J. *A Soul for Sale*. Macmillan, 1947. *One and One*. Heinemann, 1959. *Come Dance with Kitty Stobling*. Longmans, 1960. *The Great Hunger*. MacGibbon & Kee, 1966. *On the Way to the Depot*. Chatto & Windus/Hogarth Press, 1967. *About Time*. Chatto & Windus/Hogarth Press, 1970.

Kell, Richard. *Control Tower*. Chatto & Windus/Hogarth Press, 1962. *Differences*. Chatto & Windus/Hogarth Press, 1969.

Kennelly, Brendan. *Dream of a Black Fox*. Allen Figgis, 1968. *Bread*. Tara Telephone Publications, 1971.

Kerrigan, Anthony. *At the Front Door of the Atlantic*. Dolmen Press, 1969.

Kinsella, Thomas. *Another September*. Dolmen Press, 1958. *Downstream*. Dolmen Press and Oxford University Press, 1962. *Nightwalker and Other Poems*. Dolmen Press, 1968.

Kirkup, James. *The Drowned Sailor and Other Poems*. Grey Walls, 1947. *The Creation*. Lotus Press, 1951. *The Submerged Village*. Oxford University Press, 1951. *A Correct Compassion*. Oxford University Press, 1952. *A Spring Journey*. Oxford University Press, 1954. *The Descent into the Cave*. Oxford University Press, 1957. *The Prodigal Son : Poems 1956–1959*. Oxford University Press, 1959. *Refusal to Conform*. Oxford University Press, 1963. *White Shadows Black Shadows*. Dent, 1970. *The Body Servant*. Dent, 1971. *A Bewick Bestiary*. MidNAG, 1971.

Kops, Bernard. *Erica I Want to Read You Something*. Scorpion Press, 1967.

Larkin, Philip. *The North Ship*. Faber, 1966 (f.p. 1945). *Fantasy Poet No. 21*. Fantasy Press, 1954. *The Less Deceived*. Marvell Press, 1955. *The Whitsun Weddings*. Faber, 1964.

Lee, Laurie. *The Sun My Monument*. Hogarth Press, 1944. *The Bloom of Candles*. John Lehmann, 1947. *My Many-Coated Man*. Deutsch, 1955.

Lerner, Laurence. *Fantasy Poet No. 28*. Fantasy Press, 1955. *Domestic Interior*. Hutchinson, 1959. *The Directions of Memory : Poems 1958–1963*. Chatto & Windus, 1963. *Selves*. Routledge & Kegan Paul, 1969.

LONDON MAGAZINE

Art Architecture Films Theatre

Music Poetry Stories Criticism

Memoirs Posters Jazz Books

"The character of the *London Magazine* has always resided in its enthusiastic openness to ideas and new work, both traditional and avant-garde, without becoming embattled, ideological, or trendy."—*New Statesman*

"*London Magazine* is far and away the most readable and level-headed, not to mention best value for money, of the literary magazines"—*The Times*

"Alan Ross has admirably achieved what he set out to do: to provide a more detailed and considered chronicle of the cultural scene than the weeklies have the space for, and to offer interesting new work in poetry and (the *LM*'s particular strength since no one else will print them) the short story."—*Times Literary Supplement*

Subscription £5 (USA $14) a year
Single copies 90p. Illustrated.
Cheques payable to London Magazine, 30 Thurloe Place, London SW7

YOU could spend a lot of time and effort looking for the best four books of new poetry published in Britain this year

OR you could for an outlay of only £4 for the year join

THE POETRY BOOK SOCIETY

and receive a book of new poetry every quarter plus the Society's Bulletin, Special Christmas Poetry Supplement and yearly check list of new verse

Write to: The Secretary
Poetry Book Society Ltd.
105 Piccadilly
London W1V 0AU

Levi, Peter. *The Gravel Ponds*. Deutsch, 1960. *Water, Rock and Sand*. Deutsch, 1962. *Fresh Water, Sea Water*. Black Raven Press, 1966. *Pancakes for the Queen of Babylon*. Anvil Press, 1968. *Ruined Abbeys*. Anvil Press, 1968. *Life is a Platform : Death is a Pulpit*. Anvil Press, 1971.

Lindop, Grevel. *Against the Sea*. Carcanet Press, 1969.

Livingstone, Dinah. *Beginning*. Katabasis, 1968 (f.p. 1967). *Tohu Bohu*. Katabasis, 1968. *Maranatha*. Katabasis, 1969.

Logue, Christopher. *The Man Who Told His Love*. Scorpion Press, 1969 (f.p. 1958). *Songs*. Hutchinson, 1959. *Christopher Logue's ABC*. Scorpion Press, 1966. *Pax*. Rapp & Carroll, 1967. *New Numbers*. Cape, 1969. *Patrocleia*. Scorpion Press, 1969. *Twelve Cards*. Lorrimer, 1971.

Longley, Michael. *Ten Poems*. Festival Publications, 1965. *Secret Marriages*. Phoenix Pamphlet Poets, 1968. *No Continuing City: Poems 1963–1968*. Macmillan/Gill & Macmillan, 1969.

Lowbury, Edward. *Time for Sale*. Chatto & Windus/Hogarth Press, 1961. *Daylight Astronomy*. Chatto & Windus/Hogarth Press, 1968.

Lucie-Smith, Edward. *A Tropical Childhood*. Oxford University Press, 1961. *Confessions and Histories*. Oxford University Press, 1964. *Futura 10: Cloud Sun Fountain Statue*. Editions Hansjörg Mayer, 1966. *Towards Silence*. Oxford University Press, 1968. *A Girl Surveyed*. Hanover Gallery, 1971.

Lykiard, Alexis. *Robe of Skin*. Allison & Busby, 1969.

MacBeth, George. *The Broken Places*. Scorpion Press, 1963. *A Doomsday Book*. Scorpion Press, 1965. *The Colour of Blood*. Macmillan, 1967. *The Night of Stones*. Macmillan, 1968. *A War Quartet*. Macmillan, 1969. *The Burning Cone*. Macmillan, 1970. *Collected Poems 1958–1970*. Macmillan, 1971. *The Orlando Poems*. Macmillan, 1971.

MacCaig, Norman. *Riding Light*. Hogarth Press, 1955. *The Sinai Sort*. Hogarth Press, 1957. *A Common Grace*. Chatto & Windus/Hogarth Press, 1960. *A Round of Applause*. Chatto & Windus/Hogarth Press, 1962. *Measures*. Chatto & Windus, 1965. *Surroundings*. Chatto & Windus/Hogarth Press, 1966. *Rings on a Tree*. Chatto & Windus/Hogarth Press, 1968. *A Man in my Position*. Chatto & Windus/Hogarth Press, 1969.

McClymont, Davie. *Menelek*. East Kilbride Arts Centre, 1969.

MacDiarmid, Hugh. *A Drunk Man Looks at the Thistle*. Castle Wynd Printers, 1956 (f.p. 1926). *A Lap of Honour*. MacGibbon & Kee, 1967. *A Clyack-Sheaf*. MacGibbon & Kee, 1969. *Selected Poems*. Penguin, 1970. *More Collected Poems*. MacGibbon & Kee, 1970.

McGough, Roger. *Frinck, a Day in the Life of*, and *Summer with Monika*. Michael Joseph, 1967. *Watchwords*. Cape, 1969. *After the Merrymaking*. Cape, 1971.

McIlvanney, William. *The Longships in Harbour*. Eyre & Spottiswoode, 1970.

MacSweeney, Barry. *The Boy from the Green Cabaret Tells of His Mother*. Hutchinson, 1968. *Our Mutual Scarlet Boulevard*. Fulcrum Press, 1971.

Mahon, Derek. *Night Crossing*. Oxford University Press, 1968. *Ecclesiastes*. Phoenix Pamphlet Poets, 1970. *Lives*. Oxford University Press, 1972.

Manning, Hugo. *The Secret Sea*. Villiers Publications, 1962. *Encounter in Crete*. Enitharmon Press, 1971.

Mansel, Lavinia. *Already on the Hills*. Anvil Press, 1968.

Massingham, Harold. *Black Bull Guarding Apples*. Longmans, 1965. *Creation*. Sycamore Press, 1968. *The Magician*. Phoenix Pamphlet Poets, 1969. *Frostgods*. Macmillan, 1971.

Mead, Matthew. *Identities*. Migrant Press, 1964. *The Administration of Things*. Anvil Press, 1970.

Middleton, Christopher. *Torse: Poems 1949–1961*. Longmans, 1962. *Nonsequences*. Longmans, 1965. *Our Flowers and Nice Bones*. Fulcrum Press, 1969.

Milne, Ewart. *A Garland for the Green*. Hutchinson, 1962. *Time Stopped*. Plow Poems, 1967.

THE TIMES LITERARY SUPPLEMENT

The TLS reviews more books on every subject, from any source, than any other weekly literary journal.

But the TLS is more than a collection of book reviews. It also publishes articles written by some of the best-known personalities of the world of letters, and many of the most renowned thinkers of the day contribute to its pages.

The TLS is invaluable for everyone interested in the printed word.

Out every Friday. Available from any newsagent. Price 10p.

The Critical Quarterly

5,000 subscribers read our new poems and major articles on literature. Recent contributors include Ted Hughes, Philip Larkin, David Holbrook, Louis Simpson, R. S. Thomas, and Charles Tomlinson.

"It brings its audience splendid gifts."
The Guardian

"The sane, sparkling Critical Quarterly.*"*
Encounter

Price £1·50 for four issues from
Oxford University Press,
Subscription Department,
Press Road,
Neasden,
London NW10

Mitchell, Adrian. *Fantasy Poets No. 24*. Fantasy Press, 1954. *Poems*. Cape, 1964. *Out Loud*. Cape Goliard, 1969. *Ride the Nightmare*. Cape, 1971.

Moat, John. *Thunder of Grass*. Barrie & Rockliff, 1969.

Mole, John. *The Instruments*. Phoenix Pamphlet Poets, 1970.

Montague, John. *Poisoned Lands*. MacGibbon & Kee, 1961. *Tides*. Dolmen Press, 1970.

Montgomery, Stuart. *Circe*. Fulcrum Press, 1969.

Moraes, Dom. *A Beginning*. The Parton Press, 1957. *Poems*. Eyre & Spottiswoode, 1960. *John Nobody*. Eyre & Spottiswoode, 1965.

Morgan, Edwin. *Starryveldt*. Eugen Gomringer Press, 1965. *A Second Life*. Edinburgh University Press, 1968. *The Horseman's Word*. Akros Publications, 1970.

Murphy, Richard. *Sailing to an Island*. Faber, 1963. *The Battle of Aughrim* and *The God Who Eats Corn*. Faber, 1968.

Normanton, John. *The Window Game*. London Magazine Editions, 1968.

Norris, Leslie. *Finding Gold*. Chatto & Windus/Hogarth Press, 1967. *Ransoms*. Chatto & Windus/Hogarth Press, 1970.

Nuttall, Jeff. *Poems I Want to Forget*. Turret Books, 1965. *Poems 1962–1969*. Fulcrum Press, 1970.

Nye, Robert, *Juvenilia 1*. Scorpion Press, 1961. *Juvenilia 2*. Scorpion Press, 1963. *Darker Ends*. Calder & Boyars, 1969.

Oakes, Philip. *Unlucky Jonah: Twenty Poems*. Reading University, School of Art, 1954. *In the Affirmative*. Deutsch, 1969.

O'Grady, Desmond. *The Dying Gaul*. MacGibbon & Kee, 1968.

Oxley, Brian. *Twenty Five Poems*. MidNAG, 1970.

Patten, Brian. *Little Johnny's Confession*. Allen & Unwin, 1967. *Notes to the Hurrying Man*. Allen & Unwin, 1969. *The Irrelevant Song*. Allen & Unwin, 1971.

Pickard, Tom. *High on the Walls*. Fulcrum Press, 1967. *The Order of Chance*. Fulcrum Press, 1971.

Pilling, Christopher. *Snakes and Girls*. School of English Press, University of Leeds, 1970. *In all the Spaces on all the Lines*. Phoenix Pamphlet Poets, 1971.

Pinter, Harold. *Poems*. Enitharmon Press, 1968.

Pitter, Ruth. *Urania*. Cresset Press, 1950. *The Ermine: Poems 1942–1952*. Cresset Press, 1953. *Still by Choice*. Cresset Press, 1966. *Poems 1926–1966*. Barrie & Rockliff, Cresset Press, 1968.

Plath, Sylvia. *The Colossus*. Heinemann, 1960. *Ariel*. Faber, 1965. *Crossing the Water*. Faber, 1971. *Winter Trees*. Faber, 1971.

Plomer, William. *The Fivefold Screen*. Leonard and Virginia Woolf at the Hogarth Press, 1932. *Visiting the Caves*. Cape, 1936. *Selected Poems*. Hogarth Press, 1946 (f.p. 1940). *The Dorking Thigh*. Cape, 1946 (f.p. 1945). *A Shot in the Dark*. Cape, 1955. *Collected Poems*. Cape, 1960. *Taste and Remember*. Cape, 1966. *Celebrations*. Cape, 1972.

Porter, Peter. *Once Bitten, Twice Bitten*. Scorpion Press, 1961. *Words without Music*. Sycamore Press, 1968. *A Porter Folio*. Scorpion Press, 1969. *The Last of England*. Oxford University Press, 1970.

Prince, F. T. *Poems*. Faber, 1938. *Soldiers Bathing and Other Poems*. Fortune Press, 1954. *The Doors of Stone: Poems 1938–1962*. Hart-Davis, 1963. *Memoirs in Oxford*. Fulcrum Press, 1970.

Prynne, J. H. *Aristeas*. Ferry Press, 1968. *Kitchen Poems*. Cape Goliard, 1969. *The White Stones*. Grosseteste Press, 1969.

Pudney, John. *Spill Out*. Dent, 1967. *Spandrels*. Dent, 1969. *Take this Orange*. Dent, 1971.

Purcell, Sally. *The Devil's Dancing Hour*. Anvil Press, 1968. *Provencal Poems*. Carcanet Press, 1969. *The Holly Queen*. Anvil Press, 1972.

Raine, Kathleen. *Stone and Flower: Poems 1935–1943*. Nicholson & Watson PL, 1943. *Living in Time*. Editions Poetry, 1946. *The Pythoness and Other Poems*. Hamish Hamilton, 1949. *The Year One*. Hamish Hamilton, 1952. *Collected Poems*. Hamish Hamilton, 1956.

akrospoetry

Akros Poetry Magazine   25p per issue (except no. 18   40p)   90p for four issues
"the most vigorous force in modern Scots poetry making"
Alastair Mackie: Clytach: poems   £1·15 and 55p
Duncan Glen: The Individual and the 20th-Century Scottish Literary Tradition   55p
Duncan Glen: A Small Press and Hugh MacDiarmid   53p
Hugh MacDiarmid & Duncan Glen: The MacDiarmids, a conversation   43p
John C. Weston: Hugh MacDiarmid's "A Drunk Man Looks at the Thistle"   53p
Duncan Glen: In Appearances: a sequence o poems   £1·15
Duncan Glen: Clydesdale: a sequence o poems   30p
Tom Scott: At the Shrine o the Unkent Sodger: a poem   38p
Alexander Scott: Cantrips: poems   £1·13
Maurice Lindsay: This Business of Living: poems   £1·13
Maurice Lindsay: Comings and Goings: poems   40p
Iain Crichton Smith's translation of "Ben Dorain"   38p
Write for full list of Akros Publications, hardbacks and pamphlets, to:
Akros Publications, 14 Parklands Avenue, Penwortham, Preston, Lancashire, England

AGENDA

A Magazine of Poetry and Criticism

Subscription (4 issues, 1 year) £2·00 ($6)

Special issues in print:-

Ezra Pound	75p ($2)
Hugh McDiarmid	90p ($3.00)
Wyndham Lewis	£2·50 ($7)
Translation	60p ($2)
Greek Poetry	30p ($1)
W. B. Yeats/Montale	90p ($3)
Ungaretti	45p ($2)
Thomas Hardy	90p ($3.00)

Please send all orders to the Editor, AGENDA
5 Cranbourne Court, Albert Bridge Road,
London SW11 4PE

POETRY WALES

Cylchgrawn Cenedlaethol o Farddoniaeth Newydd

Editor: Meic Stephens

The renaissance of Anglo-Welsh poetry in the 'sixties was led by this national magazine. Among its contributors have been Vernon Watkins, Glyn Jones and R. S. Thomas, as well as a host of younger poets including Emyr Humphreys, Leslie Norris, Roland Mathias, Peter Gruffydd, Harri Webb, Raymond Garlick, John Ormond, Anthony Conran, Gwyn Williams, Bryn Griffiths, John Tripp and Peter Finch. There have been articles and reviews on the work of the major Anglo-Welsh poets, Dylan Thomas, Alun Lewis, Edward Thomas and David Jones. The Spring 1972 number was devoted to the work of R. S. Thomas. We have also published all the leading poets in the Welsh language— Euros Bowen, Pennar Davies, Bobi Jones, Gwyn Thomas and Derec Llwyd Morgan are a few. Poetry is flourishing in Wales today, in both English and Welsh. POETRY WALES, while keeping an informal eye on the poetry of other countries, is entirely committed to its cause.

'Beirdd byd barnant wyr o galon'

Price 38p a copy (annual subscription £1·52 for 4 numbers)

CHRISTOPHER DAVIES LTD., LLANDYBIE, RHYDAMAN, CARMARTHENSHIRE

LINES REVIEW

is now 21 years old, and continues to publish the best new writing from Scotland, along with occasional features on new writing from Europe. Special one-man issues have been devoted to Iain Crichton Smith (No. 29), Sorley Maclean (No. 34), Robert Nye (No. 38) and Derick Thomson (No. 39). 'Mixed' issues feature about four poets, plus reviews. LINES REVIEW EDITIONS is a new series of books by writers associated with LINES REVIEW. No. 1 is *The Man with the Surbahar* by Robin Fulton; No. 2 is a new collection by Iain Crichton Smith; No. 3 will be a new collection by Robert Garioch.

LINES REVIEW costs £1·00 for four issues.

LINES REVIEW EDITIONS cost 80p each.

They can be ordered from the publisher:

M. Macdonald, Edgefield Road, Loanhead, Midlothian

The Hollow Hill. Hamish Hamilton, 1965. *The Lost Country*. Dolmen Press and Hamish Hamilton, 1971.

Rattenbury, Arnold. *Second Causes*. Chatto & Windus/Hogarth Press, 1969.

Raworth, Tom. *The Relation Ship*. Goliard Press, 1967. *The Big Green Day*. Trigram, 1968. *Lion Lion*. Trigram, 1970. *Moving*. Cape Goliard, 1971.

Redgrove, Peter. *The Collector and Other Poems*. Routledge & Kegan Paul, 1960. *The Nature of Cold Weather*. Routledge & Kegan Paul, 1961. *At the White Monument*. Routledge & Kegan Paul, 1963. *The Force and Other Poems*. Routledge & Kegan Paul, 1966. *Peter Redgrove's Work in Progress*, 1968. Poet & Printer, 1969. *The Mother, the Daughter and the Sighing Bridge*. Sycamore Press, 1970. *Love's Journeys*. Second Aeon, 1971.

Reeves, Gareth. *Pilgrims*. Carcanet Press, 1969.

Reeves, James. *The Password and Other Poems*. Heinemann, 1952. *The Talking Skull*. Heinemann, 1958. *Collected Poems 1929-1959*. Heinemann, 1960. *Subsong*. Heinemann, 1969.

Reid, Alastair. *Oddments, Inklings, Omens, Moments*. Dent, 1960.

Richards, I. A. *Goodbye Earth and Other Poems*. Routledge & Kegan Paul, 1959. *The Screens*. Routledge & Kegan Paul, 1961. *Internal Colloquies*. Routledge & Kegan Paul, 1972.

Riddell, Alan. *The Stopped Landscape*. Hutchinson, 1968.

Ridler, Anne. *The Nine Bright Shiners*. Faber, 1944 (f.p. 1943). *A Matter of Life and Death*. Faber, 1959. *Some Time After*. Faber, 1972.

Riley, Peter. *Love-Strife Machine*. Ferry Press, 1969. *The Canterbury Experimental Weekend*. Arc Publications, 1971.

Robson, Jeremy. *Thirty Three Poems*. Sidgwick & Jackson, 1964. *In Focus*. Allison & Busby, 1970.

Roche, Paul. *To Tell the Truth*. Duckworth, 1967.

Ross, Alan. *The Derelict Day*. John Lehmann, 1947. *Something of the Sea*. Verschoyle, 1954. *To Whom It May Concern*. Hamish Hamilton, 1958. *African Negatives*. Eyre & Spottiswoode, 1962. *North from Sicily*. Eyre & Spottiswoode, 1965. *Poems 1942-1967*. Eyre & Spottiswoode, 1967.

Rowse, A. L. *Poems Partly American*. Faber, 1959. *Poems of Cornwall and America*. Faber, 1967.

Rudolf, Anthony. *The Manifold Circle*. Carcanet Press, 1971.

Russell, David. *Exacting Modality of the World Web*. Cafe Books, 1970.

Russell, Peter, *Visions and Ruins*. Saint Albert's Press, 1964. *Paysages Legendaires*. Enitharmon Press, 1971.

Scannell, Vernon. *Graves and Resurrections*. Fortune Press, 1948. *A Mortal Pitch*. Villiers Publications, 1957. *The Masks of Love*. Putnam, 1960. *A Sense of Danger*. Putnam, 1962. *Epithets of War : Poems 1965-1969*. Eyre & Spottiswoode, 1969. *Selected Poems*. Allison & Busby, 1971.

Schmidt, Michael. *Black Buildings*. Carcanet Press, 1969. *Bedlam and the Oakwood*. Carcanet Press, 1970. *Desert of the Lions*. Carcanet Press, 1972. *It was My Tree*. Anvil Press, 1972.

Scott, Alexander. *Cantrips*. Akros Publications, 1968.

Scott, Tom. *The Ship and Other Poems*. Oxford University Press, 1963. *At the Shrine of the Unkent Sodger*. Akros Publications, 1968.

Seddon, Alexandra. *Sparrows*. Carcanet Press, 1970.

Seymour-Smith, Martin. *Fantasy Poets No. 10*. Fantasy Press, 1952. *Reminiscences of Norma : Poems 1963-1970*. Constable, 1971.

Shayer, Michael. *Poems from an Island*. Fulcrum Press, 1970.

Shepherd, W. G. *Allies*. Anvil Press, 1968. *Sun, Oak, Almond, I*. Anvil Press, 1970.

Silkin, Jon. *The Peaceable Kingdom*. Chatto & Windus, 1954. *The Two Freedoms*. Chatto &

PHOENIX: A POETRY MAGAZINE EDITED BY HARRY CHAMBERS

(£1 for four issues)
Start your sub. with the 84 page

PHOENIX No. 8

BLACK PAPER ON POETRY ISSUE

"*Phoenix* is always alert and interesting"—*Times Literary Supplement.*

"A selection of new verse which leaves poor old London stranded and provincial"—*Alan Brownjohn* reviewing *Phoenix 6 & 7* in the *New Statesman.*

Subscribers include the University Libraries of Yale and Harvard; the Library of Congress, Washington; and the National Libraries of Ireland and Australia.

TOWARDS THE SUN

Poems and Photographs by Glyn Hughes
A PHOENIX SPECIAL . . . price 50p

"The counterpoint of accompanying photographs contributes another dimension . . . This pamphlet is well-produced and should be snapped up."—*John Fuller, The Listener.*

FORM PHOTOGRAPH BY STANLEY COOK

(No. 12 in PHOENIX PAMPHLET POETS SERIES
Price 20p paperback or £1·05 signed hardback)

"Infinitely better than anything D. H. Lawrence wrote about a classroom, and for humour, generosity and lightness of touch, almost as good as Chaucer's *Prologue.*"—*The Teacher.*

"a kind of South Yorkshire Spoon River. He writes with compassionate sincerity"—*The Use Of English.*

ECCLESIASTES BY DEREK MAHON

(No. 9 in PHOENIX PAMPHLET POETS SERIES
Price 20p paperback or £1·05 signed hardback)

Poems from Belfast by the theatre critic of *The Listener:*
"A bitter power underlies all the poems"—*Irish Times.*

Send for full details of these and
Sixteen other pamphlets of similar quality

Orders (crossed cheque/P.O. payable to PHOENIX) to/further details from:

PHOENIX · 8 CAVENDISH ROAD
HEATON MERSEY · STOCKPORT · CHESHIRE

Windus, 1958. *The Re-ordering of the Stones*. Chatto & Windus/Hogarth Press, 1961. *Nature with Man*, Chatto & Windus/Hogarth Press, 1965. *Poems New and Selected*. Chatto & Windus, 1966. *The Killhope Wheel*. MidNAG, 1971. *Amana Grass*. Chatto & Windus/Hogarth Press, 1971.

Simmons, James. *In the Wilderness and Other Poems*. Bodley Head, 1969. *Energy to Burn*. Bodley Head, 1971.

Singer, Burns. *Still and All*. Secker & Warburg, 1957. *Collected Poems*. Secker & Warburg, 1970.

Skelton, Robin. *Patmos and Other Poems*. Routledge & Kegan Paul, 1955. *Third Day Lucky*. Oxford University Press, 1958. *Begging the Dialect*. Oxford University Press, 1960. *The Dark Window*. Oxford University Press, 1962. *Answers*. Enitharmon Press, 1969. *An Irish Album*. Dolmen Press, 1969. *The Hunting Dark*. Deutsch, 1971. *Remembering Synge*. Dolmen Press, 1971.

Smith, John. *The Dark Side of Love*. Hogarth Press, 1952. *Excursus in Autumn*. Hutchinson, 1958. *A Letter to Lao Tze*. Hart-Davis, 1961. *A Discreet Immortality*. Hart-Davis, 1965.

Smith, Ken. *The Pity*. Cape, 1967.

Smith, Stevie. *Mother, What is Man?* Cape, 1942. *Harold's Leap*. Chapman and Hall, 1950. *Not Waving but Drowning*. Deutsch, 1958 (f.p. 1957). *Selected Poems*. Longmans, 1962. *The Frog Prince*. Longmans, 1966. *Some are More Human than Others*. Gaberbocchus, 1968. *Two in One*. Longmans, 1971. *Scorpion and Other Poems*. Longmans, 1972.

Stallworthy, Jon. *The Astronomy of Love*. Oxford University Press, 1961. *Out of Bounds*. Oxford University Press, 1963. *The Almond Tree*. Turret Books, 1967. *Root and Branch*. Chatto & Windus/Hogarth Press, 1969.

Stow, Randolph. *Act One*. Macdonald, 1957. *A Counterfeit Silence*. Angus & Robertson, 1969.

Tarn, Nathaniel. *Old Savage/Young City*. Cape, 1964. *Where Babylon Ends*. Cape Goliard, 1967. *The Beautiful Contradictions*. Cape Goliard, 1969. *October*. Trigram, 1969.

Thomas, D. M. *Two Voices*. Cape Goliard, 1968. *Logan Stone*. Cape Goliard, 1971.

Thomas, R. S. *An Acre of Land*. Montgomeryshire Printing Co., 1952. *Song at the Year's Turning*. Hart-Davis, 1955. *Poetry for Supper*. Hart-Davis, 1958. *Tares*. Hart-Davis, 1961. *The Bread of Truth*. Hart-Davis, 1963. *Pieta*. Hart-Davis, 1966. *Not that he Brought Flowers*. Hart-Davis, 1968.

Thwaite, Anthony. *Home Truths*. Marvell Press, 1957. *The Owl in the Tree*. Oxford University Press, 1963. *The Stones of Emptiness: Poems 1963–1966*. Oxford University Press, 1967.

Tomlinson, Charles. *Relations and Contraries*. Hand & Flower, 1951. *The Necklace*. Oxford University Press, 1966 (f.p. Fantasy Press, 1955). *Seeing is Believing*. Oxford University Press, 1960. *A Peopled Landscape*. Oxford University Press, 1963. *American Scenes and Other Poems*. Oxford University Press, 1966. *The Way of a World*. Oxford University Press, 1969.

Tonks, Rosemary. *Iliad of Broken Sentences*. Bodley Head, 1967.

Toulson, Shirley. *Circumcision's Not Such a Bad Thing After All*. Keepsake Press, 1970.

Turnbull, Gael. *To You, I Write*. Migrant Press, 1963. *Twenty Words: Twenty Days: a Sketch Book and a Morula*. Migrant Press, 1966. *A Trampoline: Poems 1952–1964*. Cape Goliard, 1968. *Scantlings: Poems 1964–1969*. Cape Goliard, 1970.

Waddington, Miriam. *Say Yes*. Oxford University Press, 1969.

Wain, John. *Mixed Feelings*. Reading University School of Art, 1951. *A Word Carved on a Sill*. Routledge & Kegan Paul, 1956. *Weep Before God*. Macmillan, 1962 (f.p. 1961). *Wildtrack*. Macmillan, 1965. *Letters to Five Artists*. Macmillan, 1969.

Walker, Ted. *The Solitaries*. Cape, 1967. *Fox on a Barn Door*. Cape, 1969. *The Night Bathers*. Cape, 1970.

Ward, J. P. *The Other Man*. Christopher Davies, 1969.

Warner, Val. *These Yellow Photos*. Carcanet Press, 1971.

STAND

a quarterly

80 pages of poetry, fiction, translation and criticism edited by Jon Silkin, Lorna Tracy, Ed Brunner, Robert Ober, and Howard Fink.

The 50th issue of STAND appeared in March 1972. Since 1952 the magazine has printed British and American poetry alongside translations that include poetry from Eastern Europe and Latin America: Blok, Voznesensky, Mandel'shtam, Hikmet, Holub, Jozsef, Radnoti, Herbert, Rozewicz, Enzensberger, Bobrowski, Neruda, Cisneros, and Vallejo.

Contributors from Britain and America include Geoffrey Hill, Michael Hamburger, Ken Smith, Jon Silkin, John Heath-Stubbs, Christopher Middleton, Norman Nicholson, John Berryman, Marvin Bell, Philip Levine, William Stafford, Nathan Whiting, Thomas Lux.

Work, accompanied by return postage, should be sent to STAND, 58 Queen's Road, Newcastle on Tyne.

Subscription: 4 issues a year
£1·25 ($3.30)
two years £2·40 ($6.50)
STAND, 58 Queen's Road,
Newcastle on Tyne
NE2 2PR

MPT MODERN POETRY IN TRANSLATION
edited by Daniel Weissbort

"This excellent magazine has, since 1965, sustained an unmodish and professional interest in the literature of other languages . . . one admirable emphasis of MPT is its stress on being informative and helpful." Douglas Dunn, *Encounter*

". . . doing such a worthwhile job in keeping open the lines of poetic communication between modern languages." Robert Nye, *The Scotsman*

MPT has given the lead, publishing in English for the first time the work of many important poets. Its back list of contributors, its special issues which are comprehensive anthologies, its informative and provocative reviews, make it an essential periodical for any reader interested in modern poetry in the widest sense.

Modern Poetry in Translation Ltd.
Subscription: 4 issues £2·00 ($6.00).
10 Compayne Gardens,
London NW6 3DH

Way, Peter. *The Pieces of a Game*. Allison & Busby, 1969.
Weissbort, Daniel. *The Leaseholder*. Carcanet Press, 1971. *In an Emergency*. Carcanet Press, 1972.
Wevill, David. *Birth of a Shark*. Macmillan, 1964. *A Christ of the Ice-Floes*. Macmillan, 1966. *Firebreak*. Macmillan, 1971.
Whigham, Peter. *The Blue-Winged Bee*. Anvil Press, 1969. *Astapovo or What Are We To Do?* Anvil Press, 1970.
Williams, Hugo. *Sugar Daddy*. Oxford University Press, 1970. *Symptoms of Loss*. Oxford University Press, 1970.
Wright, Adrian. *Waiting for Helen*. Carcanet Press, 1970. *The Shrinking Map*. Carcanet Press, 1972.

Anthologies

The Akros Anthology of Scottish Poetry 1965–1970. Ed. Duncan Glen. Akros Publications, 1970.
British Poetry Since 1945. Ed. Edward Lucie-Smith. Penguin, 1970.
Children of Albion: Poetry of the Underground in Britain. Ed. Michael Horovitz. Penguin, 1970 (f.p. 1969).
Five Quiet Shouters. Ed. Barry Tebb. Poet and Printer, 1966.
For Bill Butler. Wallrich Books, 1970.
Frontier of Going. Selected by John Fairfax. Panther Books, 1969.
A Group Anthology. Ed. Edward Lucie-Smith and Philip Hobsbaum. Oxford University Press, 1963.
The Happy Unicorns: Poetry of the Under 25's. Ed. Sally Purcell and Libby Purves. Sidgwick & Jackson, 1971.
Holding Your Eight Hands. Ed. Edward Lucie-Smith. Rapp & Whiting, 1970.
The Liverpool Scene. Ed. Edward Lucie-Smith. Donald Carroll, 1967.
London Magazine Poems 1961–1966. Selected by Hugo Williams. Alan Ross, 1966.
Mindplay: An Anthology of British Concrete Poetry. Ed. John J. Sharkey. Lorrimer, 1971.
New Lines 2. Ed. Robert Conquest. Macmillan, 1963.
The New Poetry. Ed. A. Alvarez. Penguin, 1962.
Next Wave Poets. Ed. Desmond Hertzberg. Next Wave Publications, 1969.
Next Wave Poets 2. Ed. Desmond Hertzberg. Next Wave Publications, 1970.
Penguin Modern Poets 1. Lawrence Durrell, Elizabeth Jennings, R. S. Thomas. Penguin, 1962.
Penguin Modern Poets 2. Kingsley Amis. Peter Porter, Dom Moraes. Penguin, 1962.
Penguin Modern Poets 3. George Barker, Martin Bell, Charles Causley. Penguin, 1966 (f.p. 1962).
Penguin Modern Poets 4. David Holbrook, Christopher Middleton, David Wevill. Penguin, 1963.
Penguin Modern Poets 6. Jack Clemo, Edward Lucie-Smith, George MacBeth. Penguin, 1967 (f.p. 1964).
Penguin Modern Poets 7. Richard Murphy, Jon Silkin, Nathaniel Tarn. Penguin, 1965.
Penguin Modern Poets 8. Edwin Brock, Geoffrey Hill, Stevie Smith. Penguin, 1966.
Penguin Modern Poets 10. Adrian Henri, Roger McGough, Brian Patten. Penguin, 1968
Penguin Modern Poets 11. D. M. Black, Peter Redgrove, D. M. Thomas. Penguin, 1968.
Penguin Modern Poets 12. Alan Jackson, Jeff Nuttall, William Wantling. Penguin, 1968.
Penguin Modern Poets 14. Alan Brownjohn, Michael Hamburger, Charles Tomlinson. Penguin, 1969.
Penguin Modern Poets 15. Alan Bold, Edward Brathwaite, Edwin Morgan. Penguin, 1969.
Penguin Modern Poets 16. Jack Beeching, Harry Guest, Matthew Mead. Penguin, 1970.
Penguin Modern Poets 17. David Gascoyne, W. S. Graham, Kathleen Raine. Penguin, 1970.

CARCANET PRESS

Pin Farm   South Hinksey   Oxford

". . . anyone looking for the genuinely new as opposed to the merely trendy ought to keep a close watch on their list." Robert Nye, *The Times*

"The Carcanet Press is certainly the most enterprising of the smaller publishers. It also produces its books handsomely and at reasonable prices." Elizabeth Jennings, *The Scotsman*

"Carcanet Press goes from strength to strength." Lyman Andrews, *The Sunday Times*

POETRY BOOKS FROM CARCANET

GEORGE BUCHANAN MINUTE-BOOK OF A CITY

ELIZABETH DARYUSH SELECTED POEMS

HD TRIBUTE TO FREUD

HERMETIC DEFINITION

PETER JONES THE PEACE & THE HOOK

MARGARET NEWLIN THE FRAGILE IMMIGRANTS

DAY OF SIRENS

MICHAEL SCHMIDT BEDLAM AND THE OAKWOOD

DESERT OF THE LIONS

DANIEL WEISSBORT IN AN EMERGENCY

ADRIAN WRIGHT THE SHRINKING MAP

forthcoming

MICHAEL CAYLEY THE SPIDER'S TOUCH

VAL WARNER UNDER THE PENTHOUSE

GLEN CAVALIERO THE ANCIENT PEOPLE

JAMES ATLAS (ED.) NEW AMERICAN POETS

MICHAEL SCHMIDT (ED.) NEW BRITISH POETS

poetry booklets in print and forthcoming by

JOHN BALABAN, GEORGE BUCHANAN, MICHAEL CAYLEY, MARCUS CUMBERLEGE, ELIZABETH DARYUSH, PRISCILLA ECKHARD, ROGER GARFITT, JONATHAN GRIFFIN, W. J. HARVEY, DAWSON JACKSON, NICOLAS JACOBS, PETER JONES, ISHAN KAPUR, GREVEL LINDOP, BARRY MORSE, SALLY PURCELL, GARETH REEVES, ANTHONY RUDOLF, MICHAEL SCHMIDT, ALEXANDRA SEDDON, ROBERT SHAW, VAL WARNER, DANIEL WEISSBORT, AND ADRIAN WRIGHT.

For a full list of Carcanet Press publications, including our Translations, Fyfield, and Critical books, please write to us at Pin Farm, South Hinksey, Oxford.

Penguin Modern Poets 18. A. Alvarez, Roy Fuller, Anthony Thwaite. Penguin, 1970.

Penguin Modern Poets 19. John Ashbery, Lee Harwood, Tom Raworth. Penguin, 1971.

Penguin Modern Poets 20. John Heath-Stubbs, F. T. Prince, Stephen Spender. Penguin, 1972.

Poems from Poetry and Jazz in Concert. Ed. Jeremy Robson. Souvenir Press, 1969.

Poems of the Sixties. Ed. F. E. S. Finn. John Murray, 1970.

Poetry Introduction 1. Faber, 1969.

Poetry Introduction 2. Faber, 1972.

Scottish Poetry 4. Ed. George Bruce, Maurice Lindsay, Edwin Morgan. Edinburgh University Press, 1969.

Scottish Poetry 5. Ed. George Bruce, Maurice Lindsay, Edwin Morgan. Edinburgh University Press, 1970.

Test Tube : An Anthology of Experimental Poetry. Ed. Will Parfitt. Vertigo Publications, (1969).

Typewriter Poems. Ed. Peter Finch. Second Aeon/Something Else Press, 1972.

The Young British Poets. Ed. Jeremy Robson. Chatto & Windus, 1971.

Index

THIS selective index includes page references to authors mentioned in the body of the book, to movements, small presses and magazines, and related entries. The titles of books and individual poems are not included.